ROYAL HISTORICAL SOCIETY

STUDIES IN HISTORY

New Series

T0366986

HENRY III OF ENGLAND AND THE STAUFEN EMPIRE, 1216–1272

HENRY III OF ENGLAND AND THE STAUFEN EMPIRE, 1216–1272

Björn K. U. Weiler

THE ROYAL HISTORICAL SOCIETY
THE BOYDELL PRESS

First published 2006
The Royal Historical Society, London
in association with
The Boydell Press, Woodbridge
Reprinted in paperback and transferred to digital printing 2012
The Boydell Press, Woodbridge

ISBN 978 0 86193 280 1 hardback
ISBN 978 0 86193 319 8 paperback

The Boydell Press is an imprint of Boydell & Brewer Ltd
PO Box 9, Woodbridge, Suffolk IP12 3DF, UK
and of Boydell & Brewer Inc.
668 Mt Hope Ave, Rochester, NY 14620-2731, USA
website: www.boydellandbrewer.com

A CIP catalogue record for this book is available
from the British Library

This publication is printed on acid-free paper

Contents

Publication of this volume was aided by a generous grant from the Scouloudi Foundation, in association with the Institute of Historical Research

FOR IRMGARD AND HELMUT WEILER

Acknowledgements

My debts are numerous. I would like to thank Rob Bartlett for his criticism, encouragement and equipoise of mind; Iona McCleery and Angus Stewart for digging up references, and for their occasional stylistic vetoes; Stumpy, as she never tired of hearing about Richard of Cornwall; Ruth Macrides and Michael Brown for breaking the rules, and Berta Wales for her frequent injections of sanity. The thesis, on which this volume is based, would never have been completed without the congenial atmosphere provided by the old West Port Hotel, where so much of it had been conceived, and the process of transforming it into a book could not have been embarked upon without the friendship, generosity and hospitality of Haki Antonsson, Stuart Feathers, Julian Jackson, Jill Lewis, Dirk Matten and Nick Paul. Thanks are also due to my friends and academic colleagues at Aberystwyth, for providing such a congenial and supportive environment, the Department of History at Swansea for its extended welcome, and to the historians at Durham for their timely hospitality.

I would furthermore like to acknowledge the help received from the staff and librarians at the Monumenta Germaniae Historica, the Friedrich-Meinecke-Institut für Geschichtswissenschaften at the Freie Universität Berlin, the Cambridge University Library, the library of the dean and chapter of Durham Cathedral, St Andrews University Library, the Interlibrary Loan desk at Swansea and the London Library (in particular its country officer).

I have profited from the advice and criticism of Frances Andrews, Haki Antonsson, David Carpenter, Michael Clanchy, Christoph Egger, Chris Given-Wilson, Margaret Howell, John Hudson, Ruth Macrides, John Maddicott, Michael Prestwich, Len Scales and Nicholas Vincent. Michael Brown, Stephen Church, Stuart Feathers, Ifor Rowlands, Kris Towson and the late Simon Walker read various sections or versions of this book in draft and provided stimulating criticism and advice, while Christine Linehan has undertaken the unenviable task of copy-editing the manuscript with admirable patience and helpfulness. Without their efforts, the number of errors, misreadings and mistakes – for which I alone take responsibility – would have been even greater.

It would not have been possible to undertake a PhD without generous financial assistance from the University of St Andrews, and the patient forebearance of my parents. The Royal Historical Society, the Russell Trust and the Carnegie Trust for the Universities of Scotland facilitated a number of research trips.

I would also like to thank the Master and Fellows of Corpus Christi College, Cambridge, who kindly gave permission to reproduce the sketch of

Frederick II's elephant from Matthew Paris's Chronica majora (MS 16, fo. 151v.), and the Scouloudi Foundation for supporting the publication of this book. For permission to include material which has already appeared elsewhere, I would like to thank Boydell & Brewer, Blackwell, OUP and the editors of *Historical Research* and the *English Historical Review*.

The dedication page speaks for itself.

Björn K. U. Weiler
Aberystwyth,
July 2004

Abbreviations

AfD	*Archiv für Diplomatik, Schriftgeschichte, Siegel- und Wappenkunde*
AM	*Annales monastici*, ed. H. R. Luard (RS, 1864–9)
BIHR	*Bulletin of the Institute of Historical Research*
BN	Bibliothèque Nationale, Paris
CChR	*Calendar of charter rolls preserved in the Public Record Office*, London 1903–27
CLR	*Calendar of the liberate rolls preserved in the Public Record Office: Henry III*, London 1916–64
col.	column
CPR	*Calendar of patent rolls of the reign of Henry III preserved in the Public Record Office*, London 1901–13
CR	*Close rolls of the reign of Henry III preserved in the Public Record Office*, London, 1902–38
DA	*Deutsches Archiv für Erforschung des Mittelalters*
EHR	*English Historical Review*
HZ	*Historische Zeitschrift*
JMH	*Journal of Medieval History*
mem.	membrane
MGH	Monumenta Germaniae Historica
SS	Scriptores rerum Germanicarum in folio
sep. ed.	In usum scholarum separatim editi
vern. ling.	Qui vernacula lingua usi sunt
MIÖG	*Mitteilungen des Instituts für Österreichische Geschichtsforschung*
NA	*Neues Archiv der Gesellschaft für ältere deutsche Geschichtsforschung*
PRO	Public Record Office
RHGF	*Receuil des historiens des Gaules et de la France*, ed. M. Bouquet, Paris 1738–1904
RIS	Rerum italicarum scriptores, nova series
RLC	*Rotuli litterarum clausarum in Turri Londinensi asservati*, ed. T. Duffus Hardy, London 1833–4
RS	Rolls Series
SCH	Studies in Church History
SRH	Scriptores rerum hungaricarum
TCE	*Thirteenth-Century England*
VSM	*Veterum scriptorum et monumentorum, historicorum, dogmaticorum, moralium amplissima collectio*, ed. E. Martene and U. Durand, i, Paris 1724, repr. Westmead 1969

The Holy Roman Empire, c. 1250

Introduction

For much of his reign of fifty-six years, Henry III lived under his father's shadow. When the infant Henry succeeded to the throne in 1216, his realm was in the throes of civil war. The reconstruction of England once peace had finally been established occupied the early years of his reign, and the mistrust born out of these wars continued to haunt the adult king. More important, the recovery of those lands lost by John dominated Henry's relations with the European mainland. In 1204 Philip Augustus, the king of France, had seized Normandy, Anjou and Maine. John's efforts to recover them effectively came to an end in 1214 at the battle of Bouvines, where Philip Augustus defeated the forces of Emperor Otto IV, just after Philip's son Louis had won a decisive victory over John's troops in Poitou. Within two years, Otto had been driven to the northernmost ends of Germany by his rival, Frederick of Sicily, the king of France's *protégé*. In England, John's military failure increased baronial exasperation over the king's tight fiscal control, and the apparent futility of his efforts. In 1215 the outbreak of civil war was narrowly avoided at Runnymede, where the king was forced to concede the demands of his barons by granting Magna Carta. This agreement marked, however, but a temporary halt in hostilities, and within a month John had sought the papacy's backing in freeing himself from the promises he had made. A disillusioned baronage decided to choose another king in place of John, and invited Prince Louis of France to seize the crown of England. From the moment, therefore, when the nine-year-old Henry succeeded to the throne in October 1216, he found himself confronted with a distrustful aristocracy and an inheritance stripped of some of its most lucrative and prestigious parts.

By the time of Henry's death in 1272, England was again recovering from civil unrest. In 1265, at Evesham, a group of barons under the leadership of Simon de Montfort, earl of Leicester, was defeated by a royalist force. This was but the final act in a struggle which had dominated much of Henry's reign. The king had only reluctantly agreed to confirm Magna Carta, and the charter's exact interpretation continued to vex his government of England.[1] The king's real or perceived disinclination to take the counsel of his subjects and his attempts at exploiting his juridical rights for the administration of patronage featured highly in the complaints against his government. Henry's favouritism towards his foreign relatives, most notably his wife's uncles, the

1 R. C. Stacey, *Politics, policy and finance under Henry III, 1216–1245*, Oxford 1987, 1–44; J. C. Holt, *Magna carta*, 2nd edn, Cambridge 1992, 378–405; D. A. Carpenter, 'Chancellor Ralph de Neville and plans of political reform, 1215–1258', *TCE* ii (1987), 69–80, and 'King, magnates and society: the personal rule of King Henry III, 1234–1258', *Speculum* lx (1985), 39–70, repr. in his *Reign of Henry III*, London 1996, 61–74, 75–106.

Savoyards, and his half-brothers, the Lusignans, did little to ease tensions. In 1258 this culminated in moves by a group of barons, under the leadership of Simon de Montfort, to oust the Lusignans from court, and to reform royal government. Henry III was forced to surrender control of the key posts in his administration to a baronial council. What had begun as a court intrigue soon developed a dynamic of its own and engulfed not only Henry III's domestic rule, but also, as we will see, his foreign projects.

These domestic setbacks were aggravated by a lack of success abroad. Henry never recovered his father's lands. In fact, in 1224 he suffered yet another defeat, when the new king of France, Louis VIII, occupied Poitou. Campaigns to win back the province in 1230 and 1242 failed. None the less, the continued efforts to recover these lands, and the need to find allies to be able to do so, formed a central pillar of Henry's diplomacy. Assistance in 'reclaiming his inheritance', 'restoring his rights' or 'defending his legal claims' – terms used during negotiations for a German marriage in 1225, in the aftermath of Emperor Frederick II's marriage to Henry's sister Isabella in 1235, and in preparation for the Poitevin campaign of 1242 – was what Henry most frequently sought from his intended partners. The extent to which the matter of Henry III's inheritance dominated his dealings with the rulers of continental Europe, the ways and means by which he strove to reclaim it, how he had to modify and change his plans, will thus be a central aspect of this book.

These issues will be explored against the wider background of thirteenth-century European politics at large. Outlining the degree to which Henry III's actions corresponded to the broader international context within which he acted will be a second key focus of this enquiry. To what extent did he take the initiative in his actions, and to what extent did he merely respond to external pressures? How appropriate were the means he chose to accomplish his goals? How did his initiatives compare with those of his peers and contemporaries? All this, in turn, leads to a third point that this work will consider, that is, Henry III himself. Henry III was as much part of this wider European economic, social, cultural, political and religious commonwealth as his subjects. Viewing Henry III in isolation, with a perspective limited solely to the affairs of England (or even Britain) would mean ignoring the inherently transregnal nature of thirteenth-century politics. The king of England was tied to the royal houses of Castile, France, Sicily and Germany by marriage and culture. The language spoken at his court was French, and he shared in the patronage of poets and writers with Frederick II and Louis IX.[2] As a vassal of the French king, and neighbour to the king of Castile, he could not have avoided assuming a role on the wider European stage. Moreover, like any other contemporary prince or ruler, he was expected to play his part in undertakings such as crusades, the defence of Hungary against the

---

[2] K. Bund, 'Studien zu Magister Heinrich von Avranches, I: Zur künftigen Edition seiner Werke', DA lvi (2000), 127–79.

Mongols, or supporting the Latin empire of Constantinople. In short, postu-
lating too clear a distinction between the king's domestic (i.e. English) and
his foreign (i.e. continental) concerns runs contrary to the very nature of the
milieu within which Henry III moved.[3] Finally, placing Henry III within a
broader European context will enable us to highlight some of the structural
features underpinning the political history of thirteenth-century Europe, and
to explore what terms like 'diplomacy' and 'foreign relations' actually meant
in a medieval context. First, however, let us establish the broader historical
background to the events and developments with which we will be dealing.

The framework

Throughout Henry's reign, the Holy Roman Empire featured prominently in
English royal diplomacy. To some extent that, too, was something his father
had bequeathed him. After all, the build-up to the battle of Bouvines had
witnessed the English court forging ties with the emperor, the duke of
Brabant and the count of Flanders.[4] Even the rulers of the Iberian Peninsula
had become involved (via Ferrand of Portugal, titular count of Flanders),
while Philip Augustus of France sought to employ the services of the king of
Scotland and the Welsh princes.[5] Moreover, Otto's elevation to the imperial
throne in 1209 had initially been a direct result of the manoeuvrings of John
and his predecessor, Richard the Lionheart.[6] Similar considerations guided
most of Henry's contacts with the empire. Frederick II, as will become
apparent, may well have been reluctant to side with a king whose father had
sought to deprive him of his inheritance in Sicily and the empire, but many
of the emperor's vassals displayed much greater willingness to come to
Henry's assistance. The archbishops of Cologne, the dukes of Brunswick and
Brabant, the counts of Toulouse, Provence and Savoy thus played a more
decisive part in English diplomacy than Frederick II. None the less, even in
his dealings with the imperial court the king of England achieved a number
of remarkable successes, the most notable being his sister Isabella's marriage
to Frederick II in 1235. It is, moreover, unlikely that Henry would have been

---

3   For the traditional, more hostile, view of Henry's continental endeavours, focusing on
the so-called 'Sicilian Business', see W. Stubbs, *The constitutional history of England*, 6th edn,
Oxford 1903, ii. 105, and R. F. Treharne, *The baronial plan of reform, 1258–1263*,
Manchester 1932, repr. 1971, 49–50.
4   N. Fryde, 'King John and the empire', in S. D. Church (ed.), *King John: new interpretations*, Woodbridge 1999, 335–46; R. V. Turner, *King John*, London 1994, 134–6.
5   A. A. M. Duncan, 'John King of England and the kings of Scots', and I. W. Rowlands,
'King John and Wales', in Church, *King John*, 257–71 at pp. 260–7, 273–87 at pp. 283–5.
6   The most detailed coverage has been provided by T. Holzapfel, *Papst Innozenz III,
Philipp II. August, König von Frankreich und die englisch-welfische Verbindung, 1198–1216*,
Frankfurt am Main 1991. For a summary of events in English see J. Gillingham, *Richard I*,
New Haven 1999, 311–12.

able to pursue either his brother Richard's elevation to the office of emperor-elect in 1257, or his son Edmund's short-lived Sicilian career (1254–63) without these earlier contacts, which linked him to members of the Staufen dynasty as much as to the secular and ecclesiastical elites of Germany, Burgundy, Italy and Sicily.

A study of these political and diplomatic contacts holds considerable merit in its own right, but investigating relations between Henry III and the rulers of the Holy Roman Empire also offers us the chance to sketch out the procedures and techniques by which diplomatic affairs were generally conducted in the Middle Ages. Before doing so we should, however, note some key particularities. To begin with, unlike in the case of the kings of Castile or France, there was no territorial dispute, and, unlike in the case of Scotland and France, for instance, there was no debate as to their exact hierarchical relationship. The empire mattered mainly as a potential recruiting ground for allies and supporters. Furthermore, few contemporary realms are as suitable as the empire to discuss what has been called Henry III's 'European strategy',[7] that is, his deepening involvement in the politics of the European mainland, rather than the British Isles. Indeed, the very nature and structure of the empire demands that it and its external relations are considered within as wide a framework as possible.

The Medieval or Holy Roman Empire – at a most elementary level, the three kingdoms of Germany, Italy and Burgundy – was the core of a protean political landscape, and as such defies easy definition. Although frequently referred to as the German empire, and although Germany formed its political centre, its lands and territories encompassed the borders of the modern Netherlands, Belgium, eastern and southern France, Germany, the Czech Republic, Austria, Switzerland, Luxemburg, Liechtenstein and most of Italy. Among the languages spoken in the empire were various forms of German, French, Provençal, Italian and Czech. It included towns and regions as diverse as Prague, Lyons, Marseilles, Cologne, Brunswick, Milan and Parma, Flanders, Saxony, Lombardy, Moravia, Styria and Lorraine. To varying degrees, all these lands played their part in imperial affairs, and any coverage of relations between Henry III and his imperial counterparts would thus need to take into account this range of concerns. Matters were further complicated by the fact that Frederick II was not only emperor, but also king of Sicily, king-regent of Jerusalem and claimant to a diffuse and ill-defined overlordship to the kingdoms of Cyprus and Armenia.[8] In this context, any approach

---

[7] This term was coined by M. T. Clanchy, *England and its rulers, 1066–1272*, London 1983, 230–40.

[8] For the range of Hohenstaufen interests since the reign of Emperor Henry VI (1190–7) see P. Halfter, 'Die Staufer und Armenien', in S. Lorenz and U. Schmidt (eds), *Von Schwaben bis Jerusalem: Facetten staufischer Geschichte*, Sigmaringen 1995, 187–208; J. G. Ghazarian, *The Armenian kingdom in Cilicia during the crusades: the integration of Cilician Armenians with the Latins, 1080–1393*, Richmond, VA 2000, 144, 148; P. Csendes, *Heinrich*

which limits itself to the affairs of Germany alone is a dangerously narrow one.

Initially, however, it was the German princes who mattered most to Henry III and his father. During preparations for the 1214 campaign, Provence and Languedoc had been of limited concern,[9] and few contacts had been made with the towns of Italy. This was as much a reflection of the English court's strategic needs – to attack Philip Augustus from several sides – as of the politics of contemporary Germany. Both the French and the English court had their German champions – Philip Augustus sponsored Frederick of Sicily, while John sided with Emperor Otto IV. Frederick's success after 1214 thus posed several problems for Henry III, and not the least among them was that the emperor's dependence on the Capetians' military and financial backing forced Henry to broaden his contacts within the empire. The whole range of opportunities and challenges, which this encapsulated, will become apparent once we consider the political make-up of the empire and the events prior to Henry's accession.

The divisions in Germany evident in the build-up to the battle of Bouvines are sometimes referred to as the Welf–Staufen conflict, after the two families at its centre. The Welfs, who originated in Swabia, and who had inherited the duchies of Saxony and Bavaria in the twelfth century,[10] claimed an impressive pedigree, going back to Louis the Pious's marriage with Judith in the ninth century. In addition, through a number of fortuitous marriages, the Welfs had managed to claim their place amongst the empire's most powerful families. Their fortunes declined, however, in 1180 with the fall of Henry the Lion, and their lands were reduced to the areas around Brunswick and Lüneburg, that is, the eastern parts of the modern *Land* of Lower Saxony. To reverse these losses, and to reclaim their former status were among the main concerns of Henry's descendants, and in 1198 they achieved their first success. The death of Emperor Henry VI in the previous year had triggered a division among the German princes and the elevation of two rival kings: Philip of Swabia, a Staufen, the brother of the deceased emperor, and Otto of Lüneburg, count of Poitou, Henry the Lion's second son.[11] The latter had been reared at the English court, and was rumoured to have been among the possible candidates for the succession to Richard the Lionheart.[12] After Philip's murder in 1208, Pope Innocent III crowned Otto emperor in the following year. The

---

VI, Darmstadt 1993, 170, 198; and C. Naumann, *Der Kreuzzug Kaiser Heinrichs VI*, Frankfurt am Main–Berlin 1994.

9   For more detailed coverage see N. Vincent , 'England and the Albigensian Crusade', in B. K. U. Weiler with I. W. Rowlands (eds), *England and Europe in the reign of Henry III, 1216–1272*, Aldershot 2002, 67–97 at pp. 78–85.

10 See, more generally, B. Schneidmüller, *Die Welfen: Herrschaft und Erinnerung*, Stuttgart 2000, 105–79.

11 For the most recent study of Otto's career see B.-U. Hucker, *Kaiser Otto IV*, Hanover 1990.

12 Ibid. 12–13, 16–18.

Welfs' restoration to power seemed complete. In 1210, however, when Otto attacked Sicily, a papal fief and the inheritance of Henry VI's son, Frederick, he was excommunicated, and the pope thereafter supported the candidacy of Frederick of Sicily for the imperial throne. In 1212 a diet of German princes at Nuremberg elected him king and he soon made swift progress through northern Italy and southern Germany.[13] Bouvines marked the beginning of the end for Otto,[14] and when he died in 1218, his power was largely confined to his allodial lands around Brunswick.[15]

The Staufen, named after one of their castles, also, had their power-base in Swabia.[16] From 1138 to 1197 three members of the family – Conrad III, Frederick I Barbarossa and Henry VI – occupied the imperial throne. Their territorial interests were not, however, confined to the empire alone.[17] In 1184 the Emperor Frederick Barbarossa arranged a marriage between his son, the future Henry VI, and a sister of King William II of Sicily. At the time, this had primarily been a matter of settling the simmering conflict between the Normans and the empire, but when William died in 1189 without a direct male heir, his sister claimed the Sicilian throne. Emperor Henry VI, viewing this as an opportunity to seize the Normans' inheritance in southern Italy and combine it with his imperial possessions in the north, entered Sicily, where his son, Frederick, was born in 1194. This acquisition was to prove both the apogee and the undoing of Staufen influence in Europe. When Henry VI died in 1197, the claims of the infant Frederick, although chosen as successor during his father's lifetime, were ignored. Pope Innocent III urged that the young boy's mother, rather than the German knights who had accompanied Henry VI, exercise the regency of Sicily. In the empire, the Double Election of 1198 presented an opportunity to secure the separation of imperial northern Italy from the kingdom of Sicily in the south, and it was Otto's willingness to agree to this that ultimately secured him Innocent's backing. That the kingdom of Sicily, or *regno*, was a fief held of the pope, mattered little in practice, since papal overlordship, unless backed up by military force, remained very much a legal fiction.[18] With this in mind, a separation of the imperial lands in northern Italy from the Staufens' inheritance in the south and Sicily

---

13 For the early years of Frederick's reign see W. Stürner, *Friedrich II*, Darmstadt 1992–2000, i. 137–80.

14 G. Baaken, 'Der deutsche Thronstreit auf dem IV. Laterankonzil', in K. Herbers, H. H. Kortüm and C. Servatius (eds), *Ex ipsis rerum documentis: Beiträge zur Mediävistik: Festschrift Harald Zimmermann*, Sigmaringen 1991, 509–21.

15 Hucker, *Otto IV*, 303–30.

16 For the early history of the Hohenstaufen see O. Engels, *Die Staufer*, 6th edn, Stuttgart 1994, 9–31; E. Klebel, 'Zur Abstammung der Hohenstaufen', *Zeitschrift für die Geschichte des Oberrheins* cii (1954), 137–85; and H. Bühler, 'Die frühen Staufer im Ries', in I. Eberl, W. Hartung and J. Jahn (eds), *Früh- und hochmittelalterlicher Adel in Schwaben und Bayern*, Sigmaringendorf 1988, 270–94.

17 For what follows see Csendes, *Heinrich VI*.

18 *Regestum Innocentii III papae super negotio romani imperii*, ed. F. Kempf, Rome 1947, no. 29.

may have seemed an opportunity as well as a necessity. The papacy's success was, however, short-lived, for Innocent III had ultimately to abandon what he had gained in Sicily to preserve what he had won in the empire. None the less, efforts at ensuring a separation of the imperial north from the Sicilian south remained an important feature in papal diplomacy. Frederick II, for instance, had to promise a diplomatic and dynastic separation of his Sicilian and German lands, and once the *curia* began to search for a new king of Sicily from 1253 onwards, it looked above all else for a guarantee that whoever took control of the *regno* would seek to expand no further.

The archbishops of Cologne were among the most prominent figures in diplomatic exchanges between England and the empire. Their wealth and political clout set them apart from the other princes of the empire, and their frequent involvement in the affairs of England and Germany warrants a more detailed coverage. After the fall of Henry the Lion in 1180 the prelates had been awarded the duchy of Westphalia, roughly identical with the western parts of the modern *Land* of North Rhine-Westphalia. They put this position to good use. In 1198, for instance, they had been instrumental in securing the election of Otto IV, and had taken an active role in arranging the alliance between the emperor and King John.[19] In fact, most diplomatic contacts were arranged either directly by the archbishops, or by nobles and emissaries connected to them. At the same time, their importance has sometimes been exaggerated, and they have all too often been assigned the role of a *deus ex machina*, conveniently used to explain even the most complex questions, and to postulate links and contacts where none existed.[20] The part played by the archbishops of Cologne points, however, to some important structural differences between England and the empire. Whereas Henry III and his father had little difficulty overseeing the movements of their clergy and nobles, no such control could be exercised by the emperor. The prelates and nobles of Germany, Burgundy and Italy pursued their ambitions and contacts with a large degree of autonomy.

This, in turn, leads to two preliminary points. First, coverage of English relations with the medieval empire cannot concentrate on the emperor or a particular prince alone. Secondly, this seeming anomaly in the organisation of political contacts with foreign powers in the medieval empire has given rise to doubts as to whether it is at all possible to use terms such as 'foreign

---

19 H. Stehkämper, 'England und die Stadt Köln als Wahlmacher Ottos IV. (1198)', *Mitteilungen aus dem Stadtarchiv Köln* lx (1971), 213–44; S. Zöller, *Kaiser, Kaufmann und die Macht des Geldes: Gerhard Unmaze von Köln als Finanzier der Reichspolitik und der 'Gute Gerhard' des Rudolf von Ems*, Munich 1993.
20 See, for instance, K. Wand, 'Die Englandpolitik der Stadt Köln und ihrer Erzbischöfe im 12. und 13. Jahrhundert', in J. Engel and H.M. Klinkenberg (eds), *Aus Mittelalter und Neuzeit: Festschrift S Gerhard Kallen*, Bonn 1957, 77–95. Wand's argument, in turn, has been adopted by J. P. Huffmann, *The social politics of medieval diplomacy: Anglo-German relations, 1066–1307*, Ann Arbor 2000, 249, 260, 272–3.

relations' in a medieval context.[21] It would seem that, if any political figure of some clout could enter into relations with a ruler other than the emperor, and if they could do so without fear of reprisals, this would undermine the concept of diplomacy as interaction between autonomous, inclusive and hierarchically centred political entities. German medievalists, in particular, have voiced doubts concerning the applicability of the term 'foreign relations' to political exchanges between medieval princes. It is possible, however, that their perception has been coloured by the specific conditions of the empire, themselves by no means typical. England, for once, provides an example of far more stringent control of baronial activities.

The English kings had established well-developed machinery to direct their barons' relations with neighbouring rulers. Few English magnates had power and liberty to follow Henry the Lion's example and search for allies abroad, independently of the king. William the Marshal, among the leading magnates of King John, and head of Henry III's regency council, still had been expected to ask for permission before entering into separate negotiations with Philip Augustus concerning his lands in France.[22] Similarly, in 1236 and 1237 Richard of Cornwall required permission of his brother and the barons before he could depart for a planned meeting with Frederick II. Even Simon de Montfort could not simply leave the realm in 1240, when going on crusade, without having first informed the king and his council.[23] The physical make-up of England facilitated easier – though by no means total – control of the magnates' movements, in particular as far as continental Europe was concerned, but this pattern even applies with regard to Wales, Ireland or Scotland. The king had the means, administrative, fiscal and political, to oversee the baronial contacts with those from outside his realm. The situation in France, by contrast, to some extent resembled that in the empire. Outside the Île de France, the traditional heartland of the Capetian monarchy, French magnates enjoyed a large degree of autonomy, far

---

[21] A short survey has been provided by D. Berg in *Deutschland und seine Nachbarn, 1200–1500*, Munich 1997, 47–57, and a very detailed discussion in his *England und der Kontinent: Studien zur auswärtigen Politik der Anglo-normannischen Könige im 11. und 12. Jahrhundert*, Bochum 1987, 7–23. The collection of essays, D. Berg, M. Kintzinger and P. Monnet (eds), *Auswärtige Politik und internationale Beziehungen im Mittelalter (13. bis 16. Jahrhundert)*, Bochum 2002, appeared too late to be made use of fully in the context of this study. Of particular use for our understanding of what diplomacy and international relations could mean in a medieval context is the article in that collection (pp. 47–86) by W. Georgi, 'Intra und extra: Überlegungen zu den Grundlagen auswärtiger Beziehungen im früheren Mittelalter: Wahrnehmung, Kommunikation und Handeln'. Most of the remaining articles, with the exception of K. van Eickels, 'Vom freundschaftlichen Konsens zum lehensrechtlichen Konflikt: die englisch-französischen Beziehungen und ihre Wahrnehmung im Wandel an der Wende vom Hoch- zum Spätmittelalter' (pp. 87–111), are concerned with the period from *c.* 1300 onwards.
[22] D. Crouch, *William Marshal: court, career and chivalry in the Angevin empire, 1147–1219*, London 1990, 85–6.
[23] J. R. Maddicott, *Simon de Montfort*, Cambridge 1994, 29–34.

exceeding that of their English counterparts. It was not until St Louis began to prepare his first crusade, from 1244 onwards, and in the aftermath of this campaign, that the king aimed to expand his juridical and administrative authority across his realm.[24] Until then, the Capetians' control over their magnates in no way resembled that of the king of England, but they still held a greater degree of authority than an emperor.

The emperor's – by comparison – more limited control over his noble subjects was intrinsically linked to the political structure of the medieval empire.[25] He could not press the same claims in the imperial cities of Germany and the communes of Lombardy. The king of Bohemia had to be treated differently from the duke of Limburg. While this, in turn, left individual princes a considerable degree of autonomy, it did not mean that an emperor was bereft of authority. The extent of his ability to control the actions and ambitions of his princes varied, and depended on the overall political situation – the existence of an alternative source of patronage, doubts as to the legitimacy of his rule and, quite often, the military might and the general prestige he was able to muster. For instance, when Frederick II returned from his crusade in 1229, and once peace had been arranged with the papal *curia* in 1230, his political clout far exceeded that of the adolescent emperor who, in 1220, faced rebellions in Sicily and struggled to assert his authority in Germany and Italy. As a result, the years from 1230 to 1237 witnessed an almost unprecedented expansion of imperial power into regions which had previously experienced at best a nominal form of overlordship. The same pattern applies to princely alliances with monarchs other than the emperor. In 1242, for instance, some nobles in imperial Burgundy still felt that they needed permission from Emperor Frederick II before they would join a campaign against the king of France. A thirteenth-century emperor lacked the administrative apparatus available to the English king and had to strive continuously to make his authority felt and accepted. If he failed, or if he was prevented from doing so, princely authority increased. This forms an important part of the background against which English relations with the empire have to be considered. Contacting the emperor alone was not enough.

These differences between English magnates and imperial princes reflect their differing political functions. On a very basic level, the Holy Roman Empire was an elective monarchy, that is, a group or groups of princes elected the ruler. The exact composition of that princely elite was unclear and often debated. In practice, a college of seven electors, consisting of the archbishops of Cologne, Trier and Mainz, the king of Bohemia, the duke of Saxony, the count Palatine of the Rhineland and the margrave of Brandenburg, emerged

---

24 W. C. Jordan, *Louis IX and the challenge of the crusade: a study in rulership*, Princeton 1979, 35–64; R. Bartlett, 'The impact of royal government in the French Ardennes: the evidence of the 1247 *enquête*', JMH vii (1981), 83–96.
25 For a detailed recent overview see B. Arnold, *Medieval Germany, 500–1300: a political interpretation*, London 1997, 108–16, 146–59.

in the context of the Double Election of 1257,[26] but we may assume that movements towards an electoral college had existed for some time before then.[27] At the same time, the concept of an electoral monarchy was not wholly alien to the magnates of England. In 1135, for instance, they were forced to choose between several claimants to the succession of Henry I. In 1199 some contemporary observers again stressed the electoral nature of John's elevation to the throne,[28] in 1212 rumours abounded as to the election of Simon de Montfort the elder as king[29] and in 1216 some English magnates did choose another king in Prince Louis of France.

In many ways, twelfth-century Germany provides a dynastically more stable picture than England. Although the succession was decided by a vote among the princes, this normally meant that they elected an emperor's son. Frederick Barbarossa, Henry VI and Frederick II all ensured the election of their sons as successors during their lifetime. Only when an emperor died without male issue, or in politically fraught circumstances, such as in 1198, did the princes exercise their electoral rights independently. This system only changed during the thirteenth century. With Frederick II and his offspring excommunicated, the electoral ranks of the imperial aristocracy assumed an unprecedented importance as a stabilising and arbitrating factor, and the empire did not return to a quasi-hereditary form of kingship until the late fifteenth century. During the period under consideration here, that is the second and third quarter of the thirteenth century, the princes' standing in relation to the monarch was greater than that of the English magnates. At the same time, the effect this had on imperial politics is easily exaggerated. The emperor did not face a united front of hostile princes, continuously emphasising their independence and stubbornly refusing to comply with his demands. In fact, most princes desired the exercise of stable authority as much as their English counterparts. The degree to which they were willing to submit varied, however, as did the degree to which they were expected to submit.[30]

---

[26] The classic account is that of H. Mitteis, *Die deutsche Königswahl: ihre Rechtsgrundlagen bis zur Goldenen Bulle*, 2nd edn, Darmstadt 1987. See also C. C. Bayley, *The formation of the German college of electors in the mid-thirteenth century*, Toronto 1949. W. Giese, 'Der Reichstag vom 8. September 1256 und die Entstehung des Alleinstimmrechts der Kurfürsten', *DA* xl (1984), 562–90, is also useful in the context of the Double Election.

[27] F.-R. Erkens, *Kurfürsten und Königswahl: zu neuen Theorien über den Königswahlparagraphen im Sachsenspiegel und die Entstehung des Kurfürstenkollegiums*, Hanover 2002.

[28] Matthew Paris, *Chronica maiora: the chronica maiora of Matthew Paris*, ed. H. R. Luard (RS, 1872–4), ii. 454–5.

[29] *Annals of Dunstable*, in *Annales monastici*, ed. H. R. Luard (RS, 1864–9), iii. 33. See also Vincent, 'England and the Albigensian Crusade', 75.

[30] B. Arnold, 'Emperor Frederick II, 1194–1250, and the political particularism of the German princes', *JMH* xxvi (2000), 239–52, and *Princes and territories in medieval Germany*, Cambridge 1991. 5; K. J. Leyser, 'Some reflections on twelfth-century kings and kingship', *EHR* xc (1975), 481–506. T. Reuter, 'The origins of the German *Sonderweg*? The empire and its rulers in the high Middle Ages', in A. Duggan (ed.), *Kings and kingship in medieval Europe*, London 1993, 179–211, provides a good overview.

The relative weakness of the emperor in relation to his princes was, however, not the only limitation on his political power. Being elected and crowned King of the Romans was, after all, only a first step. In order to become emperor, another hurdle had to be taken, and the newly chosen king had to be crowned emperor by the pope. Being crowned emperor had rarely been a mere routine matter, but especially from the twelfth century onwards the *curia* utilised this step to voice its own demands. These mostly concerned guarantees for the integrity and defence of papal lands and rights. From 1194 onwards, this became an even more pressing need in the light of the Staufens' acquisition of Sicily. The separation of empire and *regno* thus emerged as a recurrent feature in negotiations. In 1220, for instance, Frederick II was not crowned emperor until he promised that only one of his sons would succeed him in the empire, while another was later to take possession of Sicily. As we will see, similar conditions were put before Prince Edmund in 1254 and Charles of Anjou in 1263. To some extent, these issues arose from the specific circumstances of the imperial successions of 1198 and 1212. Yet, even under more settled conditions, an imperial coronation conveyed general obligations, most notably the duty to defend and assist the *curia*.[31]

The *curia* thus played a prominent political as well as a religious and spiritual role, and this was by no means confined to the empire: Frederick II, as well as Henry III, owed his throne to papal support.[32] Frederick's downfall was ultimately triggered by his clash with Pope Gregory IX, leading to his excommunications in 1227 and 1239, and by his inability to resolve this conflict with Gregory's successor, Innocent IV, who deposed him during the Council of Lyon in 1245. None the less, we should not reduce the *curia*'s role to mere *realpolitik*. We must also consider the wider institutional, ethical and religious framework within which the papacy acted, and this included the crusade. Expeditions directed at the liberation of the Holy Land, in particular, involved diplomatic preparations and attempts at installing a framework of rules, which sought to define the pursuit of conflicts and claims.[33] This normally involved efforts at

31 For these concepts see R. Folz, *The concept of empire in western Europe from the fifth to the fifteenth century*, trans. S.A. Ogilvie, London 1969; J. A. Watt, 'Spiritual and temporal powers', in J. H. Burns (ed.), *The Cambridge history of medieval political thought, c. 350–c. 1450*, Cambridge 1988, 367–423, and 'The theory of papal monarchy in the thirteenth century: the contribution of the canonists', *Traditio* xx (1964), 178–317; and A. Stickler, 'Imperator vicarius papae: die Lehren der französisch-deutschen Dekretistenschule im 12. und beginnenden 13. Jahrhunderts über die Beziehungen zwischen Papst und Kaiser', *MIÖG* lxii (1954), 165–212.
32 For the best overview see F. A. Cazel, Jr, 'The legates Guala and Pandulf', *TCE* ii (1987), 15–21; F. M. Powicke, *King Henry III and the Lord Edward: the community of the realm in the thirteenth century*, Oxford 1947, 1–41; and D. A. Carpenter, *The minority of Henry III*, London 1990, 254–6.
33 *Decrees of the ecumenical councils*, ed. and trans. N. P. Tanner, London–Washington, DC 1990, i. 267–71; B. K. U. Weiler, 'The *negotium terrae sanctae* in the political discourse of Latin Europe, 1215–1311', *International History Review* xxvi (2003), 1–36, and, especially for the reign of Henry III, J. M. Rodríguez García, 'Henry III (1216–1272), Alfonso X of

halting or settling conflicts until the aims of a prospective campaign had been achieved: Christians were not to fight Christians when their energies could be more profitably directed at Muslims, schismatics or heretics. Although the popes faced considerable challenges in enforcing this concept, it was none the less one which dominated the *curia's* involvement, for instance, in the conflicts between Henry III and Louis IX, or between Frederick II and his son Henry (VII) and the Lombard communes. In addition, the emperor's very role as the secular protector of the Holy See could also involve him in papal initiatives aimed at creating a political climate in the west favourable towards a *passagium* to the east.[34] In hindsight we can judge these efforts to have failed, but we must none the less consider the extent to which they informed papal responses to the emperor or the king of England, and how they in turn sought to respond to or utilise them.

Considering, therefore, the manifold restrictions on imperial authority, the heterogeneous nature of the realms over which Frederick and his successors presided, as well as their role which – at least in theory – transcended modern ideas of domestic and foreign affairs, doubts about the applicability of terms such as 'foreign relations' seem understandable. At the same time, such scepticism is rooted in a definition of 'foreign policy' which takes as its empirical basis the period after the 1648 Treaty of Westphalia, with its – relatively – clearly defined political entities and an increasingly well-developed bureaucratic, theoretical and juridical apparatus of international law. The problem lies, therefore, with the definition, rather than the phenomenon it seeks to describe. Entities like the medieval empire, however, simply do not fit this pattern. How, then, should one define diplomacy and foreign relations in a medieval context?

First, we need to accept that medieval diplomacy was highly informal. The international nature of aristocratic society blurs modern distinctions between the 'domestic' and the 'foreign', between the 'public' and the 'private' ambitions of rulers and princes. In a medieval context, therefore, the working definition of 'foreign relations' put forth by Dieter Berg seems considerably more appropriate: 'any political action by a ruler which exceeds his own immediate sphere of power and influence, and which aims to realise its goals by applying suitable instruments of political communication'.[35] This needs to be further refined to take into account the dealings of princes and magnates with foreign lords, probably best defined as those to whom they do not owe and with whom they did not share a legal, customary or political loyalty which superseded other legal, customary or political obligations. This would cover,

---

Castile (1252–1284) and the crusading plans of the thirteenth century', in Weiler and Rowlands, *England and Europe*, 99–120.

[34] B. K. U. Weiler, 'Gregory IX, Frederick II and the liberation of the Holy Land, 1230–9', in R. N. Swanson (ed.), *Holy Land and holy lands* (SCH xxxvi, 2000), 192–206.

[35] Berg, *England und der Kontinent*, 4.

for instance, dealings between the archbishop of Cologne or the count of Provence, and the king of England. At first sight this definition may seem more difficult to apply in cases such as Henry III's dealings with the count of Ponthieu or the king of Scotland. After all, as duke of Aquitaine, Henry was – at least in theory – as much a vassal of the Capetian crown as was the count of Ponthieu. Similarly, although Henry III – however grudgingly – acknowledged the autonomy of the Scottish kingdom, the king of Scotland still owed fealty for his English possessions. Contemporaries were, however, well aware of these differences, and these variations in status were played upon only if political points could be made. When Henry III came to France after concluding the 1259 Treaty of Paris, for instance, he was greeted not as a vassal of the French crown, but as a monarch of equal standing to his host, and this was positively commented upon by English and French observers alike.[36] Contemporaries were conscious of the multiple levels on which relations between rulers could be negotiated. With these qualifications in mind, Berg's definition remains applicable.

This definition, furthermore, accommodates the whole range of business conducted in medieval diplomatic exchange. In fact, for the upper echelons of medieval aristocratic society, dealing with – in the modern sense – foreign rulers was almost part of their everyday existence. Among issues requiring contacts with overlords other than one's own were marriage negotiations, the settlement of legal claims, the administration of one's estates, the planning of a crusade or payments and loans.[37] Rarely, however, did these trigger a hostile or defamatory response. An important distinction was made between peaceful dealings between a vassal and a foreign ruler and those aimed at or likely to result in undermining a vassal's overlord. This principle, in turn, also underpinned Henry III's dealings with members of the French aristocracy in 1230 and 1242: he only sought to reclaim his rights. That is, he employed a terminology which aimed to present his actions as nothing but the legitimate and rightful actions of a vassal who had been wronged by his lord. Henry III did not encourage his prospective allies to rebel against their king, but he sought their assistance in voicing his *gravamina* against an unjust lord. This also points to another important issue, that is, the difficulty of distinguishing clearly between 'private' and 'public' goals in medieval politics. Naturally, every ruler had certain obligations towards his subjects: he had to secure the safety of their borders, protect them against enemies and ensure that justice was done to them. These were, however, criteria sufficiently vague to accommodate a series of

---

36 See K. van Eickels, *Vom inszenierten Konsens zum systematisierten Konflikt: die englisch-französischen Beziehungen und ihre Wahrnehmung an der Wende vom Hoch- zum Spätmittelalter*, Sigmaringen 2002, for the wider phenomenon.

37 See also the list provided by D. Matthew, *The English and the community of Europe in the thirteenth century: the Stenton lecture 1996*, Reading 1997, 22–9. That this was not limited to secular leaders alone is illustrated by J. Burton, 'The monastic world', and Christoph Egger, 'Henry III's England and the *curia*', both in Weiler and Rowlands, *England and Europe*, 121–36, 215–32.

concerns which in a modern context would count as the king's private affairs. In Henry's case, this included his paternal inheritance in France, and in Frederick's his excommunication by the pope. Both did, however, have considerable impact on the subjects of king and emperor. Losing Poitou in 1224, for example, hampered trade, and it undermined confidence in the king's ability to protect his lands and safeguard his subjects.

When considering thirteenth-century diplomatic exchanges, it is important to remember that decisions were frequently made on an *ad hoc* basis. We should avoid seeing a detailed and finely thought-out 'grand strategy' behind every move, without necessarily claiming, as the other extreme, that medieval kings had no underlying aims and ambitions at all. Henry III's involvement in Sicily and his brother Richard's in Germany, were, as we will see, the result of chance, of opportunities which unexpectedly presented themselves, and which the king and his brother could not afford to ignore. The range of contacts, the concerns they dealt with, frequently depended on who approached the king, and on what they were able to offer at that particular moment in time. Further examples include Henry III's plans for a Bohemian marriage in 1227 or the marriage between Frederick II and Isabella in 1235. In both cases Henry III found himself confronted with developments which he had neither sought nor expected but which he and his regents were none the less quick to exploit. We thus have to be aware of the multiplicity of reasons and motivations which had led to contacts, the often accidental origin of what resulted in prolonged and difficult negotiations, and view them against their contemporary background, and avoid over-simplified explanations. None the less, although many of the contacts which triggered exchanges may have been the result of chance, they were still utilised to achieve long-term aims. In Henry's case, this primarily concerned the recovery of Normandy and Poitou. Almost any contact with the emperor or the empire's aristocracy was viewed in this light: in 1225 a German marriage was to be arranged in the hope that this would help Henry 'to restore his rights'; in 1235 Frederick's marriage with Isabella was interpreted as a first step towards 'reclaiming Henry's inheritance'; in 1246 Amadeus of Savoy's enfeoffment with lands in northern Italy was announced to the king as a first step 'towards confusing his enemies'. On Frederick's part, he did not begin to take an interest in closer ties with England until after his reconciliation with Gregory IX in 1230, and then his main concern was to ensure the financial, military and political backing which he required for the establishment of his rights in Italy, and the planned crusade. After the emperor's second excommunication in 1239, the need to ensure that Henry would not put his wealth at the *curia's* disposal, and the need to have powerful men pleading on his behalf, dominated the emperor's actions. These aims led to sometimes unduly high expectations on Henry's part, as well as Frederick's. Charting these conflicting hopes, how either the king of England or his counterparts in the empire reacted to them, and how they sought to achieve their aims none the less, will be one of the main themes of this book.

We furthermore need to remember that formal treaties and alliances were not the only means by which diplomatic relations could be conducted, nor were these necessarily always their ultimate goal. Issues such as prestige, moral and ethical obligations or dynastic necessities played as much a part as political and economic concerns. Not every privilege granted to the merchants of Cologne, for instance, indicated a new diplomatic initiative. Nor should every marriage alliance be viewed exclusively in terms of power politics. In fact, as will become apparent when dealing with the 1235 union between Frederick II and Isabella of England, a whole variety of issues could lead to the successful conclusion of this type of matrimonial diplomacy. At the same time, it would be foolish to try to establish too clear a distinction between the political and the social or economic. For Henry III and his court never left any doubt as to the ultimate political gains they hoped to draw from this union: the recovery of his continental inheritance. Similarly, when the king of England and his brother called on the dukes of Brunswick and Brabant to provide experts for the 1247 recoinage in England or the exploitation of Cornish tin mines, this should not be misconstrued as taking sides in the internal political squabbles of Germany at this particular point. None the less, as will become apparent, the choice of minters from Brunswick, rather than Cologne, was at least to some extent conditioned by the political needs and requirements of Henry III and his court. As much as we should avoid viewing every contact in merely political terms, so it would be inappropriate to ignore the political when dealing with economic, cultural or social exchanges.

Finally, neither Henry nor his contacts in Germany, Burgundy or Italy acted in a vacuum. The simmering Anglo-French conflict and the rivalry between pope and emperor were not the sole parameters which defined the course of thirteenth-century history. Henry III, as much as Frederick II, the archbishop of Cologne or the counts of Savoy, faced other rivals, internal and external, and they all had to respond to events and movements which concerned the whole of Latin Christendom. A study of Anglo-imperial relations in the thirteenth century will therefore have to take account of Anglo-Castilian relations as well as conflicts between the emperor and the nobility of the Latin kingdom of Jerusalem, Louis IX's crusading preparations as much as the affairs of the Latin empire of Constantinople. It will only be possible to understand fully relations between those two realms, if they are viewed in a broad European context. Only then can they offer more than a very specialised study of political history and only then will it be possible to see how events in various parts of Europe influenced and formed decisions and actions with which they had – at first sight – little or no connection.

This study will therefore use the diplomatic and political relations between Henry III of England and the rulers and princes of the Staufen dominions to answer a number of more general questions about the nature, structure and conduct of medieval foreign policy.[38] Its emphasis will be on the high politics of the period, and will deal with issues such as the broader ideological and structural parameters which conditioned relations between rulers; the mechanisms for establishing contacts; the means available to implement one's ambitions on the European stage, and the limitations and opportunities facing kings and princes in doing so.

A narrative of events will be central, but this narrative, in turn, will allow us to highlight three overlapping fields of analytical enquiry, that is, Henry III's place and conduct before a wider European background; the structural (i.e. political) features determining 'foreign policy' in the thirteenth century; and the mechanisms used to organise and conduct diplomatic exchanges. This book falls into three chronological segments. The first, comprising chapters 1 and 2, will take events up to 1235, the date of Isabella's marriage with Frederick II. Henry's own marriage the following year brought him into closer contact with the rulers of Languedoc, and their Savoyard relatives, thus heralding a new range of contacts. The 1235 marriage also initiated a period during which Frederick II, rather than his subjects, dominated contacts between the empire and the English court. The second part, consisting of chapters 3–5, will deal with events up to 1250, and will consider how Henry III reacted to his newfound relationship with the imperial court. In addition, we will investigate the changes which Frederick's excommunication in 1239 and his deposition in 1245 forced upon his European partners. Henry III found it increasingly difficult to muster the support he needed to realise his ambitions in France, and was required to look for allies elsewhere. This also obliged him to widen the range of contacts within the empire, while at the same time avoiding embracing either the pope or the emperor too closely. Finally, Henry's taking of the cross and Frederick's death in 1250 mark the final stage of relations between Henry III and the empire, and will occupy chapters 6–8. Henry soon competed with the kings of Aragon, Castile and France in filling the vacuum created by the demise of the Staufen, and we see him and his family take control of Sicily and the empire. In the end, this will not only broaden our understanding of England's place within Europe, but also of thirteenth-century Europe, its political structures and mechanisms, as a whole.

---

[38] For some general accounts see G. Wolf, 'Anfänge ständigen Gesandtschaftswesens schon zur Zeit Kaiser Friedrichs II?', *AfD* xxxvii (1991), 147–53; J. O. Baylen, 'John Maunsell and the Castilian treaty of 1254: a study of a clerical diplomat', *Traditio* xvii (1961), 482–91; R. I. Lustig, 'Some views on Norwegian foreign service', *Medieval Scandinavia* xi (1978–9), 212–41; D. F. Queller, *The office of ambassador in the Middle Ages*, Princeton 1967; K. Heller, 'Norwegian foreign policy and the Maid of Norway', *Scottish Historical Review* lxix (1990), 142–56; G. P. Cuttino, *Medieval English diplomacy*, Bloomington 1985, and *English diplomatic administration, 1259–1339*, 2nd edn, Oxford 1971; and P. Chaplais, *English diplomatic practice in the Middle Ages*, London 2003.

PART I

THE LEGACY OF BOUVINES, 1216–1235

1

Divergent Goals, 1216–1231

The battle of Bouvines in July 1214 was to shape the political landscape of Europe for most of the thirteenth century.[1] Emperor Otto IV lost his throne; King John was not only forced to abandon his efforts at reconquering Normandy, Anjou and Maine, but soon faced a rebellion in England as well as – in the person of Prince Louis of France – the spectre of a rival claimant to the throne.[2] The inheritance John bequeathed his infant son in 1216 was thus weakened, disputed and fragile. The main beneficiaries of Bouvines were the Capetian kings of France, who found themselves elevated to the leading ranks of European royalty. Frederick II, by contrast, spent the next decade attempting to impose his authority on the empire and Sicily, while Henry III was to spend much of his reign seeking to overcome the consequences of his father's defeat, at home as well as abroad. In many ways, the events of these years set the pattern for Henry's relations with the empire for the next thirty years.

To regain the lands lost by his father remained among the overriding ambitions of the king and his regents. When Louis VIII succeeded his father in 1223, however, he sought to emulate Philip Augustus' expansion of Capetian territories, and did so by attacking both the Plantagenets and his neighbours south of the Loire. Frederick II, on the other hand, became increasingly involved in the affairs of the Latin Kingdom of Jerusalem, an entanglement which was to result in his first excommunication in 1227, and which was to remain a dominant feature in his actions until his death in 1250. He thus had neither the inclination nor the opportunity to involve himself in the conflicts of his neighbours. These divergent concerns defined the direction of English diplomacy in relation to the Holy Roman Empire. The young king, and those leading his government, faced no easy task. They presided over a kingdom but slowly recovering from civil war. Henry III and his government showed, however, an astonishing resilience in their efforts to undo what they perceived as unjust, and to reclaim what they maintained should be rightly theirs. It was within this context that Germany began to play its part, and it is to this background that we must now turn.

---

1 See G. Duby, *The legend of Bouvines: war, religion and culture in the Middle Ages*, trans. C. Tihanyi, Berkeley 1990, for a more detailed narrative. See also Holzapfel, *Papst Innozenz III*, 306–8, and R. Hiestand, 'Von Bouvines nach Segni', *Francia* xxii/1 (1995), 59–78.
2 Holt, *Magna carta*, 188–266; Turner, *King John*, 225–37, 249–56.

England and France

In 1220 Philip Augustus agreed to a truce for four years, and recalled his son from across the Channel.[3] Henry III's regents immediately set to work. Gascony and Poitou were secured, and strenuous efforts were undertaken to restore the juridical and fiscal administration of the realm. The promise of a new start was made when, in 1220, the king was crowned for a second time, acknowledged now, too, by those who in 1216 had sided with Prince Louis.[4] England looked set for a slow, but persistent recovery. In 1223, however, Philip Augustus died. Initially, this seems to have caused a surge of optimism at the English court, in the – mistaken – belief that now was the time to claim back the young king's inheritance. The archbishop of Canterbury was sent to France to demand the return of Normandy,[5] while Henry requested support from Honorius III,[6] and Pandulph, the former legate.[7] This optimism was, as it was to turn out, ill founded, as Louis VIII was to pose an even greater threat than his father.

In spring 1224 an English embassy was sent to Paris to negotiate an extension of the 1220 truce.[8] The king of France, however, seized the opportunity, and gathered troops.[9] In June, while the English court, still unaware of Louis's moves, concentrated its resources on the siege of Bedford castle,[10] the attack on Poitou began. The county succumbed quickly, and by August La Rochelle, the key fortress in Poitou, had fallen. Even Gascony, the sole remaining territory in France under Plantagenet control, was in danger. This was to be a momentous event in the history of English relations with the mainland. From then until the Treaty of Paris (1259), the recovery of lands lost in 1204 and 1224 remained a decisive factor in determining Henry's political actions, and brought him into frequent and close contact with the rulers and princes of Germany, Burgundy, France, Languedoc, Castile, Aragon and Navarre.

The events immediately following the loss of Poitou indicate a recurrent

[3] *Diplomatic documents preserved in the Public Record Office, 1101–1272*, ed. P. Chaplais, London 1964, no. 67; *Regesta Honorii papae III*, ed. P. Pressutti, 1889, nos 1000–1; 'The annals of Southwark and Merton', ed. M. Tyson, *Surrey Archaeological Collections* xxvi (1925), 24–57 at p. 50; Carpenter, *Minority of Henry III*, 27–44, 176–9; N. Vincent, *Peter des Roches: an alien in English politics, 1205–1238*, Cambridge 1996, 135–41, 163–5.
[4] Carpenter, *Minority of Henry III*, 187–91, 200–3; R. Eales, 'The political setting of the Becket translation of 1220', in D. Wood, *Martyrs and martyrologies* (SCH xxx, 1993), 127–39 at pp. 130–9.
[5] *Chronica Johannis de Oxenedis*, ed. H. Ellis (RS, 1859), 148.
[6] *Diplomatic documents*, no. 139.
[7] Powicke, *Henry III*, 170.
[8] CPR, *1216–1225*, 484.
[9] See Carpenter, *Minority of Henry III*, 370–5, for this and the following.
[10] *Gervasii cantuarensis gesta regum continuata*, in *The historical works of Gervase of Canterbury*, ed. W. Stubbs (RS, 1879–80), ii. 113. R. Eales, 'Castles and politics in England, 1215–1224', TCE ii (1987), 23–43, is important for the wider context.

pattern.[11] Once news of Louis's attack had reached England, papal support was enlisted, and a search for potential allies began. In August 1224 Honorius III wrote to Louis VIII, reprimanding him for his actions, and demanding an immediate truce.[12] Similar exhortations were issued in February and during the summer of 1225.[13] Even Frederick II was called upon by Henry.[14] The king of France, however, refused to comply. By December 1224 it had become clear that there was little hope that Louis would surrender his gains voluntarily. That month, English proctors at the *curia* sent a report detailing how French envoys had declared that King Louis VIII would instantly cross over to England, should the pope decide in favour of Henry III, 'an impecunious minor'. They also brought other, worrying news: the papal legate in France was planning to arrange a marriage alliance between the Staufens and the Capetians.[15] The English court is said to have taken this threat so seriously that sea-towns were fortified and hostages demanded from the Cinque Ports.[16]

In January 1225 Walter Mauclerk, bishop of Carlisle, was sent to Germany to arrange a marriage between Henry III's sister and Frederick II's son. In addition, attempts were made to form a coalition of all those who had been wronged by the kings of France, including members of the French aristocracy, such as the counts of Auvergne and Clermont.[17] The fear with which Henry's court faced Louis VIII did, however, lead to a sometimes peculiar choice of allies.[18] In August 1225, for instance, Henry III wrote to Count Raymond of Toulouse, emphasising how both his ancestors and Raymond's had been persecuted and robbed by the French crown. They should, therefore, work together and stand firm against the Capetian threat. The moment was well chosen, as Raymond had just begun to recover ground lost during the Albigensian Crusade, while Louis VIII was exerting all his influence to receive papal permission to lead yet another campaign against him.[19] Henry III seems to have been aware of the dangers close links with Raymond could pose, and strict precautions were taken to keep the pact secret: the treaty document was to be kept hidden, and all further discussions in this matter

---

11 Parts of the following have appeared as B. K. U. Weiler, 'Henry III's plans for a German marriage (1225) and their context', *TCE* vii (1999), 173–88.
12 *Royal and other historical letters illustrative of the reign of Henry III*, ed. W. W. Shirley (RS, 1862–6), i, appendix v, n. 18.
13 *Regesta Honorii III*, i, no. 5575; *Epistolae saeculi XIII e regestis pontificium romanorum selectae*, ed. C. Rodenberg, MGH Epistolae, Berlin 1883–94, i, no. 267.
14 *Diplomatic documents*, no. 162.
15 Ibid. no. 153.
16 *Annals of Dunstable*, AM iii. 92–3.
17 CPR, *1216–1225*, 580. For Henry's diplomatic preparations see also Powicke, *Henry III*, 174–6.
18 On English relations with the rulers of Languedoc see also Vincent, 'England and the Albigensian Crusade', 79–80.
19 J. R. Strayer, *The Albigensian Crusades: with a new epilogue by Carol Lansing*, Ann Arbor 1992, 123–6; M. Costen, *The Cathars and the Albigensian Crusade*, Manchester 1997, 151–3.

were to be made by word of mouth alone.[20] This proved a wise move when the count was excommunicated the following year,[21] and when Honorius threatened Henry III with a similar punishment.[22] This was not, however, the only curious choice made by the young king's regents. A letter from Henry III to the count of Flanders survives in which the king suggested that they should join forces against their common foes, probably referring to the Capetians.[23] However, the count of Flanders, Ferrand of Portugal, was still in French captivity, where he had been since the battle of Bouvines in 1214. This letter may therefore have been addressed to the 'false Baldwin', who had appeared in 1225,[24] and whose supporters claimed that he was Count Baldwin, the first Latin emperor of Constantinople, who had been missing since 1205. The episode thus illustrates not only the often desperate measures the English court found itself forced to take, it also sheds new light on the English mission to Germany. After all, the archbishop of Cologne played an important, though murky, role in the affairs of the pretender.[25] The 1225 mission can be properly understood only as part of a wider diplomatic initiative.

Ultimately, the German marriage did not materialise, nor did 'Baldwin's' restoration last for long. Furthermore, Louis VIII had begun to lead a crusade against the Cathar heretics in Languedoc, thus enjoying papal protection which made a successful English initiative unlikely.[26] Consequently, Henry's court sued for peace, and a temporary truce was concluded.[27] Later that year events took yet another turn, when Louis VIII died. When this coincided with a revolt of French nobles,[28] Henry III opened negotiations with the rebels. Count Ferrand of Flanders, moreover, recently released from captivity, received confirmation of his English fiefs.[29] An opportunity had presented itself to reclaim by force what diplomacy had failed to win: the recognition of Henry's claims to Normandy and Poitou. In the end, this alliance collapsed when one of its pillars, Hugh de Lusignan, decided to make his peace with the

---

[20] *Foedera, conventiones, litterae et cujuscunque generis acta publica*, ed. T. Rymer, new edn, I/1, ed. A. Clark and F. Holbrooke, London 1816, i. 179.

[21] Roger of Wendover, *Flores historiarum*, ed. H. O. Coxe, London 1841–4, iv. 124.

[22] *Royal letters Henry III*, I, appendix v, no. 22.

[23] *Foedera*, i. 177.

[24] For the following see R. L. Wolff, 'Baldwin of Flanders and Hainault, first Latin emperor of Constantinople: his life, death and resurrection, 1172–1225', *Speculum* xxvii (1952), 281–322 at pp. 294–9. See G. L. Dept, *Les Influences anglaises et françaises dans le comté de Flandre au début du XIIIe siècle*, Ghent–Paris 1928, 156–65, for a slightly old-fashioned, but more detailed narrative.

[25] *Alberti stadensis chronica*, MGH, SS xvi. 58; *Chronica regia coloniensis*, ed. G. Waitz, continuatio iv. MGH, SS sep.ed., Hanover 1880, 255.

[26] *Royal letters Henry III*, i, appendix v, no. 22.

[27] CPR, 1225–32, 24, 74–5.

[28] Roger of Wendover, *Flores*, iv. 135. J. Richard, *Saint Louis: roi d'une France féodale, soutien de la terre sainte*, Paris 1983, 40–4; Stacey, *Politics, policy and finance*, 166; J. Le Goff, *Saint Louis*, Paris 1996, 88–95.

[29] *Foedera*, i. 187.

king of France. Henry had to send his younger brother, Richard, to conclude a truce for two more years. In 1228, when the truce came up for renewal, the English court had little choice but to comply with the papal pressure it found itself exposed to, and agreed to extend it by another year.[30] Attempts at utilising the situation in France were repeatedly thwarted by the king's allies, and the skill with which Philip Augustus and his successors managed to exploit the position they had obtained after Bouvines.

Henry III and his regents did not despair in their efforts. By November 1228 another opportunity presented itself, when Raymond of Toulouse insisted that the terms of their agreement of 1225 be fulfilled.[31] He was not the only one to approach the English court. During the Christmas court at Oxford in 1228, the archbishop of Bordeaux arrived, to speak on behalf of the aristocracy in Gascony, Aquitaine and Poitou.[32] Independently, nobles from Normandy sent representatives, and asked for Henry's support. Most prominent amongst them was Simon de Montfort, claimant to the earldom of Leicester.[33] Suddenly, the English court found the support within France it had been lacking for so long. Sensitive to papal demands, however, a good reason had to be found before war could be declared. After some sabre-rattling in March, when Henry complained about recent infringements of the truce,[34] *pro forma* negotiations began. The stakes, however, had been raised. A document survives in which Henry III outlined the demands to be made by his proctors in France.[35] He proposed three possible solutions. First, the king of England would receive back all his lands, except for Normandy. There, his holdings were to be limited to one or two dioceses which, however, could be surrendered, if need be. Alternatively, a French prince could marry Henry's sister Isabella, who was to receive Normandy and Anjou as her dowry. Finally, Henry III offered to buy back his lands. These terms would have been acceptable only if Henry could have negotiated from a position of strength, and if conceding to his demands would have meant averting an even more adverse outcome. Unsurprisingly, therefore, Queen Blanche, the regent, decided to call his bluff. Henry took his time, and did not set out for France until Easter 1230.[36] Henry's troops proceeded amidst much joy, but to little effect. In the end, all he was able to show for his efforts was the contin-

---

30 CPR, 1225–32, 213–4; *Layettes du Tresor de Chartes*, ed. H.-F. Laborde and A. Teulet, Paris 1863–1909, ii, no. 1970.

31 *Royal letters Henry III*, I, no. 279; CR 1227–31, 233.

32 See Roger of Wendover, *Flores*, iii. 79–80, for this and the following.

33 This connection has been suggested by N. Vincent, 'Simon de Montfort's first quarrel with Henry III', TCE iv (1991), 167–77 at p. 168.

34 CR, 1227–31, 234.

35 *Royal letters Henry III*, i, no. 288.

36 *Annals of Dunstable*, AM iii. 125; Roger of Wendover, *Flores*, iv. 208–9; Stacey, *Politics, policy and finance*, 173.

uing homage of the count of Brittany.[37] Queen Blanche's regime was stronger than before, and it took twelve more years before another campaign to Poitou was mooted. At the same time, the proposed negotiations also indicate the degree of flexibility and imagination at the English court. Although a show of force would have been needed to reach the desired result, Henry did not aim for a full recovery of the Plantagenet inheritance. The options proposed included a marriage alliance, the payment of a substantial sum of money, as well as a complex legal settlement. We should thus avoid viewing every contact and every diplomatic initiative merely in terms of a potential military alliance. Diplomatic gains were just as important, and just as sought after, and sabre-rattling could be little more than just that: a means of forcing negotiations, and of embarking upon them from a position of – real or pretend – strength. In the end, it was the English court's inability to show that its words were not mere posturing, which brought about an end to this particular scheme.

What may appear to be no more than a list of failed campaigns and botched initiatives none the less reveals a number of important features. We learn not only of the political preoccupations of Henry's court, but also of its methods. Plantagenet diplomacy was dominated by a desire to recover the lands lost in 1204 and 1224. To gain the necessary military or diplomatic backing to press these claims was its main objective. To this purpose, the papacy was called upon, as were the rulers of Languedoc, imperial Burgundy, Flanders and Germany. Henry's regents drew on a variety of tools in seeking to accomplish their goal, and by no means was a military recovery the only option considered or available. In all this, it is also important to note the chronology of events. Although truces were frequently declared, they were viewed as an opportunity to prepare for war, not as a step towards peace. Prolongations of such agreements were forced upon Henry III – be it by Honorius III, the fact that he was abandoned by his allies, or that he lacked the means and men to pose a serious threat – rather than sought by him. The approaching expiry date of a truce normally coincided with renewed diplomatic efforts to press Plantagenet claims. These were also the years in which English contacts with the rulers and princes of Germany peaked.

Frederick II, the papacy and the crusade

England was the least of Frederick's worries.[38] Foremost among his concerns was the planned campaign to the Holy Land and the problem of Lombardy. Germany, by comparison, posed little danger for the emperor. By 1220

---

37 Roger of Wendover, *Flores*, iv. 204–5; Stacey, *Politics, policy and finance*, 170–2; Powicke, *Henry III*, 167–8, 180–3.
38 Stürner, *Friedrich II*, i. 212–53. D. Abulafia, *Frederick II: a medieval emperor*, London 1988, 103–31, is also useful.

Frederick had safely established himself and was crowned emperor by Honorius III.[39] This also coincided with a dynastic decision which was to have considerable impact on Anglo-imperial relations. Otto IV, originally the pope's champion, had been abandoned once he laid claim to Sicily. Having rid itself of Otto, the *curia* soon found that its championing of Frederick II had exacerbated the problem. When Frederick II was crowned emperor in 1220, he thus had to promise to make his son, Henry (VII), king of the Romans,[40] to be left in Germany under the supervision of Archbishop Engelbert of Cologne and Bishop Conrad of Speyer. In theory, the Staufen domains had thus been split. This was less than what had initially been expected by the *curia*,[41] but it held the promise that, as the years passed, the potential difficulties posed by the same dynasty ruling Sicily as well as the empire could be, if not wholly resolved, so at least temporarily defused.

One of the first initiatives taken by Frederick after his imperial coronation was to ensure that friendly relations with the Capetians continued, and in November 1223 Louis and Frederick II concluded the Treaty of Catania, which confirmed the earlier concord of 1212.[42] The main clause of the document stipulated that neither Louis nor Frederick would assist rebels or those who waged war against either of them, but it also made specific reference to Henry III: the emperor was not to enter upon an alliance with the king of England or his heirs, nor would he allow anyone in his power to do so.[43] This agreement emphasised the degree to which Frederick owed his crown to the Capetians' support, and it indicates the difficulties which Henry III and his regents had to overcome. That the king of England was specifically mentioned also points to the fact that the Capetians, as much as Henry III's government, were aware that the issue of the Plantagenet inheritance had not yet been settled. The agreement, however, also caused considerable friction with the German regency, when Frederick insisted that his son, too, sign it.[44] This was to provide an opportunity, willingly taken up by the English court, and explains why so many contacts with the empire centred on the government of Germany, rather than on the emperor. In the meantime, though, Louis would not have to fear a repeat of the Anglo-German alliance of 1198–1214, and it was one of the initiatives which prepared the way for the conquest of Poitou in 1224. Although, at first sight, Frederick gained very little from this agreement, it was to prove beneficial in the long run, when a

---

39 For the general background of their relations see R. Manselli, 'Onorio III e Frederico II. revisione d'un giudizio', *Studi Romani* xi (1963), 142–59.

40 *Constitutiones et acta publica imperatorum et regum*, II: *1198–1272*, ed. L. Weiland, MGH Legum Sectio, iv, Hanover 1896, no. 70. Henry's regnal numbers are commonly put in brackets to differentiate between him and the fourteenth-century Emperor Henry VII (1308–13).

41 Stürner, *Friedrich II*, i. 242–53.

42 *Constitutiones, 1198–1272*, no. 44.

43 Ibid. no. 99; Stürner, *Friedrich II*, i.126–8.

44 *Constitutiones, 1198–1272*, no. 290.

similar compact was concluded with the regents of Louis IX in August 1227.[45] Shortly afterwards, Frederick was excommunicated and faced not only a papal invasion of Sicily, but also attempts at establishing an anti-king in Germany. This time, however, the Capetians refused to lend their backing to papal initiatives. The Treaty of Catania acknowledged not merely that Frederick had depended on the Capetians to gain his throne, but also that their backing was, if not essential, at least helpful if he wanted to keep it.

The Treaty of Catania also highlights another important element in Frederick's dealings with other rulers: his crusade.[46] In 1216 Frederick had promised to lead a new expedition to the Holy Land. By 1223 the Fifth Crusade had come to a disastrous end, when the Christians were forced out of their recently seized stronghold at Damietta. Their defeat was largely blamed on the inactivity of the emperor, and the inability of Frederick and Honorius III to settle remaining points of conflict.[47] Frederick did, however, face political problems which very frequently left him little option but to prevaricate.

By April 1223 the pope announced that Frederick had promised to lead a new expedition by the summer of 1225.[48] As the date of departure approached, it became obvious that there was little likelihood that the emperor would be able to muster a sufficiently strong contingent to lead to Palestine.[49] During the early summer of 1225 Frederick therefore opened negotiations with Honorius, with a final agreement reached in August.[50] The settlement and its clauses exemplify both the degree to which this issue dominated papal–imperial relations, and the lengths to which Frederick was willing to go to prove the sincerity of his intentions. The emperor would be excommunicated should he not set sail for the Holy Land by August 1227, while detailed provisions were made for the number of ships and the funds he had to provide.[51] To add a further incentive, he married Yolanda/Isabella, the heiress of the kingdom of Jerusalem.[52] Had he failed to set out again, he would have incurred not only the opprobrium due to a crusader who broke his vow, but also that due to a king who failed to defend his kingdom.

---

[45] Ibid. no. 115.

[46] R. Hiestand, 'Friedrich II und der Kreuzzug', in A. Esch and N. Kamp (eds), *Friedrich II: Tagung des deutschen Historischen Instituts in Rom im Gedenkjahr 1994*, Tübingen 1996, 128–49; Abulafia, *Frederick II*, 132–64.

[47] J. Powell, *Anatomy of a crusade, 1213–1221*, Philadelphia 1987, 196; U. Schwerin, *Die Aufrufe der Päpste zur Befreiung des Heiligen Landes von den Anfängen bis zum Ausgang Innozenz IV: ein Beitrag zur Geschichte der kurialen Kreuzzugspropaganda und der päpstlichen Epistolographie*, Berlin 1937, 107–8.

[48] *Epistolae saeculi XIII*, i, no. 225.

[49] Ibid. i, no. 230.

[50] *Ryccardi de San Germano cronica*, MGH, SS xix, 344–5.

[51] *Constitutiones, 1198–1272*, nos 102–3.

[52] The most elaborate account is *Chronicon St Martini turonensi*, MGH, SS xxvi, 471–2. See also Filippo da Novara, *Guerra di Federico II in oriente, 1223–1242*, ed. S. Melani, Naples 1994, cap. 20–2, 76–9; Stürner, *Friedrich II*, i. 91–8.

There is little doubt, therefore, as to the crusade's significance for Frederick's actions, and it even began to overshadow relations with his neighbours. In 1224, for instance, King Waldemar of Denmark had been captured, thus providing an opportunity to reclaim lands in north Germany then under Danish rule. Overriding the objections of Henry (VII)'s regents, the emperor ensured Waldemar's release, provided he participate in Frederick's crusade.[53] Similarly, when in early 1227 peace was made with the Lombards, the emperor was content with their promise of providing 400 knights for his expedition.[54]

Similar considerations guided Frederick's involvement in Anglo-French affairs, where he acted in close co-operation with the *curia*. Honorius III left little doubt as to the connection between a successful crusade and peace in Latin Europe. This was made explicit to Philip Augustus in April 1223, with similar words addressed to the king of England about a week later:[55] a secular vassal would lose his honour and rights if he failed to defend his lord's possessions, and a Christian knight endangered his soul by failing to defend the *patrimonium* of Christ. All Christians should, therefore, take up arms against the infidel, but in order to do so they had to observe peace amongst themselves.[56] Frederick II shared these concerns. In March 1224, he wrote to Honorius III, and complained, in particular, that few of the great men of England and France seemed willing to take the cross, unless peace were first arranged between their kings.[57] This was swiftly taken up by the *curia*. On 4 April Louis was asked to enter into a firm and permanent truce with Henry, and this request was repeated in August 1224.[58] Similarly, in February 1225, Louis was exhorted to aid Frederick II, rather than fight the king of England.[59] The timing of these papal initiatives is worth noting, coinciding, as they did, with Louis's attack on Poitou, and his threat to cross the Channel. At best, the continuing wars between England and France were a hindrance, at worst they endangered the survival of Christendom in Palestine. Settling their dispute, moreover, required energies and resources which were needed elsewhere in order to prepare for the emperor's campaign.

Foremost among the preparations of any crusader for his campaign were

---

53 *Constitutiones, 1198–1272*, no. 101; Stürner, *Friedrich II*, ii. 116–26; P. Thorau, *König Heinrich, VII., das Reich und die Territorien: Untersuchungen zur Phase der Minderjährigkeit und der "Regentschaften" Erzbischofs Engelberts I. von Köln und Herzog Ludwigs I. von Bayern, (1211) (1220–1228)*, Berlin 1998, 202–26.

54 *Constitutiones, 1198–1272*, no. 111. Interesting, for the cross-connection with England, is *English episcopal acta, IX: Winchester, 1205–1238*, ed. N. Vincent, Oxford 1994, no. 47.

55 *Epistolae saeculi XIII*, i, no. 225.

56 Ibid. i, no. 220. For the terminology see Schwerin, *Die Aufrufe*, 39–45.

57 *Acta imperii inedita saeculi XIII et XIV: Urkunden und Briefe zur Geschichte des Kaiserreichs und des Königreichs Sizilien*, ed. E. Winkelmann, Innsbruck 1880–5, i, no. 261. This was repeated in March 1225: *Diplomatic documents*, no. 162.

58 *Royal letters Henry III*, i, appendix v, no. 18.

59 *Epistolae saeculi XIII*, i, no. 267.

efforts to ensure the safety of his lands, and that included the settlement of feuds, and – increasingly – the continuation of one's dynastic line. By 1220 Frederick's son was established as king of the Romans, and internal opposition in Sicily had largely been overcome.[60] The emperor's attention, thus, turned to Italy, where his recent efforts at manifesting imperial rights had run into difficulty. Relations between Frederick and the north Italian communes had, however, been uneasy for some time.[61] Frederick did little to allay their fears. He made no secret of his hostility towards towns and communes. In June 1226, for instance, the commune recently formed at Cambrai had been outlawed, and in October communes were banned throughout imperial Burgundy.[62] In November, Henry (VII) dissolved the League of Rhenish Cities.[63] To deal with these matters, as well as the planned expedition to the Holy Land, Frederick called a diet to Cremona for 1226. Henry (VII) was to attend, and Italian support was to be mustered. The very presence of German troops, however, and the fact that the settlement of 'imperial affairs' – a phrase which previously denoted attempts at enforcing an emperor's rights within the communes – was to be discussed, caused unease.[64] It is therefore not surprising that, prior to the diet, the Lombard League was refounded. What followed has often been seen as indicating how Frederick used his crusading status primarily to serve his political ends. In June a group of German bishops excommunicated the Lombard cities for obstructing the business of the Holy Land,[65] and in July the emperor outlawed Milan and its allies.[66] However, Frederick could ill afford to alienate Honorius III yet again. In fact, it seems that the planned meeting at Cremona had been designed chiefly to whip up support for the emperor's imminent departure. Nor was

[60] D. Matthew, *The Norman kingdom of Sicily*, Cambridge 1992, 315–26; Stürner, *Friedrich II*, i. 1–83.

[61] A. Zorzi, 'La giustizia imperiale nell'Italia communale', in P. Toubert and A. Paravacini Bagliani (eds), *Federico II e le città Italiane*, Palermo 1994, 85–103; G. Tabacco, *The struggle for power in medieval Italy: structures of political rule*, trans. R. B. Jensen, Cambridge 1989, 215–16; R. L. Benson, 'Political *renovatio*: two models from Roman antiquity', in R. L. Benson and G. Constable (eds), *Renaissance and renewal in the twelfth century*, Oxford 1982, 339–86 at pp. 364–6; R. L. Benson, 'Libertas in Italy, 1152–1226', in G. Makdisi, D. Sourdel and J. Sourdel-Thomine (eds), *La Notion de liberté au moyen âge: Islam, Byzance, occident: Penn-Paris-Dumbarton Oaks colloquia*, Paris 1985, 191–213 at pp. 201–7.

[62] *Constitutiones, 1198–1272*, no. 108. See also, for a general account of the history of communes in Provence (up until the rule of Charles of Anjou), K. Schulz, '*Denn sie lieben die Freiheit so sehr . . .*': Kommunale Aufstände und Entstehung des europäischen Bürgertums im Hochmittelalter*, Darmstadt 1992, 247–74.

[63] *Constitutiones, 1198–1272*, no. 294; F. Knöpp, *Die Stellung Friedrichs II und seiner beiden Söhne zu den deutschen Städten*, Berlin 1928, 36–8.

[64] Stürner, *Friedrich II*, ii. 98–111; Abulafia, *Frederick II*, 154–63.

[65] *Constitutiones, 1198–1272*, no. 105.

[66] Ibid. no. 107. For a good secondary account see H. Kluger, *Hochmeister Hermann von Salza und Kaiser Friedrich II: ein Beitrag zur Frühgeschichte des Deutschen Ordens*, Marburg 1987, 66.

Frederick in a strong enough military position to press his claims.[67] Had the meeting been intended to mark the opening of a campaign against the Lombards, it was not only ill timed, but also ill equipped. Unsurprisingly, therefore, Frederick asked the pope to mediate, and negotiations began in October, with a final agreement reached by March 1227.[68] Frederick was left with no excuse, when his opponents agreed to safeguard his claims and possessions, and to contribute troops for his crusade.[69] Although no final settlement had been reached, a truce had been arranged, and no conceivable reason remained to delay the emperor's expedition. In fact, if Frederick failed to make true his promises yet again, it could only be a sign of his insincerity and lack of faith.

This certainly was the view taken by Honorius' successor, Gregory IX. The emperor left for Palestine in August 1227, but was taken ill three days into the journey, and returned. Gregory perceived this as yet another false excuse, and excommunicated him. Frederick decided on a high-risk strategy, and, by June 1228, set sail for Palestine regardless of his status as an excommunicate.[70] A military conquest of Jerusalem, though, had to be ruled out. The illness which had struck the emperor also killed a large part of his army, and the situation in the Holy Land, with the nobles and military orders split in their attitude to Frederick, remained volatile. Consequently, the emperor looked to achieve his goal through diplomacy. This was made easier by the fact that al-Kāmil, the sultan of Egypt, had been eager to recruit troops against his rival in Damascus, and that he had already made friendly overtures towards the Christians.[71] Even before Frederick's departure, a regular exchange of envoys had begun, thus preparing the ground for negotiations. In February 1229 an agreement was reached, awarding the Christians control over Jerusalem and a ten-year truce.[72] Although it had been achieved by

---

67 *Annales placentini gibellini*, MGH, SS xviii. 469.
68 *Ryccardi de S Germano cronica*, MGH, SS xix. 346; *Annales placentini guelfi*, MGH, SS xviii. 442–3; *Annales cremonenses*, MGH, SS xviii. 807.
69 *Constitutiones, 1198–1272*, no. 114.
70 *Annals of Margam*, AM i. 36, testifying to the interest taken in England. One of the most detailed, but generally neglected, accounts can be found in *Chronica latina regum Castellae*, in *Chronica Hispana saeculi XIII*, ed. L. C. Brea, J. A. Estévez Sola and R. C. Herrero (Corpus Christianorum Continuatio Medieualis lxxiii), Turnhout 1997, 101–3. For a detailed secondary account see H. E. Mayer, *Geschichte der Kreuzzüge*, 7th edn, Stuttgart 1989, 205–10; M. A. Aziz, 'La Croisade de l'Empereur Frédéric II et l'orient latin', in M. Balard (ed.), *Autour de la Première Croisade*, Paris 1996, 371–8; Stürner, *Friedrich II*, ii. 139–67.
71 J. Richard, *The Latin kingdom of Jerusalem*, trans. Janet Shirley, Amsterdam–New York–Oxford 1979, 232; H. L. Gottschalk, *Al-Malik al-Kāmil von Ägypten und seine Zeit: eine Studie zur Geschichte Vorderasiens und Egyptens in der ersten Hälfte des 7./13. Jahrhunderts*, Wiesbaden 1958, 144, 152–60.
72 *Annales marbacenses qui dicuntur*, ed. H. Bloch, MGH, SS sep.ed., Hanover–Leipzig 1907, 92–3. See *Constitutiones, 1198–1272*, no. 120, for the text of the agreement, and P. M. Holt, 'The treaties of the early Mamluk sultans with the Frankish states', *Bulletin of the School of Oriental and African Studies* xliii (1980), 67–76, for the contemporary context.

highly unorthodox means, Frederick could claim that he had achieved more than previous campaigns led by the papacy, and did not hesitate to utilise his success when he returned to Sicily.[73] Gregory IX found it harder to maintain a united front against the man who could claim to have freed Jerusalem, and by 1231 Frederick's excommunication was revoked.

The crusade was a major element in the emperor's diplomacy. This was partly forced upon him, but it also provided a means to settle his claims, and to avoid being drawn into the territorial squabbles of his neighbours. In this context, Henry III mattered only because the dispute over his inheritance tied up resources, and because his efforts to win allies added to Frederick's German worries.

England and Germany

Henry's regents realised that Frederick had little inclination to support their plans. Most contacts with the empire were thus arranged via Henry (VII) and Archbishop Engelbert of Cologne, or the dukes of Brabant, Brunswick and Austria, as well as the king of Bohemia. Similarly, the timing of English embassies is worth noting. They increased in frequency in the aftermath of Louis's attack on Poitou in 1224/5, in 1227, when Frederick's imminent crusade, Henry (VII)'s coming of age and the baronial rebellion against Queen Blanche coincided, and in 1229/30, during the emperor's excommunication. Henry's regents knew that their best chance of success rested with the government of Germany.

The battle of Bouvines had not put an end to exchanges between the rulers of England and Germany.[74] Regular contacts were maintained with Otto IV's half-brother,[75] while new links were established with princes such as the duke of Austria.[76] The German regency, too, continued to be in communication with the English court.[77] Frequently, the initiative appears to

---

[73] *Annales marbacenses*, 92–3.

[74] *Roll of divers accounts for the early year of the reign of Henry III*, ed. F. A. Cazel, London 1982, 34.

[75] *Diplomatic documents*, no. 28.

[76] *Foedera*, 166. The envoy has been identified as Master Bernard, provost of St Bartholomew's in Friesach, chaplain of Duke Leopold VI: E. Zöllner, 'Das Projekt einer babenbergischen Heirat König Heinrichs III von England', *Archiv für Österreichische Geschichte* cxxv (1966), 54–75 at p. 58.

[77] *RLC*, i. 471. Although the messenger, Conrad, provost of Speyer, was listed as 'envoy of the emperor', this is misleading. The bishop of Speyer was, next to the archbishop of Cologne, a leading member of the regency for Henry (VII), having previously been imperial chancellor: W. Kienast, *Die deutschen Fürsten im Dienste der Westmächte bis zum Tode Phillips des Schönen*, Utrecht 1924–31, ii. 6; F. Bienemann, *Conrad von Scharfenberg: Bischof von Speier und Metz und kaiserlicher Hofkanzler, 1200–1224*, Strasbourg 1886, passim. Similarly, Conrad is regularly attested as being in the bishop's presence, ranking amongst his closest confidantes: F. X. Remling, *Urkundenbuch zur Geschichte der Bischöfe zu Speyer*, ed. F. X. Remling, Mainz 1852–4, i, no. 139. This included both the early years, spent in the

have been taken by Henry (VII)'s government. In 1223, for instance, shortly after the Treaty of Catania had been agreed, a group of envoys arrived, led by Bernard of Horstmar and Arnold of Gymnich, two Cologne *ministeriales*, or unfree knights, with considerable experience in Anglo-imperial relations.[78] Bernard had been among Richard the Lionheart's companions during the king's captivity, and had played a significant role in Otto IV's negotiations with King John.[79] Arnold had been among Frederick's earliest supporters,[80] and continued to enjoy strong links with the imperial court. Although mostly active in the area around Aachen,[81] he also appears on the witness lists for some of Frederick's Italian charters in 1222/3.[82] Their mission was probably concerned with the Catania agreement, as Archbishop Engelbert of Cologne, head of the regency council, continued to oppose closer links with the Capetians.[83] It also initiated one of the most ambitious projects undertaken by the English king's regency: a double marriage between Henry III's sister Isabella and Henry (VII), and between Henry III and a daughter of the duke of Austria.[84]

The earliest evidence for the project coincides with alarming news from the *curia*. In December 1224, as we have seen, Louis VIII's proctors had threatened an invasion of England. On 3 January 1225 Walter Mauclerk's embassy was announced to Engelbert of Cologne and the duke of Austria.[85] He was accompanied by two officials from the English court – Henry of

emperor's entourage (*Regesta imperii: die Regesten des Kaiserreiches unter Philipp, Otto IV., Friedrich II., Heinrich [VII.], Conrad IV., Heinrich Raspe, Wilhelm und Richard, 1198–1272*, ed. J. F. Böhmer, E. Winkelmann and J. Ficker, Innsbruck 1881–1901, nos 982, 1038), as well as the young king's regency (ibid. nos 3865, 3694) and his early government (ibid. no. 4108), where he remained after the bishop's death (ibid. no. 4106). Conrad, thus, was an envoy of the regency, rather than the emperor; also, in the summer of 1222 (*RLC*, i. 506), an otherwise unidentified Brother Hamo was sent to England; one may assume that the abbot of St Augustine at Canterbury was also dealing at least with some matters of diplomatic importance when, in May 1223, he received a safe-conduct to go on pilgrimage to Cologne: *CPR, 1216–1225*, 372.

78 *RLC* i. 578.

79 J. Ficker, *Engelbert der Heilige: Erzbischof von Köln und Reichsverweser*, Cologne 1853, repr. Aalen 1985, 137–9. See also his 'Herr Bernhard von Horstmar', *Zeitschrift für vaterländische Geschichte und Altertumskunde* iv (1853), 291–306.

80 *Regesta imperii*, no. 822.

81 *Aachener Urkunden, 1101–1250*, ed. E. Meuthen, Bonn 1972, no. 251; *Urkundenbuch für die Geschichte des Niederrheins*, ed. T. J. Lacomblet, Düsseldorf 1840–58, ii, no. 99.

82 *Regesta imperii*, nos 1423, 1435, 1459.

83 W. Kienast, *Deutschland und Frankreich in der Kaiserzeit (900–1270): Weltkaiser und Einzelkönige*, Stuttgart 1975, iii. 587–9. Engelbert has triggered a relatively rich literature on his life. Most recently see J. Lothmann, *Erzbischof Engelbert I von Köln, 1216–1225: Graf von Berg, Erzbischof und Herzog, Reichsverweser*, Cologne 1993; B. Fischer, 'Engelbert von Berg, 1185–1225, Kirchenfürst und Staatsmann', *Zeitschrift des Bergischen Geschichtsvereins* xciv (1989–90), 1–47.

84 For a more detailed coverage see Zöllner, 'Das Projekt', passim; Huffman, *Social politics*, 233–41; Thorau, *König Heinrich VII*, 241–5, 251–8; and Weiler 'Henry III's plans'.

85 *CPR, 1216–1225*, 558.

Cornhill, chancellor of London, who had been involved in previous negotiations with the French court, and in 1220 had been to the papal *curia* on the king's behalf, and Nicholas de Molis, later to become seneschal of Gascony – as well the masters of the Hospitallers and the Templars in England.[86] Walter's mission had been in the planning for some time. When he arrived in Cologne, he found one of his clerics waiting for him, as well as Henry de Zudendorp, one of the archbishop's *ministeriales*, and scion of a family with a commendable record in Anglo-imperial diplomacy.[87] The mission may even have been among the issues discussed in July 1224, when Richard de Zudendorp had been in England.[88] Much of what we know about the ensuing negotiations is based on a letter by Walter to Henry III from early February 1225.[89] When Walter first met the archbishop, Engelbert pointed out that the English king was not the only one who wanted to have Henry (VII) as an in-law: recently 45,000 marks had been offered if he married a Bohemian princess, not to speak of proposals made by the king of Hungary.[90] None the less, the archbishop remained optimistic, and had already taken steps to secure the emperor's consent.

As far as the Austrian marriage was concerned, progress was less smooth. In March Henry of Cornhill wrote that his offer had been received coldly, and declared that he would rather be sent to Acre, than spend any more time with the Austrians, a 'furious people, lacking both in modesty and reason'.[91] This change in attitude – after all, the proposal had first been made by the duke[92] – may be explained by the *Chronica reinhardsbrunnensis*, which reports that Henry (VII) had been supposed to marry a Bohemian princess. As the couple were too closely related, the duke was entrusted with the princess, while a papal dispensation was secured. Instead, the duke secretly sent his own messengers, and asked for papal dispensation on behalf of his daughter. These envoys are said to have been dispatched by early March, at about the time when the English mission arrived.[93] Duke Leopold is known to have

[86] Ibid. 319–20, 484. See also M.-L. Bulst-Thiele, 'Templer in königlichen und päpstlichen Diensten', in P. Classen and P. Seibert (eds), *Festschrift Percy Ernst Schramm zu seinem siebzigsten Geburtstag*, Wiesbaden 1964, i. 289–308, in particular at pp. 297–301. For the English context see H. Nicholson, 'The military orders and the kings of England in the twelfth and thirteenth centuries', in A. V. Murray (ed.), *From Clermont to Jerusalem: the crusades and crusader societies, 1095–1500: selected proceedings of the international medieval congress, University of Leeds, 10–13 July 1995*, Turnhout 1998, 203–17.

[87] J. P. Huffman, 'Prosopography and the Anglo-imperial connection: a Cologne *ministerialis* family and its English relations', *Medieval Prosopography* xi (1990), 53–134, 59, 63. They also held lands in England: CChR, 1226–57, 215.

[88] *Regesta imperii*, no. 10923. This was followed by frequent exchanges of envoys: RLC i. 465, 471, 483, 495.

[89] *Royal letters Henry III*, i, no. 213.

[90] *Diplomatic documents*, no. 153. For the context see also F. Neininger, *Konrad von Urach († 1227): Zähringer, Zisterzienser, Kardinallegat*, Paderborn 1994, 203–72.

[91] *Diplomatic documents*, no. 163.

[92] Zöllner, 'Das Projekt', 58–9.

[93] *Chronica reinhardsbrunnensis*, MGH, SS xxx. 607.

been at the imperial court, and later Bernard of Horstmar, who had been dispatched to the emperor by Engelbert, referred to the role which the duke played in the negotiations for the planned marriage.[94] It is possible that the duke was already planning to arrange a match between his own daughter and Henry (VII). Under these circumstances, the presence of English envoys may have been viewed as cumbersome, which would explain the coldness with which the chancellor of London found himself received.

This did not bode well for the project as a whole. Walter stayed in Cologne, increasingly frustrated,[95] while the archbishop and Bernard of Horstmar assured Henry's court that matters were progressing well, and that a (positive) decision was imminent.[96] Walter was still at Cologne in July,[97] and it was not until August that he was allowed to return.[98] By that stage it must have become clear that the project had failed. Any hopes that the marriage might yet be salvaged were shattered when Engelbert was murdered on 7 November 1225.[99] On 18 November Henry (VII) married Margaret, daughter of the duke of Austria,[100] and the following year the German king, too, ratified the Treaty of Catania.[101] Not for the last time, Henry III's efforts had been frustrated.

The 1225 mission reveals a series of important features in Anglo-imperial exchanges. That Walter's negotiations dealt as much with the loss of Poitou as with the king's marriage had never been a secret. When the bishop of Carlisle first met Engelbert, he opened their conversation with a request to prevent a Staufen–Capetian marriage, and he ended his account of the meeting by reporting that the archbishop had been optimistic about Henry's chances of recovering his inheritance.[102] A marriage between Isabella and Frederick II's heir would have strengthened Henry III's position against Louis VIII, even if it did not result in a joint military undertaking. Most important, it would have undermined the position Louis had gained through the Treaty of Catania, and it would have provided a means to exert pressure on the king of France. The overall approach chosen by the king and his regents closely resembled that of John after the loss of Normandy, and Walter's embassy may thus be indicative of the personnel in charge of Henry III's government. Those who in the past had brokered the deal with the Welfs in order to recoup Normandy, were now those who sought to utilise the victorious

---

94 *Royal letters Henry III*, i, no. 213.
95 Ibid. i, no. 217; *Diplomatic documents*, no. 172.
96 *Diplomatic documents*, nos 188–9.
97 *Quellen zur Geschichte der Stadt Köln*, ed. L. Ennen and G. Eckertz, Cologne 1860–79, ii, no. 87.
98 The letter has been dated 17 August in *Foedera*, i. 190, and 27 August in *Historia diplomatica*, ii. 851.
99 *Annales elwangenses*, MGH, SS x. 20.
100 *Annales scheftlarienses*, MGH, SS xvii. 338; Thorau, *König Heinrich VII*, 262–7.
101 *Constitutiones*, *1198–1272*, no. 290, 11.6.1226.
102 *Royal letters Henry III*, i, no. 213.

33

Staufen for the recovery of Poitou. The personnel, as well as the methods, of Henry's early diplomacy was identical to that of his father's reign. Walter Mauclerk, for instance, had been John's envoy to the *curia*,[103] while the marriage negotiations as such had been supported by both Peter des Roches, bishop of Winchester, and Hubert de Burgh.[104] Thus, despite their often bitter conflict over access to royal patronage,[105] they fundamentally agreed as to the ways and means by which Henry's inheritance could be recovered. This extended to the empire, as even the envoys dispatched by Henry (VII)'s regents shared above all their earlier involvement in contacts between Otto IV and John, and – as in the build-up to Otto's candidacy in 1198 and thereafter – it was the archbishop of Cologne who was the driving force behind these negotiations. At the same time, Henry's government did not blindly follow past precedent. The means by which they sought to realise their goals aimed primarily at a diplomatic, rather than a military solution. The king's regents aimed to isolate the king of France by thwarting his diplomatic initiatives, but they lacked the resources for an armed expedition across the Channel. In this context, potential gains to be drawn from Walter's mission – even if merely that Henry (VII) would not confirm the Treaty of Catania, and that a marriage alliance between Capetians and Staufens could be scuppered – were well worth holding out for. Success did not necessarily entail that Henry III took an Austrian wife. All that mattered was that Henry (VII) did not marry a Capetian princess.

Under these circumstances, Walter's mission was a successful attempt at preventing a potentially disastrous outcome. Furthermore, both the timing and the destination were well chosen. It was obvious that Frederick was unlikely to favour closer ties with the Plantagenets. The settlement of 1220 had, however, given a considerable degree of autonomy to the German regency, and the extent of the emperor's control had caused repeated friction between the two. The proposed marriage was thus mooted at a time when it seemed that these rifts could be turned to Henry III's advantage. Engelbert had little reason to support Louis VIII. In the early thirteenth century the Capetians directed their ambitions not only westwards, against the Plantagenets, but also eastwards, into imperial Burgundy and the Maas region, the latter an area where the see of Cologne had long-standing interests.[106] A marriage between Henry (VII) and a Plantagenet princess may thus

---

[103] *Diplomatic documents*, no. 19.

[104] *RLC* i. 465; *Royal letters Henry III*, i, no. 207.

[105] Vincent, *Peter des Roches*, 184–228; F. A. Cazel, 'Intertwined careers: Hubert de Burgh and Peter des Roches', *Haskins Society Journal* i (1989), 173–81.

[106] For the increasing hostility see W. Stürner, 'Der Staufer Heinrich, (VII) (1212–1242): Lebensstationen eines gescheiterten Königs', *Zeitschrift für Württembergische Landesgeschichte* liii (1993), 13–33 at p. 21. See also H. Stehkämper, 'Der Reichsbischof und Territorialfürst, 12. und 13. Jahrhundert', in P. Berglar and O. Engels (eds), *Der Bischof in seiner Zeit: Bischofstypus und Bischofsideal im Spiegel der Kölner Kirche: Festschrift Joseph Kardinal Höffner*, Cologne 1986, 95–184 at pp. 133–8, for Cologne's territorial interests.

have been perceived as a means of countering Capetian influence in that region. Engelbert's murky role in the affairs of the 'false' Baldwin points in a similar direction: although he avoided associating himself directly with the pretender, he was none the less perceived as someone likely to lend his support, and he thus became Baldwin's first port of call. Other reasons, though, have to be taken into account as well: Cologne's traditionally strong trading links with England faced increasing competition from other German towns, and closer political ties with England might thus have been viewed as a way of gaining an advantage over these rivals from Lübeck, Hamburg and Bremen, or the domains of the duke of Brabant.[107] Furthermore, there was an ongoing conflict as to what exactly Frederick's role was in relation to the German regency.[108] Although in theory he had handed over the affairs of Germany to his son, in practice he continued to dictate the young king's actions.[109] Once Henry (VII) came of age, this was to lead to renewed conflict, but even during his minority, tensions occurred.[110] Engelbert's insistence on pursuing the project of an Anglo-German marriage, and his efforts at preventing Henry (VII) from adopting his father's stance towards the Capetians, may thus have been an attempt to assert the independence of the regency council, and to escape its increasing domination by the emperor.

The 1225 mission was well timed in another respect, too. Henry (VII) had reached a marriageable age, while his father was under pressure to complete his crusading preparations. Traditionally, these included the continuation of a crusader's dynastic line. Henry VI, for instance, had sought to ensure his youngest son's coronation before departing on crusade.[111] Walter was thus sent when the emperor could be expected to have other things on his mind than meddling in the affairs of Germany, and at a time when it seemed likely that his eldest son would soon be married. Nor was the English court the only one to realise this, as Engelbert had explained to Walter: the kings of Bohemia and Hungary had also approached the regency, and we have seen how the papal legate in France had been eager to arrange a marriage. The regents of the infant king of England acted in competition with their Capetian rivals, but they pursued their goals through means which were no different from those used by any other prince in thirteenth-century Europe.

---

107 N. Fryde, 'Deutsche Englandkaufleute in frühhansischer Zeit', Hansische Geschichtsblätter xcvii (1979), 1–14 at p. 6.

108 W. Goez, 'Möglichkeiten und Grenzen des Herrschens aus der Ferne in Deutschland und Reichsitalien, 1152–1220', in T. Kölzer (ed.), Die Staufer im Süden: Sizilien und das Reich, Sigmaringen 1996, 93–112 at pp. 97–9.

109 W. Goez, 'Friedrich II und Deutschland', in K. Friedland, W. Goez and W. J. Müller (eds), Politik, Wirtschaft und Kunst des staufischen Lübeck, Lübeck 1976, 5–38 at pp. 20–6; Stürner, Friedrich II., i. 16–30.

110 Stürner, 'Der Staufer Heinrich (VII)', 21.

111 See Csendes, Heinrich VI, 58–73, 171–8, for the examples of Frederick Barbarossa and Henry VI.

The project of a double marriage had been undertaken at a point and under circumstances which offered hopes for its successful conclusion. At the same time, these very circumstances also hold the key to understanding why the project ultimately failed. One almost suspects that Henry's regents expected this to happen. Although contacts with Germany were frequent and wide-ranging, no evidence survives for an English mission contacting Frederick. This was an apt reflection of political realities. The emperor had left little doubt as to his reluctance to be involved in the conflict between Plantagenets and Capetians. Concluding the Treaty of Catania was little more than an acknowledgement of the Capetians' support in gaining him his throne, and Frederick stayed clear of offering more than his supportive neutrality to Louis VIII. We may assume that he eyed proposals for a French marriage for his eldest son as warily as those for an English union. By accepting either, Frederick would have risked being perceived as supporting one against the other, and such a step might have conjured up memories of the events after Henry VI's death, when Philip Augustus and King John had tried to utilise the German Double Election by supporting rival candidates. This was no mere speculation. When Henry (VII) rebelled against his father in 1234/5, he tried to secure supporters by suggesting, amongst others, a marriage alliance with the Capetians.[112] Furthermore, alienating Louis VIII would have gained Frederick little. Although relations with Louis were less cordial than they had been with Philip Augustus,[113] Henry III, 'an impecunious minor', as Louis's envoys allegedly had put it in 1224, had nothing to offer in exchange. He could have contributed neither to the emperor's crusade, nor to a strengthening of his and his family's position in Germany. To Frederick, arranging an Austrian marriage for Henry (VII) may thus have been the means to avoid being drawn into the Anglo-French conflict.

In 1227 a marriage – between Henry III and Agnes of Bohemia – was on the cards again. This time, though, circumstances seemed more auspicious. Frederick was expected to leave for Palestine at any moment, while Henry (VII) was at last taking personal control of his kingdom. Once again, the initiative appears to have been taken by the archbishop of Cologne. Although the duke of Bavaria had taken over as regent after Engelbert's murder,[114] the prelate's successor, Henry of Mühlenark, continued to dominate exchanges. This is illustrated by the appearance of familiar figures, such as the Zudendorps and Conrad of Speyer, among imperial envoys, but also stretched into previously uncharted territory.[115] The Zudendorps owed their loyalty, as we have seen, primarily to the archbishops of Cologne, while

112 *Annales marbacenses*, 96.
113 *Layettes*, ii, no. 1716.
114 *Burchardi et Cuonradi urspergensis chronicon: continuatio*, MGH, SS xxiii. 381; H. Flachenecker, 'Herzog Ludwig der Kelheimer als Prokurator König Heinrichs, VII', *Zeitschrift für Bayerische Landesgeschichte* lix (1996), 835–48.
115 *CLR, 1226–40*, 15, 17: Gerard de Colonia.

Conrad of Speyer had been in England at least once between 1220 and 1224. Moreover, as a member of the bishop of Speyer's household, he had played a prominent part both in Frederick's government and in that of his son. These men had been selected for their diplomatic experience, and they reflected both the continuing influence of the archbishop, and the close interest taken in relations with England by members of the young king's government. Whoever wanted to enter into close relations with England had to ensure the services of the archbishop. This is particularly well illustrated by the man chosen by the king of Bohemia as his envoy to Henry, Count Arnold of Hückeswagen.[116] Between 1234 and 1238 Arnold was to play a significant role at the Bohemian court, and became a prominent and regular attestor to royal charters.[117] The count's main distinction, however, seems to have been his family's ties with the archbishops of Cologne. The Hückeswagen originated in the Lower Rhineland which had brought them into close contact with the see of Cologne:[118] Arnold's father appears on the witness-lists of Archbishop Adolf of Cologne in 1205, while Arnold himself witnessed a grant by Archbishop Engelbert to the abbey of Altenberg, made at some point between 1218 and 1225.[119] Arnold's son and heir, in turn, joined the chapter of St Gereon at Cologne.[120] We may thus assume that Arnold had been selected both for his position at the Bohemian court, and because of his family's ties with Cologne. The archbishop's role was also underlined when Henry III asked him specifically for his advice about how to proceed in his marriage negotiations.[121] Even if Engelbert had failed to assert his independence from Frederick, he had certainly enshrined his see's dominant role in relations with England.

Although negotiations had been conducted for some time prior to Arnold's arrival,[122] Henry was to remain without a spouse,[123] this despite the fact that in 1227 he seemed set to obtain what he had failed to achieve

---

116 Ibid. 36.

117 *Regesta diplomatica nec non epistolaria bohemiae et moraviae, 600–1253*, ed. K. J. Erben, Prague 1854, nos 833, 862, 873, 889, 923, 932; appendix no. 9.

118 H. Stoob, 'Bruno von Olmütz, das mährische Städtenetz und die europäische Politik von 1245 bis 1281', in H. Stoob (ed.), *Die mittelalterliche Städtebildung im südöstlichen Europa*, Cologne–Vienna 1977, 90–129, 101 n. 34. I am grateful to Dieter Wojtecki for this reference. The connection with Cologne has been overlooked by J. P. Huffman, *Family, commerce and religion in London and Cologne: Anglo-German emigrants, c. 1000–c. 1300*, Cambridge 1998, and *The social politics of medieval diplomacy: Anglo-German relations, 1066–1307*, Ann Arbor 2000.

119 *Urkundenbuch zur Geschichte der mittelrheinischen Territorien*, ed. H. Beyer, L. Eltester and A. Goerz, Koblenz 1874, nos 15, 128.

120 *Urkundenbuch des Stiftes St Gereon zu Köln*, ed. P. Joerres, Bonn 1983, nos 121, 156.

121 *Foedera*, i. 185.

122 *Regesta imperii*, no. 10970; RLC ii. 126.

123 This was not the end of contacts with the count, though: CLR, *1226–40*, 36, 68, 88, 110, 235; CR, *1227–31*, 107–8. For a later account see *Some new sources for the life of Blessed Agnes of Bohemia, including a XIV century Latin version and a XV century German version of her Life*, ed. W. W. Seton, Aberdeen 1915, 70. I am grateful to Jörg Dendl for this reference.

before: a marriage, as well as a political alliance with the empire. In April he wrote to Henry (VII), the duke of Bavaria and the archbishop of Cologne, acknowledging the mission of Conrad of Speyer, and the offer of a confederation with the empire.[124] It seems that the German court had taken the initiative. In his letter to the young king, Henry III referred to the proposal as having first been made by Conrad of Speyer, while the duke of Bavaria was assured of the king's gratitude for his promised support in concluding the alliance. It seems likely that negotiations for the Bohemian marriage had been undertaken in this context. The king of England was, however, to be disappointed yet again. In September 1227 Henry III announced to the prelates and princes of the empire assembling at Antwerp that he would send a high-ranking embassy.[125] No further record survives, however, either for the planned meeting or the proposed alliance. As in 1225, the timing of these contacts and the context within which they were organised hold the key to understanding the reasons for their ultimate failure.

As far as the English court was concerned, the marriage formed part of an attempt to utilise the troubled situation in France, where the infant Louis faced resistance among his barons, and the fact that the truce was about to expire, for a recovery of Henry's lands.[126] Moreover, with the death of Louis VIII the Treaty of Catania was up for renewal once more, while in March 1227 Henry (VII)'s coming of age had been celebrated with the coronation of his wife at Aachen.[127] Even if Henry (VII)'s government would not participate in any military undertakings, friendly relations with the German government would have isolated Louis IX diplomatically. This would have followed the example of Louis VIII, who in 1223 had similarly assured himself of Frederick II's tacit support, before attacking the lands of the infant king of England. Furthermore, with Frederick aiming to set sail for the Holy Land by midsummer, it was to be expected that Henry (VII) would be able to act more freely. It seems plausible that the motives on the German side were similar to those in 1225: an attempt to assert Henry (VII)'s independence, as well as the need to strengthen Cologne's position. These were also the reasons why little came of this. Frederick's imminent departure certainly offered the opportunity for Henry (VII) to act more independently. By September 1227, however, when the proposed meeting at Antwerp was to take place, the emperor had just returned to Sicily, and was excommunicated by the pope. Under these circumstances, Frederick continued to dominate German affairs, and it became politically inopportune to alienate the Capetians. Equally, Gregory IX warned Henry III that he was willing to mediate, but he would not permit open war. The pope said as much when he wrote to Louis IX and Henry III in May 1227. Louis was encouraged to do

124 *Foedera*, i. 185; *Historia diplomatica*, iii. 322.
125 CPR, 1225–32, 161–2.
126 H.-P. Geh, *Insulare Politik in England vor den Tudors*, Husum 1964, 32–3.
127 See also Thorau, *König Heinrich VII*, 298–301.

justice to the king of England,[128] while Henry was warned that the king of France was under the pope's special protection.[129] This had the desired effect: in June Henry suggested that they extend the truce.[130]

The emperor's excommunication soon embroiled much of Latin Europe. It forced Henry III, who by then had officially come of age, to try to avoid being drawn into the papal–imperial conflict, but without alienating either party. A letter sent to the sultan of Damascus, in which the Muslim ruler was requested to set free Christian prisoners, presents the closest evidence for active involvement by the royal court in Frederick's crusade.[131] Henry preferred to mediate. In February 1228 he wrote to Gregory and Frederick, warning that the enemy of mankind was jeopardising the crusade by sowing discord between Frederick and the Church.[132] Henry III implored the pope to consider that it would be impossible to lead a crusade without the emperor and that Frederick should thus be taken back into the Church.[133] In July, after the emperor had departed for the Holy Land, Henry exhorted him to make his peace with the papacy, and to petition humbly to be taken back into the Christian fold.[134] Not for the first time, those who sought to procure a settlement between emperor and pope resorted to the very imagery which in the past the *curia* had used to urge them to settle their conflicts, and to focus their attention on the Holy Land instead. Neither pope nor emperor, however, would allow the English court to remain neutral.

As soon as Frederick had left for Palestine in 1228, Gregory IX declared him deprived of the Sicilian throne, and sent an army against the *regno*, led by the emperor's estranged father-in-law, Jean de Brienne, and manned mostly by the Lombard communes.[135] To sustain this momentum it became, however, necessary to solicit additional funds. Gregory IX, therefore, sought to muster the Church's resources.[136] In France, for instance, the clergy had to hand over the tenth originally collected for Louis VIII's Albigensian Crusade.[137] In 1229 it was England's turn.[138] In April the collection of a tenth

---

128 *Les Registres de Gregoire IX*, ed. L. Auvray, Paris 1896–1955, no. 86.
129 Ibid. no. 95.
130 *CPR, 1225–32*, 213–14.
131 *CR, 1227–31*, 94.
132 Ibid. 93–4. This was probably in response to an imperial embassy which had arrived the day before: *CLR, 1226–40*, 69.
133 *CR, 1227–1231*, 93.
134 *Royal letters Henry III*, i, no. 272. The day before, on 14 July, Reiner de Insula, the emperor's envoy, had been promised 100s: *CLR, 1226–40*, 91. This implies continuing contacts.
135 *Annales scheftlarienses maiores*, MGH, SS xvii, 339; *Chronica Johannis de Oxenedis*, 159; Roger of Wendover, *Flores*, ii. 381 (testifying to the interest taken in England).
136 W. E. Lunt, *Financial relations of the papacy with England to 1328*, Cambridge, Mass. 1939, 191.
137 *Annals of Dunstable*, AM iii. 114.
138 *Annals of Winchester*, AM ii. 85, s.a. 1228.

on all the goods of the clergy began, 'for the sustenance of the war against Frederick, emperor of the Romans'.[139] That proved insufficient.[140] For 29 April 1229 a meeting was thus called to Westminster, where the papal chaplain overseeing the taxation tried to whip up support. The clergy agreed reluctantly to contribute, but the laity refused. It would be mistaken, though, to view this as a token of sympathy for Frederick. The objections raised were directed not at the purpose for which these funds were raised, but against an additional burden of taxation, so soon after the subsidies granted in 1225.[141] In addition, agreeing to a lay subsidy for papal campaigns may have been viewed as setting a dangerous precedent. Nor was Henry III willing to send troops. No record survives for English knights fighting alongside papal armies against the emperor in southern Italy. Equally, however, Frederick's propaganda was ignored in England.[142]

Gregory's actions, though, were not confined to sending an army against Frederick's lands in Sicily. Efforts were undertaken to undermine the emperor's support in Germany.[143] A legate was sent, whose mission has been associated with efforts to replace Henry (VII) with Otto of Lüneburg, heir to the Welfs' claims.[144] Traditionally, it has been assumed that Henry III played a major part in these proceedings,[145] based on a series of letters written by the king on behalf of his German relative. In early March 1229 Henry III wrote to Otto,[146] probably in response to an embassy he had recently received from Brunswick,[147] and expressed his joy at hearing of Otto's recently obtained liberty. He continued to elaborate on their similar fortunes: Otto had been

---

139 *Annals of Tewkesbury*, AM i. 73; 'Annals of Southwark and Merton', 56; *Annals of Dunstable*, AM, iii. 114–15.

140 See Roger of Wendover, *Flores*, iv. 125–6, for what follows.

141 F. A. Cazel, 'The fifteenth of 1225', *BIHR* xxiv (1967), 67–79; Carpenter, *Minority of Henry III*, 379–82.

142 Not that he did not try: *Chronica maiora*, iii. 152–3.

143 *Annals of Dunstable*, AM iii. 113; *Albrici abbatis Trium Fontium chronica*, MGH, SS xxiii. 602; E. Winkelmann, 'Zwölf Papstbriefe zur Geschichte Friedrichs II. und seiner Nachkommen', *Forschungen zur deutschen Geschichte* xv (1875), 373–89, no. 5. J. B. Freed, *The friars and German society in the thirteenth century*, Cambridge, Mass. 1977, 140; *Annales scheftlarienses maiores*, MGH, SS xvii. 339.

144 *Albrici abbatis Trium Fontium chronica*, MGH, SS xxiii, 926; *Registres Grégoire IX*, no. 6151.

145 E. Winkelmann, 'Die Legation des Kardinaldiakons Otto von S. Nicolaus in Deutschland, 1229–31', *MIÖG* xi (1890), 28–40; A. Michels, *Leben Ottos des Kindes, ersten Herzogs von Braunschweig und Lüneburg*, Einbeck 1891, 17–30; F. Trautz, *Die Könige von England und das Reich, 1272–1348*, Heidelberg 1961, 104; J. Ahlers, *Die Welfen und die englischen Könige 1165–1235*, Hildesheim 1987, 263–5; K. A. Frech, 'Ein Plan zur Absetzung Heinrichs, (VII.): die gescheiterte Legation Kardinals Otto in Deutschland, 1229–1231', in S. Lorenz and U. Schmid (eds), *Von Schwaben bis Jerusalem: Facetten staufischer Geschichte*, Sigmaringen 1995, 89–116.

146 *CR, 1227–31*, 233.

147 Brother William de Hospitali of Lüneburg and brother Waremact who received 100 marks on 5 March: *CLR, 1226–40*, 121.

prevented from claiming his rights, and Henry from obtaining his inheritance. In this context, Henry assured his cousin that he would work for his welfare and honour. Furthermore, the young Welf was requested to send envoys by Pentecost so that Henry III could enter into further communication.

Most recently, attention has been drawn to the following passage: 'Scire etiam vos volumus quod prompti sumus et semper parati ad quecumque commodum vestrum respiciunt et honorem, *quem a nostro non reputamus alienum.* (For we want you to know that we are willing and always ready for whatever concerns your comfort and honour, *which we do not consider to be different from our own.*)' This has been interpreted as indicating plans to elevate Otto to quasi-royal status, thus suggesting that the king of England participated in papal initiatives to promote the young Welf as king in Henry (VII)'s stead.[148] Some credence has been given to this argument by the steps Henry III was to take next. After receiving an envoy from Otto,[149] the king wrote to Gregory IX in April 1229.[150] Thanking the pope for his support in freeing Otto from captivity, he then requested that the young Welf, who was praised for his piety and undoubted loyalty to the Holy See, be recommended to the German princes.[151]

The phrasing of Henry III's letters allows, however, for a different interpretation, once we take into account the language employed by the king and its contemporary political, legal and literary context; the political initiatives undertaken by Henry III; and the wider framework of events. Let us begin by placing the phraseology of Henry's letter in context. The king of England did not promise the duke of Brunswick that he would make him king. All Henry did was assure Otto that, to him, Otto's honour was his honour, too. In contemporary usage, honour could refer to status and prestige as much as to legal claims, and should not be read as indicating an equality in rank. Henry's letter formed part of a contemporary diplomatic discourse of honour and friendship.[152] Furthermore, the question remains of what Henry III referred to when writing about Otto's 'recent captivity' and the rights he had been denied. Otto the Child was the surviving son of emperor Otto IV,[153] and sole heir to the remaining Welf domains in Germany. In 1227 he had been captured in battle, and was not to be released until 1229, and even then only after pressure from Gregory IX. By then, Otto also faced opposition concerning his ducal title and his rights to several lands he claimed as part of

---

148 Frech, 'Ein Plan', 100.
149 *CPR, 1225–32*, 243; *CLR, 1226–40*, 123.
150 *CR, 1227–31*, 234–5.
151 Kienast, *Die deutschen Fürsten*, ii. 50.
152 van Eickels, *Vom inszenierten Konsens*, passim.
153 For what follows see E. Boshof, 'Entstehung des Herzogtums Braunschweig-Lüneburg', in W.-D. Mohrmann (ed.), *Heinrich der Löwe*, Göttingen 1980, 249–74 at pp. 265–7, and Stürner, *Friedrich II*, i. 312–16.

his inheritance.[154] This forms part of the context within which Henry III's efforts have to be placed. The king of England had promised to assist the young prince in asserting his rights and inheritance, and so he did. Otto may have turned to his English cousin because of the links between the English court and Henry (VII)'s government. That Henry III turned to the *curia* may have been based on the fact that the archbishop of Bremen was the main challenger to Otto's claims, which made the pope the appropriate addressee for such an intervention. Finally, when Frederick initiated the process which led to the restoration of Otto's rights and title in September 1234, the phraseology used was similar to that employed by Henry III.[155] Henry sought to aid Otto in reclaiming his inheritance, and not to promote the Welf's candidacy for a throne which Otto was unwilling, and which he would have been unable, to seize.

Henry III undoubtedly drew political benefits from his involvement, as it extended the group of imperial princes whose services might be called upon in future. Otto sent envoys to England in September 1229,[156] and arrived himself in July 1230.[157] He certainly was not treated as a prospective fellow-royal. When he reached England, Henry was campaigning in France, and so Otto had to stay in London,[158] where, as one chronicler puts it, his great length and height were commented upon.[159] Henry did not hasten his return, and Otto was forced to wait until October before he met the king. His visit's most palpable result was a series of trading privileges.[160] Otto's primary concern was probably to utilise Henry's extensive contacts in Germany, thus taking up the king's promise to support him in recovering his rights and inheritance. One may also speculate whether he may have aimed at reclaiming some of the lands formerly held by Otto IV,[161] who had once held the title of count of Poitou. The timing of the young Welf's visit, coinciding with Henry III's Breton campaign, may be suggestive. Should this have been the case, no record survives, not least because Henry's expedition failed to achieve its aim. All this seems, however, a more likely explanation for these contacts than Otto's presumed resurrection of the Welfs' imperial aspirations.

There is little indication that Henry III promoted Otto's candidacy among his German contacts. No reference to this matter was made in dealings with the king of Bohemia or the archbishop of Cologne. In fact, the English court was quite willing to let slip by opportunities for mustering support, as is illus-

---

154 See Schneidmüller, *Die Welfen*, 274–9, for a more detailed coverage.
155 *Constitutiones, 1198–1272*, no. 186.
156 *CLR, 1226–40*, 143.
157 *CR, 1227–31*, 366; Roger of Wendover, *Flores*, ii. 199–200.
158 *Annals of Dunstable*, AM iii. 125.
159 Roger of Wendover, *Flores*, ii. 385.
160 *CPR, 1225–32*, 415.
161 Ahlers, *Die Welfen*, 169–78; Hucker, *Otto IV.*, 13–21; R. Favreau, 'Otto von Braunschweig und Aquitanien', in *Heinrich der Löwe und seine Zeit: Herrschaft und Repräsentation der Welfen, 1125–1235* (exhibition catalogue), Munich 1995, ii. 369–76.

trated by its dealings with the duke of Brabant. Despite regular contacts, the issue of the duke's English fiefs overshadowed relations.[162] As Duke Henry had sided with Philip Augustus after Bouvines, he had been deprived of the honour of Eye, his main possession across the Channel. In the early 1220s efforts were made to improve relations, and a series of letters from the duke and Engelbert of Cologne survive,[163] petitioning the English court to restore the duke's lands. In October 1229, however, Hubert de Burgh received Eye in safekeeping for the duke's heirs.[164] This grant seems to have caused some unease at the ducal court, as a safe-conduct from December 1229 survives for the duke and his son on coming to England.[165] Whether this visit was completed remains doubtful, the only indication being a trading privilege granted in February 1230 at the duke's instigation, which did not necessarily require his presence in England.[166] The duke's visit would have provided an opportunity to extend relations with Germany, and to utilise them on Otto's behalf, but the surviving evidence does not suggest that either Otto's candidacy or the general situation in Germany had been given much thought.

Although it seems unlikely that Henry III involved himself directly in the internal affairs of Germany and the empire, we can none the less observe a hiatus in contacts with Henry (VII) and the emperor. Several messengers from Frederick or his son are listed as arriving between February and July 1228,[167] that is immediately prior to Frederick's crusade, but then diplomatic exchanges ceased until February 1230, shortly before Gregory and the emperor resumed negotiations.[168] At the same time, this need not necessarily be a sign of growing hostility. During these months papal efforts to undermine Frederick's regime were at their most intensive, while the English court was primarily concerned with finding allies for the imminent campaign in France, an undertaking to which the Staufen seemed unlikely to contribute. Moreover, too close a rapport with the excommunicated Staufen would have been an unwise move at this stage, as the pope's support was still needed for settling the questions surrounding Henry's own inheritance. Finally, we need to consider what possible interest Henry III could have had in undermining the Staufen in Germany. After all, Henry (VII) had shown great eagerness to forge closer links with England. He was more likely to prove a reliable ally than a reluctant anti-king who lacked both the military and the political muscle to make true his claims.

Although Henry III did not achieve what he had hoped for – an alliance with Germany – the years from 1225 to 1231 were not wasted. The English

---

162 G. Smets, *Henri I duc de Brabant, 1190–1235*, Brussels 1908, 199–201.
163 *Diplomatic documents*, nos 151, 152, 157, 158.
164 *CChR, 1216–1272*, 101.
165 *CPR, 1225–32*, 323.
166 Ibid. 328. In itself, the grant only confirmed privileges already made out in October 1229: ibid. 268–9, 277.
167 *CLR, 1226–40*, 68, 69, 91.
168 Ibid. 169.

court had renewed old ties, and it had won new and influential allies: the king of Bohemia, the archbishop of Cologne, the duke of Brabant and the (future) duke of Brunswick. In Germany, support for closer ties with the Plantagenets grew. Already in 1224/5, Frederick had encountered opposition from the German regency concerning the Treaty of Catania, and two years later, when Henry (VII) came of age, the young king's government actively sought closer ties. It may therefore have seemed as if these could be more fully utilised, once emperor and pope were reconciled. This, in turn, was indicative of the conservatism which defined English diplomacy during these years, both in the strategy pursued and in the choice of allies. This is not surprising, considering that Hubert de Burgh and, to a lesser extent, Peter des Roches, had dominated John's relations with continental Europe, and that they continued to do so under his son. It would be mistaken, however, to view this as blind conservatism, reluctant to face the realities posed by Frederick II's success. Henry and his regents were aware that they could only hope to forge closer ties with the empire by sidestepping the emperor. They tried to do exactly that by exploiting the differences between Frederick and his son's government. More importantly, they, too, had learned from their mistakes: Henry's regents may have sought to sidestep the emperor, but they stopped well short of seeking to determine who that emperor might be. Their plans failed because they underestimated the weight Frederick still carried in German affairs, but also, and more importantly, due to the pressures the emperor found himself exposed to. Frederick had little reason to abandon those who had financed his bid for the throne, while the needs of his planned expedition to the Holy Land, the difficulties he faced in Lombardy and his increasingly fragile relations with the *curia* would have made any involvement in the affairs of England or France unwise. There would have been little to gain, and much to lose. It remained to be seen whether this would change, once Frederick II had returned from the Holy Land and once the conflict between pope and emperor had been resolved.

2

Marriage Politics and the Crusade, 1231–1235

When Frederick returned to Sicily in 1229, the papal campaign against him quickly collapsed.[1] By April 1230 negotiations had begun for a peace with the Lombard communes,[2] and simultaneously pope and emperor treated about a revocation of Frederick's excommunication. A final agreement was reached by 1231, which initiated a period of concord between Gregory and Frederick.[3] This co-operation was, however, forced upon, rather than sought by them. It depended on their willingness to set aside their conflicting conceptions of papal and imperial lordship respectively, and the best means to achieve that was by concentrating on preparations for another crusade. This had various consequences for the king of England. Henry (VII) lost his significance. As in all his domains, the emperor sought to reassert and exercise his imperial rights in full, and this meant that Henry (VII)'s independent governance in Germany became little more than a legal fiction. An alliance, like the one envisaged in 1227, thus had little chance of success. Henry III, in turn, beset by domestic problems and short of funds, was in no position to challenge his Capetian adversaries, and had to settle for a series of truces instead. He thus lacked the incentive to forge closer ties with the court of Henry (VII), and the regular exchanges which we have witnessed up to 1228 ceased. Once more, Henry III concentrated on the archbishop of Cologne, and the dukes of Brunswick and Brabant. At the same time, the king's court also made its first, informal contacts with Frederick. Little, though, could have prepared Henry for the emperor's announcement in 1234 that he wanted to marry Isabella Plantagenet. Once placed within the context of papal–imperial relations during these years, Frederick's marriage proposal will seem less sudden and unexpected, and it is to this context that we should therefore turn next.

---

1 *Chronica Johannis de Oxenedis*, 159, 160; *Willelmi chronica andrensis*, MGH, SS xxiv. 770, s.a. 1230; R. Hiestand, 'Ierusalem et Sicilie rex: zur Titulatur Friedrichs II', *DA* lii (1996), 181–9 at pp. 184–5; Stürner, *Friedrich II*, ii. 170–81.
2 *Constitutiones, 1198–1272*, no. 125.
3 Ibid. nos 126–49; Kluger, *Hochmeister*, 141–61; Stürner, *Friedrich II*, ii. 181–9.

Emperor and pope

The new spirit of papal–imperial concord was most visible in dealings with the commune at Rome and the Lombard towns and in the affairs of the Latin kingdom of Jerusalem, but it also extended to the emperor's interests in Burgundy, and the government of Germany. In the light of later events, notably Frederick's second excommunication in 1239, it is easy to view these years as at best a prelude, or at worst as indicative of papal double-dealing.[4] Seen in their contemporary context, matters become more complex. Gregory and Frederick had not suddenly become friends. Rather, they were bound by ties of mutual dependence. The emperor needed papal support to subdue his many foes, foremost amongst them the Italian communes. Similarly, Gregory viewed Frederick's success of 1229 as merely preliminary, a breathing period, allowing for the spiritual, political and logistic preparation of a new campaign to the Holy Land. This, more than anything else, brought pope and emperor together. That this concord broke down eventually is something which we, blessed with hindsight, can judge to have been inevitable. The situation may not have appeared the same to contemporaries, and the events of 1231–5 ought to be considered with this in mind.[5]

The *curia* continued to stress the precarious state of the Holy Land. In April 1231, for instance, Henry III was admonished to make peace with Louis IX, as the king of Persia was planning to destroy the Christian faith in Africa,[6] with a similar request submitted to Louis in May 1233.[7] The connection between peace in Europe and the success of a future crusade was stressed once more in spring 1234: a new crusade was soon to be launched, and its success depended upon peace among the rulers of Christendom.[8] This formed part of wider preparations for the new campaign. These included renewed efforts at pacifying Christendom, as well as attempts at creating a state of religious purity and dogmatic orthodoxy. It was during the early 1230s that Gregory commissioned his *Decretales*, a canon law collection which remained in use until the early twentieth century, and that he began to formalise the legal procedures for the interrogation and prosecution of suspected heretics.[9] An armed pilgrimage to Jerusalem could be successful only if the combatants

---

4 Abulafia, *Frederick II*, 290–320; T. C. van Cleve, *The Emperor Frederick II of Hohenstaufen: immutator mundi*, Oxford 1972, 231–3.

5 This has been elaborated in Weiler, 'Frederick II, Gregory IX and the Holy Land', 192–206, on which parts of this chapter are based.

6 *Epistolae saeculi XIII*, i, no. 438. The historical context of this remains unclear: see Mayer, *Kreuzzüge*, 226; R. S. Humphreys, *From Saladin to the Mongols: the Ayyubids of Damascus, 1193–1260*, Albany 1977, 214–20; Gottschalk, *Al-Malik al-Kāmil*, 160–7; P. M. Holt, *The age of the crusades: the Near East from the eleventh century to 1517*, Harlow 1986, 63–6; *Albrici abbatis Trium Fontium chronica*, MGH, SS xxiii. 603.

7 *Royal letters Henry III*, i, appendix v, no. 31.

8 *Registres de Gregoire IX*, nos 1801–2.

9 Ibid. nos 2099–102, 2121, 2127

were true Christians, untainted by heterodoxy. Even a union of the Greek and Latin Churches was attempted.[10] This followed, almost to the letter, the canons of the Fourth Lateran Council. Then, too, the institutional and spiritual renewal of Latin Christendom, the battling of heretics and schismatics, had been perceived as leading towards the ultimate goal of an armed pilgrimage to Jerusalem.[11] Nor were Gregory's references to the affairs of the Holy Land idle talk: in September 1234 the pope called for a new crusade to start once Frederick's truce had expired, and by November the preaching of the cross had begun in Ireland, France, Germany and Lombardy.[12] Time was needed to muster the necessary financial and military resources, to allow for the recruitment of troops, the collection of funds and the settlement of legal and political disputes.

Preparations made by Gregory and Frederick also included efforts to foster stronger links with the Muslim rulers of north Africa. On 20 April 1231 the emperor concluded a truce with the ruler of Tunisia.[13] They agreed to release prisoners, and to make amends for damages inflicted by pirates. The problem of Muslim corsairs also involved the pope, who, in August 1231, requested al-Kāmil's support in freeing merchants from Ancona.[14] Moreover, efforts were made to win or convert potential allies. In February 1233, for instance, the sultan of Damascus was requested to allow the mendicants to preach the Gospel, and to accept Christianity.[15] For March 1235, an embassy from the sultan of Iconium is reported as visiting Rome, discussing the possibility of an alliance, and conveying the sultan's promise to assist the Christians in recovering all lands they had lost under Saladin.[16] Attempts to convert the people east of the river Volga were made, and the earliest contacts with the Mongols were initiated.[17] The success of Frederick's strategy in 1229, in itself by no

---

10 J. Doran, 'Rites and wrongs: the Latin mission to Nicaea, 1234', in R. N. Swanson (ed.), *Unity and diversity in the Church* (SCH xxxii, 1996), 131–44.

11 *Decrees of the ecumenical councils*, i. 230–80; H. Roscher, *Papst Innocenz III. und die Kreuzzüge*, Göttingen 1969, 27–50.

12 *Epistolae saeculi XIII*, i, nos 605–6; *Pontificia hibernica: medieval papal chancery documents concerning Ireland, 640–1261*, ed. M. Sheehy, Dublin 1962–5, no. 214; *Registres Gregoire IX*, nos 2204–9. *Annals of Dunstable, AM*, iii.142, refer to the beginning of crusade preaching in England s.a. 1235; *Chronica maiora*, iii.288.

13 *Constitutiones, 1198–1272*, no. 153. Note also the imperial embassy sent in 1235: *Extraits du Collier de perles*, in *Receuils des historiens des croisades: historiens orientaux*, ii, Paris 1880, 196. Ibn Wasil reports continuing friendly relations between Frederick and the Aiyyubid rulers of Cairo: *Arab historians of the crusades*, ed. and trans. F. Gabrieli, English trans. E. J. Costello, London 1969, 276; C. Hillenbrand, *The crusades: Islamic perspectives*, Edinburgh 1999, 337–40.

14 *Regesta regni hierosolymitani (1097–1291)*, ed. R. Röhricht, Innsbruck 1893–1904, repr. New York n.d., i, no. 1025.

15 *Epistolae saeculi XIII*, i, no. 512. In May, similar petitions were directed towards the caliph of Baghdad and the sultan of Morocco: ibid. nos 527–8.

16 *Registres Gregoire IX*, no. 2473.

17 H. Dörrie, 'Drei Texte zur Geschichte der Ungarn und Mongolen', *Nachrichten der Akademie der Wissenschaften in Göttingen (Philosophisch-Historische Klasse)* (1956), 125–202

means unprecedented, set an example which was willingly taken up by the *curia*.

Returning Jerusalem to Christian control had helped to end Frederick's excommunication, and, despite the hostile reception it initially received,[18] greatly increased his standing within Latin Christendom. Frederick's position was, however, under threat from two sides: the agreement of 1229 had been a truce, not a final settlement, and he faced opposition from the nobles of *Outremer*. Frederick's difficulties in the east rested with his unwillingness to accept the limits of his own claim to the title of king of Jerusalem, which, after all, he only held by right of his wife Isabella, and on behalf of their son Conrad.[19] This was combined with Frederick's reluctance to acknowledge that in the Holy Land, unlike in Sicily or Germany, the monarch was – at least in theory – ruler *primus inter pares*.[20] For instance, he refused to accept the role traditionally exercised by the nobility of Palestine in appointing a regent, and sent his Sicilian marshal, Richard Filangieri, instead. He similarly disregarded the barons when handing out lands regained in 1229.[21] Frederick

---

at pp. 151–62; J. Richard, *La Papauté et les missions d'orient au moyen âge, XIIIe–XVe siècles,* Rome 1977, 37–41. See also K.-E. Lupprian, *Die Beziehungen der Päpste zu islamischen und mongolischen Herrschern im 13. Jahrhundert anhand ihres Briefwechsels,* Vatican City 1981, nos 1–3, 5; T. Allsen, 'Prelude to the western campaigns: Mongol military operations in the Volga-Ural region, 1217–1237', *Archivum Eurasiae Medii Aevii* iii (1983), 5–24.

[18] A. Sommerlechner, *Stupor mundi? Kaiser Friedrich II. und die mittelalterliche Geschichtsschreibung,* Vienna 1999, 263–308.

[19] H. E. Mayer, 'Kaiserrecht und Heiliges Land', in H. Fuhrmann, H. E. Mayer and K. Wriedt (eds), *Aus Reichsgeschichte und nordischer Geschichte,* Stuttgart 1972, 193–208 at p. 195; Hiestand, 'Ierusalem et Sicilie rex', 181; for the problems posed by 'foreign' marriages of the queens of Jerusalem see B. Hamilton, 'King consorts and their entourages from the west from 1186 to 1250', in H. E. Mayer (ed.), *Die Kreuzfahrerstaaten als multikulturelle Gesellschaft,* Munich 1997, 13–24. For a contemporary, hostile account see *Gestes de chiprois,* ed. G. Raynaud (Publications de la Société de l'orient latin: série historique, v, 1887, repr. Osnabrück 1968), 76–83, 83–99, 105, 112–46; *Continuation de Guillaume de Tyre dite du manuscrit de Rothelin,* in *Receuil des historiens des croisades: historiens occidentaux,* ii, Paris 1859, 526 (Eng. trans. by J. Shirley in *Crusader Syria in the thirteenth century: the Rothelin continuation of the history of William of Tyre with part of the Eracles or Acre text,* Aldershot 1999, 37, chapter 19); Filippo da Novara, *Guerra,* caps 39–43, 100–4; *Acta aragonensia: Quellen zur deutschen, italienischen, französischen, spanischen, zur Kirchen- und Kulturgeschichte: aus der diplomatischen Korrespondenz Jaymes II (1291–1327)* (including vol. iv, *Nachträge*), ed. H. Finke, Munich 1908–33, iv, no. 1; G. N. Bromiley, 'Philip of Novara's account of the wars between Frederick II of Hohenstaufen and the Ibelins', *JMH* iii (1977), 325–38; P. W. Edbury, *John of Ibelin and the kingdom of Jerusalem,* Woodbridge 1997, 41–57, and *The kingdom of Cyprus and the crusades, 1191–1374,* Cambridge 1991, 55–65.

[20] J. Prawer, *The Latin kingdom of Jerusalem: European colonialism in the Middle Ages,* London 1972, 102; S. Melani, 'Lotta politica nell'Oltremare franco all'epoca di Federico II', in *Federico II e le nuove culture: atti del XXXI convegno storico internazionale, Todi, 9–12 ottobre 1994,* Spoleto 1995, 89–111.

[21] Most of these went to the Teutonic Knights, rather than their former owners: Anonymous, 'Quatre Pièces relatives à l'ordre teutonique en orient', *Archive de l'orient latin* ii (1884), 164–9, no. 3; D. Wojtecki, 'Der Deutsche Orden unter Friedrich II', in Fleckenstein, *Probleme um Friedrich II,* 187–224 at pp. 187–8; J. C. Riley-Smith, 'The

thus alienated some of the kingdom's most important families. In particular the Ibelin lords of Beirut, one of the most influential families of *Outremer*, soon became a focal point for those opposing the Staufen regime.[22] To some extent a crusade could be used to overcome this resistance. When Gregory came to support Frederick against the rebels, for instance, he did so because they impeded the planned crusade. Just as the crusade of 1227 had been used to overcome the resistance of the Lombards, so a campaign which success-fully reasserted Christian control of Palestine would have given Frederick the prestige, as well as the means of patronage, to deal with his opponents. Last but not least, Frederick was the king of Jerusalem, and thus bound by obliga-tions greater than those of ordinary crusaders.[23]

In the Holy Land, Gregory fully backed the emperor. In August 1231 he wrote to Frederick who, for the first time, was addressed as king of Jerusalem (in itself a major concession on the pope's part),[24] and promised his full support;[25] in June 1232 Gregory reprimanded the patriarch of Jerusalem for supporting the rebellion against Frederick;[26] in July the military orders and the Church of *Outremer* were ordered to fight against those who disobeyed the emperor.[27] Gregory continued to support Frederick, even after Filangieri had been defeated and after the Ibelins had brought much of the kingdom under their control. In August 1234 he admonished Jean de Ibelin to make amends for the insults he had done to the emperor, or to seek papal arbitra-tion.[28] Gregory made clear whose claims he deemed to be the better. This could not have come as much of a surprise: even the best equipped and manned crusade would achieve little if the crusader states remained inter-nally divided. It was only when Frederick failed to win a decisive victory, and when his continuing conflict with the Ibelins threatened the planned crusade itself, that Gregory ceased in his unquestioning support for him.

A similar spirit of co-operation prevailed in dealings with the Lombard communes. The *curia's* support was, however, less unquestioning, and Gregory urged peace and compromise, rather than condemning those resisting Frederick. This still marked a momentous shift in papal attitudes. In fact,

---

Templars and the Teutonic Knights in Cilician Armenia', in T. S. R. Boase (ed.), *The Cilician kingdom of Armenia*, Edinburgh 1978, 92–117 at pp. 111–15; P. Hilsch, 'Der deut-sche Ritterorden im südlichen Libanon: zur Topographie der Kreuzfahrerherrschaften Sidon und Beirut', *Zeitschrift des Deutschen Palästina-Vereins* xcvi (1980), 174–89, and Walter Hubatsch, 'Der deutsche Orden und die Reichslehnschaft über Zypern', *Nachrichten der Akademie der Wissenschaften in Göttingen (Philologisch-Historische Klasse)* (1955), 245–306 at pp. 251–79.

22 Abulafia, *Frederick II*, 175–80, 190–4.
23 See Prawer, *Latin Kingdom*, 108, for a more critical view.
24 Hiestand, 'Jerusalem et Sicilie rex', passim.
25 *Epistolae saeculi XIII*, i, no. 450.
26 Ibid. i, nos 467–8; R. Röhricht, *Geschichte des Königreichs Jerusalem (1100–1291)*, Innsbruck 1898, 797–828.
27 *Epistolae saeculi XIII*, i, no. 477.
28 *Registres Gregoire IX*, no. 2045.

when announcing his reconciliation with the emperor, the pope found it necessary to assure the communes that this was not a betrayal of his Lombard allies.[29] Gregory was soon forced to arbitrate. The Italian communes and their representatives had been summoned to a number of meetings in 1231,[30] which were to culminate in a diet at Ravenna. Although Frederick emphasised that this had been planned with the pope's advice, the list of participants and the diet's agenda caused unease. Frederick's son was to attend with a contingent of German princes, and the meeting's objective was the 'establishment of peace and prosperity in Italy'.[31] The presence of German troops and an agenda whose phrasing echoed the very imperial claims which the Lombard League had sought to resist, did little to assure the communes. The towns blocked the Alpine passes and prevented Henry (VII) from attending.[32] In the end, Frederick was forced to seek papal mediation. Negotiations began in March 1232, but a final agreement was not reached until October 1233.[33] It is worth noting that, as in the truce of 1227, one of the clauses stipulated that the League provide knights for the emperor's use in the Holy Land.[34] This agreement was a reluctant compromise which patched over the differences between emperor and communes, without claiming to resolve them. Viewed in the context of papal crusading policy, however, it was a small step towards the pacification of Christendom. All the *curia* expected was that hostilities ceased for long enough for the planned crusade to get under way.[35] Nor should we be surprised at Gregory's rather different handling of the opposition to Frederick II in Italy and Christian Syria. The communes had provided the pope with the financial and military backing to lead his wars against Frederick, and their wariness of any attempt at establishing firm imperial control was a fundamental safeguard for the continuing political independence of the Holy See. Gregory IX could not and probably did not want to support open rebellion against the emperor. Neither, though, could he abandon his old allies and support the emperor in all his demands against the Lombards.

The complexity of the papacy's dealings with Frederick is further illustrated by developments in Rome itself, in particular the question of communal self-government.[36] Much of that centred on defining what the

---

[29] Constitutiones, 1198–1272, no. 149.

[30] Ibid. nos 151–2.

[31] Ibid. no. 155.

[32] van Cleve, Emperor Frederick II, 361.

[33] Constitutiones, 1198–1272, nos 161–9, 176–82; Kluger, Hochmeister, 168–9.

[34] Constitutiones, 1198–1272, no. 182.

[35] Codes diplomaticus dominii temporalis sancti sedis, ed. A. Theiner, Rome 1861–2, i, nos 177–8; W. Maleczek, 'Das Frieden stiftende Papsttum im 12. und 13. Jahrhundert', in J. Fried (ed.), Träger und Instrumentarien des Friedens im hohen und späten Mittelalter, Sigmaringen 1996, 249–332 at pp. 287–97.

[36] P. Partner, The lands of St Peter: the papal state in the Middle Ages and the early Renaissance, Berkeley 1972, 249–54; M. Thumser, 'Friedrich II und der römische Adel', in Esch and Kamp, Friedrich II, 425–38 at pp. 431–3.

exact balance of power was between the pope as secular lord of Rome and the citizens. A final break occurred in 1234. The citizens maintained that all the papacy's possessions were part of the dominions of the city of Rome, and as such had to be under communal control. This was unacceptable to Gregory, and preparations began to solve the problem by force. In October and November the *curia* started to muster troops in Germany for a campaign against the Romans, to be led by the emperor.[37] In December the Churches of France, Castile and Aragon were asked for support,[38] as was the English clergy.[39] English chroniclers emphasise the prominent role of Peter des Roches, bishop of Winchester, during the campaign.[40] The reasons for Peter's involvement will be dealt with in greater detail at a later stage. Suffice it to say here that his involvement was not a sign of warming relations between the English court and the emperor, but the result of Peter's fluctuating political fortunes which by then, and not for the first time, had driven him into exile.[41] What this episode does illustrate, however, is the degree to which pope and emperor collaborated, and the extent to which they were mutually dependent. Frederick needed Gregory in Palestine and Lombardy, while the pope required help to deal with the political challenges he faced in his own domains.

The emperor's relations with his son and the affairs of Languedoc illustrate the fragile nature of this concord, and the effect it had on the political structure of the empire. Frederick's involvement in Gregory's war against the Romans was cut short by his son's rebellion.[42] Since Henry's failure to attend the diet at Ravenna relations between father and son had taken a turn for the worse. In April 1232, during a meeting at Aquileia, the king was forced to swear an oath of loyalty to the emperor. To make Henry (VII)'s humiliation complete, the German princes were authorised to rebel against him, should he show any sign of disobedience in future. Furthermore, Henry (VII) had to petition Gregory to be excommunicated should he ever again oppose his father's decisions.[43] This left Henry no room for manoeuvre. When he concluded a treaty of mutual friendship and support with the Lombard

37 *Registres Gregoire IX*, nos 2146, 2224–56, 2259–80, 2291–2.
38 Ibid. nos 2344–73. See also the account in *Chronica latina regum castellae*, 109–10.
39 *Annals of Tewkesbury*, AM i. 94; Matthew Paris, *Chronica maiora*, iii. 288.
40 *Annals of Southwark*, MGH, SS xxvii. 432; *Annals of Tewkesbury*, AM i. 95; *Annals of Dunstable*, AM, iii. 142. However, Matthew Paris names the count of Toulouse as leader of the papal armies: *Chronica maiora* iii. 304.
41 Vincent, *Peter des Roches*, 470–2.
42 Stürner, 'Der Staufer', 26–30; K. Borchardt, 'Der sogenannte Aufstand Heinrichs (VII) in Franken 1234/5', in K Borchardt and E. Bünz (eds), *Forschungen zur bayerischen und fränkischen Geschichte: Festschrift Peter Herde*, Würzburg 1998, 53–119; Stürner, *Friedrich II*, 286–309; C. Hillen, *Curia regis: Untersuchungen zur Hofstruktur Heinrichs (VII) 1220–1235 nach den Zeugen seiner Urkunden*, Frankfurt am Main 1999, 214–19.
43 *Constitutiones, 1198–1272*, no. 170.

League,[44] he had reached the point of no return. In spring 1235 the emperor entered Germany, while Gregory IX threatened excommunication to those assisting the rebels.[45] Henry's support crumbled, and in July 1235, he was imprisoned and exiled to Apulia.[46] The compromise agreed in 1220, awarding Frederick control over the empire on condition that his son rule Germany, had failed, not the least because Frederick was unwilling to cede authority in deed as well as name.

The affairs of imperial Burgundy followed a similar pattern. As soon as peace had been arranged with Gregory IX, the emperor stated his claims.[47] The full weight of imperial authority was to be felt, and in September 1234 the count of Toulouse received a confirmation of his fiefs and was granted the margravate of Provence.[48] In this, Frederick followed a petition made by the king of France to the pope.[49] Frederick's influence in the region is also evident in the presence of both the counts of Toulouse and Provence at a diet at Hagenau in late 1235.[50] They led the largest contingent of Burgundian nobles attending a meeting outside Arles since the days of Frederick Barbarossa. Their participation was an achievement in itself, as in the past the ongoing feud between the counts had thwarted all efforts at peace-making.[51] The emperor used his new-found influence to manifest his claims even in regions which in the past had at best witnessed a nominal exercise of imperial lordship. Nor were these efforts confined to the lands listed above. In Germany the emperor, too, aimed at establishing a basis for firmer royal control than had existed before: in 1235 the *Mainzer Reichslandfrieden* was issued, listing and defining the juridical responsibilities and rights of the emperor in his German homelands. The document, which remained among the core constitutional documents of the Holy Roman Empire until its dissolution in 1806, was in part aimed at strengthening the monarch's position by underlining his role as the final arbiter of legal disputes and conflicts.[52]

---

44 *Annales placentini gibellini*, MGH, SS xviii. 810; *Annales bergomates*, MGH, SS xviii. 497; *Constitutiones, 1198–1272*, nos 325–8.

45 *Registres Gregoire IX*, nos 2445–6.

46 *Annales scheftlarienses maiores*, MGH, SS xvii. 340.

47 *Constitutiones, 1198–1272*, nos 159–60, 175.

48 *Layettes*, ii, no. 2309.

49 *Epistolae saeculi XIII*, i, nos. 577, 625–6.

50 *Continuatio IVa, Chronica regia*, 267–8; Kienast, *Die deutschen Fürsten*, ii. 34.

51 *Registres Gregoire IX*, no. 2427.

52 A. Buschmann, 'Landfriede und Verfassung: zur Bedeutung des Mainzer Reichslandfriedens von 1235 als Verfassungsgesetz', in *Aus Österreichs Rechtsleben in Geschichte und Gegenwart: Festschrift Ernst C. Hellbling*, Salzburg 1971, 449–72; H. Angermeier, 'Landfriedenspolitik und Landfriedensgesetzgebung unter den Staufern', in Fleckenstein, *Probleme um Friedrich II*, 167–86; Stürner, *Friedrich II*, ii. 311–16; E. Klingelhöfer, *Die Reichsgesetze von 1220, 1231/32 und 1235: ihr Werden und ihre Wirkung im deutschen Staat Friedrichs II*, Weimar 1955; H. Koller, 'Zur Diskussion über die Reichsgesetze Friedrichs II', *MIÖG* lxvi (1958), 29–51.

Frederick's dealings with the barons of the Holy Land and his son in Germany, his relations with the communes of northern Italy and the lords and nobles of Burgundy, follow a distinctive pattern. They sought to extend, manifest and strengthen his authority in all those lands which nominally fell under his control, and they did so with reference – sometimes specific, sometimes by implication – to the needs of the Holy Land. The question remains, however, whether these objectives were as mutually exclusive to him as they might seem to us. Unless proper control had been established over his various domains, Frederick would be unable to lend the planned expedition his full support. In many ways his actions are reminiscent of Frederick Barbarossa's preparations for the Third Crusade, which entailed a temporary pacification of Italy, the establishment of a general peace in Germany and further expansion into Burgundy.[53] Similarly, the ruthlessness with which Henry VI had established his claims over Sicily was part of his crusading preparations, as well as stating his claims to be William II's true successor,[54] while Louis IX and Henry III, too, were to use their crusading vows to secure and expand their and their families' possessions. If compared to his father's and grandfather's undertakings, the main difference appears to be that Frederick II did not die before the crusade got under way or before it reached its goal.[55] If viewed within a medieval context, we see Frederick emerge as a monarch who lived, thought and acted within the same parameters as his contemporaries.[56] Part of this *Weltbild* was, and was to remain for a long time, the defence of Christian lands in *Outremer*. Closely entwined with this was the realisation that Frederick II and Gregory IX could only work together with the interests of *Outremer* as guiding principle. Until 1235 at least it was the emperor who benefited most from this, but Gregory IX lent his support with the expectation that the emperor would repay him by assisting the *curia*

---

53 *Arnoldi abbatis lubecensis chronica*, MGH, SS xxi. 170; R. Hiestand, 'Precipua tocius christianissimi columpna: Barbarossa und der Kreuzzug', in A. Haverkamp (ed.), *Friedrich Barbarossa: Handlungsspielräume und Wirkungswesen des staufischen Kaisers*, Sigmaringen 1992, 51–108 at pp. 52–8.
54 Csendes, *Heinrich VI*, 144–58, 179–88; R. Hiestand, 'Kingship and crusade in twelfth-century Germany', in A. Haverkamp and H. Vollrath (eds), *England and Germany in the high Middle Ages*, Oxford 1996, 236–65, at pp. 253–61.
55 For the wider context of Frederick's religiosity see H.M. Schaller, 'Die Frömmigkeit Kaiser Friedrichs II', in *Das Staunen der Welt: Kaiser Friedrich II von Hohenstaufen, 1194–1250: Schriften zur staufischen Geschichte und Kunst*, xv, Göppingen 1996, 128–51; J. M. Powell, 'Frederick II and the Church: a revisionist view', *Catholic Historical Review* xlviii (1962), 487–97, and 'Frederick II and the Church in the kingdom of Sicily 1220–1224', *Church History* xxx (1961), 28–34; H. Beumann, 'Friedrich II. und die heilige Elisabeth: zum Besuch des Kaisers in Marburg am 1. Mai 1236', in *Sankt Elisabeth: Fürstin-Dienerin-Heilige*, Sigmaringen 1981, 151–66, repr. in his *Ausgewählte Aufsätze, 1966–1986*, ed. J. Petersohn and R. Schmidt, Sigmaringen 1987, 411–26; and J. Petersohn, 'Kaisertum und Kultakt in der Stauferzeit', in J. Petersohn (ed.), *Politik und Heiligenverehrung im Hochmittelalter*, Sigmaringen 1994, 101–47 at pp. 115–18, 133–8.
56 See also Abulafia's key thesis, *Frederick II*, 438–9.

where necessary, but, above all, that he would continue to work for another campaign to the east.

Where did this leave Henry III? Henry (VII), had been politically isolated. At best, the king of England may have hoped that Frederick's interest in the affairs of imperial Burgundy might lead to a *rapprochement*. After all, Languedoc had come under increasing domination by the Capetians, and frequently, especially during Louis VIII's reign, at the emperor's expense.[57] Moreover, by granting Raymond of Toulouse the margravate of Provence, Frederick was rewarding one of the English king's most loyal allies. Should Henry have entertained such hopes, he was to be disappointed. Louis IX and Frederick II acted in unison. The grant to Raymond of Toulouse coincided with a petition to this effect made by the king of France, whose brother, after all, was to inherit the county on Raymond's death.[58] The emperor's primary objective was to establish a firmer grip on the affairs of imperial Burgundy, and he had little reason to fear Capetian influence in the region. Frederick also made sure that his renewed interest in the kingdom of Arles was accompanied by efforts to strengthen his ties with Louis, and in May 1232 the Treaty of Catania was confirmed once more.[59] There was thus little indication that Frederick would change his stance. In many ways, the circumstances which had forced his hand before the crusade were now even more pressing, but, unlike Louis IX, there was little that Henry III could contribute.

Henry III and Louis IX

The hope that Poitou, Anjou and Normandy might yet be recovered had not been abandoned. Henry III was, however, unable to embark on a campaign of conquest, and had to settle for a series of truces instead. This was as much the result of political problems he faced in England, as of persistent papal pressure.[60] In April 1231, shortly after an understanding had been reached with Frederick II, Gregory IX wrote to Henry III urging him either to make peace with Louis IX or to prolong the existing truce,[61] with similar exhortations sent to the king of France in May 1233.[62] The pope even involved himself directly in negotiations: in 1233 the archbishops of Paris and Sens, as well as

---

[57] *Chronica Magistri Guillemi de Podio Laurentii*, ed. J. Duvernoy, Paris 1976, repr. Toulouse 1996, 124.

[58] *Registres Gregoire IX*, nos 4782–92. The significance of this for the English court is attested by the fact that a version of the Treaty of Paris was enrolled on the Gascon register: *Gascon register A (series of 1318–1319)*, ed. G. P. Cuttino and J.-P. Trabut-Cussac, London 1975, no. 344.

[59] *Constitutiones, 1198–1272*, nos 174, 313; Le Goff, *St Louis*, 116–18.

[60] *CR, 1231–4*, 559.

[61] *Epistolae saeculi XIII*, i, no. 438.

[62] *Royal letters Henry III*, i, appendix v, no. 31.

the bishops of Salisbury and Winchester, received papal letters ordering them to facilitate an agreement. This formed part of the papacy's peacemaking efforts in preparation for the 1239 crusade, a connection underlined by another papal missive from February 1234: Louis and Henry should come to terms, as the Holy Land depended on peace among the Christian princes.[63] Henry III faced a papal attitude not unlike the one Frederick II encountered in Lombardy. A conflict which was not amenable to a quick and peaceful solution, or where such a settlement could be achieved only through a prolonged and costly military campaign, consumed resources which were more urgently needed elsewhere. A truce, however unsatisfactory or preliminary, was preferable to yet another war.

Henry III left no doubt that any agreement was to be temporary. While negotiations for a peace continued, preparations began for military action. In April 1234 troops had been mustered to assist the count of Brittany in a rebellion against the king of France.[64] His allies, though, deserted Henry III as quickly as he had won them, and in September the count submitted to Louis IX.[65] Similarly, in August 1234, Henry's stepfather, Hugh de Lusignan, agreed on a settlement with Louis IX.[66] The king of France promised not to enter a truce unless the count's claims against the king of England concerning the island of St Oleron had been settled. This was to prove a major obstacle,[67] and a final agreement was not reached until late July 1235.[68] A complicated system of arbitration was put in place to deal with violations of the peace, thus foreshadowing the Treaty of Paris (1259). Even then, the truce was not fully ratified until early 1236.[69] The truce of 1235 was to form the pattern for similar agreements for almost a generation. At the time, however, it was not a blueprint for peace, but merely a means of postponing the final recovery of Henry's inheritance.

The English court continued to look for allies in France. Most important, plans were made for a marriage between Henry III and the count of Ponthieu's daughter and heiress.[70] After consultations with the *curia*, as well as the regents of Louis IX and Queen Blanche, the king's intentions were made public in April 1235.[71] Soon after, Henry's almoner was sent to

---

63 *Registres Gregoire IX*, nos 1801–2.
64 CR, *1231–4*, 558; Stacey, *Politics, policy and finance*, 176–7.
65 Powicke, *Henry III*, 184.
66 *Layettes*, ii, no. 2307.
67 CR, *1234–7*, 160–1; *Treaty rolls, 1234–1325*, ed. P. Chaplais, London 1955, no. 65; CPR, *1232–47*, 110.
68 *Diplomatic documents*, no. 239; CR, *1234–7*, 192.
69 *Foedera*, i. 221; CR, *1234–7*, 158.
70 Howell, *Eleanor of Provence*, 10–11.
71 *Treaty rolls*, no. 5. Henry announced a mission headed by William of Kilkenny and Robert Surecote, vaguely defined as dealing with urgent matters on which the pope's counsel was needed. Presumably, this included the planned marriage: CPR, *1232–7*, 94; *Treaty rolls*, no. 61.

Ponthieu, probably in order to finalise arrangements.[72] By early summer, however, problems occurred. According to Matthew Paris, the marriage failed, among other reasons, because of opposition from Louis IX.[73] The prospect of an English king acquiring the strategically important county of Ponthieu must have caused some unease, especially when considering that Count Simon, an ally of King John at Bouvines, had only been allowed to exercise control of his county again in 1231, and then only after promising that he would not marry off his children without royal consent.[74] At the same time, it seems that Henry III was playing a double game. Although he and Count Simon of Ponthieu had entered a legally binding agreement, the king also contacted Count Amadeus of Savoy. Henry explained that he had been prevented from marrying the count's niece, daughter of the count of Provence, because he had already exchanged vows concerning another bride. In the meantime, however, Henry had heard of an impediment to their proposed marriage. Amadeus was therefore asked to ensure that his niece would not marry someone else.[75] This probably referred to the king and Simon's daughter being related within the canonically prohibited degrees of consanguinity. Negotiations to secure a papal dispensation had, however, been conducted for quite some time, before Henry announced his intentions, and strenuous efforts had to be made by the English court to counteract the ongoing process at the *curia*. On the very day the letter was sent to Amadeus of Savoy, Henry III contacted his proctors in Rome and ordered them not to pursue the matter any further.[76] In July the king's agents were informed that the council had decided to postpone the planned marriage. Therefore, they were ordered 'not to breathe a word about it to any living soul'.[77] By August the *curia's* support had been enlisted,[78] and in early October Henry wrote to the count of Provence, announcing envoys to draft a marriage treaty.[79] By Christmas, he was married.[80]

We will probably never know for certain why Henry III changed his mind. Matthew Paris may have reflected anxieties at the French court as to the possible consequences of Plantagenet control of Ponthieu, but proceedings at the *curia* seem to have progressed well, and should Louis IX have made serious objections, there would have been no need to order Henry's proctors to act in such a secretive manner. It is equally difficult to see the advantages

---

[72] *Treaty rolls*, no. 64.

[73] Matthew Paris, *Chronica maiora*, iii. 327–8.

[74] J. W. Baldwin, *Aristocratic life in medieval France: the romances of Jean Renart and Gerbert de Montreuil, 1190–1230*, Baltimore 2000, 58–60.

[75] *Treaty rolls*, no. 70.

[76] Ibid. no. 72.

[77] Ibid. no. 75.

[78] Ibid. nos 76–8. However, it is worth noting that Henry's betrothal to the daughter of Simon of Ponthieu was not finally nullified by the *curia* until August 1252: *Foedera*, i. 284.

[79] *Treaty rolls*, no. 84.

[80] CR, *1234–7*, 339; Howell, *Eleanor of Provence*, 12–21.

of a Provençal marriage. Not only did Henry risk alienating his traditional ally in Languedoc, the count of Toulouse, he also got very little in exchange. His marriage portion was never formally settled,[81] and his wife would have been only one of several claimants to her father's inheritance. At best, Henry may have hoped to offset Capetian influence at the flanks of Gascony, or maybe, as has been suggested, exchange any lands he might receive for territories in Normandy or Poitou.[82] He may also have reacted to Louis IX's marriage with another of the count's daughters in 1234. Be this as it may, these dealings underline the extent to which Henry refused to give up hope of a future role in France.

Prospective marriages were not the only means by which Henry III tried to strengthen his influence along the borders of Capetian France. He continued to maintain friendly relations with the count of Toulouse. Parallel to negotiations with the count of Provence, an envoy from Raymond arrived in England in October 1235. Henry's response to the count's embassy seems sufficiently conspiratorial to assume that possible moves against Louis IX had been amongst the issues discussed: Henry's envoy would convey the king's answer verbally, as the roads were too dangerous to commit anything to writing.[83] How effective such an alliance would have been remains debatable. Raymond's heiress had married Alphonse of Poitiers in 1234, making Louis's brother the prospective heir of Toulouse. At the same time, as later events would show, Raymond was far from willing to accept this as inevitable, and he continued to pose problems to Louis's authority in the region until his death. Some evidence survives for other contacts. The count of Guines came to England,[84] and the countess of Flanders was requested to repay a loan of £50 made by King John to the citizens of Ghent.[85] These are unlikely to indicate any plans being hatched by the English court concerning a campaign in France. The count of Guines was one of the most successful mercenary leaders of his age, and his help may have been required in Henry's campaign against the rebellious Richard Marshal, while insisting on the repayment of loans which had been made twenty years earlier may point to the increasing financial strains facing him. Henry's dealings with the countess also illustrate the diplomatic difficulties he encountered. Louis IX strengthened his hold not only over traditional addressees of Henry's anti-Capetian diplomacy, but on dependent rulers, such as the countess of Flanders.[86] Under these circumstances, the king of England had little option but to sue for peace.

Diplomatic setbacks were not, however, the only reason for a lack of

---

81 *Treaty rolls*, nos 24–5.
82 Stacey, *Politics, policy and finance*, 180–1.
83 CPR, 1232–47, 129.
84 Ibid. 86, 94, 97.
85 *Royal letters Henry III*, i, no. 397. For the wider background see T. H. Lloyd, *The English wool trade in the Middle Ages*, Cambridge 1977, 20–3.
86 D. Nichols, *Medieval Flanders*, London 1992, 151–6.

military initiative on Henry III's part. England was beset by political difficulties, and during 1233–4 the king faced the most serious rebellion of magnates since Magna Carta,[87] originating in the king's refusal to grant Richard Marshal access to all of his inheritance. The marshal soon formed an alliance with Llewelyn ap Iowerth, thus threatening Henry both along England's western borders and in the south-east. Furthermore, Peter des Roches, bishop of Winchester, at the time in charge of the king's government, had lost support by his treatment of Hubert de Burgh, whom he had imprisoned on trumped up charges of treason, including that he had conspired to scupper the marriage plans of 1225.[88] By spring 1234 Henry III was also encountering strenuous opposition from the English episcopate, led by Edmund Rich, the new archbishop of Canterbury, who threatened to excommunicate him should he not make peace with the earl marshal.[89] Aggravated by his continuing financial malaise, Henry remained unable to respond to the raids of the marshal and his allies. In 1234 a compromise was agreed, Peter des Roches was sent into exile, and only the marshal's sudden death spared Henry III further humiliation. In these circumstances, Henry lacked the means and the backing to embark upon adventures abroad. This inability to plan the recovery of his continental inheritance also had implications for Henry's dealings with the Staufen and their subjects.

Frederick II and Henry III

After Frederick's return from crusade, hopes that his predicaments might be used to Henry III's advantage proved unfounded: Henry (VII) was in no position to challenge his father. Still, contacts had not come to a complete halt. In January 1231, for instance, the bishop of Cambrai received guarantees for his safety on coming to England,[90] and in 1232 the duke of Limburg visited the shrine of St Thomas at Canterbury.[91] The latter may indicate continuing relations with Cologne, as the duke remained among the archbishop's most trusted allies. A similar connection is suggested by a grant of trading privileges to the merchants of Cologne from April 1231.[92] Unlike earlier grants,

---

[87] Vincent, *Peter des Roches*, 375–9, 399, 417–34; B. Smith, 'Irish politics, 1220–1245', TCE viii (1999), 13–21; B. Wilkinson, 'The council and the crisis of 1233–4', *Bulletin of the John Rylands Library* xxvii (1942–3), 384–93.

[88] D. A. Carpenter, 'The fall of Hubert de Burgh', *Journal of British Studies* xix (1980), 1–17, repr. in his *Reign of Henry III*, 45–60.

[89] *Chronicon de Lanercost, 1201–1346*, ed. J. Stevenson, Edinburgh 1839, 42; C. H. Lawrence, *St Edmund of Abingdon: a study of hagiography and history*, Oxford 1960, 124–32; Powicke, *Henry III*, 134–7.

[90] CR, 1227–31, 466. A Simon de Cambrai is referred to in October 1231 as a customary recipient of the king's alms: *Memoranda rolls 16–17 Henry III preserved in the Public Record Office*, ed. R. Allen Brown, London 1991, no. 206. No further identification could be made.

[91] *Foedera*, i. 205.

[92] CPR, 1225–32, 431.

this time concessions were awarded for an unspecified length of time. Amongst the other agents of English relations with the empire, the duke of Brunswick played only a subordinate role, with envoys from the ducal court recorded in August 1231 and July 1233.[93] No evidence survives, though, to illuminate the purpose of their mission. Apart from these, some familiar names appear, like that of the count of Hückeswagen, whose wife had sent envoys to the English court in 1233.[94] This may have been related to earlier proceedings concerning a Bohemian marriage, and to rumours about Henry (VII)'s alleged plan to divorce his wife, and to marry Agnes of Bohemia instead.[95] They may also have been an attempt to win patronage from the English court in recognition of past services. The duke of Brabant, on the other hand, played no part at all, and in February 1231 Henry's brother Richard was granted the duke's English lands.[96] Although contacts continued, their scale and frequency were but a dim reflection of those during the years before 1231.

Henry (VII)'s diminishing importance coincided with a surge of English interest in Frederick. In November 1232 a messenger from Thomas of Acerra, who had been involved in the diplomatic preparations for Frederick's crusade, when he negotiated with al-Kāmil, and who was later to play a significant role in the administration of the Latin kingdom of Jerusalem,[97] arrived in England.[98] This may indicate high-ranking contacts, but no evidence survives to illuminate the background of his mission. Nor was this the only contact. In March 1233 Henry III complied with a petition from the emperor and promised £30 to assist Lando, a nephew of the archbishop of Messina, in his studies at Paris.[99] It would none the less be reading too much into the sources to deduce from this that the emperor was now considered a diplomatic channel for English interests.[100] What these visits certainly did indicate, however, was the eminent role played by Peter des Roches in English politics.

After losing out against Hubert de Burgh in 1225, the bishop had left for the Holy Land, where he had come to prominence in the emperor's crusade. He accompanied Frederick when he entered Jerusalem, and some, mostly

93 CR, 1227–31, 545; CLR, 1226–40, 224.
94 CLR, 1226–40, 235.
95 Casum S. Galli continuatio iii, MGH, SS ii, 180; Annales wormatienses, MGH, SS xvii, 43.
96 CChR, 29.
97 Powell, Anatomy of a crusade, 199; M. Ohlig, Studien zum Beamtentum Friedrichs II: in Reichsitalien von 1237–1250 unter besonderer Berücksichtigung der süditalienischen Beamten, Kleinheubach am Main 1936, 43–5, 166–8, J. Riley-Smith, The feudal nobility and the kingdom of Jerusalem, 1174–1277, London 1973, 182–3.
98 CLR, 1226–40, 189.
99 CR, 1231–4, 303. Little is known about Lando, but his uncle had been among Frederick's chief advisors, while also being close to Honorius III and Gregory IX: N. Kamp, Kirche und Monarchie im staufischen Königreich Sizilien, Munich 1973–82, i. 926–30.
100 For an opposing view see Huffman, Social politics, 249.

English chroniclers, list him among the leaders of the expedition.[101] Returning to Europe with the emperor, Peter was involved in negotiations with Gregory IX during 1230–1. The *Annals of Tewkesbury* probably exaggerate when they state that the bishop pacified Frederick and Gregory,[102] but independent evidence survives to link Peter with the proceedings. In August 1230 he was one of the envoys confirming the demands made by the cardinal of Santa Sabina, the pope's negotiator, to the emperor.[103] This suggests that Peter had been amongst a number of men chosen by both parties and deemed capable of finding a settlement for the remaining points of conflict. His selection also indicates the high regard in which both Frederick II and the *curia* held him. This earlier involvement in imperial politics may explain the contacts established with the imperial court during the early 1230s. The count of Apulia probably met Peter during Frederick's crusade, while the archbishop of Messina most likely dealt with him in the course of the negotiations of 1229–31.[104] This impression is also strengthened by the kind of petitions Henry's government received, such as that on Lando's behalf. The embassies reaching England certainly point to personal ties.[105] No treaties were discussed or alliances planned. Still, the possibility that Peter sought to utilise his good standing with the emperor to Henry III's advantage should not be ruled out. The fact that Henry (VII) solicited French rather than English support during his rebellion, may also be a case in point.[106] Peter was certainly adept at calling in favours from old friends. Matthew Paris, for instance, reports that in 1233 he had asked for the emperor's support in the planned election of John Blund as archbishop of Canterbury.[107] Similarly, despite serious misgivings as to the treatment of Hubert de Burgh, Gregory IX came to Peter's aid when his position became increasingly difficult. Closer ties were certainly forged; the question remains whether this would have been the case without Peter's involvement.

Even the bishop of Winchester's prominent role did not prepare Henry III for what happened next. In November 1234, after negotiations which may have been under way since September,[108] Frederick II officially announced

---

[101] K. R. Giles, 'Two English bishops in the Holy Land', *Nottingham Medieval Studies* xxxi (1987), 46–57; Vincent, *Peter des Roches*, 229–58; C. Tyerman, *England and the crusades, 1095–1588*, Chicago 1988, 99; *Annals of Margam*, AM i. 37; *Annals of Dunstable*, AM iii. 126–7; *Willelmi chronica andrensis*, MGH, SS xxiv, 768; *Epistolae saeculi XIII*, i, no. 384.
[102] *Annals of Tewkesbury*, AM i. 76.
[103] *Constitutiones, 1198–1272*, no. 141.
[104] Kamp, *Kirche und Monarchie*, 929.
[105] Peter des Roches and Frederick II also shared in their patronage of Henry de Avranches: Vincent, *Peter des Roches*, 246–7; E. Winkelmann, 'Reisefrüchte aus Italien und anderes zur deutsch-italienischen Geschichte', *Forschungen zur deutschen Geschichte* xviii (1878), 469–92 at pp. 482–92; Bund, 'Studien zu Magister Heinrich'.
[106] *Annales marbacenses*, 96.
[107] For the election and Peter's role see Matthew Paris, *Chronica maiora* iii. 243, and Vincent, *Peter des Roches*, 365–71.
[108] TNA: PRO, E 372–8 mem. 13.

his intention to marry the king's sister Isabella.[109] An embassy led by Peter de Vinea, Frederick's chief councillor,[110] was sent to arrange the details. If possible, he was to be joined by the archbishop of Cologne. The emperor was very specific in what he had to offer: he would take Isabella as his wife, and would keep her with all the dignity appertaining to an empress. She would be given the Mazara valley and the honour of Mount San Angelo, as other queens of Sicily had had it,[111] in exchange for a dowry of 30,000 marks. By mid-December, Peter had reached England.[112] However, he travelled alone. Henry of Mühlenark, the archbishop of Cologne, played no part in the proceedings. Negotiations proceeded quickly, and in late February 1235 Henry III announced his sister's imminent marriage.[113] At last, and wholly unexpectedly, the king of England received what he had been working for for so long, with so much effort and so little success: an alliance with the Staufen.

In late spring 1235, an embassy led by Duke Henry of Brabant arrived in England to escort the king's sister to Germany.[114] The archbishop of Cologne and two high-ranking members of the Teutonic Knights accompanied the duke.[115] Isabella's imminent departure provided an opportunity to reward old friends and to seek new allies. On 24 April the Teutonic Knights were promised an annual rent of 40 marks.[116] Most important, on 7 May, the duke of Brabant was promised that, should he or his son return within a month from Michaelmas 1235, or by Easter 1236, they would receive the honour of Eye.[117] That this involved overturning an earlier grant made to the king's brother attests to the importance which the king attached to good relations with the duke. Henry seems to have had great hopes for this alliance. In October, after news of the duke's death had reached England, Henry assured the duke's son that Eye could still be his.[118] To underline the sincerity of his intentions, Richard de Zudendorp received confirmation of a grant which Duke Henry once had made concerning the town of Laxfeld.[119] Furthermore,

---

109 *Historia diplomatica*, iv. 503–6.
110 On his career see also Ohlig, *Studien*, 133–7.
111 The same lands had been promised to Henry II's daughter Joanna in 1177: *Chronica Magistri Rogeri de Houdene*, ed. William Stubbs (RS, 1868–71), ii. 94–8. I am grateful to Ellen Godfrey for this reference. For Isabella see W. Kowalski , *Die deutschen Königinnen und Kaiserinnen von Konrad III bis zum Ende des Interregnums*, Weimar 1913, 31–4.
112 *Foedera*, i. 221.
113 Ibid. i. 224–5; *Treaty rolls*, nos 1, 4.
114 *Treaty rolls*, no. 19.
115 Ibid. no. 20; Matthew Paris, *Chronica maiora*, iii. 320. The Teutonic knights played a similar role in Frederick's marriage with Constance of Aragon: J. Powell, 'Frederick II, the Hohenstaufens and the Teutonic Order in the kingdom of Sicily', in M. Barber (ed.), *The military orders: fighting for the faith and caring for the sick*, Aldershot 1994, 236–44.
116 CChR, 200. The full text is in H. Koeppen, 'Die englische Rente für den deutschen Orden', in *Festschrift Hermann Heimpel*, Göttingen 1972, 402–21 at pp. 413–14.
117 CPR, 1232–47, 103.
118 *Treaty rolls*, no. 83.
119 CChR, 215.

trading privileges were issued to the duke's merchants,[120] while one of his clerks was promised an annual payment from the exchequer.[121] Others, too, were rewarded for their services.[122] Although old friends were not forgotten, new friendships were eagerly created.

Frederick's choice of emissaries reflected the history of English contacts with Germany. Although Peter de Vinea led negotiations, Isabella's escort consisted of the archbishop of Cologne and the duke of Brabant. The latter's importance is further underlined by the fact that one of the Teutonic Knights who accompanied the mission, Giles Bertaud, originated from Brabant.[123] Similarly, on the English side, with Peter des Roches in exile once again, it fell to Walter Brewer, the bishop of Exeter, and second leader of the English contingent during the emperor's crusade, to escort Isabella across the Channel. Only the duke of Brunswick was conspicuous by his absence. This was, however, not a sign of cooling relations nor of the duke's lessening significance. Rather, Otto of Lüneburg was about to be granted what he and his family had been fighting for ever since the fall of Henry the Lion in 1184: to be taken back into the ranks of the imperial nobility.[124] After his wedding at Worms,[125] Frederick proceeded towards Mainz, where he presided over the diet which witnessed the final reconciliation between Staufen and Welfs. Since September 1234 a commission had been investigating Otto's claims to the Welf inheritance.[126] In August 1235 he was granted the lands of his uncle, and was made duke of Brunswick.[127] This was as much a reward for Otto's loyalty during the emperor's excommunication and Henry (VII)'s rebellion, as it was yet another step towards pacifying the emperor's homelands as well as his domains in Burgundy and Italy.

The way the union of 1235 had been brought about did not lack irony. For years Henry had been trying to forge closer ties with the empire. Throughout, the best means of reaching his goal had been to side-step Frederick II and turn to his son and the German princes instead. Over and over again it was

---

[120] CPR, 1232–47, 103, 108.

[121] Ibid. 110.

[122] Ibid. 130.

[123] Giles Bertaud, or Berthaut, was the scion of a noble Brabantine family in the area around Mecheln: Koeppen, 'Die englische Rente', 404–5; K. van Eickels, *Die Deutsch-ordensballei Koblenz und ihre wirtschaftliche Entwicklung im Spätmittelalter*, Marburg 1995, 29–30.

[124] *Annales marbacenses*, 97; Boshof, 'Die Entstehung', 264–6.

[125] Matthew Paris dates the wedding to 20 July: *Chronica maiora*, iii. 324; the *Annals of Tewkesbury* to around the feast of St Barnabas: AM i. 98; the *Annals of Worms* to 15 July: *Annales wormatienses*, MGH, SS xvii. 44. This latter date is indirectly confirmed by a letter from the bishop of Hildesheim to the pope: *Historia diplomatica*, iv. 730. For the ceremony itself see *Chronica maiora*, iii. 321–7; Huffmann, *Social politics*, 252; Stürner, *Friedrich II*, ii. 309–11; C. Wolf di Cecca, 'Der Brautschatz der Isabella von England 1235 mit besonderer Berücksichtigung der Brautschatzkrone', *AfD* xli (1995), 137–45.

[126] Boshof, 'Die Entstehung', 269; Schneidmüller, *Die Welfen*, 279–84.

[127] *Constitutiones, 1198–1272*, no. 197.

the emperor's unwillingness to involve himself in the rivalry between Plantagenets and Capetians which had caused Henry's schemes to falter. Then, just as Henry (VII) was effectively deprived of his royal status, Frederick announced his intention of marrying a Plantagenet princess. In many ways, this is illustrative of the tight reins with which he governed Germany, and of his strengthened position since returning from the Holy Land. It was the success of his crusade, too, which allowed Frederick II to disregard at least some of the worries this marriage caused his old Capetian friends. None the less, the abruptness with which he changed direction requires some further analysis. What exactly had been his reason for marrying Isabella Plantagenet?

It seems that the English court had been surprised by Frederick abandoning his traditional stance towards the Plantagenets. There was no bargaining over the conditions he had made concerning Isabella's marriage portion, and no attempt at receiving further guarantees of political collaboration. The prize on offer was too valuable to risk it by making demands. None the less, Henry and his court made clear what they expected to gain from this alliance. Ever since Peter de Vinea's arrival in England, hopes abounded that the proposed marriage might be used against Louis IX. In December 1234 Henry wrote to Frederick II, expressing his hope that, as he had helped the emperor to obtain his honour and advantage, Frederick would do the same for him.[128] Probably in February 1235, a similar letter was sent to the cardinal of St Praxedis, who was asked to ensure that emperor and pope would aid Henry in restoring his honour and rights.[129] These expectations are also reflected in the *Annals of Dunstable*'s account of the marriage: the emperor had promised to assist Henry in the acquisition and defence of his rights.[130] This certainly expressed the prevalent attitude amongst those close to the king: the marriage was a stepping stone towards the recovery of Anjou, Poitou and Normandy.[131]

The emperor's motivation is more difficult to ascertain. After all, he must have been aware of English expectations that his marriage could be utilised against Louis IX. At the same time, no evidence survives to suggest that he was about to abandon his Capetian allies.[132] In fact, the emperor took great care to assure Louis that his marriage would not end their friendship. In April 1235, informing the king of France of the planned wedding, Frederick declared that he was to continue his alliance with the Capetians, and suggested that he and Louis IX meet in the near future.[133] Gregory IX, too,

---

128 *Foedera*, i. 221.
129 *Treaty rolls*, no. 14.
130 *Annals of Dunstable*, AM iii. 142.
131 Stacey, *Politics, policy and finance*, 180.
132 For a different view see Wand, 'Die Englandpolitik', 87; Kienast, *Die deutschen Fürsten*, ii. 67–74.
133 *Historia diplomatica*, iv. 539–40.

assured the king of France that no harm was to come from this union.[134] Furthermore, attempts were made to settle the Anglo-French conflict. In a letter, probably written in June 1235, Henry III referred to a suggested meeting between the rulers of England, Germany and France.[135] This can be linked to the planned conference at Vaucouleurs, to which we will return in the next chapter. Frederick was aware of the implications that his marriage might have for relations with the Capetians, and that a settlement of the differences between Henry III and Louis IX would have to form part of its diplomatic context.

This still does not explain why Frederick was willing to enter a union which, despite his best efforts, was viewed as potentially threatening by the Capetians. A number of explanations have been put forth, none of them entirely convincing. To give a few examples: the marriage was interpreted as aiming to put an end to the old conflict between Welfs and Staufen.[136] On the other hand, by 1235 the Welfs' loyalty was beyond doubt, and Frederick II had initiated moves for a final settlement before opening negotiations with Henry III. It has even been suggested that the union was to prevent Henry (VII) from receiving English subsidies,[137] but Henry had approached the Capetians, not England for support. Fritz Trautz suggests that it may have been an attempt at linking Frederick to a ruler of proven loyalty to the Holy See.[138] However, in 1234 Henry III had faced excommunication, not the emperor. Although this does not mean that none of these reasons may have played their part in Frederick's or the *curia*'s deliberations, it seems that other, equally important reasons have so far been overlooked.[139] To reach a better understanding of events, the wider political and diplomatic context of this marriage has to be considered. Most important, we should address the role played by Gregory IX.

Neither the emperor nor Henry III had left any doubt about the pope's involvement in arranging this marriage.[140] When Frederick II first announced his intentions, he described himself as acting 'ad tractatum et ordinationem karissimi patris nostri domini Gregorii (at the insistence and

134 Ibid. iv. 538–9.
135 *Royal letters Henry III*, i, no. 393.
136 E. H. Kantorowicz, *Frederick II*, trans. E. O. Lorimer, London 1931, 406; Abulafia, *Frederick II*, 242.
137 Kienast, *Die deutschen Fürsten*, ii. 75.
138 Trautz, *Die Könige*, 104.
139 Other examples include Frederick's assumed need of an heir: Abulafia, *Frederick II*, 237; Trautz, *Die Könige*, 104. See, however, H. Decker-Hauff, 'Das Staufische Haus', in *Die Zeit der Staufer: Geschichte-Kunst-Kultur* (exhibition catalogue), Stuttgart 1977–9, iii. 339–74.
140 Nor did the papal court: *Vita Gregorii IX*, in P. Fabre, L. Duchesne and G. Mollat (eds), *Le 'Liber censuum' de l'église romaine*, Paris 1889–1952, ii. 8–36 at p. 27; A. Paravicini Bagliani, 'La storiografica pontificia del secolo XIII: prospettive di ricerca', *Römische Historische Mitteilungen* xxviii (1976), 45–54 at pp. 52–3.

command of our father, [Lord] Gregory').[141] This was repeated in the emperor's letter to Louis IX from April 1235: during a meeting the previous summer, the pope had suggested Isabella as Frederick's wife.[142] He was not exaggerating the importance of the pope's role. Gregory took an active role in the negotiations. In December 1234, for instance, Gregory wrote to Henry III and announced that Frederick was to ask for Isabella as his wife.[143] A similar point was made in the marriage contract publicised on 27 February: Isabella had been given in marriage to Frederick II on the pope's advice.[144] This was repeated when the king of England wrote to the cardinal of St Praxedis the same month.[145] Taking into account his repeated exhortations to Louis IX and Henry III to arrange peace, it seems unlikely that he had intended the marriage to be the opening shot in a war against Louis IX. This is underlined by a letter from Pope Gregory to Louis IX from September 1234, after the marriage between Frederick and Isabella had first been mooted: so as not to impede the business of the Holy Land, peace ought to be made with Henry III.[146] Why then did both Gregory and Frederick favour an English marriage?

It may be worth considering overall papal policy during these years. As we have seen, a crusade to the Holy Land remained at the centre of papal concerns, and the pacification of Christendom was an integral part of preparations for it. England and France were not the only subjects of papal arbitration. In January 1235, for instance, Gregory IX had urged the archbishop of York and the bishop of Carlisle to arrange a peace with Scotland.[147] Peace was to be established across Christendom. Not all of the pope's efforts aimed at a permanent settlement of conflicts. In fact, it appears that the *curia* would have seen its aims fulfilled if peace lasted long enough for the campaign to get under way. This pattern had been evident in his dealings with Frederick and the Lombard League, it was to dominate his actions in *Outremer* after 1235 and it was one of the most basic elements in papal crusading diplomacy. With this proviso in mind, Gregory's support for the Anglo-German marriage seems perhaps less surprising. If nothing else, the Staufen were linked to the Plantagenets, while still being firmly tied to the Capetians. Potentially, this could mean forging a formidable alliance to be mobilised for the needs of the Holy Land. Even if this might have been overly optimistic, the emperor's influence with Henry III and Louis IX could none the less be used to broker, if not a permanent, at least a temporary settlement of the rivalry between Capetians and Plantagenets which had beset past expeditions to the Holy Land. Moreover, it would allow the crusade to harness the financial and mili-

---

141 *Historia diplomatica*, iv. 503.
142 Ibid. iv. 539–40.
143 *Foedera*, i. 220.
144 *Treaty rolls*, no. 1.
145 Ibid. no. 4. The point was repeated in a letter from Henry III to Gregory IX from April 1235: *Foedera*, i. 225–6.
146 *Registres Gregoire IX*, no. 2180.
147 *Foedera*, i. 214–15.

tary might of three of the Latin west's most powerful kingdoms. As we will see, this was not entirely unrealistic. Furthermore, it made moves like that by Louis VIII in 1224, when the king of France had used the Treaty of Catania as a means to prepare for the conquest of Poitou, more difficult to accomplish. Frederick would not have supported Henry III against Louis IX, but equally the latter would risk relations with the emperor were he to follow his father's example.[148]

Where does this leave the emperor? As with Henry III's Savoyard marriage, we will perhaps never find a wholly satisfactory answer. Unlike the king of England or Gregory's later biographer,[149] Frederick did not put his expectations into writing, beyond vague references to the honour and utility which he hoped to draw from this union. The affairs of the Holy Land certainly played their part in Frederick's deliberations, even if he did not intend to participate himself in the planned campaign.[150] The English alliance also brought other much needed gains. Its financial benefits were considerable,[151] and the payment of Isabella's dowry was to dominate exchanges between Plantagenets and Staufens over the following years. Frederick needed funds to finance his campaigns in Italy and Palestine. Similarly, the marriage gave Frederick additional standing within Latin Christendom, with some important consequences. In 1238, for instance, English troops fought alongside the emperor's against the Lombard League. The marriage between Frederick and Isabella gave Gregory IX the hope that peace could be arranged in time for his planned crusade, it gave Henry III the expectation that Frederick's support could be won against the Capetians, and it gave the emperor much needed funds, troops and prestige.

In many ways, these years represented an interlude. Any hopes that Frederick's return from *Outremer* might open new opportunities for Henry III proved to be unfounded. Still, contacts had not come to a complete halt. Henry III continued to be approached by envoys from Brabant, Brunswick and Cologne, while first, informal ties were forged with the emperor. The grand schemes, though, pursued in the years before Frederick's crusade, were missing. We can, furthermore, see the role played by personal friendships, as for example in the dealings with the nephew of archbishop Lando, in the parts played by Walter Brewer or Peter des Roches. Equally, traditions

---

[148] This, in itself, followed an established tradition of papal peace diplomacy: C. M. Rousseau, 'A papal matchmaker: principle and pragmatism during Innocent III's pontificate', *JMH* xxiv (1998), 259–71.

[149] *Vita Gregorii IX*, ii. 27: Gregory had aimed to show his love for the emperor.

[150] It may be worth considering, for instance, Frederick's letter to the archbishop of Trier from July 1234, just a few months before he embarked on negotiating his marriage: he announced that he was planning to visit Germany the following summer, and that he would be accompanied by a legate to preach the cross: *Acta imperii selecta: Urkunden der Deutscher Könige und Kaiser, 928–1398, mit einem Anhange von Reichssachen*, ed. J. F. Böhmer, Innsbruck 1870, no. 303.

[151] Trautz, *Die Könige*, 105.

mattered: envoys, such as the Zudendorps, were chosen for their previous experience. Finally, these contacts were conditioned by the wider political situation in Europe. It is doubtful whether, without the crusade, the emperor would ever have considered an English marriage. It certainly caused unease at the court of Louis IX, and, as we will see, resulted in several attempts at settling the simmering conflict between Plantagenets and Capetians. To some extent, therefore, relations between Henry III and Frederick II were built on shaky foundations.

PART II

GRAND EXPECTATIONS, 1235–1250

3

Allied Against All Men, 1235–1239

Isabella's marriage heralded a new era in Anglo-imperial relations,[1] and the years until Frederick's excommunication in 1239 stand out for the frequency and intimacy of contacts. The emphasis on a possible alliance against the Capetians, which had dominated exchanges up to 1230, was, though not absent, much more muted. On the surface, at least, Anglo-imperial relations were dominated by the affairs of Italy, the collection of Isabella's dowry and the Holy Land. The depth and range of contacts went well beyond what had been achieved during the 1220s, as evident, for instance, in the increasingly flowery style of Henry's foreign correspondence, which has been linked to the prolonged presence of Peter de Vinea in England.[2] Similarly, in 1236, when Frederick II opened an investigation into accusations of ritual murder against the Jewish community at Fulda, he drew on the expertise of the king of England.[3] These contacts extended beyond the fiscal and political. Henry III and Frederick II seem to have embarked on an animated exchange about falconry,[4] and the English court continued to act as patron to clerics from Sicily.[5] Frederick sought to maintain the spirit of friendship with a number of exotic gifts, including a camel and a leopard.[6] All of this indicates a qualitative as well as a quantitative shift in relations between them.

This transformation is also evident in the diminishing significance of the German princes. Not surprisingly, it was Frederick II who stood at the centre

---

1   The quotation in the title of this chapter, 'Confederati sumus (. . .) contra omnes homines' is from Henry III in a letter to Gregory IX, outlining his relationship with Frederick: *Treaty rolls*, no. 48.
2   E. H. Kantorowicz, 'Peter de Vinea in England', MIÖG li (1937), 43–88 at pp. 58–9. However, the influence exercised by the papal chancery should also be noted: G. Barraclough, 'The English royal chancery and the papal chancery in the reign of Henry III', MIÖG lxxii (1954), 365–78. The continuing presence of Peter and of Walter of Ocra was related to the need to collect Isabella's dowry, ultimately overseen by Walter of Ocra and Giles Bertault: CPR, *1232–47*, 146, 368; CR, *1234–7*, 509–10, 571–4; *Treaty rolls*, no. 55; F. Liebermann, 'Zur Geschichte Friedrichs II. und Richards von Cornwall', NA xiii (1888), 217–22 at pp. 217–18.
3   *Royal letters Henry III*, ii, no. 418; *Annales erphordenses fratrum praedicatorum*, in *Monumenta erphesfurtensia saec. XII, XIII, XIV*, ed. O. Holder-Egger, MGH, SS sep.ed., Hanover–Leipzig 1899, 92; F. Battenberg, *Herrschaft und Verfahren: politische Prozesse im mittelalterlichen römisch-deutschen Reich*, Darmstadt 1996, 30–3; Stürner, *Friedrich II*, ii. 321–6.
4   CPR, *1232–47*, 139; CR, *1234–7*, 296.
5   CPR, *1232–47*, 219.
6   Matthew Paris, *Chronica maiora*, iii. 324–5, 334, 369.

71

of the king's initiatives. The regents, acting on behalf of the emperor's second son, Conrad IV, who was formally elected king in 1237, played only a supporting part. Moreover, those, like the archbishops of Cologne, who had played such an important role during the 1220s, largely disappear from the record.[7] Instead, the majority of contacts were conducted by and with members of the imperial court. The emperor drew on men like the imperial chamberlain, Henry of Aachen,[8] and other members of the family of the mayor of Aachen,[9] or Hugh de Castello Novo, a medium ranking official in his Sicilian administration.[10] Exchanges were not, however, limited to bureaucrats and minor knights, as perhaps best exemplified by Walter of Ocra, who oversaw the collection of Isabella's dowry in 1236 and 1237.[11] Since 1236 Walter had been Frederick's chaplain, acting as one of the emperor's foremost diplomats and, next to Peter de Vinea and Thaddeus de Suessa, chief advisors.[12] His presence therefore testifies to the significance now attached by the emperor to relations with England, and may point to the fact that Frederick may have been expecting more than merely funds from Henry. Many of the men who were sent to England continued to play a significant role. Peter de Vinea, for instance, recipient of an annual retainer from Henry III, was to be called upon in preparation for the 1242 Poitevin campaign. Similarly, Frederick II, too, sought to widen his contacts in

[7] The exception is 1237, when Gerard de Zuydendorp was in England: *CLR, 1225–40*, 263.

[8] Henry is referred to as 'imperialis aulae marescallus'. This poses problems of identification: J. Ficker, 'Die Reichshofbeamten der staufischen Periode', *Sitzungsberichte der Philosophisch-Historischen Klasse der (k. k.) Österreichischen Akademie der Wissenschaften zu Wien* xl (1862), 447–549 at p. 466, suggested that as the 'de Aquis' were usually chamberlains, not marshals, this must refer to Henry of Pappenheim. However, it is equally likely that an English scribe had been making a mistake. Henry of Aachen (Aeys being the Anglo-Norman word for Aachen) was a prominent figure, involved in negotiations with France (*Regesta imperii*, no. 1986), and later prothonotary: *Quellen zur Geschichte der Stadt Köln*, ii, no. 222. I am grateful to David Trotter and Julie Kerr for discussing this point.

[9] Henry visited England in 1236 and 1239: *Foedera*, i. 224; *CLR, 1226–40*, 359. For Henry's family see *Aachener Urkunden*, nos 8, 254; E. Meuthen, 'Die Aachener Pröpste bis zum Ende der Stauferzeit', *Zeitschrift des Aachener Geschichtsvereins* lxxviii (1966–7), 5–95 at pp. 60–84. Another member of his family, the advocate of Aachen, is recorded as being in England in June 1236: *Historia diplomatica*, iv. 884–5. For William, the advocate of Aachen, Henry's brother, see *Aachener Urkunden*, no. 122. A third member of this family also made an appearance, in December 1237, when a 'Gerardus de Aquis tricamerarius noster' was announced as the emperor's envoy to crusaders from France: *Historia diplomatica*, v. 141.

[10] *CR, 1234–7*, 301. Who exactly he was remains obscure. In 1255, however, Innocent IV mentioned Hugh de Castronovo in a letter outlining the actions to be taken against Manfred and Frederick Lancea in Sicily: *Acta imperii inedita*, ii, no. 1044. The envoy 'Hugh', mentioned in 1237, may have been the same person: *CLR, 1226–40*, 250.

[11] *Treaty rolls*, nos 53–5; *CPR, 1232–47*, 145, 146, 188; *CLR, 1226–40*, 265, 268, 269, 275, 276, 278; *CR, 1234–7*, 466.

[12] For his diplomatic career see Kamp, *Kirche und Monarchie*, i. 128–32; H. Hartmann, 'Die Urkunden Konrads IV', *AfD* xviii (1944), 38–163 at pp. 134–47; and Wolf, 'Anfänge', 147–53.

England. We know, for instance, that he took special care to maintain links with Richard of Cornwall, but his hospitality and generosity also extended to other members of the English aristocracy, such as Simon de Montfort.[13] These English contacts, in turn, were repeatedly called upon after the emperor's excommunication in 1239, and after his deposition in 1245. Friendly relations between emperor and king thus involved members of their respective households, but they also carried with them expectations that favours would be returned.

Frederick II was to count on Henry's financial and diplomatic backing in his dealings with the Italian communes and the papacy. In fact, the English court went to great lengths to accommodate the emperor's political and military needs. At the same time, this, too, was perceived as a means to an end: the recovery of Normandy and Poitou. Although these expectations were never voiced directly to the emperor, they loomed in the background, and filtered through to those, like Matthew Paris, who had access to the court, and recorded its hopes and expectations. Frederick, by contrast, appears to have perceived Henry III as one ally among many. To gauge fully the standing of the king in relation to the emperor, therefore, contacts between the two will have to be considered against the background of Frederick's increasingly complex relationship with Gregory IX, the Lombard communes and the affairs of imperial Burgundy.

Imperial diplomacy

Frederick's marriage had begotten problems as well as opportunities, especially in his relations with Louis IX. It is therefore not surprising that he stepped up his efforts to broker a more permanent settlement between the kings of England and France. In 1236 he called a meeting between himself, Henry III and Louis IX to Vaucouleurs, on the borders between France and the empire.[14] Matthew Paris described the meeting vaguely as designed to deal 'with urgent matters, concerning the Empire as well as other kingdoms'.[15] The meaning of this passage is clarified in a letter from Henry III to Frederick, in which he thanked the emperor for his efforts to broker a peace between Capetians and Plantagenets.[16] It appears, therefore, that a – at least temporary – settlement of Louis's and Henry's conflicting claims was to form part of the meeting. Furthermore, it has to be viewed within the broader context of papal and imperial diplomacy, much of which centred on the planned crusade. The conflict between Plantagenets and Capetians threat-

13 Matthew Paris, *Chronica maiora*, iii. 480, 487.
14 For the tradition of meetings at Vaucouleurs see I. Voss, *Herrschertreffen im frühen und hohen Mittelalter: Untersuchungen zu den Begegnungen der ostfränkischen und westfränkischen Herrscher im 9. und 10. Jahrhundert sowie der deutschen und französischen Könige im 11. bis 13. Jahrhundert*, Cologne–Vienna 1987, 79–83.
15 Matthew Paris, *Chronica maiora*, iii. 393.
16 *Treaty rolls*, no. 53.

ened to embroil the emperor, but also, and more importantly, it endangered continuing Christian control of the Holy Land.

That Frederick's plans ultimately failed was, however, as much due to Henry III's reluctance to forego his claims in France, as it was to the difficulties which Frederick faced at home. In early January 1236 Henry III declared that he would not participate in the meeting.[17] He himself was preoccupied with other matters, while the barons were reluctant to let his brother Richard leave the realm, unless sufficient guarantees could be given for his safety. In February the emperor's invitation was finally declined.[18] The barons, Henry explained, had refused to give Richard permission to leave, and his presence could not be spared, as campaigns in Scotland, Wales and Ireland were imminent. Matthew Paris elaborates on this: as Richard was the king's heir, and as nobody knew whether the king's wife would bear children, he should not be exposed to the dangers of a meeting with Louis IX.[19] On their own, none of these reasons seems entirely convincing. After all, Louis was in a similar position (he was barely of age and as yet without a son from his 1234 marriage). It might be a plausible speculation that a failure of the Vaucouleurs conference had been perceived as the lesser of two evils. It seemed unlikely that Louis IX would concede what Henry III really wanted: a return of his paternal inheritance. Not attending the meeting at all would have caused less affront to the emperor than resisting his efforts at mediation. Moreover, using the truce forced upon Henry in 1235 to muster the means and men necessary for a military campaign, may have seemed a more promising option. We also need to keep in mind the difficult political situation he faced in England. Since 1234 Henry had faced repeated political crises at home, and had even fallen out with his brother.[20] In short, he lacked the fiscal and political strength to pursue his ambitions on the continent, and would have negotiated from a position of considerable weakness. Causing a delay, under these circumstances, would have been the best alternative. In a way, this would also have been reminiscent of the 1225 marriage negotiations, where the success of Mauclerk's mission rested not with its declared aim (a double marriage), but with scuppering a Capetian–Staufen marriage.

The emperor, though, had not yet abandoned hope, and called for another meeting. In April 1237 Henry announced to the emperor that Richard and other English nobles would attend the meeting at Vaucouleurs.[21] The second

---

[17] Ibid. no. 93; Kienast, *Die deutschen Fürsten*, ii. 226–8.
[18] *Royal letters Henry III*, ii, no. 419.
[19] Howell, *Eleanor of Provence*, 2; Matthew Paris, *Chronica maiora*, iii. 340.
[20] See R. R. Davies, *The age of conquest: Wales, 1063–1415* (originally published as *Conquest, coexistence and change: Wales, 1063–1415*, Oxford 1987), Oxford 1991, 298–9; M. Brown, 'Henry the Peaceable: Henry III, Alexander III and royal lordship in the British Isles, 1249–1272', in Weiler and Rowlands, *England and Europe*, 43–66; R. Frame, 'King Henry III and Ireland: the shaping of a peripheral lordship', *TCE* iii (1991), 179–202; Powicke, *Henry III*, 147–55; N. Denholm-Young, *Richard of Cornwall*, Oxford 1947, 32–7.
[21] *Treaty rolls*, no. 53.

conference, too, failed to materialise, with Matthew Paris providing the most detailed version of events.[22] Richard was to be accompanied by the arch-bishop of York and other prelates and nobles. Some unease had been caused by the fact that the king of France had been amassing forces near Vaucouleurs, but the party decided to set out none the less. However, when they reached Dover, imperial envoys brought news that the conference had been postponed until the following year.[23] Matthew's report is confirmed by another source. In the late thirteenth century, William de Nangis described the planned meeting and reported that, just before it, Louis's younger brother Robert had married a daughter of the duke of Brabant. As this was to be followed by Robert's enfeoffment with the county of Artois, many nobles attended the festivities.[24] The emperor, however, seeing that so many armed men accompanied Louis, cancelled the meeting. According to William, this was a sign of God's good will towards the king, as it was suspected that the emperor had evil designs on the kingdom of France. Much of this may have been written in the light of Frederick's later reputation. However, Frederick faced political difficulties in Germany and Italy which may have required a postponement, and which were probably among the affairs of the empire referred to by Matthew Paris.

Since 1235 Gregory IX had been trying to arrange a truce between the emperor and the Lombard League. This put him in an increasingly difficult position, as Frederick II's demands for a heavy fine and the excommunication of all those who refused to make peace met with equally stubborn resistance from the Lombards. At this point, the pope could ill afford to alienate either party and, in the end, he had little option but to continue pressing the case for a peaceful settlement.[25] Consequently, Gregory tried to arrange a series of meetings between Frederick II's proctors and those of the rebelling towns.[26] In many ways, this was a race against time, and increasingly placed the pope in a situation in which a neutral stance was difficult to maintain. The emperor had intended to lead a campaign to northern Italy in 1236, but post-poned it at Gregory's instigation.[27] A planned meeting at Viterbo failed when Frederick's representatives left before those of Milan and its allies arrived. In June, another attempt was made, but when Frederick was forced to intervene in the wars against the duke of Austria, this caused yet another delay.[28] Once

---

22 Matthew Paris, Chronica maiora, iii. 393–4.
23 Imperial envoys, Walter of Ocra and Giles Bertaud, are known to have been at the royal court between 17 June and 6 July 1237 to collect Isabella's dowry: CLR, 1226–40, 275, 276, 278; CPR, 1232–47, 188; CR, 1234–7, 466; Treaty rolls, nos 54–5.
24 William de Nangis, Gesta sanctae memoriae Ludovici regis Franciae, RHGF xx, Paris 1840, 309–465 at pp. 424–6. See also Chronicon Alberici, 591. For Frederick's response see Acta imperii inedita, ii, no. 26.
25 Epistolae saeculi XIII, i, nos 691–2.
26 Kluger, Hochmeister, 172–7.
27 Historia diplomatica, iv. 876.
28 F. Hausmann, 'Kaiser Friedrich II und Österreich', in Fleckenstein, Probleme um

he returned to Italy, new efforts were undertaken to find a peaceful settlement, and in April and May 1237, at around the time when Richard of
Cornwall and his entourage were told that the meeting at Vaucouleurs had
been called off, a number of high-ranking imperial officials were sent to the
pope, 'pro facto Lombardie'.[29] However, Frederick's patience began to wear
thin. While proceedings continued at the *curia*, preparations were made for a
military solution. The emperor's prospects for success seemed good. During
1235–6 he had taken control of several towns – Bergamo, Verona, Vicenza
and Padua all accepted his rule in 1236.[30] Milan and its allies were thus
increasingly isolated. If peace could not be arranged by diplomatic means, it
certainly could be achieved by victory in battle. Milan's hopes thus began to
centre on the prospect of a break between pope and emperor. In the meantime, though, Frederick achieved a decisive victory when he intercepted a
party led by the Milanese at Cortenuova in 1237.[31] This resulted in one of
the worst defeats in Milan's history. Its *podestà*, the head of the city government, was executed, and the *carroccio*, the symbol of communal identity, sent
to Rome as a trophy.[32] Frederick saw the opportunity to establish his
authority in Lombardy. In July 1238 he rejected a papal offer to mediate, as he
could not accept anything but the Lombards' unconditional surrender.[33]
Considering these events, Matthew's statement that the second meeting at
Vaucouleurs had been postponed at the emperor's instigation seems credible.
At stake was not only Frederick's control over the imperial towns in northern
Italy, but also his relationship with the *curia*, and settling the conflict
between Plantagenets and Capetians would have become a less pressing
concern.

The fact that Frederick's toughened stance after Cortenuova had little
immediate impact on his standing with the papacy does not mean that we
should ignore, or that the emperor had been unaware of, the strain his attitude put on their relations.[34] In fact, events in Lombardy point to the fragility
of the papal–imperial concord. In September 1236, for instance, the emperor

---

Friedrich II, 225–308 at pp. 245–64; K. Brunner, 'Zum Prozess gegen Herzog Friedrich II,
von 1236', *MIÖG* lxxviii (1970), 260–73; Stürner, *Friedrich II*, ii. 331–4.
[29] *Ryccardi de S Germano cronica*, MGH, SS xix. 374; *Epistolae saeculi XIII*, i, no. 707.
[30] *Annales scheftlarienses maiores*, MGH, SS xvii. 340; *Annales bergomates*, MGH, SS xviii.
810; *Annales mantuani*. MGH, SS xix. 21; J. P. Grundman, *The popolo at Perugia,
1139–1309*, Perugia 1992, 81–3; G. M. Varanini, 'La marca trevigiana', and M. Ronzani,
'Pisa e la Toscana', both in Toubert and Paravacini Bagliani, *Federico II*, 48–64, 65–84.
[31] *Annales bergomates*, MGH, SS xviii. 810.
[32] *Chronicon imaginis mundi*, Monumenta Historiae Patriae Scriptores, v, Turin 1848, col.
1579. For the role of the *carroccio* see H. Zug Tucci, 'Il carroccio nella vita communale
Italiana', *Quellen und Forschungen aus italienischen Archiven und Bibliotheken* lxv (1985),
1–104, and E. Voltmer, 'Nel segno della croce: il carroccio come simbole del potere', in
*Militia Christi e crociata nei secoli XI–XIII: atti della undecima settimana internazionale di studio,
Mendola, 26 Agosto–1 Settembre 1989*, Milan 1992, 193–207.
[33] *Acta imperii inedita*, i, no. 351.
[34] Stürner, *Friedrich II*, ii. 458–66.

criticised Gregory: while he was asking for ecclesiastical censures against the Lombard rebels, all he got in response were complaints about his alleged maltreatment of the Sicilian Church.[35] Earlier on the same year, Gregory had accused Frederick of various transgressions, to which the emperor responded by listing what he considered the injustices committed by the Holy See.[36] Frederick's confidence in the pope's neutrality was certainly not increased when Cardinal James of Praeneste, a staunch supporter of the League, was appointed papal legate in Italy. In a letter probably dating from February 1237, the emperor announced that he was sending Herman of Salza as his envoy. However, Herman was to deal only with Gregory himself, not the legate.[37] The spirit of co-operation that had guided the actions of emperor and pope since 1231 began to wear thin.

Simultaneously, papal and imperial interests began to clash in Provence. In April 1236 Gregory IX ordered the count of Toulouse to go to the Holy Land for five years if he wanted to avert his excommunication.[38] In May he requested Louis IX's help against the count.[39] Gregory did this at a time when Frederick was aiming to strengthen his authority over Languedoc. From 1238, the conflict escalated. In August Gregory IX ordered the citizens of Avignon not to ally themselves with the count of Toulouse against the count of Provence, or to support the imperial seneschal.[40] Furthermore, the communes of Arles and Marseilles were ordered to fight Frederick's seneschal, as was the count of Provence.[41] Gregory considered the fight against Catharism more important than Frederick's claims to imperial overlordship in Languedoc. Gregory's actions were the more dangerous, as the count of Toulouse was Frederick's most reliable ally in the area.[42] Frederick, however, decided to disregard papal interference, and continued to state his claims. In January 1238 he granted a series of privileges to the citizens of Avignon,[43] and in June he complained to Gregory about the appointment of James de Praeneste as legate in Provence.[44] However, the affair also shows that pope and emperor were still capable of settling their conflicts peacefully. The legate was ordered to absolve the count of Toulouse from all ecclesiastical censures,[45] and Frederick decreed that his edicts against heresy be promul-

---

35 *Registres Grégoire IX*, no. 3361.
36 *Epistolae saeculi XIII*, i, nos 695–701.
37 *Acta imperii inedita*, ii, no. 25.
38 *Epistolae saeculi XIII*, i, no. 688.
39 *Registres Grégoire IX*, no. 3138. This request was repeated the following year: *Epistolae saeculi XIII*, ii, no. 706.
40 *Registres Grégoire IX*, nos 3802–3.
41 Ibid. nos 3804–6.
42 Matthew Paris, *Chronica maiora*, iii. 491.
43 *Historia diplomatica*, v. 158–60; J. Chiffoleau, 'I ghibellini de regno di Arles', in Toubert and Paravicini Bagliani, *Federico II*, 364–88.
44 *Acta imperii inedita*, i, no. 349.
45 *Epistolae saeculi XIII*, i, no. 731.

gated in the kingdom of Arles.[46] Their relationship was not yet wholly doomed.

A similar picture emerges concerning Frederick's difficulties in the Holy Land. One of the emperor's major conflicts had been with the commune of Acre. In 1236 a compromise had been arranged with Gregory's help.[47] As long as the prospect that the planned crusade would get under way remained, co-operation continued. That very project, however, soon began to divide Gregory and Frederick. The pope had been planning another expedition to Palestine, to begin in 1238.[48] The emperor, though, insisted that his truce should be observed, and the campaign should not start until 1239. In November 1237 Gregory announced to Frederick that the crusaders were to set sail by June 1238.[49] Simultaneously, he addressed prominent ecclesiastical circles in Sicily and asked them to persuade the emperor to support his crusading plans.[50] Frederick refused to comply, and announced that he was sending one of his officials to the crusaders assembling in France to expound his reasons for asking them to postpone their expedition.[51] By 7 December he could announce to the pope that the crusaders had agreed not to begin their campaign until the truce had expired.[52] In the end, Gregory complied. Frederick, however, was never to participate in the expedition. In March 1239 he was excommunicated for a second time. The ensuing wars left little room for an adventure like the one he had undertaken in 1228, and it was left to a number of French and English nobles to sustain the crusading effort. Still, Gregory and Frederick had fallen out, not over the question of whether, but rather of when the crusade should take place.

These differences over the affairs of Burgundy, Italy and the Holy Land illustrate the problems at the heart of papal–imperial relations. Gregory had been willing to help and assist Frederick, but if the emperor harboured heretics or if he flatly rejected papal efforts at pacifying Lombardy, this could not be accepted. Equally, Frederick claimed that his actions were only aimed at putting an end to the very problems, which had hampered his freedom of action in the past. The battle of Cortenuova had presented the opportunity to solve the Lombard problem while he was also on his way to establishing effective imperial authority in Burgundy. At the same time, it would be mistaken to view relations between Frederick and Gregory as drifting inescapably towards the excommunication of 1239. There still was room for compromise.

---

[46] *Acta imperii inedita*, i, no. 351.
[47] *Historia diplomatica*, iv. 808. A later, dubious, source relates that Gregory IX then authorised the military orders and the Italian communities in Genoa to assist the citizens of Acre: Riley-Smith, *The feudal nobility*, 207.
[48] *Epistolae saeculi XIII*, i, no. 688.
[49] *Historia diplomatica*, v. 126–8.
[50] *Epistolae saeculi XIII*, i, nos 714–15.
[51] *Historia diplomatica*, v. 140–2.
[52] Ibid. v. 139–40.

This, in short, was the context within which Anglo-imperial relations during these years have to be placed. As far as Frederick was concerned, his dealings with Henry III formed but part of a wider series of initiatives to secure the support of his fellow monarchs. We may assume that the meetings at Vaucouleurs, apart from settling the conflict between Henry III and Louis IX, were also to have formed part of wider efforts concerning Lombardy and *Outremer*. They certainly would have conformed to a general pattern. In July 1236, for instance, King Bela of Hungary, probably acting at Frederick's request, wrote to Gregory IX and asked him not to support the Lombards, as this would damage both the Church and the Christian princes.[53] Henry III, similarly, played a significant diplomatic as well as military role. In June 1236 he asked the pope not to support the Lombard rebels against their lord, the emperor,[54] with similar requests, Matthew Paris reports, repeated in 1238.[55] It appears that the king of England acted in close co-operation with his brother-in-law. He thus, for instance, announced to Frederick that he had sent Baldwin de Vere and Bartholomew Pecche to further the emperor's cause at the *curia*.[56] We should also note that Simon de Montfort, in Rome to seek dispensation for his marriage with Henry's sister, contacted the imperial court before proceeding to the *curia*.[57] Henry and Frederick, in short, acted in unison, and the king of England, his family and magnates, like many of their peers across Europe, pleaded on Frederick's behalf. In the case of Henry III, such support also included more palpable gifts. Matthew Paris reports how, in 1238, a contingent of English troops under the leadership of Henry de Trubleville, seneschal of Gascony, was sent to Italy.[58] Henry brought not only knights, but also funds: in February 1238 he received £73 from the exchequer 'pro auxilio sororii regis imperatoris Alemannorum',[59] and in February 1239, Florentine merchants received 1,000 marks that they had lent to the bishop-elect of Valence, 'for the expedition of the king's affairs in Italy when he was there in the emperor's army'.[60] Henry III was not alone. In many ways, the campaign of 1238 marked the *apogee* of Frederick's standing within Latin Christendom. Also participating was Baldwin de Guines;[61] the king of Hungary had been ordered to provide troops;[62] and Flemish and Spanish knights fought on Frederick's side.[63] Moreover, some later sources report that

53 A. Huillard-Brehouilles, 'Examen des chartes de l'église romaine contenues dans les rouleaux de Cluny', *Notices et extraits des manuscrits de la Bibliothèque imperiale* xxi/2 (1865), no. 34, cited after Kluger, *Hochmeister*, 174 n. 67.
54 *Treaty rolls*, nos 39, 43–5.
55 Matthew Paris, *Chronica maiora*, iii. 485.
56 *Historia diplomatica*, iv. 884–5.
57 Matthew Paris, *Chronica maiora*, iii. 487; Maddicott, *Simon de Montfort*, 23, 56, 75, 109.
58 Matthew Paris, *Chronica majora*, iii. 485–6, 491–2.
59 CR, 1237–42, 30.
60 CLR, 1226–40, 365.
61 Kienast, *Die deutschen Fürsten*, ii. 85.
62 *Constitutiones*, 1198–1272, no. 206.
63 *Regesta imperii*, no. 2375a.

the sultan of Egypt and Vatatzes, emperor at Nicaea, had sent contingents.[64] This testifies to the success of Frederick's diplomacy. He could justly claim to act in unison with the secular leaders of Christendom. This provides the background to the planned conferences at Vaucouleurs, and it establishes the framework within which relations between Frederick II and Henry III were conducted. The king of England mattered as the empress's brother, but also as someone who could aid Frederick politically, financially and militarily. At the same time, Henry III remained only one among several sources of support, and Frederick continued to avoid offering the king what he really wanted: assistance in recovering his continental inheritance.

Frederick's campaigns in Lombardy also explain another dominant feature in his exchanges with Henry III: the collection of Isabella's dowry. By the thirteenth century, imperial campaigns in Italy were based less on feudal levies than on the hiring of mercenaries, thus greatly increasing the cost of warfare.[65] Moreover, military action alone was not enough. Allies had to be won and rewarded. The payment of specified sums of money became a feature of increasing regularity in the treaties between medieval rulers. In 1229, for instance, Henry III had offered financial payments as one way of receiving back Normandy and Poitou, and the 1259 Treaty of Paris was to stipulate the sums Louis IX was to pay out to Henry III in exchange for an end to Plantagenet claims on Normandy and Poitou. 30,000 marks were, therefore, a prize which could not be set aside easily, and we should not be surprised to see that most of the surviving evidence for contacts between the imperial and the English courts concerned Isabella's dowry. This appears to have caused some embarrassment to the king. In June 1236, for instance, Henry asked for a postponement of the next instalment.[66] He seems to have had little success, as in August he requested Gregory IX's help in extracting funds from his Irish subjects.[67] In late April 1237 Henry put all payments on hold, until 10,000 marks owed to Frederick for the previous Easter term had been delivered.[68] He even had to allow Frederick's proctors to oversee the collection of funds in Ireland. In fact, the financial difficulties the king faced during these years led to an important political concession in England, and in January 1237 Henry III once again confirmed Magna Carta, in exchange for a grant of taxation.[69] Although all this marked a considerable improvement, we should not exaggerate Henry's importance to the emperor. There is little to distin-

---

[64] *Annales placentini gibellini*, MGH, SS xviii. 479. However, this statement could have been influenced by later events. Ibn Wasil does not record any military aid: *Arab historians*, 276.

[65] P. Thorau, 'Der Krieg und das Geld: Ritter und Söldner in den Heeren Kaiser Friedrichs II', *HZ* cclxviii (1999), 599–634.

[66] *Treaty rolls*, no. 40.

[67] Ibid. no. 101.

[68] CLR, *1225–40*, 265; *Treaty rolls*, no. 55.

[69] Holt, *Magna carta*, 394–5; F. M. Powicke, *The thirteenth century, 1216–1307*, 2nd edn, Oxford 1961, 73–5, 97–9.

guish between the way Henry III was treated and how other potential allies fared. Frederick's concerns had changed little since the Treaty of San Germano: he sought to establish his authority across all his domains, and realising that this was going to cause increasing problems with the papacy, he called upon his fellow-monarchs to back his efforts. As far as relations with England were concerned, the emperor certainly saw his marriage pay the dividends he may have expected, but the question remains to what extent Henry III had come any closer to seeing his hopes fulfilled.

Plantagenet hopes

Although a truce had been agreed in 1235, the English court seems to have hoped that Frederick would join a campaign against the Capetians. In 1236, for instance, Matthew Paris reports that Frederick had requested Richard of Cornwall to come to Vaucouleurs to fight the French.[70] Matthew frequently drew on information from the inner circles of the royal court – including Henry and his brother – and his statement may thus reflect expectations held by the king and his court.[71] Henry III certainly continued his efforts to find allies against Louis IX, but met with repeated setbacks. In 1237, for instance, Robert of Artois married a daughter of the duke of Brabant,[72] and another of Louis IX's brothers the heiress of Toulouse,[73] while in 1234 Louis himself had married one of the daughters of the count of Provence.[74] The duke and Raymond of Toulouse had frequently been courted by Henry. The duke's Capetian marriage sealed Plantagenet efforts at drawing him into a web of allies on the eastern borders of Louis's kingdom. Raymond probably had little choice regarding this marriage, as it had been stipulated in the 1229 Treaty of Paris, but Henry had to face up to the prospect that Toulouse would soon pass into Capetian hands.

Still, it was not all gloom. In January 1236 the marriage between Eleanor of Provence, daughter of Count Raymond Berengar, and Henry III was celebrated at Westminster.[75] In the long term, the most important result of this union was that it brought Henry III into close contact with the counts of Savoy, thus gaining him the advice of a family with greater knowledge of the structures and under-currents of European politics than most members of his

---

70 Matthew Paris, *Chronica maiora*, iii. 340.
71 R. Vaughan, *Matthew Paris*, Cambridge 1958, 13–17; H.-E. Hilpert, *Kaiser- und Papstbriefe in den Chronica majora des Matthaeus Paris*, Stuttgart 1981, passim, and 114–20.
72 William de Nangis, *Gesta*, 524.
73 *Albrici abbatis Trium Fontium chronica*, RHGF xxi. 691.
74 E. L. Cox, *The eagles of Savoy: the house of Savoy in the thirteenth century*, Princeton 1974, 44.
75 *Annals of Burton*, AM i. 253; *Annals of Waverley*, AM ii. 316; Howell, *Eleanor of Provence*, 14–18.

court.[76] A series of advantageous marriages had brought the Savoyards, who originated in the border regions of northern Italy and modern Switzerland, lands and relatives as far afield as Bern, Asti, Aix-en-Provence and Lyon, and tied them closely to the royal houses of England and France.[77] It would be mistaken, though, to view them exclusively in terms of the potential benefits Henry III might have drawn from this connection. In fact, he was only one among several claimants to their loyalty, as is perhaps best illustrated by Thomas of Savoy who, in 1237, married the countess of Flanders.[78] According to a later French source, the countess's chosen spouse had initially been Simon de Montfort, but because Simon was a vassal of King Henry, Louis IX put pressure on her to marry Thomas instead.[79] It seems unlikely that Louis would have favoured Thomas over Simon had he been perceived as a stalwart of Plantagenet interests. After all, he was Louis's uncle by marriage as much as Henry's. Thus, even the traditional payment of 500 marks to the count, which the king had reinstated in 1239, did not sway Thomas when Henry asked for his military support during the Poitevin campaign of 1242/3.[80] Moreover, the count also held considerable parts of his territories in fief from the emperor. Thomas's freedom of action was thus curtailed by the fact that he was count only in right of his wife, by the pressure Louis IX and the Capetians could exert on the rulers of Flanders, by his familial obligations towards the king of England and by the services he owed to Frederick II. Similar pressures applied to other members of the family. Although the Savoyards were to play a prominent part in the conduct of Henry's diplomacy, we need to be aware that their wide-ranging connections brought with them limitations as well as opportunities.

As the case of William of Savoy, the bishop elect of Valence, will show, the queen's relatives were not simple pawns, but had ambitions and pursued projects of their own. William was among those of Eleanor's relatives who were to play the most prominent part in English affairs,[81] acting, for instance, as one of the leaders of the English contingent during the emperor's 1238 campaign.[82] It was only his death in 1239 which prevented him from assuming an even more prominent role.[83] None the less, William caused as many problems as he helped to solve. In 1238, for example, the chapter of Liège Cathedral split over the election of a new bishop, with Otto, the provost of Aachen Cathedral, and William of Savoy as the chief

76 Stacey, *Politics, policy and finance*, 182.
77 Howell, *Eleanor of Provence*, 1–3; Cox, *Eagles of Savoy*, 33–79.
78 *Annales laubiensum continuatio*, MGH, SS iv. 26; *Annales aquicintini*, MGH, SS xvi. 504.
79 *Albrici abbatis Trium Fontium chronica*, RHGF xxi. 619.
80 Stacey, *Politics, policy and finance*, 181–2.
81 J. Chevalier, *Quarante Années de l'histoire des évêques de Valence au moyen âge: Guillaume et Philippe de Savoie (1226 à 1267)*, Paris 1889, 3–41. For relations with the Savoyards in general see references in Howell, *Eleanor of Provence*.
82 Matthew Paris, *Chronica maiora*, iii. 485–6, 491–2.
83 Ibid. iii. 623.

contenders.[84] The political situation in the region at the time is important. It has been suggested that Thomas, the new count of Flanders, may have had a hand in this election, as he and the late bishop had been close allies.[85] There is, however, little evidence to suggest Henry III's involvement. Even Matthew Paris, who would not normally let pass an opportunity to comment on the king' patronage of his foreign favourites,[86] records no involvement. It seems, rather, that Gregory IX was the driving force behind William's candidacy. Matthew, for instance, reports that the pope had offered the bishopric to William during a visit to Rome, possibly undertaken in the context of the 1238 Lombard campaign.[87] The sole piece of evidence linking the king of England directly to the affair is a petition from Otto, provost of Aachen, on behalf of a clerk of the duke of Brabant, Henry de Rumenham, sent probably in March 1239.[88] This suggests that Henry III was not perceived as someone hostile to Otto's candidacy. Otherwise, there would have been no point in choosing Otto to plead Henry's case with him. This is given some credence by the fact that, since 1235, Otto and his family had become one of the chief conduits for Anglo-imperial diplomacy. As with the plans mooted in 1229 to elect Otto the Child as anti-king, there is no evidence to suggest an active role by Henry III in supporting those hostile towards the emperor. In fact, support from the English court for William's bid would have placed it in direct opposition to the emperor, contrary to the approach hitherto pursued by the king and his advisors: Henry III had spent considerable funds to assist Frederick in Lombardy, he had sent troops to fight alongside those of his brother-in-law; and he had pleaded with Gregory IX not to aid those who resisted the emperor. Henry's Provençal marriage certainly opened new channels of influence, but it also meant that the king was drawn into a whole range of conflicts and rivalries which, at times, stood in direct opposition to what he was hoping to achieve.

William's case illustrates a recurrent pattern in the English court's attitude towards Frederick. Henry left little doubt that he hoped ultimately to be able to draw on the emperor's support in pursuing his claims to Normandy and Poitou. However, the reluctance with which the emperor reacted to these expectations, and the fact that Frederick was preoccupied with the affairs of Lombardy and *Outremer*, brought Henry III into a position in which he could but seek to oblige Frederick in the hope that his favours be returned at some point in the future. He did so by sending men and funds, and by interceding on the emperor's behalf with Pope Gregory. In addition, he took great care

---

84 P. Thorau, 'Territorialpolitik und fürstlicher Ehrgeiz am Niederrhein zur Zeit Kaiser Friedrichs II und König Konrads IV: das Lütticher Schisma von 1238', in Herbers, Kortüm and Servatius, *Ex ipsis rerum documentis*, 523–46.
85 Cox, *Eagles of Savoy*, 70.
86 In 1239, for instance, Matthew was to blame the outbreak of a war between the counts of Toulouse and Provence on Thomas of Flanders: *Chronica maiora* iv. 19–24.
87 Ibid. iii. 539.
88 *Diplomatic documents*, no. 250.

not to alienate the emperor, even if this involved, as in the next and final example, the welfare of his own agents.

When Gregory IX excommunicated Frederick for a second time in 1239, he listed among his reasons the alleged maltreatment of Peter Saracenus, described as Henry III's envoy.[89] The affair remains murky, but merits attention, as it exemplifies the increasingly fragile nature of the concord between Frederick and Gregory, as well as the difficulties this could pose to those, like Henry III, who got caught in between. In June 1238 Gregory IX wrote to Frederick, and demanded Peter's immediate release.[90] In July Frederick responded and declared that Peter would not be freed, as he had sought to sow discord between the emperor, the pope and the king of England.[91] No evidence survives to illuminate the nature of Peter's alleged crimes. At best the timing of the episode may point towards a connection with the emperor's Lombard campaign. Matters are further complicated by the fact that Peter, the descendant of a noble Roman family,[92] had acted as Henry's proctor at the *curia* since the days of Honorius III.[93] Only in March 1238, three months before the pope first intervened on Peter's behalf, had the king written to Gregory IX about – unspecified – business which Peter was to conduct on his behalf.[94] There clearly were strong links with the English court, but Henry III does not appear to have been overly concerned about his proctor's imprisonment. No evidence survives to suggest that efforts were made to help Peter, even though the episode was widely known.[95] No letters to the emperor survive, no envoys were sent. This seems unusual, but it may indicate Henry's reluctance to alienate Frederick. Just as William of Valence had not been able to count on the king's support in pursuing his ambitions in Liège, so Peter could expect little help from his English employer. The affair also highlights the mutual distrust which began to permeate relations between pope and emperor. This was not the only incident of its kind. However, while matters such as Gregory's involvement in the affairs of Languedoc, or Frederick's attempts to delay the departure of the crusade could still be settled amicably, by the summer of 1238, it seems, there was less and less room for compromise. Like many others, Henry III was caught in the midst of this escalating conflict, and like them he would soon have to weather an even fiercer storm.

---

[89] Matthew Paris, *Chronica maiora*, iii. 558–9.
[90] *Epistolae saeculi XIII*, i. 730.
[91] *Acta imperii inedita*, i, no. 351.
[92] Kamp, *Kirche und Monarchie*, ii. 597.
[93] *Treaty rolls*, nos 30–3; *Diplomatic documents*, nos 25, 121, 182–3, 190, 192, 203; *CPR, 1226–47*, 147. Peter and his family had also received lavish rewards from the royal court: *CLR, 1226–40*, 281, 287, 315, 371, 416; *CPR, 1232–47*, 190, 412; *CR, 1234–7*, 68, 145, 235, 257, 439.
[94] *CPR, 1232–47*, 235.
[95] Matthew Paris, *Chronica maiora*, iii. 526; *Annals of Dunstaple*, AM iii. 148.

Frederick II drew considerable benefits from his marriage. Henry III, though, remained only one among a number of allies. This, in combination with the needs of *Outremer* and the problems of Lombardy, limited the support Frederick could lend. That the king of England did not formally press the emperor for more support should also come as no surprise. A truce had been agreed in 1235, and Henry lacked the means to embark on any major activities on the continent. It would be equally mistaken, however, to ignore the wider international context of the actions of Henry and Frederick, foremost among them a new crusade. Frederick's 1228/9 campaign had secured Christian possession of Jerusalem for the first time in over a generation. The 1239 crusade was thus no ordinary expedition, but aimed at expanding and securing the largest expanse of Christian lands in Syria since the battle of Hattin in 1187. Not surprisingly therefore, large numbers of English magnates also participated in it,[96] giving Henry an additional interest in supporting the activities of his brother-in-law. Normandy and Poitou remained a dominant feature in the king's European diplomacy, but their recovery was intertwined with other concerns, not the least the needs and ambitions of those whose support Henry hoped to muster. We should not let the absence of more palpable gains for or demands by Henry III deceive us as to the nature of Anglo-imperial relations. We have witnessed the formation of links, contacts and friendships which were to be called upon repeatedly over the next decade and beyond.

96 S. Lloyd, *English society and the crusade, 1216–1307*, Oxford 1988, 83–4, 244–5; Maddicott, *Simon de Montfort*, 38–41; Denholm-Young, *Richard of Cornwall*, 38–44.

4

The Dragon and the Little Snake, 1239–1245

In March 1239 Gregory IX excommunicated Frederick for the second time.[1] The emperor responded by drawing on the contacts and allies he had won since 1229. He called upon his fellow monarchs to intercede on his behalf, but also asked them not to lend the *curia* their financial or military backing. Frederick had, however, lost the initiative, and most of his diplomatic activities were concerned with responding to, rather than forestalling Gregory's moves. It certainly would be mistaken to view events as drifting inescapably towards the 1245 Council of Lyon and the final showdown between Innocent IV and Frederick II. None the less, the extent of Gregory's hostility towards the emperor, and the range of initiatives he took to enforce Frederick's excommunication, far exceeded what had gone before, in 1227–31. To Henry III this meant that he found himself placed awkwardly between the emperor and the Holy See. He was unwilling to challenge the pope directly. At the same time, the king relied on Frederick's support for his brother's crusade, and he had not yet given up hopes for a military recovery of Poitou and Normandy. Frederick, in turn, was to depend increasingly on Louis IX, who sought to exploit the fact that both pope and emperor needed his support. Thus, just when the time seemed ripe for Frederick to lend the king of England the support he so eagerly expected, the emperor faced a situation which left little room to meet Henry's expectations. The challenges confronting Henry differed little from those facing other monarchs, as did the steps he took to meet them. To some extent, events during these years mirrored those of 1227–31, but with an important difference. Even then, Henry III had sought to avoid becoming involved in the conflict. Ten years on, the political context had changed. Henry was now on a friendly footing with Frederick II himself, rather than with those who viewed the English court as a means of settling their grievances with the emperor, or of asserting their independence from him. The conflict also involved the king's sister, and threatened the realisation of the very project that had brought him to lend his unquestioning support to Frederick over the previous five years: the recovery of his parental inheritance. Henry could no longer stay aloof.

---

[1] The title of this chapter is a reference to a comment allegedly made by Innocent IV, referring to Henry III's complaints about the actions of papal commissioners in England: 'contrito enim vel pacificato dracone [i.e. Frederick II], cito serpentuli [i.e. Henry III] conculcabuntur': Matthew Paris, *Chronica maiora*, iv. 423.

Searching for allies: the political background

Immediately after pronouncing Frederick's excommunication, Gregory began to search for candidates to replace him as emperor.[2] Those approached included Robert of Artois, the younger brother of Louis IX,[3] as well as the king of Denmark's son.[4] Gregory IX's efforts soon centred on the king of France. On 21 October 1239 he wrote to Louis IX and his mother, praising Louis for his interest in the Holy Land, but then explaining that it would be even more meritorious if Louis were to fight those, like Frederick, who attacked the Church from within.[5] Gregory was not content with merely declaring the emperor expelled from the community of the faithful, but – building on his experiences of Jean de Brienne's abortive campaign – sought to use this to inflict the greatest possible political damage on his foe.

Gregory quickly carried the struggle into all of Frederick's domains. Unlike the emperor's first excommunication in 1227, the second had at least some impact in Germany. The archbishop of Mainz, recently appointed guardian for Frederick's son Conrad IV, assumed leadership of the anti-Staufen forces.[6] The newly elected archbishop of Cologne, Conrad of Hochstaden, too, was forced into the anti-imperial camp.[7] By 1240, however, much of this opposition seems to have been overcome. In May, the German bishops and princes wrote to pope and emperor, urging them to make peace.[8] They also sent an embassy to press for negotiations, led by the master of the Teutonic Knights, Herman of Salza, a reliable ally of the emperor, who had been involved in previous dealings with the *curia*.[9] By 1241 the situation had changed again, when the archbishop of Mainz led troops against Frederick's partisans,[10] and

---

2   *Chronica regia coloniensis continuatio S Pantaleonis v*, in *Chronica regia coloniensis*, 274–5; *Ryccardi de S Germano cronica*, MGH, SS xix. 378; William de Nangis, *Gesta*, RHGF xx. 330.

3   Matthew Paris, *Chronica maiora*, iii. 624–7.

4   *Albrici abbatis Trium Fontium chronica*, RHGF xxi. 625. The question remains, however, to what extent these reports were coloured by hindsight. Matthew Paris, for instance, did not start writing the parts dealing with events after 1236 until after 1246: Hilpert, *Kaiser- und Papstbriefe*, 30–2.

5   *Layettes*, ii, nos 2835, 2836.

6   Goez, 'Friedrich II und Deutschland', 30.

7   M. Werner, 'Prälatenschulden und hohe Politik im 13. Jahrhundert', in H. Vollrath and S. Weinfurter (eds), *Köln: Stadt und Bistum im Reich des Mittelalters: Festschrift Odilo Engels*, Cologne–Weimar–Vienna 1993, 511–70, passim, at pp. 545–51 for Conrad; M. Kettering, 'Die Territorialpolitik des Kölner Erzbischofs Konrad von Hochstaden (1238–1261)', *Jahrbuch des Kölnischen Geschichtsvereins* xxvi (1951), 1–84.

8   *Constitutiones*, 1198–1272, nos 225, 228, 229 (for the prelates), 226, 227, 230–2 (for the secular princes).

9   *Annales erphordenses*, in *Monumenta erphesfurtensia*, 98.

10   *Annales zwifaltenses maiores*, MGH, SS x. 60; *Annales Sancti Truberti*, MGH, SS xvii. 294; Matthew Paris, *Chronica maiora*, iv. 188.

in 1244, while negotiations continued between pope and emperor, he travelled his diocese to whip up support against the latter.[11] It was not until after
Frederick's deposition in 1245, however, that these efforts began to cause
serious problems. Although a number of prelates opposed Frederick, the
majority of secular princes remained loyal. The archbishop of Mainz's
successor as guardian for Conrad, for instance, was Henry Raspe, Landgrave
of Thuringia, who did not desert the emperor's cause until 1246, when he was
elected anti-king.

In the kingdom of Burgundy, though, the pope soon found willing allies. In
September 1239 Frederick opened proceedings against Raymond Berengar of
Provence, who was accused of allying himself with the emperor's foes in the
city of Arles and of expelling Frederick's vicar in Arles and Vienne.[12] This
was followed by attempts to forge an alliance against him, including the
count of Toulouse, and the commune of Avignon.[13] Initially, this proved
successful,[14] and the king of France was asked for help against the count of
Provence.[15] Raymond Berengar, in turn, was quick to realise the benefits of a
closer alliance with the papacy, and in November 1239 he promised to
support the pope against Frederick.[16] Alberic of Troisfontaines also refers to
this papal connection: in response to unrest caused by heretics in Provence,
he reported, James of Praeneste had called a council where it was decided
that a French army should be sent to fight the opponents of Raymond
Berengar.[17] Louis's involvement soon put an end to the imperial advance.[18]
Early in 1241, the count of Toulouse had to succumb to the needs of self-pres-
ervation and declared that he would assist the Church against the emperor.[19]
This did not mean the end of his relations with Frederick: after the election
of Innocent IV, he was one of the emperor's proctors in negotiating with the
new pope,[20] and he was to intercede on Frederick's behalf at the Council of
Lyon. By then, the counts of Toulouse and Provence had also overcome their
divisions and fought alongside Henry III against Louis IX.[21] At the time,
though, this presented a serious setback for Frederick. One of his most reliable allies had been forced to submit, while Louis used his power to back not
the emperor, but Gregory IX.

The Holy Land was another area in which Gregory IX gained ground.[22] In

11 *Annales erphordenses*, in *Monumenta erphesfurtensia*, 99.
12 *Constitutiones, 1198–1272*, no. 222.
13 *Historia diplomatica*, v. 403–6.
14 *Layettes*, ii, no. 2842; *Historia diplomatica*, v. 1022–3.
15 *Historia diplomatica*, v. 406–7.
16 Ibid. v. 488–9.
17 *Albrici abbatis Trium Fontium chronica*, RHGF xxi. 628.
18 P. Belperon, *La Croisade contre les albigeois et l'union du Languedoc à la France
(1209–1249)*, Paris 1967, 427–31; Chiffoleau, 'I ghibellini de regno di Arles', 364–88.
19 *Historia diplomatica*, v. 1101–2.
20 *Constitutiones, 1198–1272*, no. 248.
21 Matthew Paris, *Chronica maiora*, iv. 190.
22 Riley-Smith, *The feudal nobility*, 207–13, and D. Jacoby, 'The kingdom of Jerusalem and

1243 Conrad, Frederick's son with Isabella/Yolanda, came of age, and was supposed to take over the government of his realm. Frederick, however, refused to relinquish control and continued to dominate the affairs of Jerusalem. The *baillie*, for instance, appointed by Conrad, was Count Thomas of Acerra, a Sicilian nobleman. The emperor's control over the kingdom had, however, been severely weakened. The authority of the *baillie* was increasingly confined to Tyre, which, too, was lost to the rebels in 1243.[23] Gregory lent those opposing Frederick his full support. Papal mandates were sent to the military orders, the Italian communities in Acre, and to Genoa, exhorting them to fight Frederick. When the rebels decided to appoint their own *baillie*, their decision to elect the queen of Cyprus was confirmed by the Holy See.[24] Effectively, although Conrad continued to issue edicts and to appoint officials for the Latin kingdom until his death in 1254,[25] Staufen rule in Palestine was at an end. Gregory IX had thus seriously weakened Frederick's position in Burgundy and the Holy Land, inroads had been made into Germany and a number of Italian communes had been won over.[26]

The *curia* also managed to thwart a series of alliances pursued by Frederick. Most important among these were plans for a marriage between Conrad IV and a Capetian princess, and – after the death of Empress Isabella in 1241[27] – between Frederick II and the heiress of Austria. Neither undertaking proceeded beyond a preliminary stage. In June 1243 Walter of Ocra was sent to France to arrange a marriage between Conrad IV and a daughter of Louis IX, but no further evidence survives for this project.[28] Had it been successful, it certainly would have strengthened Frederick's hand in negotiations with Innocent IV, thereby also underlining the king of France's role in the conflict. That, in turn, might have put Louis in a difficult position, but it also provided opportunities to further his own ambitions, and ultimately, as we will see, was to bring the whole of Languedoc under his family's control.[29]

the collapse of Hohenstaufen power in the Levant', *Dumbarton Oaks Papers* xl (1986), 83–101.

23 *Crusader Syria*, 129, 131–2 (chapters 52, 55).

24 *Andrae Danduli ducis venetiarum chronica per extensum descripta*, ed. E. Pastorello, RIS xii/1, Bologna 1925–40, 301; J. Richard, 'Pairie d'orient latin: les quatres baronnies des royaumes de Jérusalem et de Chypre', *Revue historique de droit français et etranger* (1950), 67–88, repr. in his *Orient et occident au moyen âge: contacts et relations (XIIe–XVe s.)*, London 1976; D. Jacoby, 'La dimensione imperiale oltremare: Federico II: Cipro e il regno di Gerusalemme', in M. S. C. Mariani and R. Cassano (eds), *Federico II: immagine e potere*, Bari 1995, 31–5.

25 H. E. Mayer, *Die Kanzlei der lateinischen Könige von Jerusalem*, Hanover 1996, 366–7; H. Hartmann, 'Die Urkunden Konrads IV.', *AfD* xviii (1944), 38–163 at p. 135.

26 *Cronica di Antonio Godi Vicentino*, ed. G. Soranzo, RIS viii/2, Città di Castello 1908, 13.

27 *Rolandini patavini cronica in factis et circa facta marchiae trivixane*, ed. A. Bonardi, RIS viii/1, Città di Castello 1903–8, 75.

28 *Historia diplomatica*, vi. 95–8.

29 Le Goff, *Saint Louis*, 163–9.

Frederick's hopes for an Austrian marriage also failed.[30] Deliberations to turn the duchy into a kingdom, promulgated in June 1245, were probably connected to his marital plans,[31] and were mooted at about the same time as the emperor's proctors opened negotiations with the duke. If this was expected to sway the ducal family into supporting him, Frederick was to be disappointed. If Matthew Paris is to be believed, his prospective spouse was so horrified at the idea of being married to a persistent apostate that she refused his overtures.[32] Other projects, such as plans for a Provençal marriage, also pursued in 1245, met with equally little success. However, it was not all doom. In 1242 the emperor married one of his illegitimate daughters to John III Vatatzes, the Byzantine emperor at Nicaea.[33] This provided Frederick with an important ally on the eastern flank of Venice, one of the leading supporters of both the *curia* and the Lombard League.[34] More important, he secured a truce between Baldwin of Constantinople, the Latin emperor, and Vatatzes.[35] As this provided a much needed respite for the Latin empire, it may not come as a surprise that Emperor Baldwin was among those arguing most persistently in favour of Frederick's excommunication being lifted.[36] Being unable to offer a symbolic gesture of comparable impact to the liberation of Jerusalem, the emperor found it harder to counter the *curia's* diplomatic offensive. At the same time, he proceeded along familiar lines. Frederick courted those who in the past had spoken out on his behalf, and even if another crusade was out of the question, his daughter's marriage to Vatatzes, and the emperor's subsequent involvement in the affairs of Constantinople still point to his efforts to be seen as a defender of Latin Christendom.

This conflict was one of words as well as deeds. Frederick soon realised the

---

[30] Hausmann, 'Friedrich II. und Österreich', 268–74.

[31] *Constitutiones, 1198–1272, no. 261.*

[32] Matthew Paris, *Chronica maiora*, iv. 474–5. See also *Bartholomaei scribae annales*, MGH, SS xviii. 217.

[33] Matthew Paris, *Chronica maiora*, iv. 299, 357; S. Brezeanu, 'Notice sur les rapports de Frédéric II de Hohenstaufen avec Jean III Vatatzès', *Revue des études sud-est européennes* xii (1974), 583–5; C. Marinesco, 'Du Nouveau sur Constance de Hohenstaufen, impératrice de Nicée', *Byzantion* i (1924), 451–9; A. Kiesewetter, 'Die Heirat zwischen Konstanze-Anna von Hohenstaufen und Kaiser Johannes III. Batatzes von Nikaia (Ende 1240 oder Anfang 1241) und der Angriff des Johannes Batatzes auf Konstantinopel im Mai oder Juni 1241', *Römische Historische Mitteilungen* xli (1999), 239–50; F. Tinnefeld, 'Byzanz und die Herrscher des Hauses Hohenstaufen', *AfD* xli (1995), 105–27.

[34] The *podestà* of Milan, executed at Cortenuova, was the doge of Venice's son: *Andrae Danduli*, 296. In 1231 the doge had allied himself with Jean de Brienne: *Urkunden zur älteren Handels- und Rechtsgeschichte der Republik Venedig mit besondere Beziehung auf Byzanz und die Levante*, ed. G. L. Tafel and G. M. Thomas, Vienna 1856–7, ii, no. 277; H. Chone, *Die Beziehungen Kaiser Friedrichs II zu den Seestädten Venedig, Pisa, Genua*, Berlin 1902.

[35] *Regestes des empéreurs latins de Constantinople (1204–1261/72)*, ed. B. Hendrickx, Thessalonika 1988, no. 212.

[36] Matthew Paris, *Chronica maiora*, iv. 371, 431, 447.

dangers posed by papal propaganda, and quickly tried to counteract it.[37] From
the beginning the imperial chancery produced missives which aimed to reject
and disprove accusations levelled at Frederick, and sought to turn them
against the *curia* instead. Thanks to Matthew Paris, many of the materials
addressed to the English court survive. The letter sent to Richard of Cornwall
in April 1239 may serve as example for the general thrust of the emperor's
claims. Frederick's excommunication was declared to be a rejection of God
and everything that was just. While the emperor was willing to prove his
orthodoxy, the pope refused to hear him. In fact, claimed Frederick, as
Gregory was allying himself with the Lombards who were known harbourers
of heresy, the pope himself had become a heretic and friend of heretics.[38] The
accusations which had been levelled at the emperor were now directed
against those who opposed him, and Gregory was declared guilty of the very
crimes of which he had accused Frederick. These letters were disseminated
across Latin Christendom,[39] and were frequently combined with specific
requests. In October 1239, for instance, the barons of England were
petitioned to prevent papal legates from collecting funds for use against
Frederick.[40] Furthermore, the emperor demonstrated his own orthodoxy by
doing publicly what he had been accused of not doing. Instances include
privileges for the Hospitallers in the kingdom of Arles – one of the points in
Gregory's bull of excommunication had been the emperor's persecution of
the military orders.[41] Similarly, imperial support was promised to those
preparing for crusades to the Holy Land, while the pope was blamed for the
emperor's inability to participate himself.[42] Not Frederick, but Gregory
endangered Christendom. Similar arguments were used during the Mongol
attacks on eastern Europe in 1241,[43] and after the fall of Jerusalem to
Khwarīzīm Turks in 1244.[44] It is particularly worth noting how Frederick

37 H. Wieruszowski, *Vom imperium zum nationalen Königtum: vergleichende Studien über die publizistischen Kämpfe Kaiser Friedrichs II und König Philips des Schönen mit der Kurie*, Munich–Berlin 1933; P. Segl, 'Die Feindbilder in der politischen Propaganda Friedrichs II. und seiner Gegner', in F. Bosbach (ed.), *Feindbilder: die Darstellung des Gegners in der politischen Publizistik des Mittelalters und der frühen Neuzeit*, Cologne–Weimar–Vienna 1992, 41–71; R. Brentano, 'Western civilization: the Middle Ages', in H. D. Lasswell, D. Lerner and H. Speier (eds), *Propaganda and communication in world history*, Honolulu 1974, i. 552–95; H. Wolfram, 'Meinungsbildung und Propaganda im österreichischen Mittelalter', in E. Zöllner (ed.), *Öffentliche Meinung in der Geschichte Österreichs*, Vienna 1979, 13–26; Stürner, *Friedrich II.*, 470–80.
38 Matthew Paris, *Chronica maiora*, iii. 575–89.
39 Ibid. iii. 590.
40 *Historia diplomatica*, v. 467–9.
41 Ibid. v. 323–6; A. J. Forey, 'The military orders and holy war against Christians in the thirteenth century', *EHR* civ (1989), 1–24.
42 *Historia diplomatica*, v. 359–62, 396–8.
43 Ibid. v. 1139–43 (to the senate of Rome), 1143–5 (to the king of Hungary); Matthew Paris, *Chronica maiora*, iv. 112–19 (to Henry III).
44 Matthew Paris, *Chronica maiora*, iii. 300–5; *Annales pragenses* i, MGH, SS ix, 171; *Annales neresheimenses*, MGH, SS x, 23. For a Muslim account see *Ayyubids, Mamlukes and*

stressed the needs of the Holy Land, thereby not only playing on the immediate concerns of his fellow monarchs – Richard of Cornwall went on crusade
in 1239, and Louis took the cross a few years later – but also appealing implic-
itly to his record. He wrote as emperor, as the one who had secured Christian
control of Jerusalem, and the one most capable of ensuring that it continued.

Furthermore, letters from those who could bear witness to Frederick's
orthodoxy were disseminated. Matthew Paris, for instance, recounts how
Walter of Ocra tried to convince the English clergy in 1244 not to send funds
to the pope by reading out letters from the Latin emperor of Constantinople
and the count of Toulouse, testifying to the emperor's orthodoxy and devotion.[45] Finally, letters were sent, like the one to Ferdinand of Castile in
September 1240, in which the emperor gave an account of his recent victories.[46] His cause was not merely just, but successful, too. The ease with which
opposition could be overcome testified to the impious motives of his foes. All
this served a twofold purpose, aiming both to prevent Gregory IX from
gaining the support of Frederick's fellow monarchs, and to secure their
backing for the emperor instead. Unless other rulers intervened on Frederick's behalf, the pope was unlikely to agree to a peaceful settlement. Papal
and imperial propaganda alike was aimed not merely at justifying a particular
course of action, but at enlisting the support of their respective neighbours,
friends and relatives.

The European response

Contemporaries, it seems, assumed that the emperor's excommunication was
only temporary and that the underlying conflict could be resolved quickly.[47]
If Matthew Paris is to be believed, the quest for a settlement involved the
upper echelons of the papal court. In late 1239, he claimed, a papal legate
urged a truce with Frederick, and suggested that a general council be held the
following Easter to settle the matter peacefully and amicably.[48] A similar
account is given in the *Annals of Dunstable*: the patriarch of Jerusalem had
been working to broker a peace, but without success. However, at the instigation of Cardinal John de Columbna, a peace proposal had been accepted, and

---

crusaders: selections from the Tarikh al-Duwal wa'l-Muluk of Ibn al-Furat, ed. U. Lyons, M. C.
Lyons and J. S. C. Riley-Smith, Cambridge 1971, ii. 3–4. I am grateful to Angus Stewart for
this reference.
[45] Matthew Paris, *Chronica maiora*, iv. 371.
[46] *Historia diplomatica*, v. 1047; Matthew Paris, *Chronica maiora*, iv. 126.
[47] Stürner, *Friedrich II*, ii. 502–9; G. A. Loud, 'The case of the missing martyrs: Frederick
II's war with the Church, 1239–1250', in D. Wood (ed.), *Martyrs and martyrologies* (SCH
xxx, 1993), 141–52. For a more critical view see Stacey, *Politics, policy and finance*, 182.
[48] Matthew Paris, *Chronica maiora*, iv. 59.

a general council was to be convened.[49] Some credibility is lent to these accounts by the fact that John broke with the pope in 1241 over Gregory's reluctance to negotiate with Frederick.[50] If nothing else, this suggests that attempts to find a swift solution to the struggle were made, and that even the members of the *curia* were split as to the course of action to be taken. Gregory could not rely on the full support even of his own immediate circle. In the end, it was the emperor himself who provided the pope with an opportunity to prolong the conflict.

Support for the idea of holding a general council to resolve the differences between pope and emperor appears to have been widespread.[51] Matthew Paris, for instance, reported that Louis IX refused to act against Frederick, unless his guilt had first been proven before a general council.[52] In March 1239 Frederick himself suggested to the cardinals that he would be willing to let their differences be decided before such a meeting,[53] and in June he sent two bishops, probably in order to deal with this matter.[54] By September 1240, however, Frederick rejected the idea as a ploy designed to give the Lombards a respite before they began to wage war again. Simultaneously, the emperor raised the stakes and declared his willingness to negotiate for a proper peace, but refused to include the Lombards in it,[55] a proposal which was unlikely to be accepted by Gregory IX. Gregory's refusal would of course only have helped to press home the point Frederick and his chancery had been aiming to make all along: that the emperor's excommunication was a matter not of maintaining or enforcing orthodoxy, but of papal treachery. Some of Frederick's reasoning, though, seems to have been based on sincere worries about the direction which the council would take, and he went to great lengths to prevent it from meeting. He described the proposed assembly as yet another attempt to further war, not peace,[56] and warned the prelates planning to participate that they would be viewed as enemies of the empire.[57] In the end, the imperial fleet intercepted and captured those sailing to Rome.[58] This was to cause some friction in the emperor's relations with Louis IX, as by far the largest contingent of prelates incarcerated by Frederick had come from France. In the short run, though, the most immediate danger had been averted. Gregory was deprived of an opportunity to air his grievances before, and have his actions condoned by, a general assembly of the Church.

---

49 *Annals of Dunstable*, AM iii. 154–5.
50 *Ryccardi de S Germano cronica*, MGH, SS xix, 381.
51 See B. Roberg, 'Der Konzilsversuch von 1241', *Annuarium Historiae Conciliorum* xxiv (1992), 286–319, for a more critical view of Frederick's actions. See also Stürner, *Friedrich II*, ii. 496–502, and *Chronica de Mailros*, ed. J. Stevenson, Edinburgh 1835, 151–3.
52 Matthew Paris, *Chronica maiora*, iii. 624–6.
53 *Constitutiones, 1198–1272*, no. 214.
54 *Ryccardi de S Germano cronica*, MGH, SS xix. 377.
55 Matthew Paris, *Chronica maiora*, iv. 65–8.
56 *Historia diplomatica*, v. 1075–7.
57 Matthew Paris, *Chronica maiora*, iv. 68–71.
58 Ibid. iv. 120–5.

Still, diplomatic efforts to find a peaceful solution continued, and they gained an added sense of urgency in 1241 when several German princes tried to organise a crusade against the Mongols.[59] This involved not only pleas for help, but also efforts to bring Frederick and Gregory to some sort of understanding. Duke Frederick of Austria took the initiative and wrote to the kings of Castile, Aragon, England and France, asking them to come in person to fight the Tartars.[60] When he approached the pope, Gregory expressed his sadness about the duke's recent misfortunes, but only gave an evasive answer as to the prospect of peace with Frederick.[61] The king of Hungary, next to the duke of Silesia the main victim of Mongol attacks in the west, was equally unsuccessful. Frederick stated that he would be unable to help as long as the pope waged war on him,[62] and Gregory gave him the same reply he had given Duke Frederick.[63] Significantly, these letters reflect the themes which permeated papal and imperial propaganda. Just as the duke of Austria and the king of Hungary viewed a settlement of the conflict as a precondition for the successful defence not just of their own lands, but of the whole of Christendom, so Frederick and Gregory each utilised these arguments to cast moral opprobrium on the other. While Frederick was to blame his inability to assist the Christians in Central Europe on Gregory's intransigence, the pope claimed that overcoming his imperial foe was an essential precondition before action could be taken against Christendom's external enemies.[64]

When Gregory IX died in 1241 it seemed as if the conflict would soon be resolved. In a letter to Henry III, Frederick declared that, as the man who had brought disunity and war to Christendom had died, the prospect of peace had arisen. Once a new pope had been chosen, the emperor expected to be once again accepted as the faithful son and protector of the Church.[65] However, when Innocent IV was elected in June 1243, he immediately confirmed Frederick's excommunication.[66] To some extent, this was to be expected. After

---

[59] *Continuatio garstensis*, MGH, SS ix. 597; P. Jackson, 'The crusade against the Mongols (1241)', *Journal of Ecclesiastical History* xlii (1991), 1–18; D. Morgan, *The Mongols*, Oxford 1986, 175–98; K. Rudolf, 'Die Tartaren 1241/1242: Nachrichten und Wiedergabe: Korrespondenz und Historiographie', *Römische Historische Mitteilungen* xix (1977), 79–107.

[60] *Historia diplomatica*, v. 1216–18.

[61] *Epistolae saeculi XIII*, i. no. 823.

[62] *Historia diplomatica*, v. 1143–5. See also Z. J. Kosztolnyik, *Hungary in the thirteenth century*, New York 1996, 151–216; *Rogerii carmen miserabile*, ed. L. Juhasz, SRH ii, Budapest 1938, 543–88; *Planctus destructionis regni Hungariae per Tartaros*, ed. L. Juhasz, ibid. 589–98.

[63] *Epistolae saeculi XIII*, i, no. 826.

[64] The Mongol invasion soon began to feature in anti-imperial propaganda: Matthew Paris, *Chronica maiora*, iv. 119–20; C. Burnett, 'An apocryphal letter from the Arabic philosopher al-Kindi to Theodore, Frederick II's astrologer, concerning Gog and Magog, the enclosed nations, and the scourge of the Mongols', *Viator* xv (1984), 151–67.

[65] *Historia diplomatica*, v. 1165–7. A similar letter was then sent to most western rulers: *Das Brief- und Memorialbuch des Albert Behaim*, ed. T. Frenz and P. Herde, MGH, Briefe des späten Mittelalters, i, Munich 2000, no. 35.

[66] K. Hampe, 'Ein ungedruckter Bericht über das Konklave von 1241 im römischen

all, the conflict had been continuing for too long to warrant an easy solution, and all, it seems, Frederick II may have hoped for, was that the new pontiff would enter into those negotiations which Gregory IX had so persistently refused to embark upon. The emperor, therefore, remained undeterred, and sent proctors to the *curia* to sue for peace regardless.[67] The same year Frederick also addressed letters to the emperor of Constantinople, Louis IX, the duke of Brabant and other rulers,[68] assuring them that, with the new pope, peace could be arranged. Again, Frederick proved more optimistic than Innocent. In August 1243 the pope declared that it was impossible that Frederick's envoys be allowed into his presence, as they had had intercourse with excommunicates, and were thus themselves excommunicates.[69] Innocent was determined to continue his predecessor's unremitting stance. Frederick was only to be allowed back into the fold of the faithful once he submitted unconditionally and fully to the sentence which the pope was to impose upon him. Moreover, the *podestàs* of Treviso and Faventia, leading exponents of the Lombard League, were assured that Innocent would not agree on a peace with the emperor, unless they were part of it.[70] The pope would have been aware that these conditions were unlikely to be accepted by Frederick. None the less, negotiations continued,[71] and in March 1244 the conditions for the emperor's submission were made public. Their acceptance by the emperor testifies to the urgency with which Frederick was searching for peace. He had to take back into his favour all those who had rebelled against him, and had to accept a papal judgement on how the Lombard question was to be resolved. Furthermore, although Frederick had to forgive all acts committed by his enemies, the pope would decide what amends the emperor had to make for the crimes and outrages he and his partisans had committed.[72] Frederick accepted Innocent's conditions, and announced this to his son Conrad,[73] and to Henry III.[74] By June, however, dealings had reached a dead end, and

---

Septizonium', *Sitzungsberichte der Heidelberger Akademie der Wissenschaften* (*Philosophisch-Historische Klasse*) (1913), 1–34; Stürner, *Friedrich II*, ii. 509–18; Matthew Paris, *Chronica maiora*, iv. 256.

67 *Ryccardi de S Germano cronica*, MGH, SS xix. 384; *Constitutiones, 1198–1272*, no. 239; C. Rodenberg, 'Die Friedensverhandlungen zwischen Friedrich II und Innocenz IV, 1243–1244', in *Festgabe für Gerold Meyer von Knonau*, Zürich 1913, 165–204; Stürner, *Friedrich II*, ii. 518–33.

68 *Historia diplomatica*, vi. 90–2 (to the Latin emperor of Constantinople), 95–8 (Louis IX), 98–9 (the duke of Brabant), 93–5. See J. R. Sweeney, 'Unbekannte Briefe Kaiser Friedrichs II. im Codex Indianensis der Werke Senecas', DA xlv (1989), 83–108, no. 1, for unspecified other rulers.

69 *Constitutiones, 1198–1272, no. 241*.

70 *Les Registres d'Innocent IV*, ed. E. Berger, Paris 1884–1919, nos 127, 136, 158.

71 A. Folz, *Kaiser Friedrich II. und Papst Innocenz IV.: ihr Kampf in den Jahren 1244 und 1245*, Strasbourg 1905.

72 *Constitutiones, 1198–1272, no. 245*.

73 Ibid. no. 249.

74 Matthew Paris, *Chronica maiora*, iv. 332–6.

Innocent left Rome. It seems that Frederick had begun to lose patience. He raised the stakes and declared that he would not comply with the conditions proffered by Innocent's proctors unless he first received letters of absolution. In the meantime, Genoa offered the pope its fleet should he seek to escape from the emperor's lands. This Innocent accepted, and fled first to Genoa and then Lyon,[75] thereby administering a serious blow to Frederick's standing in the west. After a year of negotiating and the publicly declared willingness of Innocent IV to take Frederick back into the Church, the pope had been forced to flee Rome. Matthew Paris is our most outspoken source for these events. Although he wrote some time after 1244, it is none the less obvious how he was trying to cope with the conflicting accounts of Frederick and his actions. All too frequently, he was willing to blame papal propaganda, the *curia's* greed and corruption for the emperor's undertakings. Even Matthew found it impossible to excuse the failure of negotiations in 1244, and described the emperor's actions as motivated by hubris and greed: it was Frederick's fault, and Frederick's fault alone, that the conflict continued.[76] We may assume that he was not alone in taking this view.

Contemporaries did not, however, merely stand by, watching this conflict as disinterested observers. They urged a settlement, and they sought to use the conflict to their own advantage. In this context much has been made of Louis IX's arbitration attempts.[77] We will return to his role later, but we have already seen how Louis performed a careful balancing act between a quest for peace, and one for territorial aggrandisement. Louis himself emphasised his neutrality when he asked Frederick II to set free the prelates imprisoned in 1241.[78] There is no evidence for funds or troops being sent against the emperor. Louis did, however, try to utilise the conflict to further his own ends in Languedoc, and in this he was by no means alone. In September 1239, for instance, King Fernando of Castile had announced to the pope that he was sending his heir to the emperor to demand the duchy of Swabia, which he claimed as the inheritance of his deceased wife, a daughter of Philip of Swabia. He also assured Gregory that he was not abandoning his traditional loyalty towards the Holy See. In fact, should the emperor not comply with his demands, Castilian knights would join the papal armies.[79] In December, however, he announced an embassy by the abbot of Sahagún in order to

[75] *Chronicon marchiae tarvisinae et lombardiae*, ed. L. A. Bottegli, RIS viii/3, Città di Castello 1914–16, 16–17; Matthew Paris, *Chronica maiora*, iv. 354–6; *Bartholomaei scribae annales*, MGH, SS xviii, 212–13; *Chronica regia coloniensis continuatio S Pantaleonis v*, in *Chronica regia coloniensis*, 285–6.

[76] Matthew Paris, *Chronica maiora* iv. 269, 357; Sommerlechner, *Stupor mundi*, 27–9; Vaughan, *Matthew Paris*, 147–8.

[77] Kienast, *Deutschland*, 611–13.

[78] *Historia diplomatica*, vi. 18–20.

[79] Ibid. v. 545–6. F. Giunta, 'Federico II e Ferdinando III di Castiglia', in P. Grierson and J. W. Perkins (eds), *Studies in Italian medieval history* (Papers of the British School at Rome xxiv/n.s. xi, 1956), 137–41.

reconcile pope and emperor.[80] The king and his son eventually switched sides when, in 1245, Innocent IV declared that he would grant the Infante of Castile all the help he needed, if he could prove his claims.[81] After nearly six years of unsuccessful attempts at mediating, the rulers of Latin Christendom began to accept that the conflict was unlikely to end soon, and began to see it as an opportunity to further their own ambitions. It is worth noting the similarities in the actions of Ferdinand and Louis. Swabia was the price for Fernando's support, and, ultimately, whoever was willing to pay it was able to count on the king of Castile. Louis IX, similarly, used his position to solicit grants and concessions from both parties. As we will see, the biggest gain he was to make would be the county of Provence in 1246. Even before then, the emperor's weakening hold on Burgundy and the *curia's* lack of military force could be turned to the Capetians' advantage. Both pope and emperor were in a position in which they were hard pressed to grant favours to those whose allegiance they sought to win. To some, like the duke of Austria and the king of Hungary, this proved unfortunate. To others, like Louis IX or Fernando III, it provided a welcome opening. How did Henry III seek to cope with this situation?

The role of Henry III

Henry III and his subjects were embroiled in this conflict from the start. A papal legate had been dispatched to England not long before Frederick's excommunication, so as to muster the financial resources of the English Church,[82] and several chroniclers complained of the *thesaurus non modicus* which the legate collected.[83] That was not, however, the sole concern of the legate. The consecration of St Paul's in 1239, for instance, was used to propagate the emperor's excommunication.[84] It also seems that the legate toured various religious houses, probably to oversee the collection of funds, but also to communicate the reasons for the pope's excommunication of Frederick.[85] Propaganda was not directed merely at rulers and princes, but had to be disseminated as widely as possible to be effective. The legate soon encountered difficulties. When he demanded that the indigenous clergy should follow the example of foreign beneficiaries and grant a fifth, he met with

80 *Reinado y diplomas de Fernando III*, ed. Julio Gonzalez, Cordoba 1980–6, iii. no. 659.
81 *Epistolae saeculi XIII*, ii, no. 180; *Historia diplomatica*, vi. 340–2.
82 *Chronica regia coloniensis continuatio S Pantaleonis v*, in *Chronica regia coloniensis*, 274; Matthew Paris, *Chronica maiora*, iv. 4–5, 9–11, 15, 35–8, 43 (s.a. 1240): D. M. Williamson, 'Some aspects of the legation of Cardinal Otto in England, 1237–41', EHR lxiv (1949), 145–73; Lunt, *Financial relations*, 197–205.
83 *Annals of Winchester*, AM ii. 88; *Annals of Dunstable*, AM, iii. 154.
84 *De antiquis legibus: cronica maiorum et vicecomitum Londoniarum*, ed. T. Stapleton (Camden, 1846), 8; Matthew Paris, *Chronica maiora*, iii. 545.
85 Matthew Paris, *Chronica maiora*, iii. 568–9.

protest. During a council at Reading, the prelates refused to comply.[86] Matthew Paris uses this to paint a highly uncomplimentary picture of the king. When the nobles of England protested against papal extortions, the king refused to act,[87] and when the abbots came to complain about the activities of a curial money-collector, he threatened to imprison those who resisted papal demands.[88] Even allowing that Matthew may have exaggerated the degree of the king's compliance, Henry's unwillingness to confront the *curia* seems remarkable. Funds were, however, only among several issues, and relations between emperor and king were more complex than the question of papal taxation may lead us to believe.

Naturally, Frederick, too, sought to woo Henry III and his barons. In October 1239 the emperor wrote to the nobility of England, and invoked the solidarity of the English barons: this struggle was not merely a matter between pope and emperor, but concerned all princes. Frederick complained about his excommunication being made public in England, and exhorted the barons to move the king to assist his brother and fellow-prince.[89] Similar requests were put forth in 1240. Matthew Paris reports that imperial envoys had been sent to Henry III, carrying letters requesting that Frederick's excommunication not be made public in England, that the papal money-collectors be expelled and the funds collected retained. Although Henry refused to comply, he wrote to Gregory IX, and advised the envoys to leave the country.[90] This is confirmed by several sources, and Henry's court clearly remained in close contact with that of the emperor. In February 1240, for instance, one of Frederick's emissaries, a Hugh Chabet,[91] is recorded as being in England. Furthermore, an entry in the liberate rolls for 1241, in which a merchant from Florence received 300 marks to be handed over to the king's envoys soon to arrive 'at the court of Rome and that of the emperor',[92] suggests continuing efforts at mediation. Even more intriguingly, this mission followed within days of the departure of Walter of Ocra from England.[93] It seems plausible

---

[86] Ibid. iv. 9–10.

[87] Ibid. iv. 11.

[88] Ibid. iv. 36.

[89] *Historia diplomatica*, v. 467–9.

[90] Matthew Paris, *Chronica maiora*, iv. 4–5.

[91] CLR, *1226–40*, 448, 450; CR, *1237–42*, 172; *Receipt and issue rolls for the twenty-sixth year of the reign of King Henry III, 1241–2*, ed. R. C. Stacey, London 1992, 85. He was also referred to in Frederick's letter to the English barons (*Historia diplomatica*, v. 468), and is mentioned by Matthew Paris as an imperial envoy (*Chronica maiora*, iv. 19). He remains obscure: in a document issued after 1 September 1247, Ugo Chamboctus is mentioned as one of a group of people responsible for the castle at Bari: *Acta imperii inedita*, i, no. 918; in January of that year Ugo Capasino was ordered to investigate a quarrel between the abbeys of San Filippo de Fragula and St Marie de Maniaci: ibid. i, no. 391. The papal legate is known to have left England in December 1240: CLR, *1240–5*, 17.

[92] CLR, *1240–5*, 81.

[93] *Receipt and issue rolls*, 82. Walter of Ocra returned in 1241: Matthew Paris, *Chronica maiora*, iv. 160–2; *F. Nicholai de ordine fratrum praedicatorum annales*, ed. T. Hog, London 1845, 226; *Receipt and issue rolls*, 81; CLR, *1240–5*, 79, 80.

that this embassy had been dispatched either in response to, or in close co-operation with, the emperor's representative. We would thus be mistaken to limit our inquiry to Henry's financial relations with the *curia*. Like most of his peers and contemporaries, he sought to maintain a precarious balance. While he felt unable to resist papal demands for money, there is no evidence that he provided Gregory IX with armed men for his campaigns against the emperor. More important, Henry's financial assistance went hand in hand with concerted diplomatic efforts, efforts moreover, which appear to have been undertaken in close co-operation with Frederick.

Henry III's compliance with papal demands obviously worried Frederick. However, in many respects the king's attitude was not much different from that of, for instance, Louis IX. He tried to avoid getting involved, and he hedged his bets. Henry, too, supported the planned council, and sent envoys to accompany the English prelates preparing to attend it.[94] This could not have come as a surprise. Quite apart from the religious dimension, the king also had profoundly pragmatic reasons for seeking to curry papal favour. During the late 1230s and early 1240s he had encountered repeated difficulties in his government of the English Church. Several attempts at filling the vacant see of Canterbury had resulted in stalemate and prolonged litigation at the papal court; when a new archbishop was eventually chosen in Edmund Rich, he frequently fell out with the king;[95] similarly, after Peter des Roches's death in 1238, the Winchester canons kept rejecting the king's favoured candidate. Henry thus required the *curia*'s backing to tackle his domestic problems, and also to realise his long-standing ambition of recovering his continental inheritance. Finally, we should not ignore the fact that the king of England ultimately owed his kingdom and his throne to the papal court. All this militated against Henry actively supporting his brother-in-law, especially at a time when it would seem that the conflict might be resolved as soon as Gregory IX were replaced by a pontiff more amenable to the interventions of the emperor's fellow-princes.

English attitudes only began to change with the pontificate of Innocent IV. When, in 1244, the new pope asked for further contributions for his campaigns against Frederick, he met with stubborn resistance. The prelates decided that they could not grant funds to be used against the emperor, because a general council of the Church had not yet found him guilty of heresy.[96] We should not read this as voicing sympathies for Frederick. Rather, they voiced unease about yet more financial demands from the papacy. Frederick II quickly sought to exploit dissatisfaction in England. During a meeting at London, intended to deal with papal requests for aid, Walter of Ocra was present.[97] That an imperial envoy was allowed to speak at a meeting

---

94 Matthew Paris, *Chronica maiora*, iv. 125
95 See Lawrence, *St Edmund*, 166–79.
96 *Annals of Burton*, AM i. 265.
97 Walter seems to have come to England repeatedly between January and November

also attended by the pope's emissary points to a minor diplomatic victory. According to Matthew Paris, Walter implored the assembled prelates not to support the papacy. Letters from the count of Toulouse and the Latin emperor of Constantinople were read out to testify to Frederick's orthodoxy. Furthermore, should the king heed the emperor's advice, Walter promised, the annual tribute to Rome would be abolished, and all other complaints against the Holy See would be dealt with.[98] It is difficult to distinguish between what may have been Walter's statement and what were Matthew's own grievances. The gist of Walter's reported speech, though, coincides with the points made by Frederick on other occasions. This conflict was not merely a matter for him and the pope, but was of concern to all princes and rulers. At stake was not merely his throne, but the freedom and independence of every Christian lord, the liberty of the Holy Land and the spiritual welfare of Latin Christendom.

Walter did press Frederick's case with some success. First of all, Henry III took a more active diplomatic role. The possibility of a truce was probably among the issues discussed by Nicholas de Bolevill, who was sent to the imperial court in November 1244. The fact that this happened two days after arrangements had been made to provide for Walter de Ocra's return journey suggests that Nicholas was to accompany him to the imperial court.[99] In March 1245 Frederick referred to letters he had recently received from Henry III,[100] and in June the king of England requested that Innocent delay proceedings at Lyon until Henry's envoys had returned from the emperor.[101] With Innocent IV's departure from Italy, the king of England increased his diplomatic efforts, and he acted in unison with Frederick. This was due to a number of reasons. Although Isabella had died a few years earlier, her son with Frederick was still alive, and was destined to play a more prominent role in the administration of Sicily. In fact, according to the emperor's 1250 testament, he was to receive either the kingdom of Burgundy or that of Jerusalem,[102] both of which held considerable interest for Henry III. Secondly, as we will see, the king's need to win supporters in Languedoc ultimately centred on the emperor, and a military recovery of his inheritance remained impossible without Frederick's backing. Henry's diplomatic undertakings of 1244 and 1245 thus conformed to a familiar pattern: until at least 1245 most western monarchs avoided siding too openly with either pope or emperor. They either sought to use the promise of support to further their

---

1244: *CLR*, 1240–5, 275, 277. It remains unclear whether he stayed there for the whole of the time, as in May another envoy from the emperor arrived: ibid. 232.

[98] Matthew Paris, *Chronica maiora*, iv. 371–2. See also Hilpert, *Kaiser- und Papstbriefe*, 132–53.

[99] *CLR*, 1240–5, 278.

[100] *Historia diplomatica*, vi. 267–8.

[101] *CR*, 1242–7, 356.

[102] *Constitutiones*, 1198–1272, no. 274.

own territorial ambitions, while at the same time urging moderation and compromise, as Louis IX and Fernando had done, or, as Bela of Hungary, argued that the continuing conflict between Frederick and the *curia* tied up resources better used for the defence of Christendom.

Moreover, the king's continuing loyalty to the pope was by no means entirely harmful to the emperor's affairs.[103] The very fact that Henry had been reluctant to confront the *curia* directly, his willingness to contribute financially towards the papacy's campaigns and his proven loyalty to the Holy See, made him a suitable candidate to intervene on Frederick's behalf. His position resembled that of Baldwin of Constantinople, who, too, combined loyalty to (and dependence on) the papal court with a desire to see Frederick taken back into the Church. Moreover, his usefulness was not limited to the papal court alone. Baldwin's backing for Frederick, for instance, had been made known in England and thereby helped to emphasise the support Frederick could muster among those who were in the forefront of defending Latin Christendom. This, in turn, served a twofold purpose. First, it helped to refute accusations made by Gregory IX and Innocent IV about the emperor's alleged consorting with the enemies of Christendom. Secondly, the purpose of these letters had been to persuade other rulers, too, to intercede with the *curia* on Frederick's behalf. The emperor of Constantinople could testify to the Staufen's concern for the beleaguered Christians of *Outremer* and *Romania*. Henry III, renowned already among contemporaries for his piety,[104] probably served a similar purpose. In this context it is worth noting that at least one of the emperor's missives to the English king survives in the annals of the Scottish Cistercian abbey of Melrose,[105] which may suggest that Henry III's court was involved in disseminating this particular text. In short, men like Henry and Baldwin were useful, as they possessed the trust of pope and emperor alike, but also because their pleading on Frederick's behalf reached, and was designed to reach, an audience which extended well beyond the papal court.

Negotiating between pope and emperor was made more difficult by the fact that some familiar mechanisms of peacemaking could not be applied. Commonly arbitrators, if of sufficient might and standing, could bring about a settlement and guarantee its enforcement by threatening to use their political or military power against those who violated it.[106] That option was, however, difficult to use in the case of pope and emperor, and all Frederick's fellow monarchs could do was plead, and, in the meantime, seek to use the

---

103 For a different view see Huffman, *Social politics*, 261–2, 265, 267.
104 B. K. U. Weiler, 'Henry III through foreign eyes: communication and historical writing in thirteenth-century Europe', in Weiler and Rowlands, *England and Europe*, 137–62; E. A. Bond (ed.), 'Historiola de pietate regis Henrici III', *Archaeological Journal* xvii (1860), 317–19.
105 *Chronica de Mailros*, 171–6.
106 H. Kamp, *Friedensstifter und Vermittler im Mittelalter*, Darmstadt 2001, 186–215.

situation to their own advantage. Henry III and his court were no exception, as illustrated by Richard of Cornwall's crusade, and the Poitevin campaign of 1242–3.

From an early stage, Richard of Cornwall had become embroiled in the squabble over the date and direction of a new crusade. While Gregory IX wanted to redirect the earl's campaign towards Constantinople,[107] Frederick insisted that it assist the Christians in Palestine instead. Furthermore, as early as February 1238 the emperor had written to Richard and repeated his reasoning for delaying the expedition until 1239.[108] In addition, he asked him to pass through Sicily on his way. In November, Gregory wrote to Richard of Cornwall, Louis IX and Henry III, exhorting them to channel their resources towards the Latin empire of Constantinople, rather than the Holy Land,[109] while the legate in England was ordered to induce Richard to campaign in Greece.[110] However, although the king of England was to give some support to the Latin emperor,[111] none of the English crusaders was willing to comply with the pope's wishes. If Matthew Paris is to be believed, Richard continued to encounter papal resistance to his campaign once he reached the mainland. While at Arles he met the papal legate who ordered him to delay his departure. Richard, however, decided to proceed, and left for Palestine from Marseilles, nominally under imperial control, and dispatched envoys to the emperor to keep him informed of his progress.[112] We should not, however, read too much into the fact that Richard ultimately heeded the emperor's call, and went to Palestine instead of Greece, or that he fought his campaign in close consultation with the emperor. That he campaigned in the Holy Land rather than Greece reflected a general preference among crusaders, while other crusaders, too, continued to accept Frederick's authority as nominal king of Jerusalem.

Once in the Holy Land, Richard continued to act in co-operation with the emperor. His main achievement was to conclude the negotiations, initiated by Theobald of Champagne, for another truce with the sultan of Egypt, rather than entering into an alliance with Damascus, as propagated – mostly – by the emperor's opponents in Palestine.[113] In fact, in a letter from 1245,

---

[107] R. Spence, 'Gregory IX's attempted expeditions to the Latin empire of Constantinople: the crusade for the union of the Latin and Greek Churches', *JMH* v (1979), 163–76; P. Segl, ' "Stabit Constantinopoli": Inquisition und päpstliche Orientpolitik unter Gregor IX', *DA* xxxii (1976), 209–20.

[108] Matthew Paris, *Chronica maiora*, iii. 471–2.

[109] *Registres Gregoire IX*, nos 4605, 4607–8.

[110] Ibid. no. 4609.

[111] *CPR, 1232–47*, 217.

[112] Matthew Paris, *Chronica maiora*, iv. 11, 46–7.

[113] *Annals of Waverley*, AM ii. 328; S. Painter, 'The crusade of Theobald of Champagne and Richard of Cornwall, 1239–41', in R. L. Wolff and H.W. Hazard (eds), *The later crusades, 1189–1311*; K. M. Setton (ed.), *A history of the crusades*, iv, Madison–Milwaukee–London 1969, 463–86; P. Jackson, 'The crusades of 1239–41 and their after-

Frederick referred to Richard as having signed the treaty on his behalf.[114] Furthermore, the earl's negotiations occurred while Egyptian envoys are known to have been in Sicily,[115] which suggests some degree of co-operation. This is further illustrated by the distribution of lands regained by the truce. Ascalon, for instance, was handed over to the imperial *baillie*, rather than to the council or those who previously controlled the town, and Richard remained at Ascalon until a representative of Frederick's arrived to take it under the emperor's control.[116] The earl of Cornwall continued to view Frederick as the rightful ruler of Jerusalem.

In this context we ought to consider a letter, probably written in 1241, in which the leaders of the anti-imperial opposition suggested that Simon de Montfort – rather than the emperor's appointee – act as regent for the infant Conrad IV.[117] The document should not be over-interpreted, though. Simon had close links with Frederick: while he went to *Outremer*, his wife stayed behind as the emperor's guest,[118] and he had received letters of support from Frederick when travelling to the *curia* some years earlier. Relations between them were quite clearly far from hostile. In addition, Simon counted several members of the aristocracy of Cyprus and *Outremer* among his kin, including Philip de Montfort, lord of Tyre and Toron, who also played a leading role in the anti-imperial opposition.[119] In short, Simon was a candidate acceptable to both parties, partly because he was untainted by the rivalries of Syrian politics, but also because he possessed a distinguished crusading pedigree, and because he was the leader of the next major crusading contingent arriving in Palestine.[120] Moreover, we should not exaggerate Simon's links with the English court: first of all, he had been forced into exile prior to his crusade,[121] and – unlike Richard of Cornwall – there is little evidence that he performed a semi-official role on the emperor's behalf. Simon's proposed role in Syria, as

math', *Bulletin of the School of Oriental and African Studies* l (1987), 32–60; H. Koch, *Richard von Cornwall: erster Theil, 1209–57*, Strasbourg 1887, 50–3; *Gestes des chiprois*, 122–4; M.-L. Bulst-Thiele, 'Zur Geschichte der Ritterorden und des Königreichs Jerusalem im 13. Jahrhundert bis zur Schlacht bei La Forbie am 17. Okt 1244', *DA* xxii (1966), 197–226 at p. 202.
114 *Historia diplomatica*, vi. 239.
115 Ibid. v. 433.
116 Riley-Smith, *The feudal nobility*, 207–8; *Crusader Syria*, 128–9 (chapter 51); S. Tibble, *Monarchy and lordships in the Latin kingdom of Jerusalem 1099–1291*, Oxford 1989, 38–40, 73, 86–7.
117 R. Röhricht, 'Acte de soumission des barons du royaume de Jérusalem à Frédéric II (7 mai 1241)', *Archives de l'orient latin*, ii (1881), 402–3; P. Jackson, 'The end of Hohenstaufen rule in Syria', *BIHR* lix (1986), 20–36.
118 Matthew Paris, *Chronica maiora*, iv. 7, 44–5.
119 Maddicott, *Simon de Montfort*, 30; Edbury, 'The de Montforts'.
120 Mayer, 'Kaiserrecht', 196–208. The letter also indicates the difficulties faced by the anti-imperial camp in Palestine: during the summer of 1241, Richard Filangieri had begun to make ground and almost captured Acre: Riley-Smith, *The feudal nobility*, 208.
121 Maddicott, *Simon de Montfort*, 29.

well as Richard's actions in *Outremer*, may still indicate the degree to which Frederick was viewed as a legitimate ruler by the majority of the secular aristocracy of the west.

On his return from Palestine, Richard stopped at the papal *curia* where he sought to negotiate a settlement between Frederick and Gregory.[122] Matthew Paris, who probably used information received directly from either the earl or members of his household, provides a more detailed picture. Frederick asked Richard to deal with Gregory IX, but the earl achieved little. Having spent another two months in the emperor's presence, 'quasi filius cum patre (as if they were father and son)', Richard returned to England.[123] The earl of Cornwall, it seems, did not act on his own, for during these months a number of missions departed from Henry's court for Italy. We do not know exactly how Richard and his brother sought to broker peace between pope and emperor, the arguments they used and the offers they made. We may assume that their reasoning was no different from that of Louis IX, the king of Hungary or the duke of Austria. What is certain, however, is that, like his fellow-rulers, Henry III was reluctant to side openly with either. Instead, he sought to arbitrate, and tried to utilise their predicaments to further his own goals.

In Henry's case, this meant the recovery of his continental inheritance, as exemplified by his abortive invasion of Poitou in 1242. Since 1239 the French court had formally begun to manifest its claims to those lands formerly held by the Plantagenets. In addition, the king's remaining territories began to pose difficulties. In 1241, for instance, the seneschal of Gascony came to England, and is said to have warned that, unless the king appear in person, the duchy, too, would be lost.[124] This referred both to increasing unrest in the region, and to recent moves by Louis IX. This was followed by an invasion of the lands of Henry's stepfather, the count of La Marche.[125] Furthermore, the king of France began to move on Saintes and other places in Gascony.[126] This triggered immediate diplomatic activity at the English court. In 1242 an agreement was drawn up with the count of Toulouse in which they promised mutual assistance against their enemies.[127] This was a major success for Henry III, and the result of efforts at peacemaking he had undertaken some years before.[128] Moreover, allies were sought on the eastern borders of France, including the count of Geneva.[129] Furthermore, Peter of

---

[122] Matthew Paris, *Chronica maiora*, iv. 144.

[123] Ibid. iv. 144–8.

[124] Ibid. iv. 15.

[125] *Annals of Dunstable*, AM iii. 157.

[126] *The chronicle of Walter of Guisborough, previously edited as the chronicle of Walter of Hemingford or Hemingburgh*, ed. H. Rothwell (Camden, 1957), 177.

[127] William de Nangis, *Historia albigensium*, RHGF xix. 193–225; xx. 764–76 at xx. 768–9. See also CPR, *1232–47*, 319.

[128] *Layettes*, no. 415.

[129] CPR, *1232–47*, 306.

Savoy was sent to imperial Burgundy,[130] while another envoy was accredited to Theobald of Champagne and the king's Savoyard relatives.[131] According to Matthew Paris, the kings of Aragon and Castile were considered as potential allies,[132] as was the king of Portugal.[133] Henry thus aimed at a wide-ranging alliance, covering the eastern and southern flanks of Capetian France. He drew on those who, like himself, held legitimate grievances against the Capetian crown, but he also sought to enlist the support of his widely spun network of relatives and dependants. Favours were called upon, and Frederick II was to be no exception.

The campaign was to prove unsuccessful, and nearly ended in Henry being taken captive by Louis.[134] The king of France quickly overcame the threat posed by the count of Toulouse, and forced him, as well as the count of La Marche, back into the Capetian fold. What was the emperor's role in all this? An imperial envoy left England in May 1242, just before Henry set out on campaign,[135] and Frederick soon found himself the object of repeated overtures from Henry III. In June two English envoys were sent to 'Italy and Apulia'.[136] It seems that their mission was in part a response to the earlier embassy of the emperor – in one copy of their letter of accreditation they are referred to as dealing with 'certain articles sometime treated of by the envoys of the emperor'.[137] A second copy is more specific and describes their mission as 'to enter into a treaty between the emperor and him [Henry III] of peace and truce, war and concord against all men, conventions made on the king's part with the Church of Rome excepted'.[138] This was elaborated on further in a separate letter which Henry sent to Frederick in September. He complained of his betrayal by the count of Provence, and requested that the emperor punish his vassal. Furthermore, many in Burgundy would be willing to assist Henry, if the emperor allowed them to do so.[139]

The phrasing of both the accreditation for the king's envoys, and his subsequent letter to the emperor, merit further consideration. Henry did not request Frederick's active involvement. In theory, at least, all he asked for was that the emperor exert stricter control over his vassals (and make them keep their promises), and that he allow those who were willing to side with Henry to do so. It is tempting to view this as the king's court acting in realisation of

---

130 *Foedera*, i. 242.

131 *CPR, 1232–47*, 433.

132 Matthew Paris, *Chronica maiora*, iv. 204. Henry tried to win over the king of Castile: *CR, 1237–42*, 529.

133 *CLR, 1240–5*, 155.

134 C. Bémont, 'La Campagne de Poitou, 1242–1243: Taillebourg et Saintes', *Annales du Midi* v (1893), 289–314; Stacey, *Politics, policy and finance*, 171–200; Vincent, 'England', 82–3. Matthew Paris, *Chronica maiora*, iv. 188–92, 197–9, 202–26, 230–1.

135 *CLR, 1240–5*, 134.

136 *CPR, 1232–47*, 308.

137 Ibid. 309.

138 Ibid. This mandate was confirmed and reissued in July 1242: ibid. 311.

139 *CR 1237–42*, 530–2.

the complex situation facing Frederick: he would be able to lend Henry his support, while at the same time avoid attacking Louis IX. This possibility, in turn, implied in the letter from September 1242, would have required a less firm commitment than the one envisaged when the king's envoys had first been sent. There remains, however, a danger of reading too much into the available evidence. We do not know, for instance, to what extent the idea that the aristocracy of imperial Burgundy was merely waiting for the emperor's permission before attacking the Capetians was wishful thinking on Henry's part. Moreover, the king and his court may have had undue expectations of Frederick's ability to influence Burgundian politics. Much more significant in the context of this study was the passage in which Henry III limited the degree to which he was prepared to go in assisting Frederick: their alliance was to be directed against 'all men, conventions made on the king's part with the Church of Rome excepted'. To some extent this passage was not unusual: most similar agreements safeguarded the claims of the overlord of one or both parties.[140] Still, it indicates the limits of Henry III's ability to aid his brother-in-law.

Henry sought to draw on the full range of his political and diplomatic contacts. Also in September, the count of Toulouse met the emperor at Melfi, and we may assume that English requests for help were among the issues discussed.[141] Negotiations continued well into the New Year, and in January 1243 envoys were accredited to Frederick,[142] while some imperial messengers, already in England, were asked to advance 'the matter' with the emperor, and to keep the English court informed about their progress.[143] Even the king's deceased sister was invoked: in January 1243 Henry III wrote to the emperor, announcing that he had concluded an alliance with the count of Toulouse, and requesting that Frederick give his counsel. Furthermore, he requested that the emperor 'recall to his memory the last words of I. his wife, the king's sister, and fulfil them in deed'.[144] What exactly Isabella's last words were we do not know, but we may assume that they had aimed at encouraging the emperor to support his brother-in-law. The range and persistence of diplomatic dealings with Frederick far exceeded any other initiative undertaken before or during the campaign. Hopes were riding high, and in Henry's eyes, at least, an alliance with Frederick was more than a distant and elusive goal.

The king also sought to activate links with members of Frederick's innermost circle. In June 1242, for example, Peter de Vinea was promised £40-worth of lands in England, 'in consideration of his services and deserts'.[145] This was the more generous an act in that Peter had received his

---

[140] W. Heinemeyer, 'Studien zur Diplomatik mittelalterlicher Verträge vornehmlich des 13. Jahrhunderts', *AfD* xiv (1935–6), 321–413.
[141] *Ryccardi de S Germano cronica*, MGH, SS xix. 383.
[142] *CPR, 1232–47*, 357.
[143] *CLR, 1240–5*, 169; *CPR, 1232–47*, 399.
[144] *CPR, 1232–47*, 399.
[145] Ibid. 309.

annual fief of 40 marks as recently as May.[146] Furthermore, in January 1243, Peter de Vinea was requested 'to lay these letters and the king's request before the emperor and to be diligent in advancing the king's cause'.[147] These efforts highlight the inherently personal nature of most diplomatic exchanges in our period. When Peter and Walter had received their money fiefs in 1235, this was partly a reward for their role in arranging and overseeing the wedding of the king's sister. In addition, however, it opened channels of communication, and entailed the expectation that those who received the king's money would support him in turn. This was by no means unusual. Frederick II, similarly, expected that his many gifts to Richard of Cornwall and other barons, or the hospitality offered to Simon de Montfort during the 1230s, would lead them to plead his case. Moreover, the king now had what he had been lacking in 1225 and 1227, that is, if not the ear of the emperor himself, at least that of someone who did.

In the end, the campaign's most palpable benefit was to be Richard of Cornwall's marriage to Sanchia of Provence, the third of Count Raymond's four daughters, in early 1243.[148] The alliance with the emperor failed to materialise. Being – however indirectly – implicated in an attack on the Capetians would have gained Frederick little. He was still hoping to end his excommunication. That, however, depended on the attitude of the new pope, and after the imprisonment of his prelates and envoys it would have been unwise to alienate Louis IX even further. Moreover, Frederick faced a deteriorating situation in Palestine, and Jerusalem could only be held by a concerted European effort, which would have to include the king of France. Still, we should not dismiss Henry's actions too easily. Although the emperor faced a situation which made it difficult for him to side with his English relatives, from Henry's perspective the time had come to reap the rewards of his earlier support. We have to remember that, in 1242, the conflict between Frederick and the papacy seemed at its end.[149] Gregory IX had died, and it was considered likely that whoever succeeded him would receive the emperor back into the Church. Louis's actions in Languedoc could certainly not have endeared him to the emperor. After all, Louis's chief victim had been Raymond of Toulouse, traditionally one of Frederick's closest allies in the region. By contrast, Henry's financial, diplomatic and military support exceeded that which Frederick had received from any other European monarch. As before, the king of England's undertakings were well timed and well prepared. They failed because of circumstances over which the king could have had little control. In the long term, Frederick's failure to come to Henry's assistance would force a reorientation of royal diplomacy upon the

---

146 *CLR, 1240–5*, 128.
147 *CPR, 1232–47*, 399.
148 *Annals of Waverley*, AM ii. 330.
149 Thumser, 'Friedrich II', 436–7.

king. There is, however, no evidence to suggest that a 'growing estrangement in Anglo-imperial diplomatic relations resulted' from these developments.[150] Quite the contrary: joint diplomatic initiatives increased in frequency and intensity during the years immediately following the Poitevin campaign. Henry III and his court continued to support the emperor; they intervened on his behalf with the *curia*, they negotiated and pressed for a peaceful settlement, and refused to lend either Gregory IX or Innocent IV their full backing.

Between 1239 and 1245 Frederick remained the main channel of communication with the empire. The imperial aristocracy played a negligible role, and contacts were largely confined to economic affairs and exchanges with those under the rule of princes, rather than the princes themselves. An otherwise anonymous messenger, for instance, represented the duke of Brunswick,[151] while relations with the duke of Brabant were limited to Henry de Rumenham, who came to collect the rent Henry III had been asked to grant in 1239.[152] It is worth noting that Henry avoided associating himself with those, like the archbishop of Cologne, who were hostile to the emperor.[153] Frederick may have hoped in vain for more whole-hearted support from his brother-in-law, but neither could those who opposed his rule count on the veiled or open backing of the king of England. With the exception of a messenger from Conrad IV, recorded in late 1241, who had probably been sent in the context of the planned crusade against the Mongols,[154] no further evidence survives for direct contacts with the imperial aristocracy. Henry III

---

[150] Huffman, *Social politics*, 265.

[151] *CLR, 1240–5*, 55.

[152] Ibid. 47. The duke of Brabant also made an indirect appearance during the Poitevin campaign. The war was partly conducted by raiding the ships of enemy merchants (*CPR, 1232–47*, 309). This, in turn, required the issue of safe-conducts for 'friendly' vessels. Amongst those issued in 1242, merchants from Brabant feature highly (ibid. 302, listing various merchants as being 'of the power' of the emperor and the duke of Brabant). In a mandate from August 1242 a number of Brabantine merchants are referred to by name, and it is stated that the duke of Brabant had sent letters guaranteeing similar safe-conducts to English merchants in his lands (ibid. 302).

[153] There was, however, an indirect link with the Church of Cologne, rather than its prelate. In 1239/40, Albrecht Suerbeer of Cologne was installed as archbishop of Armagh, probably by Cardinal Otto of St Nicholas. He stayed in Ireland until 1246, when he was transferred to Prussia-Livonia: Matthew Paris, *Chronica maiora*, iv. 49; J. A. Watt, *The Church and the two nations in medieval Ireland*, Cambridge 1970, 113; T. W. Moody, F. X. Martin and F. J. Byrne (eds), *A new history of Ireland* ix, Oxford 1984, 269. I am grateful to Robin Frame for sharing his expertise on the history of late medieval Ireland. The connection between Ireland and Cologne has been overlooked by Huffman, *Family* and *Social politics*.

[154] *CLR, 1240–5*, 93. It is a matter of speculation whether Bartholomew of Hoveden, sent to Denmark and Saxony in 1240 to collect goshawks, was also on a diplomatic mission: ibid. 240.

felt no need to look for allies outside the emperor's inner circle. Frederick could rely on the king of England's diplomatic support, as long as he did not expect him to challenge the pope directly. Henry III in turn continued to view Frederick as a potential ally, likely to come to his assistance, once peace had been restored with the see of St Peter.

5

On Shifting Ground, 1245–1250

In 1245, during the general council assembled at Lyon, Pope Innocent IV declared Frederick II deposed, and stripped of his dignities as emperor, king of Sicily and king-regent of Jerusalem. Efforts to put this into practice dominated European politics over the following decades. In the case of England, although the king avoided associating himself with the anti-kings Henry Raspe and William of Holland, this coincided with a broadening of contacts in Germany and Italy. After ten years during which Frederick II had dominated exchanges with the empire, others came to the fore once more. In addition, Henry suffered a series of setbacks: the count of Provence died in 1245, and in 1246 his lands fell to Louis IX's younger brother, Charles of Anjou; the count of Toulouse died in 1247; while the succession struggle in Flanders threw the county into turmoil and brought most of it under Capetian domination. Henry III found himself deprived of the very pillars on which previous attempts at recovering his inheritance had rested, and was forced to find new ways of pursuing his claims.

Frederick and his foes

Matthew Paris provides the most detailed account of events at Lyon. Although the council is mostly associated with the depositions of Frederick II and of King Sancho of Portugal, it was above all a crusading council, and the planning and financing of a new campaign thus occupied a large part of the proceedings.[1] This reflected a series of worrying developments: in 1244 the Khwarīzīm Turks had sacked Jerusalem, while most Christians in Central Europe lived in expectation of renewed attacks by the Mongols.[2] Other issues were, however, dealt with, too. The English bishops, for instance, used the opportunity to press for the canonisation of Edmund Rich, the late arch-

---

[1] *Annals of Dunstable*, AM, iii.167; Matthew Paris, *Chronica maiora*, iv. 430–73; *Decrees of the ecumenical councils*, 295–301; Stürner, *Friedrich II*, ii. 533–9. For the general problem on sources for the First Council of Lyon see W. E. Lunt, 'The sources for the First Council of Lyon', *EHR* xxxiii (1918), 72–8; 66–88; K. E. Lupprian, 'Papst Innocenz IV und die Ayyubiden: Diplomatische Beziehungen von 1244 bis 1247', in W. Fischer and J. Schneider (eds), *Das Heilige Land im Mittelalter: Begegnungen zwischen Orient und Okzident*, Neustadt-an-der-Aisch 1982, 77–82.

[2] Matthew Paris, *Chronica maiora*, iv. 430–1.

bishop of Canterbury,[3] and to present a list of *gravamina* concerning papal demands.[4] They also attended, as Henry III put it to Frederick, to broker an understanding with the pope.[5] Apart from the prelates, Ralph FitzNicholas, William Cantilupe, Philip Basset and the earl of Norfolk were present as the king's and the barons' proctors.[6] Ralph FitzNicholas, the king's seneschal, had been on diplomatic missions to Rome in 1229,[7] to the barons of France in 1230 and 1233,[8] and had been among those negotiating the truce which ended the Poitevin campaign in 1243.[9] William Cantilupe was steward of the king's household, and had acted as Henry's regent in 1242–3,[10] while in 1245 Philip Bassett was at the beginning of an illustrious career which ultimately was to see him made justiciar in 1261, and act as proctor during the Lord Edward's crusade in 1270–1. The Bigod earls of Norfolk ranked among the most important of the king's magnates, surpassed only by Richard of Cornwall in political clout. The composition of Henry's embassy, with its experienced officials and high-ranking magnates, thus testified to the importance attached to these proceedings by the English court, and highlights the care with which the king of England intended to perform his role as intermediary. The council opened in July, attended, according to one chronicler, by 250 prelates,[11] mostly from France.[12]

The situation of the Christian diaspora dominated proceedings.[13] The patriarch of Constantinople began by outlining the manifold difficulties facing Latin Christendom in Greece, where the Latin empire had come under increasing pressure from John Vatatzes. The bishop of Beirut, who gave an account of the problems besetting the Church in *Outremer*, followed. Next came Innocent IV's summary of the state of the Roman Church. It had many enemies, he claimed, most dangerous among whom, however, worse even than the Tartars and Saracens, was the emperor. This led to detailed accusations concerning Frederick's various misdemeanours, and his proctors' equally swift rebuttal. Eventually, the emperor's agents managed to secure a respite to consult with their lord. It seems, however, that Frederick saw little chance for a peaceful settlement. He denied the judicial basis of the council, and his proctors declared that the pope's only purpose in convening it had

---

3 *Annals of Bermondsey*, AM iii. 460; *Annals of Worcester*, AM iv. 434; Lawrence, *St Edmund*, 3.
4 Matthew Paris, *Chronica maiora*, iv. 440–5.
5 CR, *1242–7*, 356.
6 CPR, *1232–47*, 463; *F. Nicholai annales*, 234.
7 CPR, *1225–32*, 243–4.
8 *Diplomatic documents*, nos 225–6, 234–5.
9 Ibid. no. 254.
10 Powicke, *Henry III*, 190, 780, 783.
11 *Annales erphordenses*, in *Monumenta erphesfurtensia*, 100; 140 according to Matthew Paris, *Chronica maiora*, iv. 432.
12 *Annales scheftlarienses maiores*, MGH, SS xvii. 342.
13 The following is mostly based on Matthew Paris, *Chronica maiora*, iv. 430–40.

been to destroy the emperor, for he acted as both accuser and judge.[14] Unsurpisingly, Innocent rejected their argument, and declared Frederick deprived of his royal and imperial offices.

The participation of English proctors as such did not denote enmity towards or cooling relations with the emperor.[15] To expect the king of England not to send his agents, would mean expecting him to ignore the council's religious and political significance, as well as the various difficulties he faced at home. While many of the prelates were concerned with papal demands for money,[16] Henry III was confronted with the far more serious threat of English prelates complaining directly to the pope about his government of the Church. In June 1245, for instance, those setting out for Lyon had to swear 'not to attempt anything against the king's crown and dignity'.[17] Furthermore, one of the issues discussed at the council was the proposed canonisation of Edmund Rich, of paramount interest to the king. The synod was, therefore, dealing with issues which directly concerned the king and required the presence of his proctors. Moreover, Henry could not intercede on the emperor's behalf, or press for a peaceful settlement, unless represented by his agents. Finally, we should not forget that, although a settlement of the papal–imperial dispute was among the issues to be discussed, neither Frederick nor most of the attending clergy seem to have expected the emperor's deposition.

That Henry III was trying to arbitrate between Frederick and the pope is corroborated by a number of sources.[18] It was explicit in the authorisation he gave to his representatives 'to treat peace between the Church of Rome and the emperor'.[19] Moreover, an unpublished exchange of letters between king and emperor, recently uncovered by Nicholas Vincent,[20] also points to Henry's role as an arbitrator. In July 1244 Frederick had appointed the king of England to be his representative at the forthcoming council, with the brief of negotiating a settlement with the pope.[21] This was then extended to Henry's proctor, Master Lawrence of St Martin, and included Frederick's assurance that he planned to attend the council in person.[22] Innocent IV in turn accepted Lawrence's appointment, with specific reference to his brief of

---

[14] F. Kempf, 'Die Absetzung Friedrichs II. im Lichte der Kanonistik', in Fleckenstein, *Probleme um Friedrich II*, 345–60; R. H. Helmholz, *The spirit of classical canon law*, Athens, GA–London 1996, 257–83.

[15] For a contrary view see Huffman, *Social politics*, 268.

[16] Powicke, *Henry III*, 282–3; *Councils and synods with other documents relating to the English Church, II/1: 1205–65*, ed. F. M. Powicke and C. R. Cheney, Oxford 1964, 391–5.

[17] *CPR, 1232–47*, 463.

[18] *CR, 1242–7*, 356.

[19] *CPR, 1232–47*, 463.

[20] Professor Vincent first presented his findings at the Durham conference on thirteenth-century England in September 1999, but they have not yet been published. All manuscript references are based on the transcripts kindly provided by Professor Vincent.

[21] Marquess of Bath MS, Longleat House, muniments no. 10590, fo. 5r.

[22] Ibid.

negotiating a settlement with Frederick II.[23] Quite clearly, English participation in the council was not only accepted by the emperor: it was actively encouraged. It is, furthermore, tempting to view the pope's support for Henry's efforts as further indication that a final showdown had by no means been inevitable. Frederick's promise to attend the council certainly points to the expectation on his part that a peaceful solution might yet be found.

Matthew Paris gives a detailed account of the role of Henry's proctors in the proceedings. When Frederick's representative, Thaddeus de Suessa, requested two weeks to consult with the emperor, it was at the insistence of French and English bishops that Innocent granted a respite.[24] After Frederick's refusal to acknowledge the jurisdiction of the synod, the English were those arguing most fervently in his favour.[25] Finally, when Frederick's deposition was announced, the English proctors argued in support of his offspring, as the sons could not be punished for the sins of their fathers.[26] Although Matthew may have exaggerated the degree to which English and French prelates led the opposition to Innocent's decision, the general picture seems convincing, and is in its broad outlines confirmed by other evidence. Neither Henry III nor Louis IX had an interest in prolonging the conflict. It must have seemed unlikely that the Staufen could easily be expelled from Germany, when Gregory had failed so badly even in Lombardy. Whoever was to challenge Frederick would thus require strong support from outside Germany; this in turn posed the danger of escalating the conflict even further. To Henry's court, this must have borne an uncanny resemblance to the events of 1197–8. Louis IX, in turn, had taken the cross in 1244, and thus had every reason to press for moderation: a protracted struggle between pope and emperor would tie up resources much more urgently needed for the recovery of the Holy Land.

Matthew's statement as to the emperor's children is also revealing. The son born of Isabella and Frederick, and called Henry, was only one of three legitimate male children begotten by Frederick. The emperor played upon any expectations the English king might have had as to the future role of his nephew. In 1247, for instance, he wrote to Henry III, announcing that his nephew was to be made vicar of Sicily, and, as part of a settlement with Innocent IV, was to be baptised by the pope.[27] In addition, the boy wrote to his uncle, apologising that he had not been in contact earlier, and promising to do so now that he was of sufficient age and power.[28] Matthew probably exag-

---

23 Ibid. fo. 5v.
24 Matthew Paris, *Chronica maiora*, iv. 437.
25 Ibid.
26 Ibid. iv. 439.
27 *Historia diplomatica*, vi. 502–3. For delayed baptism, although drawing on much earlier examples, see J. Smith, 'Religion and lay society', in R. McKitterick (ed.), *The new Cambridge medieval history*, II: *c. 700 – c. 900*, Cambridge 1995, 654–80 at p. 657; Helmholz, *Spirit of classical canon law*, 200–28.
28 *Historia diplomatica*, vi. 504. Henry's elevation is confirmed by an entry in the registry of Frederick II: *Acta imperii inedita*, i, no. 919.

gerated when he described the young Henry as having been honoured and singled out before all others by Frederick.[29] The emperor's testament, however, lists him as heir should Conrad, Frederick's son with Isabella de Brienne, die without children. Moreover, he was to receive either the kingdom of Burgundy or that of Jerusalem.[30] Although these were the weakest links in the Staufens' empire, Henry III's nephew was none the less ensured a significant role in the affairs of the empire, and, by holding Burgundy, would have become the overlord of the counts of Provence and Toulouse, and thereby a potentially useful ally to his uncle. Henry III had been trying to play on the emperor's emotions when asking for help in Poitou, and Frederick did likewise, by using Isabella's only son to enlist English backing against the pope. Innocent IV, in short, could not count on the full backing of the secular rulers of Latin Christendom.

Frederick's reference to his son's imminent baptism by Innocent IV suggests that hopes for a peaceful settlement had not been abandoned. This point is worth further consideration. In April 1246 two cardinals had been sent to Sicily, authorised to relax the emperor's sentence of excommunication.[31] By the end of May, however, the pope wrote 'to the whole of Christendom' that Frederick's purgation had been found insufficient. None the less, he was invited to come to Lyon to clear himself in person.[32] Maybe even to the pope's surprise, Frederick accepted the offer. After the death of Henry Raspe earlier the same year,[33] he is said to have intended to settle his difficulties with Innocent in person, and proceeded through Lombardy towards the Alps.[34] A letter from Archbishop Boniface of Canterbury to Peter of Savoy reveals the pressures which forced Innocent to offer a settlement: Louis IX had complained of papal extortions, a renewed invasion of Hungary by the Mongols seemed imminent and the college of cardinals was divided about its policy towards Frederick.[35] Due to their family links, which included Innocent's host, the archbishop-elect of Lyon, Boniface and Peter had access to information not always available to others. We may assume that it had been in the context of the planned visit to Lyon that Frederick had intended to have his son baptised. However, when the emperor reached Turin in spring 1247 he heard that Parma, an imperial stronghold, had fallen, and was forced to return.[36] Only luck saved Innocent.[37] Still, this was not the end of imperial attempts at making peace, and Henry III played his full part in them. In June

---

[29] Matthew Paris, *Chronica maiora*, v. 99.
[30] *Constitutiones, 1198–1272*, no. 274.
[31] *Registres Innocent IV*, no. 1976.
[32] Ibid. no. 1988.
[33] *Annales erphordenses* in *Monumenta erphesfurtensia*, 101.
[34] *Bartholomaei scribae annales*, MGH, SS xviii. 221.
[35] Matthew Paris, *Chronica maiora, liber addimentorum: chronica maiora*, vi.131–3.
[36] *Chronica regia coloniensis continuatio S Pantaleonis v*, in *Chronica regis coloniensis*, 290; Stürner, *Friedrich II*, ii. 564–77.
[37] *Acta imperii inedita*, ii, no. 1040; *Brief- und Memorialbuch*, nos 97–100.

1247 Robert de Anketil was dispatched to the papal court 'for a second time', and was to be accompanied by various messengers from the emperor.[38] This suggests concerted efforts by the king of England and his brother-in-law, not unlike those in the years immediately preceding the Council of Lyon. Matthew Paris refers to another attempt made by Frederick in 1248.[39] The following year, after the death of one of Frederick's illegitimate sons, yet another embassy was sent to the pope.[40] This, too, met with little success: in April 1249 the papal legate in Italy was assured that no peace would be made with Frederick.[41] The last arbitration attempt is recorded for 1250, just a few months before Frederick's death.[42] Innocent proved as unrelenting an opponent of the emperor as his predecessor.

After Frederick's deposition, renewed efforts were made to replace him.[43] Within a year, Conrad IV's former guardian, Landgrave Henry Raspe of Thuringia, was elected king of the Romans, but died without having made much of an impact.[44] In fact, the Staufen managed to strengthen their grip on Germany when Conrad IV married a daughter of the duke of Bavaria in 1246.[45] It was during the months after Henry Raspe's death that Frederick pursued once more the hope that he might be able to settle peacefully his conflict with Innocent. In this he was to be disappointed when, by September 1247, the pope ordered the German princes to elect yet another anti-king in Count William of Holland.[46] William's wide-ranging family connections, including the duke of Brabant and the bishop of Liège, made

---

[38] CLR, 145–51, 127.

[39] Matthew Paris, Chronica maiora, v. 22–3.

[40] Ibid. v. 70–1.

[41] Epistolae saeculi XIII, ii, no. 681; xxii.

[42] Matthew Paris, Chronica maiora, v. 99–100.

[43] M. Stimming, 'Kaiser Friedrich II. und der Abfall der deutschen Fürsten', HZ cxx (1919), 210–49; G. Käser, 'Papst Innocenz IV. und der deutsche Gegenkönig Heinrich Raspe', in W. Müller, W. J. Smolka and H. Zedelmaier (eds), Universität und Bildung: Festschrift Laetitia Boehm, Munich 1991, 25–31; J. Kempf, Geschichte des deutschen Reiches während des grossen Interregnums, 1245–1273, Würzburg 1893, 14–40. For the propaganda employed see K. Hampe, 'Über die Flugschriften zum Lyoner Konzil von 1245', Historische Vierteljahresschrift xi (1908), 297–313; P. Herde, 'Ein Pamphlet der päpstlichen Kurie gegen Kaiser Friedrich II. von 1245/46', DA xxiii (1967), 468–538; H. M. Schaller, 'Die Antwort Gregors IX. auf Petrus de Vinea I, 1, "Collegerunt pontifices" ', DA xi (1954/5), 140–65, and 'Eine kuriale Briefsammlung des 13. Jahrhunderts mit unbekannten Briefen Friedrichs II. (Trier, Stadtbibliothek Cod. 859/1097)', DA xviii (1962), 171–213.

[44] Chronica regia coloniensis continuatio S Pantaleonis v, in Chronica regia coloniensis, 288–90; Annales veterocellenses, MGH, SS xvi. 431; Annales ensdorfenses, MGH, SS x. 5; Registres Innocent IV, no. 1993; Stürner, Friedrich II., ii. 548–55; D. Hägermann, 'Studien zum Urkundenwesen König Heinrich Raspes (1246/7)', DA xxxvi (1980), 487–548.

[45] Annales augustani minores, MGH, SS x. 9.

[46] Continuatio Laurentii de Leodio gesta, MGH, SS x. 525; Annales erphordenses, in Monumenta erphesfurtensia, 101–2; Hermanni abbati altahensis annales, MGH, SS xvii. 394. For previous relations between Holland and the empire see K. van Eickels, 'Die Grafen von Holland und das Reich im 12. und 13. Jahrhundert', Rheinische Vierteljahresblätter lx (1996), 65–87.

him a more formidable force to be reckoned with.[47] In 1248, to the surprise of Conrad IV and his supporters, William laid siege to Aachen,[48] and after several months entered the town to be formally crowned king of the Romans.[49] Initially, the anti-king's victory was of symbolic rather than military significance. The resting-place of Charlemagne and the traditional venue for the coronation of emperors-elect had fallen to the pope's partisans. None the less, despite William's defeat by Conrad the following year,[50] this proved to be a turning point. Conrad IV remained confined mostly to the south of Germany, and in 1251 he abandoned his lands north of the Alps altogether and left for Sicily. Innocent had achieved a first victory.

Innocent pursued a similar policy in the Holy Land. In 1246 the king of Cyprus took over his mother's role as hereditary regent of Jerusalem, and appointed his own *baillie* in opposition to the emperor's candidate.[51] The following year Innocent granted a request that the kingdom of Cyprus, nominally held as a fief from the empire, would instead be held from the pope.[52] Frederick could do little to prop up his or his son's regime in Palestine, and had to be content with emphasising his rightful claims to Jerusalem. He did so by taking an active role in the preparations for Louis IX's crusade: in September 1245 he wrote to the nobles of France, announcing that he had asked Louis to plead with Innocent IV on his behalf. He also offered that either he or his son Conrad would personally lead a crusade to Palestine, once peace had been arranged.[53] A similar letter was then addressed to the whole of Christendom.[54] Thaddeus de Suessa had made the same promise at the Council of Lyon, and he had been equally unsuccessful. In 1246 the emperor went one step further: he would spend the rest of his life in Palestine, if the pope agreed to revoke his excommunication and deposition.[55] Frederick tried to show the sincerity of his promises: in November, officials in Sicily were ordered to provide Louis with horses, arms, victuals and whatever else he might need, and to let him and his *familiares* pass through the *regno* without molestation.[56] To have the king of France set out to the Holy Land via Sicily

[47] Matthew Paris, *Chronica maiora*, iv. 624–5; B. Keilmann, 'Papst Innocenz IV. und die Kirche von Worms: Anmerkungen zur päpstlichen Personalpolitik am Beginn des Interregnums', *Archiv für mittelrheinische Kirchengeschichte* xl (1988), 43–66, especially at pp. 44–6, 48–54; K. E. Demandt, 'Der Endkampf des staufischen Kaiserhauses im Rhein-Main-Gebiet', *Hessisches Jahrbuch für Landesgeschichte* vii (1957), 102–64; Kempf, *Interregnum*, 90–178; O. Hintze, *Das Königtum Wilhelms von Holland*, Leipzig 1885.

[48] *Annales erphordenses*, in *Monumenta erphesfurtensia*, 102.

[49] *Gesta abbatum trudonensium continuatio* iii, MGH, SS x. 396; *Chronica regia coloniensis continuatio S Pantaleonis v*, in *Chronica regia coloniensis*, 291–2; Matthew Paris, *Chronica maiora*, v. 17, 25–7.

[50] Matthew Paris, *Chronica maiora*, v. 90.

[51] *Andrae Danduli chronica*, 301.

[52] *Historia diplomatica*, vi. 506–7.

[53] *Constitutiones, 1198–1272*, no. 264.

[54] *Layettes*, ii, no. 3380.

[55] Ibid. iv. 523–4.

[56] *Historia diplomatica*, vi. 465–6, 466–7.

would have been a major diplomatic victory. However, Louis was aware of these implications, and instead set out from Marseilles, by then under his brother's control. He continued to avoid taking sides. In early 1247 Louis promised that he would not act in a way that would prejudice the rights of Conrad IV or anyone else.[57] This fell equally short of guaranteeing Staufen claims in *Outremer*, and of recognising the emperor's deposition by the pope. Similarly, in 1248 Louis responded to the emperor's request that any lands reconquered would be handed over to Conrad, by stating that he would not act to the prejudice of either Conrad IV or any other Christian.[58]

Imperial manifestos repeatedly emphasised that it was necessary to have Frederick involved in planning a crusade, and that he was fully prepared to lead the Christian forces in Palestine. Matthew Paris gives the text of a letter, allegedly written by the sultan of Egypt in 1246 in response to papal attempts at concluding a truce. In this the sultan stated that he would not enter such an agreement unless the emperor were part of it. Matthew goes on to state that Innocent accused Frederick of fabricating the letter.[59] Frederick certainly tried to emphasise how willing he was to fight the Muslims, and how only the pope's unholy machinations prevented him from doing so. In August 1248, for instance, the king of England was informed of how the emperor's efforts to come to the help of a beleaguered Christendom had been thwarted by Innocent.[60] Similar complaints were directed to Louis IX in early spring 1249. Frederick particularly complained about the mendicants who, rather than converting Muslims, sowed dissension among Christians instead.[61] Similarly, Blanche, the queen-regent of France, was informed of

---

57 Ibid. vi. 500–2.

58 VSM, 1299–1301.

59 Matthew Paris, *Chronica maiora*, iv. 566–8. Ibn al-Furat, although a much later source, also refers to the ways in which Frederick tried to utilise his contacts amongst the Muslim to further 'Frankish' aims. He states that Frederick had secured Louis IX's release after the disaster at Damietta and on his way back to France: *Ayyubids*, ii. 37. This causes chronological difficulties, as Frederick was dead by the time Louis left for France. However, elements of Frederick's propaganda are also found in Muslim accounts and thus add colour to the emperor's claims. Similarly, Joinville reports how his Muslim captor rejoiced at hearing that he was Frederick's distant cousin, how he was accordingly treated with great honours: Jean de Joinville, *Histoire de Saint Louis*, ed. N. de Wailly, Paris 1890, 133–4. For a recent discussion see J. M. Powell, 'Frederick II and the Muslims: the making of an historiographical tradition', in L. J. Simon (ed.), *Iberia and the Mediterranean world of the Middle Ages: studies in honour of Robert I. Burns, S. J.*, Leiden 1995, 261–9; J. P. Lomax, 'Frederick II, his Saracens, and the papacy', in J. V. Tolan (ed.), *Medieval Christian perceptions of Islam*, London–New York 2000, 175–97; C. T. Maier, 'Crusade and rhetoric against the Muslim colony of Lucera: Eudes de Chateauroux's *Sermones de rebellione sarracenorum Lucherie in Apulie*', *JMH* xxi (1995), 343–85. For an overview of Muslim sources about the Staufen see H. L. Gottschalk, 'Der Untergang der Hohenstaufen', *Wiener Zeitschrift für die Kunde des Morgenlandes* liii (1957), 267–82.

60 *Historia diplomatica*, vi. 644–6.

61 Ibid. vi. 710–13. D. Berg, 'Staufische Herrschaftsideologie und Mendikanten-spiritualität: Studien zum Verhältnis Kaiser Friedrichs II zu den Bettelorden', *Wissenschaft*

how the pope's actions prevented Frederick from coming to Louis's assistance.[62] Matthew Paris reports that Frederick was not alone in thinking that the pope's reluctance to negotiate jeopardised the state of Christendom. In 1246 Cardinal John of Toledo, an English Cistercian,[63] is said to have complained to Innocent IV that the Church was beset by many foes, among whom he numbered Tartars, Muslims and Greeks. Therefore, the pope should make peace with the emperor.[64] Frederick's offers of leading a crusade were the best means by which to ensure his reconciliation with the Church, and to enlist the diplomatic support to force Innocent into negotiations. Just as he had been able to overcome his first excommunication in 1227 by negotiating a treaty which returned Jerusalem to Christian rule, and just as he had sought to profit from his role in the affairs of the Latin Empire of Constantinople, so the offer of a prolonged crusade was intended to demonstrate the sincerity of his intentions, and to put pressure on the papal *curia*. By doing so he used the language initially deployed by the *curia* against him, and he appealed to values and moved within a framework of political action that he shared with his peers and contemporaries.

The ascendancy of Capetian France

Only Louis IX rivalled Henry III in the frequency of his peacemaking efforts: around Christmas 1245 Innocent IV and Louis met at Cluny. If Matthew Paris is to be believed, Frederick seized the opportunity, and sent messengers to Louis, putting forth his proposal that he would go to the Holy Land, once he and his sons had been accepted back into the Church.[65] That Frederick had been in touch with Louis is confirmed by the fragment of a letter, probably dating from February 1246, in which the emperor outlined the manifold tribulations he had suffered at the *curia*'s hands.[66] However, this is the only evidence for contacts between France and the emperor in early 1246. Later that year, on the other hand, both the pope and Frederick wrote to Louis. Referring to an embassy the king of France had sent to negotiate between them, Innocent declared that he was willing to grant Frederick the opportunity to prove his devotion to the Church.[67] This effort met with little success,

und Weisheit li (1988), 26–51, 185–209; G. Barone, 'La propaganda antiimperiale nell'Italia federiciana: l'azione degli Ordini Mendicanti', in Toubert and Paravacini Bagliani, *Federico II*, 278–89.

[62] *Historia diplomatica*, vi. 746–8.

[63] See H. Grauert, 'Meister Johann von Toledo', *Sitzungsberichte der königlich-bayerischen Akademie der Wissenschaften* (1901), 113–325 at pp. 113–65 for the historical John.

[64] Matthew Paris, *Chronica maiora*, iv. 578–9.

[65] Ibid. iv. 523–4.

[66] *Historia diplomatica*, vi. 389–90. See also the, undated, letter in *Chronica de Mailros*, 164–76.

[67] *Epistolae saeculi XIII*, ii, no. 257; É. Berger, *Saint Louis et Innocent IV: étude sur les rapports de la France et du Saint-Siège*, Paris 1893, 238–67.

and in December Frederick complained of how his petitions had been refused by the *curia*.[68] In 1248 another attempt was made, when Louis set out on crusade,[69] while both Frederick and Louis's brothers urged a settlement after Louis was taken captive at Damietta.[70] Ultimately it was their failure to convince Innocent that brought them to approach Henry III, who took the cross himself in March 1250.[71] The precarious state of the Holy Land was to be the means by which peace could be created. At Lyon Innocent had argued that Frederick's deposition was not an end in itself, but a first step towards addressing the many dangers facing Christendom. The emperor and the king of France, too, argued that these threats could only be overcome once the conflict between Frederick and Innocent had been resolved, but they proposed a dramatically different solution. That both Louis and the emperor stressed the needs of the Holy Land was no coincidence, but merely reflected a common set of values,[72] espoused by the pope, as much as Henry III, Frederick II, the king of Hungary or the Latin emperor of Constantinople.

The emperor did not stop at trying to involve Louis in peace negotiations. Already in 1246, mention had been made of a Franco-imperial alliance. The king of France referred to the offer early in 1247, when he wrote to Frederick that he had made secret communications concerning the matter to the emperor's messenger.[73] What form this alliance was to take remains obscure. The best Louis could do was to insist that the pope welcome the emperor back into the Church, but he could not and would not offer his political or military support. In 1247, for instance, when Frederick marched on Lyon, Innocent IV could count on military protection from the king of France.[74] Furthermore, Louis does not appear to have hindered French knights fighting against the emperor in Germany, although this may have been a question of whether he had the ability to control them or not.[75] Similarly, the king of France tried not to be too closely associated with Frederick II. He refused to be involved in the squabbles among the inhabitants of the Latin kingdom of Jerusalem, and he refused the offer of setting sail from Sicily. At the same time, at least one contemporary observer thought that Frederick's planned expedition to Lyon had initially been undertaken at the suggestion of Louis IX. Even more intriguing is the reason given: Louis was afraid that the conflict between pope and emperor might harm his crusade.[76] The king of

---

68 *Historia diplomatica*, vi. 472.
69 *Bartholomaei scribae annales*, MGH, SS xviii. 225; Matthew Paris, *Chronica maiora*, v. 22.
70 Matthew Paris, *Chronica maiora*, v. 70.
71 Ibid. v. 175, 188–9; Jordan, *Louis IX*, 25–30.
72 Weiler, 'Negotium', passim.
73 *Historia diplomatica*, vi. 500–2.
74 *Acta imperii inedita*, ii, no. 1040; *Historia diplomatica*, vi. 544–7; F. Pagnotti, 'Niccolò da Calvi e la sua Vita d'Innocenzo IV', *Archivio della reale società romana di storia patria* xxi (1898), 7–120 at pp. 98–9.
75 *Registres Innocent IV*, no. 4060.
76 *Bartholomaei scribae annales*, MGH, SS xviii. 221.

France would not commit himself to the forced overthrow of either pope or emperor. The requirements of his planned expedition forced Louis to adapt the stance and to use the arguments which previously the papacy had used to broker peace among the Latin princes.

Between 1245 and 1250 Louis also laid the foundations for the Capetians' ascendancy in Europe. He did so not by failing to capture Jerusalem or to reconcile pope and emperor, but by a ruthless expansion of his family's lands and influence. As in the case of Frederick II or later that of Henry III, a crusade coincided with a strengthening of royal lordship and dynastic control over all of a ruler's domains. This, in turn, had important repercussions for Henry III. Louis's most important acquisition was Provence. In August 1245 the count of Provence died, leaving his youngest and still unmarried daughter Beatrice as his heiress.[77] This resulted in a mushrooming of politically-motivated suitors, including Raymond of Toulouse,[78] the emperor,[79] the king of Aragon[80] and Charles of Anjou. All this came to an end when, quite unexpectedly, Charles of Anjou married Beatrice in January 1246. The Provençal inheritance had probably been dealt with when king and pope met at Cluny in 1245. What exactly happened there remains obscure: Matthew Paris viewed the council as designed to solve the papal–imperial conflict,[81] whereas William de Nangis described it as having been motivated by the king's pious desire to meet the pope.[82] In a minute analysis, Gerd Baaken has shown how the Provençal question was used by Innocent to woo Louis IX.[83] Assuming the role of guardian to the young girl, Innocent promised his support in obtaining the county for the Capetians. In exchange, the pope may have hoped to win a more ardent ally in Louis IX. Matters progressed quickly. On 28 December Charles of Anjou received papal dispensation for his marriage, and on 31 January the union was celebrated at Aix.[84] Simultaneously, troops were dispatched to the county.[85] Although Louis never declared himself openly against Frederick, Charles of Anjou complied with papal claims and avoided doing homage to the emperor. At the same time, the union caused new difficulties. In April 1244 Count Raymond had pawned several castles to Henry III, in exchange for a loan of 4,000 marks.[86] After the county had passed to the Capetians, the king of England demanded

---

[77] Matthew Paris, Chronica maiora, iv. 545–6.
[78] Layettes, ii, no. 3382; William de Nangis, Historia, RHGF xx. 770.
[79] Acta imperii inedita, ii, no. 47; Bartholomaei scribae annales, MGH, SS xviii. 218–19.
[80] William de Nangis, Gesta, RHGF xx. 454.
[81] Matthew Paris, Chronica maiora, iv. 484.
[82] William de Nangis, Gesta, RHGF xx. 352–4.
[83] G. Baaken, 'Die Verhandlungen von Cluny (1245) und der Kampf Innocenz' IV gegen Friedrich II.', DA l (1994), 531–79 at pp. 532–59; Berger, Saint Louis, 139–70.
[84] Baaken, 'Die Verhandlungen von Cluny', 557.
[85] Matthew Paris, Chronica maiora, iv. 545–6.
[86] Receuil des actes des comtes de Provence appartenant à la maison de Barcelone, ed. F. Benoit, Monaco 1925, ii, no. 373.

control over these lands, or a repayment. The issue began to feature in nego-tiations between Henry III and Louis in 1246,[87] involved the dispatch of English envoys to Languedoc[88] and even went – unsuccessfully – before the papal court.[89] To Louis, his control over Provence meant an end to the recur-rent threat of unrest emanating from his southern borders. More important, the marriage limited Henry III's room for manoeuvre, as by now the counties of Toulouse and Provence were controlled by cadet branches of the Capetian royal family.

The king of England suffered further setbacks when, in 1247, Hugh de Lusignan died, thus depriving him of yet another pillar in his anti-Capetian diplomacy. The Capetians also cemented their position in Flanders.[90] In 1212 countess Margaret had married Burchard de Avesnes, who, however, at the time, had been in holy orders. The union produced two children, John and Baldwin, who were later declared illegitimate. Margaret's second marriage, to Walter de Dampierre, was also annulled, as the spouses were too closely related. After the countess's death in 1244, the succession dispute began. Both the Avesnes and the Dampierre children demanded that they succeed to the counties of Flanders and Hainault. They soon became embroiled in the papal–imperial conflict, with John de Avesnes requesting help from Frederick, and his half-brothers relying on Louis IX and Innocent IV. A compromise was suggested in 1246, granting the county of Hainault to John de Avesnes, and Flanders to William de Dampierre, but this found little favour with the warring brothers. None the less, the Dampierres maintained their control over most of Flanders, and, dependent as they were on Capetian support, remained unlikely to join any future undertakings against Louis IX.

Louis's successes provide the background for some of the contacts Henry III continued to have with the mainland. In December 1246, for instance, Joan of Flanders complained to Henry that he harboured those plotting against her.[91] This is given some credence by the fact that, in April 1250, John de Avesnes received a safe-conduct on coming to England.[92] Similarly, the same year messengers of the commune of Marseilles, at the time rebelling against Charles of Anjou, were received in England,[93] and, while on crusade, Louis had to ask the pope several times to warn Henry III against attacking the lands of a crusader.[94] Finally, a number of former officials of Count

---

87 Matthew Paris, *Chronica maiora*, iv. 506.
88 *CLR, 1245–51*, 13.
89 *Registres Innocent IV*, no. 1967.
90 The following is based on H. S. Lucas, 'John of Avesnes and Richard of Cornwall', *Speculum* xxiii (1948), 81–101; Nicholas, *Medieval Flanders*, 150–69.
91 *Royal letters Henry III*, ii, no. 442 (but printed between letters 448 and 450).
92 *CPR, 1247–58*, 62.
93 P. Herde, *Karl I. von Anjou*, Stuttgart 1978, 32; J. Dunbabin, *Charles I of Anjou: power, kingship and state-making in thirteenth-century Europe*, London 1998, 46–8; Schulz, *Denn sie liebten*, 271; *CLR, 1245–51*, 314.
94 Matthew Paris, *Chronica maiora*, v. 23, 26, 346.

Raymond of Toulouse, including his seneschal, continued to be supported by the English court.[95] This casts doubt on the assumption that Henry had abandoned his ambitions in France. Although we do not know to what extent these contacts were based on the initiative of the English court, the fact remains that Henry was still perceived as someone likely to provide help against the Capetians. This, in turn, underlines the wisdom in Louis's IX's decision to take control of Provence and Toulouse. If Henry III wanted to recover his continental inheritance, new means and new friends had to be found.

Henry III and his friends

Under Innocent IV there was no let-up in papal demands for money from the English Church.[96] In 1247 Innocent IV sent legates across Europe to preach the cross against Frederick,[97] and this continued until the emperor's death in December 1250.[98] This was combined with further requests for financial help,[99] which caused considerable chagrin in England. In 1245, if Matthew Paris is to be believed, the nobles estimated that annual payments to Rome amounted to 60,000 marks.[100] Paying to fund the pope's campaigns in Germany and Italy was, however, only one among many grievances: in 1246, for example, the English abbots had protested about papal provisions of benefices in England.[101] The extent of the discontent may be gleaned from the orders which Archbishop Boniface is said to have received from Innocent in September 1249: even those who secretly spoke in favour of the emperor were to be excommunicated.[102] It would be a mistake to read this simply as evidence of English support for Frederick. Criticising the pope for his actions was a means by which disapproval of the *curia's* financial demands could be expressed, but, equally, a means by which those censuring the pope could be accused of supporting the emperor. The issue at stake was not necessarily Innocent's unrelenting stance – even Matthew Paris, for instance, one of the pope's most outspoken critics, stayed well clear of endorsing Frederick's propaganda – but that he expected the English Church to pay for it.

Innocent's activities in England also brought several imperial missions to Henry's court. In July 1246 Frederick sent two envoys,[103] carrying with them a letter to the nobles of England. His excommunication, the emperor

---

95 Vincent, 'England', 84 and n. 141.
96 Matthew Paris, *Chronica maiora*, iv. 577.
97 Ibid. iv. 612; *Registres Innocent IV*, no. 3002.
98 *Registres Innocent IV*, nos 4265, 4269.
99 Ibid. no. 2997.
100 Matthew Paris, *Chronica maiora*, iv. 419; Powicke, *Henry III*, 276–82.
101 Matthew Paris, *Chronica maiora*, iv. 532; Egger, 'Henry III's England'.
102 Matthew Paris, *Chronica maiora*, lib. add.: *chronica maiora*, vi. 171–4.
103 *CLR, 1245–51*, 68.

explained, had been unjust, and he promised to help Christendom against its many foes, if only the pope would make peace with him.[104] At about the same time Walter of Ocra wrote to Henry III, and recounted Frederick's recent successes in Italy and Germany.[105] However, once again Henry was reluctant to resist papal demands.[106] Later that year, probably in an attempt to press his master's case in person, Walter visited England.[107] In August 1248 the emperor was once again complaining to Henry III that his efforts at making peace with Innocent had been thwarted by the pope.[108] Imperial missions continued to be received: in July and November 1246,[109] June 1247[110] and January 1250,[111] not counting visits by Walter of Ocra and various letters addressed to Henry III from the imperial court.[112] The emperor's deposition by no means signalled an end to his relations with Henry III, and the king continued to emphasise his friendly relations with the emperor.[113] Like most of his contemporaries, he was unwilling to abandon Frederick, but neither was he prepared to commit himself to a cause which would bring him into direct conflict with the *curia*.

Henry's German contacts exemplify the complexity of his stance. The archbishop of Cologne, the driving force behind the elections of Henry Raspe and William of Holland, remained conspicuously absent from English records. This is the more worth noting, as the king drew on his contacts in Germany to a degree unparalleled since 1235. Even men like the dukes of Brunswick and Brabant, whose role had so suddenly ceased with Isabella's marriage, found themselves courted again. At the same time, in a series of moves which heralded a change in the means, though not the objectives, of Henry's activities on the mainland, he did not seek out these contacts to further his ambitions in France, but to strengthen and expand his position in Britain and Gascony, and he pursued these contacts in addition to forging closer links with the rulers of the Iberian Peninsula.

Let us begin by looking at dealings with the duke of Brunswick. In April 1245 Francis de Bren was sent as the king's envoy to Brunswick,[114] which resulted in a ducal embassy to England shortly afterwards.[115] Although no further exchange of envoys is reported until 1248, Henry, listed as the arch-

---

104 Matthew Paris, *Chronica maiora*, iv. 538–44.
105 Ibid. iv. 575–7.
106 Ibid. iv. 577–8.
107 *CLR, 1245–51*, 94, 95; *CPR, 1232–47*, 493.
108 *Historia diplomatica*, vi. 644–6.
109 *CLR, 1245–51*, 68, 95.
110 Ibid. 127.
111 Ibid. 271.
112 The last payment of his and Peter de Vinea's annual fief is recorded in 1248: *CPR 1247–58*, 26.
113 *CR, 1247–51*, 88.
114 *CLR, 1245–51*, 43.
115 Ibid. 46, 48, 53; *CR, 1242–7*, 421.

deacon of Bremen, appeared regularly to collect his annual fee.[116] Although Bremen was not within the duke's domains, it was situated within his wider sphere of political influence. Another envoy from the duke did not arrive in England until August 1250.[117] The exact purpose of these contacts is difficult to ascertain, but at least some light is shed on them by a mandate, issued in June 1248: Jordan of Brunswick was authorised, with the consent of Richard of Cornwall, 'to bring from beyond seas to England at the king's expenses all persons who know anything of mintage and exchange of money, to do what belongs to their several duties in the kingdom'.[118] This refers to the earl of Cornwall's control over the coinage, assumed in 1247.[119] Considering that, since the days of Henry the Lion, the dukes had exercised control over the once rich silver mines at Goslar, and taking into account their traditionally good relations with England, they seem an obvious choice to provide the necessary expertise. Furthermore, although Goslar had long ceased to produce silver, it still produced ore, and the legal and technical framework developed there remained a standard across Europe, adopted at around that time by, among others, the king of Bohemia.[120] This choice was also significant in political terms. The archbishops of Cologne, for instance, oversaw the production and minting of one of the most widely used currency units of thirteenth-century Germany, and by 1247 their significance certainly exceeded that of the Welf dukes. Unlike the rulers of Brunswick, however, Conrad of Hochstaden had taken an active role in the political struggles of Germany, and had assumed the political leadership of the anti-Staufen forces. The Welfs, on the other hand, avoided being drawn into this political turmoil.[121] None of this does, of course, constitute definite proof of the king's attitude. None the less, the circumstantial evidence strongly suggests that their attitude towards Frederick and the Staufen remained an important

---

[116] CR, 1242–7, 26, 99, 165. This Henry is difficult to identify. In April 1247 Henry 'son of Vologard, consul of Bremen' received a papal mandate that he was to be granted a prebend in the diocese or commune of Bremen: Epistolae saeculi XIII, ii. no. 328. Bremisches Urkundenbuch, ed. D. R. Ehmck and W. von Bingen, i, Bremen 1873, lists only two archdeans named Henry, one Henry of Tossem, appearing around 1259/60, and another from c. 1280. However, the first Henry, before being made dean of Bremen had been a canon there and archdeacon of Hadeln. Neither candidate thus fits chronologically. However, in March 1246, a Henry of Tossem, without being given a title, witnessed a grant by the archbishop of Bremen to the abbey of Oberholz: ibid. i, no. 233.

[117] CLR, 1245–51, 302; CR, 1247–51, 316.

[118] CLR, 1245–51, 194; CPR, 1247–58, 21.

[119] CPR, 1232–47, 503, 505, 511; Denholm-Young, Richard of Cornwall, 58–67; N. Fryde, 'Silver recoinage and royal policy in England, 1180–1250', in E. van Cauwenberghe and F. Irsigler (eds), Münzprägung-Geldumlauf und Wechselkurse; Minting, monetary circulation and exchange rates, Trier 1984, 11–19; R.J. Eaglen, 'The evolution of coinage in thirteenth-century England', TCE iv (1991), 15–24, at pp. 17–18, 20–2; Huffman, Family, commerce, 41–55.

[120] P. Spufford, Money and its use in medieval Europe, Cambridge 1988, 111, 119.

[121] Schneidmüller, Die Welfen, 285.

criterion in Henry's selection of partners in the empire. This impression is further strengthened when considering Henry's dealings with the duke of Brabant.

Within four weeks of having been sent to the north of Germany, Francis de Bren was announced as the king's envoy to the duke of Brabant.[122] This initiated a period of intense diplomatic activity: by August 1247 messengers of the duke left England,[123] followed in October by another English mission to Brabant.[124] In August of the following year, two of the duke's knights were sent as the king's messengers.[125] One of them, Walter de la Hast, is recorded once again in May 1249.[126] The reasons for this sudden reawakening of interest in the duke may have been twofold. In November 1245 reference was made in a mandate for the king's treasurer to 'knights and others from over-seas and the lands of the count of Flanders'.[127] This refers to foreign merce-naries hired for campaigns in Scotland and Poitou, and these may have included knights from Brabant. In 1252, for instance, when returning to Gascony, Simon de Montfort is said to have been offered troops by the duke.[128] More important, though, were the plans for a marriage between the king's eldest son, Edward, and one of the duke's daughters.[129] Matthew Paris gives the only contemporary account of these plans. In 1247, he wrote, John Maunsel was sent to Brabant to arrange the proposed union. However, the project failed, for reasons unknown.[130] Considering the duke's political affili-ation may go some way towards illuminating the cause of the mission's failure. Initially, Duke Henry III of Brabant had remained loyal to Frederick. In 1243, for instance, he had been among those to whom the emperor expressed his great optimism that the election of Innocent IV would herald the end of his excommunication,[131] and in July or August 1246 Walter of Ocra referred to the duke as having been present at the imperial court.[132] At the same time, his family connections put Duke Henry into a difficult posi-tion. One of his daughters was married to Otto of Bavaria, thus making him an in-law of Conrad IV, while another had been married to Henry Raspe, Frederick II's first anti-king.[133] Furthermore, Henry Raspe's successor, William of Holland, was a distant relation,[134] and he therefore became

---

122 CLR, 1245–51, 57.
123 Ibid. 139.
124 Ibid. 149: Prior John of Newburgh.
125 Ibid. 198.
126 Ibid. 236.
127 CR, 1242–7, 372.
128 Matthew Paris, Chronica maiora, v. 210.
129 M. Prestwich, Edward I, London 1988, 9; Howell, Eleanor of Provence, 110–11.
130 Matthew Paris, Chronica maiora, iv. 623–4.
131 Historia diplomatica, vi. 98–9.
132 Matthew Paris, Chronica maiora, iv. 577.
133 Chronicon Alberici, RHGF xxi. 629.
134 Gesta abbatum trudonensium, continuatio iii, MGH, SS x. 395–6.

quickly embroiled in the papal–imperial conflict. In 1246 the duke was among those who were exhorted by the pope to elect Henry Raspe as anti-king.[135] That in itself does not mean that he had been a supporter of Henry's candidacy. Similar letters had been addressed to the dukes of Brunswick, Bavaria and Saxony, as well as the margraves of Meissen and Brandenburg, none of them known to be ardent supporters of the anti-king. In fact, around Pentecost 1247, Duke Henry had been one of those the emperor had called upon in preparations for his planned journey to Lyon.[136] Later that year, however, he is listed, together with the archbishops of Mainz, Cologne, Trier and Bremen, as having elected William of Holland.[137] When exactly he changed sides is unclear. An early indication may have been a privilege from April 1247, in which Innocent IV granted one of the duke's messengers the rights of legitimate birth, despite his illegitimate descent.[138] Within a couple of months, Duke Henry led William's troops. In August 1247 the papal legate in Germany was ordered to waive canonical restrictions concerning the marriage plans of several of the duke's knights, as they had taken the cross against Frederick.[139] In November the duke himself was granted remission of his sins for fighting the emperor.[140] The failure of English negotiations with Brabant would thus have coincided with the duke assuming a leading role in William of Holland's government, and we may assume that this influenced the king of England and his court. There were, of course, other reasons, too. King Henry III was in a financially desperate situation, and the need to find a sizeable dowry for his eldest son certainly played a part in negotiations when the ducal court contacted him about the planned marriage again in 1252. None the less, this points to a reluctance at Henry III's court to forge closer ties with the anti-Staufen camp in Germany, and it was certainly aware of the duke's role in Germany. Matthew Paris, for instance, lists him as a possible candidate to succeed Henry Raspe.[141] Although Frederick did not receive the degree of support he may have expected, he could rest assured that neither would his enemies.

A similar picture emerges when we consider English activities in Italy. In January 1246 Count Amadeus of Savoy did homage to Henry III for Susa, Avigliana, St Maurice-sur-Isère and Bard, that is, a series of towns and fortifications controlling important passes across the Alps, in exchange for an annual payment of £1,000.[142] The deal had been brokered by Peter de Aigueblanche, the Savoyard bishop of Hereford. The arguments with which he tried to warm the king's heart towards the arrangement are worth noting:

135 Registres Innocent IV, no. 1970.
136 Chronica regia coloniensis continuatio S Pantaleonis v, in Chronica regia coloniensis, 286.
137 Ibid. 286–7.
138 Epistolae saeculi XIII, ii, no. 314.
139 Ibid. ii, no. 425.
140 Ibid. ii, no. 470.
141 However, he does so s.a. 1251: Matthew Paris, Chronica maiora, v. 201.
142 Ibid. iv. 550; CPR, 1232–47, 469.

the count would wage war on any of the king's enemies, and Henry III should make as many friends and subjects as possible to confound his foes.[143] These lands certainly would have been of strategic significance with regard, for instance, to Provence, and this is emphasised by Amadeus' confirmation of the grant, also found in the Longleat collection: he vowed to damage the enemies of the king and his heirs as much as he could.[144] We should, however, avoid oversimplifying Henry's motivation. Recovering his inheritance certainly played its part. Although no attempts were made to reclaim his inheritance by force, the king was none the less in contact with those – like the Avesnes brothers or the citizens of Marseilles – who, too, had an axe to grind with the Capetians. Controlling a number of Alpine passes could have been useful, and it was this particular purpose which was emphasised both by the king's emissary, and the recipient of his grant. Furthermore, the grant coincided with the political turmoil in Provence after Raymond's death, and the agreement was reached at about the time – in January 1246 – when Charles of Anjou married Beatrice of Provence. In addition, though, this enfeoffment was a means of rewarding the king's Savoyard relatives, and it was so in more senses than one. The financial gains made by Amadeus were considerable, but it also enabled him and his brother Thomas to extricate themselves from an increasingly difficult political situation.[145] Their allegiance was owed to neither pope nor emperor, but to the king of England alone.

The grant caused political as well as financial problems. There was a tradition of English involvement in the area,[146] but Henry still disposed of lands nominally under the emperor's jurisdiction. Matthew Paris, for instance, stressed specifically that the count received these lands from Henry without prejudice to imperial claims.[147] If nothing else, this implies some concern as to the emperor's reaction. Henry III and the Savoyards were treading dangerous ground. After all, the latter were split between Peter of Savoy, the archbishop-elect of Lyon, and thus a member of Innocent IV's inner circle, and Amadeus, who for some time had been prevaricating between emperor and pope. In 1244, for instance, he had ignored Frederick's orders, and had ensured that Innocent could safely pass through his lands to Lyon.[148] In 1247, on the other hand, he tried to utilise the emperor's reliance on his services for the advancement of his own interests, and joined the camp of Frederick's supporters. When the emperor proceeded on Lyon, the count refused to let him pass through his territories, unless he first received certain privileges.[149]

---

143 *Diplomatic documents*, no. 254.
144 Marquess of Bath MSS, muniments no. 10590, fo. 5r.
145 Trautz, *Die Könige von England*, 106–8.
146 Cox, *Eagles of Savoy*, 151.
147 Matthew Paris, *Chronica maiora*, iv. 550.
148 *Chronicon marchiae tarvisinae et lombardiae*, RIS viii/3, 17.
149 *Bartholomaei scribae annales*, MGH, SS xviii. 221.

This led to a series of negotiations, with first results announced in April 1247, and symbolised by the marriage between Amadeus' daughter Beatrice and Manfred, the emperor's illegitimate son.[150] The grant thus formed part of the wider preparations Frederick had undertaken for his planned march on Lyon. The counts of Savoy continued to play an important role in imperial politics. In November 1248, for example, the count's brother, Thomas, received various towns and castles, including Turin, and was made imperial vicar for the lands north of Pavia.[151] Frederick also appointed Thomas and Amadeus as his proctors in arranging peace with Innocent IV.[152] Unlike the duke of Brabant, the counts of Savoy remained loyal to the emperor, and this, as well as their relationship with Henry III, helps to explain the intensity of contacts.

This episode is also helpful in demonstrating Henry III's diminishing dependence on Frederick. Instead, he turned to his relatives, and sought to reopen old channels of communication. Like Louis IX, the king of England was willing to disregard imperial rights if, by so doing, he advanced his own ambitions. He was, however, not prepared to assist those who were openly hostile to Frederick. Those who remained neutral, or who sided with Frederick, were far more likely to be contacted. Furthermore, Henry extended his contacts at a time when the Staufen had begun to lose their grip on Germany and Italy. Like others, too, Henry was trying to further his own goals, and he became ready to fill the vacuum which was slowly beginning to open at the heart of the Staufen empire.

The years between 1245 and 1250 also witnessed a strengthening of relations with the Iberian peninsula. Embassies to and from Aragon are recorded in February, May and June 1246, May 1248 and 1249,[153] to and from Castile in May and August 1246, April 1247 and May 1249.[154] Little evidence survives as to what exactly these missions had been about, although we may assume that they were related to events in Portugal, where King Sancho's deposition in 1245 had resulted in civil war. That soon began to involve other rulers on the peninsula, divided roughly between those allied with Louis IX and those who sought to find support elsewhere.[155] The king of Aragon had also played a part in the struggles over the inheritance of Provence, and the rulers of Castile took a close (and not always friendly) interest in the affairs of Gascony. In short, events in Iberia mattered to the king of England.

---

[150] *Historia diplomatica*, vi. 526–8; *Forschungen zur Reichs- und Rechtsgeschichte Italiens*, ed. J. Ficker, Innsbruck 1868–74, iv, no. 405.

[151] *Acta imperii inedita*, i, nos 407–10, 411–13; *Historia diplomatica*, vi. 658.

[152] *Constitutiones, 1198–1272*, no. 271.

[153] *CLR, 1245–51*, 26, 27, 177, 236.

[154] Ibid. 73, 75, 117, 119, 120, 123, 232.

[155] E. Peters, *The shadow king: rex inutilis in medieval law and literature, 751–1327*, New Haven 1970, 135–69; J. Mattoso, 'a crise de 1245', in his *Portugal medieval: novas interpretações*, 2nd edn, Lisbon 1992, 57–76. My thanks to Iona McCleery for these references.

Henry III's Iberian connections also brought him into close but indirect contact with Frederick II. In late 1242, for instance, while the king was in Poitou, safe-conducts were issued for a Castilian envoy bringing horses to Frederick's court, and for an imperial envoy escorting a rouncy to Italy.[156] Contacts between Castile and the empire had been frequent, despite a temporary cooling of relations after Frederick's deposition. In 1245/6 Alfonso (the future IX) had sent an envoy to the imperial court, dealing, among others matters, with the Provençal inheritance,[157] and in the summer of 1250 the king of Castile formed part of Frederick's wider diplomatic efforts to ensure his reconciliation with Innocent.[158] Even in Iberia Henry's contacts centred on those who were at least neutral in their relationship with the emperor.

Henry's activities increased not only in the Mediterranean, but also in Britain. To some extent this was a response to the difficulties he faced in France, where his allies had died, and where Louis IX had been successful in incorporating their lands into the Capetians' domains. Equally, though, Henry responded to opportunities as they arose, and he proved himself Louis's equal in seizing a chance to strengthen and augment his position and that of his family. Ireland, Wales and Scotland were as important to Henry III as Toulouse, Flanders and Provence were to Louis IX. In Ireland, for instance, the death of several barons without heirs led to a strengthening of the royal domain, and in the mid-1240s Henry III embarked on a number of campaigns in Ireland and Wales, while in 1247 he arranged for a marriage between the future Alexander III of Scotland and an English princess.[159] To some extent, therefore, these were years of stabilisation when the king sought to overcome the setbacks he had suffered abroad, and strove to augment his position at home. This does not mean that hopes for an eventual recovery of his inheritance had been abandoned. None the less, the financial constraints he suffered at home, the political embarrassment of the Poitevin campaign, in combination with Louis's successful expansion of Capetian territories into Languedoc, as well as the fact that Louis's crusading status awarded him special protection by the *curia*, reduced the king's room for manoeuvre. Under these circumstances, reasserting Plantagenet claims in Britain, and seeking to improve ties with the rulers of Castile and Aragon, were all he could do.

The king and his court did not meekly suffer the setbacks they experienced, but actively responded by exploring different approaches and by seeking to forge new links. Henry III never wavered in his loyalty to Frederick, but he was increasingly prepared to utilise the emperor's predicament

---

156 *CPR, 1232–47*, 330, 350, 398.
157 *Acta imperii inedita*, ii, no. 47.
158 *Historia diplomatica*, vi. 769–71.
159 Brown, 'Henry the Peaceable'; Frame, 'Henry III and Ireland', 193–6; Davies, *Age of conquest*, 300–7.

to further his own and his family's ambitions. When Languedoc was finally lost to the Capetians, the king of England explored new ground by strengthening his contacts in the Mediterranean, drawing on his Savoyard relatives as well as the rulers of Christian Iberia. In response to the Staufens' difficulties in Germany, the English court resumed dealings with the rulers of Brunswick and Brabant. At the same time, it stayed clear of associating itself with those hostile to Frederick II. Henry's actions conformed to a pattern common among his contemporaries, many of whom, too, began to fill the political vacuum at the heart of the Staufen empire: Louis IX by consolidating his hold on Languedoc, the rulers of Castile and Aragon by laying claim to Provence or Swabia, and the relatives of Henry's wife by strengthening their position at the borders of Italy, Germany and Burgundy. This laid the foundations for events after Frederick's death, when the Plantagenets, Alfonso X and the Capetians alike strove to secure for themselves as large a part of the emperor's inheritance as possible. In fact, in the years following the emperor's death, it seemed for a while as if the king of England would be able to outdo his peers by laying claim to the biggest prize of all: the Staufen empire itself.

PART III

FROM STAUFEN TO PLANTAGENET? 1250–1272

6

Roles Reversed, 1250–1254

1250 marked a watershed. Frederick II died in December, and none of his successors was able to muster a similar degree of power and prestige. Their weakness soon resulted in attempts by various European rulers – Louis IX, Alfonso of Castile and Henry III chief among them – to fill the political vacuum created by the emperor's death. Plans for a military recovery of Henry's continental inheritance had not been abandoned, but with most of Henry's allies dead, and their lands firmly in Capetian hands, these ambitions seemed impossible to fulfil by force alone. Instead, the king began to search for diplomatic solutions, and he directed his attentions elsewhere, as symbolised by his declaration in March 1250 that he was to lead a campaign to the Holy Land. This crusade came to dominate his actions over the following years. Neither the king's acceptance of the crown of Sicily on behalf of his son Edmund in 1254, the so-called *negotium Sicilie* or Sicilian Business, nor the baronial uprising of 1258 put an end to his crusading ambitions. Preparations for this campaign included efforts to settle relations with the Capetians, and brought the English court into ever closer contact with the rulers of the Mediterranean.

In this context, relations with Germany and the empire underwent a fundamental change. At last, the rulers of Germany were willing to offer the English king what he had desired for so long: an alliance against Louis IX. Henry, though, was now too preoccupied with his planned expedition to Palestine. The emperor's death thus heralded a reversal of roles: instead of courting, Henry was being courted. He did not abandon his neutral stance in the ongoing wars between the emperor's sons and the *curia*, but his motivation for doing so had changed. An involvement in the internal squabbles of the empire was increasingly perceived as a waste of resources and men more needed elsewhere. The most remarkable development of these years was, however, that, after thirty years during which Henry and his court had looked to the empire as a potential recruiting ground for allies, he and his family assumed control of that very empire – Edmund through the crown of Sicily, and Richard of Cornwall by becoming king of the Romans. Ironically, Henry achieved this at a time, when the motivation which had driven him in the past no longer held sway.

England, Germany and the empire

In Germany, Frederick's death marked the ascendancy of William of Holland and the demise of Conrad IV. William soon won support even from within the Staufens' traditional heartland, and he gained recognition abroad. In 1251, for instance, Duke John of Burgundy did homage to William for Lausanne and Besançon, thus gaining him a stronghold in the eastern parts of the kingdom of Burgundy.[1] This alliance soon increased in significance when one of the duke's daughters married into the duke of Brabant's family in 1253,[2] and his son into that of the burgraves of Nuremberg in 1255.[3] Not only did this strengthen William's position along the western borders of the empire, he also gained control over Nuremberg, once a centre of Staufen power.[4] The erstwhile anti-king had thus successfully filled the void left by Frederick II. His triumph was completed in 1252, when William celebrated his marriage to one of the duke of Brunswick's daughters, thus gaining ground in the north of Germany. More important, he decided to repeat his election as king of the Romans. This time, those who in the past had either ignored or opposed his royal status, confirmed his elevation.[5] Only Duke Louis of Bavaria, Conrad's father-in-law, remained hostile. However, when Louis murdered his wife in 1253,[6] he was left ostracised and deprived of political clout. Not only had those joined William's camp who in the past remained aloof from the conflict, but his opponents were left as political and moral pariahs.

William quickly decided to use this momentum for a campaign against the countess of Flanders. In July 1253 an army led by Baldwin de Avesnes inflicted a disastrous defeat on the combined forces of the countess and her Capetian allies, and the Dampierre brothers were captured.[7] The triumph was, however, short-lived. Soon after the battle, Countess Margaret offered Hainault to Charles of Anjou, and agreed to pay his expenses in recovering it, and in early 1254 Charles conquered the county without encountering

---

[1] *Layettes*, iii, no. 3935.
[2] *Annales parchenses*, MGH, SS xvi. 607.
[3] *Layettes*, iii, no. 4186.
[4] G. Pfeiffer, 'Der Aufstieg der Reichsstadt Nürnberg im 13. Jahrhundert', *Mitteilungen des Vereins für die Geschichte der Stadt Nürnberg* xliv (1953), 14–24; J. Kraus, 'Die Stadt Nürnberg in ihren Beziehungen zur Römischen Kurie während des Mittelalters', *Mitteilungen des Vereins für die Geschichte der Stadt Nürnberg* xli (1950), 1–153 at p. 3; *Die Zeit der Staufer* (exhibition catalogue), Stuttgart 1977–9, iv, maps 5, 7, 9.
[5] *Annales erphordenses*, in *Monumenta erphesfurtensia*, 111–12; Mitteis, *Die deutsche Königswahl*, 185–193; Hintze, *Königtum*, 46–56.
[6] *Annales saxonici*, MGH, SS xvi. 431.
[7] *Annales marchianenses*, MGH, SS xvi. 616; *Annales neresheimenses*, MGH, SS x. 24; *Annales erphordenses*, in *Monumenta erphesfurtensia*, 112; Matthew Paris, *Chronica maiora*, lib. add.: *chronica maiora*, vi. 252–5; v. 392, 437.

much resistance.[8] William had to give in. Louis IX, asked to arbitrate, decreed that both the Dampierre and the Avesnes brothers take their lands as fiefs from the count of Anjou, thus extending Capetian control into the empire. The Avesnes brothers remained reluctant to accept this settlement, and efforts to undo the results of the 1254 campaign remained at the heart of William's diplomacy. It was against this background that William's court approached that of Henry III.

Conrad IV soon realised that he had little chance of securing his position north of the Alps, and left for Sicily.[9] He gained swift recognition from most Apulian towns and nobles. In addition, negotiations began with Innocent IV.[10] If Matthew Paris is to be believed, these included plans for a marriage between Henry, Frederick II's son by his marriage with Isabella Plantagenet, and a papal niece.[11] However, Innocent was unwilling to acknowledge the rights of any Staufen claimant. As soon as news of Frederick's death had reached the *curia*, the preaching of a crusade against Conrad had begun.[12] Similarly, the Sicilian aristocracy was exhorted not to adhere to any of Frederick's sons.[13] While Conrad was attacked in Italy, measures were taken further to undermine his German base. In 1253 William was asked to enforce an earlier decision which deprived Conrad of the duchy of Swabia,[14] and the duke of Brabant was promised that the Church would never enter into peace with its enemies, as long as Conrad 'who acts as if he were emperor in Germany, remains adorned with the royal dignity'.[15]

It was only after a series of military defeats that Innocent began to consider negotiating with Conrad. The Staufen was granted a respite to allow him to prove his orthodoxy, as a step towards proper negotiations.[16] In the end, the young king's deposition and excommunication were confirmed. Innocent was, however, spared having to enforce his decision, as Conrad died in May

---

8   For this and what follows see Hintze, *Königtum*, 118–34; Herde, *Karl I*, 35–6; Dunbabin, *Charles I of Anjou*, 37–9.

9   *Annales ianuenses*, MGH, SS xviii. 230; G. Zeller, *König Konrad IV in Italien, 1252–1254*, Bremen 1907; S. Runciman, *The Sicilian Vespers: a history of the Mediterranean world in the thirteenth century*, Cambridge 1958, 26–38; O. Engels, *Die Staufer*, 6th edn, Stuttgart 1994, 187–91.

10   C. Rodenberg, *Innocenz IV und das Königreich Sicilien, 1245–1254*, Halle 1892, 113–26.

11   Matthew Paris, *Chronica maiora*, v. 274–5. He continues to explain that the project failed because the Sicilian nobles were unwilling to countenance such a slight on the dignity of the imperial dynasty. This was probably a veiled attack on Henry III, rather than a straightforward record of events in Sicily: B. K. U. Weiler, 'Matthew Paris, Richard of Cornwall's candidacy for the German throne, and the Sicilian Business', *JMH* xxvi (2000), 70–91.

12   *Registres Innocent IV*, no. 5032.

13   Ibid. no. 5339.

14   *Epistolae saeculi XIII*, iii, no. 186.

15   *Registres Innocent IV*, no. 6397.

16   *Epistolae saeculi XIII*, iii, no. 255; Matthew Paris, *Chronica maiora, lib. add.: chronica maiora*, vi. 298–304. See also ibid. v. 448–9.

1254. This left the pope free to pursue his aims in Sicily, and he triumphantly entered Naples, where he stayed until his death in November 1254.[17] At the time, it may have seemed as if the Staufen had finally been defeated. Of Frederick's heirs, only Conradin, a two-year-old safely confined to the duke of Bavaria's lands, and Manfred, Frederick's illegitimate son, remained. In Germany, William of Holland was at the height of his power, and in Sicily, Henry III, a loyal son of the Church, was to establish a new dynasty.

It was within these parameters that Henry III conducted his relations with Germany and the empire. These contacts were, however, mostly confined to the dukes of Brabant and Brunswick, and largely concerned with matters of trade and commerce. Dealings with the power behind William's throne, Conrad of Hochstaden, the archbishop of Cologne, had come to a complete halt, and no evidence survives to suggest any links between the prelate and the English court. In a striking parallel to relations before 1235, contacts with Germany were mostly arranged via the imperial aristocracy, rather than the king himself. As far as William was concerned, it is probably safe to assume that the main motivation behind his contacts with the king of England was a need for allies in Flanders. When Henry III stayed in Gascony in 1253-4, for instance, he received an envoy from John de Avesnes,[18] the claimant to the county and one of the leading members of William's entourage. It remains unclear, though, whether the English court had encouraged these overtures. Normally, contacts centred on the traditional addressees of English diplomacy in Germany. In April 1252 and May 1253, for instance, Master Geoffrey, a clerk of the duke of Brunswick, received a fee at the exchequer,[19] which could imply some regularity of contacts between the ducal court and that of Henry III. Geoffrey may also have brought news of William's recent successes in Germany, including his marriage to one of the duke's daughters. Another messenger, a knight from Brunswick, arrived in December 1252,[20] and stayed until early January 1253.[21] That a certain degree of cordiality prevailed in relations with the Welf is implied by the fact that this embassy was given robes 'sicut valletis regis', like one of the king's servants.[22] Such displays of generosity were normally confined to specific occasions, aiming to underline the particular importance of the issues discussed, or of those received.[23] The period of the knight's sojourn in England also witnessed the build-up to William's campaign in Flanders, and it may, thus, have been

---

[17] *Chronicon marchiae tarvisinae et lombardiae*, RIS viii/3, 24.

[18] CR, *1253-4*, 261.

[19] CLR, *1251-60*, 43-4, 128.

[20] CR, *1251-3*, 296.

[21] CLR, *1251-60*, 97.

[22] CR, *1251-3*, 296; F. Lachaud, 'Liveries of robes in England, c. 1200-c. 1300', EHR cxi (1996), 279-98.

[23] The similarities between the gifts received by the envoy from Brunswick in 1252/3, and those on display in 1257, during the archbishop of Cologne's visit, are worth noting; CR, *1256-9*, 207.

concerned with attempts at winning military and diplomatic backing from Henry III. As had become customary in dealings with the Welfs, though, political issues were not as important as commercial relations. A knight from the duke is recorded as visiting again in September 1253,[24] but this time probably in connection with the matter of various North German merchants imprisoned in July,[25] which would explain why he contacted the regents in England, rather than the king in Gascony.

A similar pattern emerges in relations with the duke of Brabant, who continued to play a prominent part in imperial affairs. In early 1251 the duke had been asked by the *curia* to lead yet another crusade against Conrad,[26] and he was one of William's most important allies during the 1253 campaign in Flanders.[27] At the same time, closer links with England continued. When returning to Gascony in 1252, for instance, Simon de Montfort was offered troops by the duke.[28] Furthermore, the project of a Brabantine marriage for Edward was mooted once more.[29] Little is known about these negotiations, and any hope of success was frustrated when Edward married the king of Castile's sister in 1254. This suggests that, despite cooling relations with the court of William himself, contacts continued with those who had traditionally been at the centre of English diplomacy in Germany. However, should William's supporters have hoped that their links could induce Henry to challenge Louis IX, they were to be disappointed.

Henry only got involved in German affairs to further the ambitions of his and his wife's family, as illustrated by a letter from spring 1253, in which the king insisted that William return Bern and other places, currently held by the counts of Kiburg, to Peter of Savoy.[30] At the time, the Savoyards were performing yet another balancing act. Matthew Paris reports that Thomas of Savoy had been involved in arranging a truce between the Staufen and Innocent IV in 1252,[31] and in February 1254 it was at the count's instigation that Conrad had been granted a respite for negotiations by the pope.[32] By the time of Conrad's death, however, the count was firmly siding with the papacy: on 30 May 1254 Innocent IV ordered William of Holland to grant Thomas possession of a castle between Asti and Alexandria.[33] Henry's intercession on Peter's behalf was primarily a matter of exercising patronage on behalf of his Savoyard relatives,[34] in the light of their projected role in Henry's crusade –

---

[24] CPR, 1247–58, 222.
[25] CR, 1251–3, 494, 495.
[26] Matthew Paris, *Chronica maiora*, v. 260.
[27] Ibid. *lib. add.*, vi. 253.
[28] Ibid. v. 210.
[29] CR, 1247–51, 527.
[30] Ibid. 457.
[31] Matthew Paris, *Chronica maiora*, v. 301.
[32] *Epistolae saeculi XIII*, iii, no. 255.
[33] *Documenti sulle relazioni tra la casa di Savoia e la Sancta Sede nel medio evo* (1066–1268), ed. P. Fontana, Turin 1939, no. 157.
[34] On their interests in the region see Cox, *Eagles of Savoy*, 201–4, and E. Tremp, 'Auf dem

after all Peter remained one of the most important recruits the king had been able to muster.[35] It also seems unlikely that Henry could have hoped for much success with his petition, as relations with William went from bad to worse.[36] In November and December 1254, for example, mandates were issued to arrest merchants from Holland and Zeeland, as English merchants imprisoned there had not yet had their goods restored, despite William's promises.[37] Furthermore, also in December 1254, the homage done by the countess of Flanders for an annual fee of 500 marks was acknowledged.[38] Not only was Henry reluctant to support William against the Capetians and their allies, he also forged stronger links with those hostile to the German king. As we will see, this tentative *rapprochement* with Louis was intrinsically linked to Henry's planned crusade. In this context, the overtures received from William and the Avesnes brothers were at best a nuisance, and at worst a potential threat to the far more important undertaking of a campaign to Jerusalem.

Conrad IV did not fare much better. Until his involvement in the Sicilian Business, Henry stayed clear of the conflict between Staufen and papal supporters in Italy. Contacts were sporadic, and focused on the affairs of Sicily, where Henry III's nephew, Henry, had assumed an increasingly important role. Matthew Paris, our main source for these contacts, maintains that Conrad had thanked Richard of Cornwall, when he rejected the *curia*'s offer to become king of Sicily in 1253.[39] Interestingly enough, an embassy from Conrad is recorded as being in England by March 1253,[40] only a few months after Richard had received the papal offer. More importantly, the same day Conrad's envoy was attested, Henry III sent one of his officials to Apulia.[41] In addition, Matthew states that Richard, still hesitant about accepting the crown, consulted Conrad concerning the affairs of Sicily.[42] Whether the English mission was, in fact, to consult Conrad on how best to overthrow his regime, may be open to question. It was probably concerned with the prospects of the king's nephew, and a possible solution for the ongoing war between Innocent IV and Conrad. It was during these months, after all, that Thomas of Savoy had been involved in arranging negotiations between the Staufen and the *curia*, and among the issues then discussed had been a marriage between young Henry and a member of Pope Innocent's family. This

Weg in die Moderne: Peter II. von Savoyen und die Anfänge der Territorialstaatlichkeit im 13. Jahrhundert', *Zeitschrift für Historische Forschung* xv (1998), 481–507.
[35] *CPR, 1247–58*, 197; Howell, *Eleanor of Provence*, 132–5; *CPR, 1247–58*, 188.
[36] For an opposing view see Huffman, *Social politics*, 272–3.
[37] *CR, 1254–6*, 3, 13.
[38] At the time Henry III was Louis IX's guest in Paris, and her homage may thus have been connected to this visit: *CPR, 1247–58*, 387; *Annals of Burton*, AM i. 329.
[39] Matthew Paris, *Chronica maiora*, v. 361.
[40] *CLR, 1251–60*, 114.
[41] Ibid.
[42] Matthew Paris, *Chronica maiora*, v. 361

does not seem unlikely. A few years later, for instance, members of the papal *curia* were to propose a marriage between a daughter of Manfred and Prince Edmund. Even if the king of England and his court had an interest in acquiring the Sicilian throne, this did not rule out the possibility of closer ties with Conrad and the Staufen.

Henry III certainly took an interest in the affairs of his nephew, and in this context it is worth considering one of the reasons which Matthew Paris gave for Earl Richard's refusal of the Sicilian throne: that it would have deprived Prince Henry of his inheritance.[43] Little is known of Henry, except that he played an important part in the administration of Sicily, and that he died in 1253.[44] Contacts between the English and the Staufen court may have also been concerned with fears for his safety, alluded to by Matthew Paris. For Henry's death soon began to play its part in the propaganda against Conrad. A Genoese source, for instance, alleged that Conrad had strangled his brother after returning to Sicily.[45] This was rejected by Matthew Paris,[46] who in turn attributed those rumours to the pope who was trying to sow discord between the king of England and his Apulian in-laws.[47] He goes on to blame Innocent for the young boy's death: after the Sicilian nobles had heard of Richard being offered their realm, they conspired against the boy.[48] We certainly should not take this at face value: almost any event described from 1254 onwards was used by Matthew Paris to illustrate either the king's incompetence, or the pope's immorality and ruthlessness.[49] None the less, should Henry's or Richard's involvement in the affairs of Sicily have constituted a threat to the young boy, this could explain the English mission from March 1253, as could plans for a negotiated settlement between Innocent and Conrad. As such, it conforms to an established pattern: contacts were used, to some extent refreshed and expanded, but any direct involvement in the conflicts between William of Holland and the Capetians, or between Conrad IV and the papacy, was limited to interceding on behalf of Henry III's relatives. Ultimately, it was his crusade that mattered most to the king of England. The precedence accorded to the affairs of the Holy Land also led to a significant decision in the context of Henry III's relations with Conrad IV:

---

43 Ibid. v. 347.

44 *Regesta imperii*, no. 4616c; *Nicolai de Jamsilla historia de rebus gestis Friderici II imperatoris ejusque filiorum*, ed. L. A. Muratori, Milan 1726, 499; M. Thumser, 'Der König und sein Chronist. Manfred von Sizilien in der Chronik des sogenannten Nikolaus von Jamsilla', in *Die Reichskleinodien: Herrschaftszeichen des Heiligen Römischen Reiches*, Göppingen 1997, 222–42.

45 *Annales ianuenses*, MGH, SS xviii. 230.

46 Matthew Paris, *Chronica maiora*, v. 448.

47 Ibid. v. 460.

48 Ibid. v. 432.

49 Vaughan, *Matthew Paris*, 146–7; K. Schnith, *England in einer sich wandelnden Welt (1189–1259): Studien zu Roger Wendover und Matthäus Paris*, Stuttgart 1974, 152; Weiler, 'Matthew Paris'.

he intended to set sail from Marseilles, not, as his brother and Simon de Montfort had done, from Sicily.[50] Even when Henry III did get drawn into the affairs of Sicily in 1253–4, this was an engagement which had not been actively sought by him, and one which at the time was largely perceived as little more than a stepping-stone towards his planned crusade.

The king's crusade

In March 1250 Henry III took the cross. Although he never went to the Holy Land, diplomatic and financial preparations for his campaign dominated the years up to 1254.[51] Despite the great care taken in planning the campaign, which was to set sail by June 1256,[52] it was criticised by contemporary and later observers alike, and was viewed as the shallow promise of a fickle king who was soon to abandon the liberation of the Holy Land for a preposterous claim to the throne of Sicily.[53] This ignores, however, the extent to which the Sicilian Business initially formed part of the king's crusading venture. Moreover, the surviving evidence leaves little doubt as to the sincerity of Henry's intentions.[54] It was not until the English court realised the extent of the problems facing it in Sicily, that the king requested a commutation of his vow from fighting the Muslims in Palestine to fighting the Staufen in Sicily. Even then, however, this was viewed as leading towards, rather than as being undertaken in place of, a campaign to *Outremer*.

Henry's preparations were thorough and wide-ranging. Great care was taken to put the campaign on a firm financial footing, and to ensure its logistics and infrastructure. Early contacts were made with the prelates of the Holy Land, the kings of Cyprus and Armenia, the prince of Antioch and other Palestine nobles, the Italian communes of Genoa, Pisa and Venice, and the military orders.[55] The king of Cyprus effectively controlled what was left of the Latin kingdom. The king of Armenia, although increasingly pushed into an uncomfortable position between the Mongols and the Mamluks, remained among the few Christian rulers still holding out against the Muslims, while the Italian maritime cities were needed for the shipment of regular supplies and for naval protection,[56] and only the military orders had the infrastructure and military expertise needed to maintain a sustained military effort in the

[50] CPR, 1247–58, 188.
[51] A. Forey, 'The crusading vows of the English King Henry III', Durham University Journal lxv (1973), 229–47; Lloyd, 'King Henry III'.
[52] CR, 1251–3, 201–2, 214.
[53] Matthew Paris, Chronica maiora, v. 101; R.C. Stacey, 'Crusades, crusaders and the baronial gravamina of 1263–4', TCE iii (1989), 137–50. Lloyd, 'Henry III', cites earlier verdicts.
[54] See Lloyd, 'Henry III', 110–22, on which much of the following is based.
[55] CPR, 1247–58, 158.
[56] Foedera, i. 285.

Holy Land.[57] We should also note that Henry III's announcement of his plans roughly coincided with a meeting of the Dominican general chapter in London.[58] By the mid-thirteenth century, the friars had become an integral element in the recruitment and organisation of crusades.[59] More important even, the king's announcement occurred at a time when both Louis IX and his regents in France were eager to recruit additional crusaders. Henry III now saw an opportunity to rival Louis in his concern for the Holy Land, as well as the political gains he hoped to draw from it. As with Frederick II in 1229, a successful recovery of Jerusalem would have gained Henry the prestige and political clout to press more successfully for the restitution of his inheritance. In Henry's eyes, the road to Rouen led through Jerusalem.

Henry's efforts were not, however, confined to the provisioning of ships and the recruitment of men. Guaranteeing the infrastructure of a campaign was only one of the tasks facing a royal crusader. Of equal importance was the need to safeguard the integrity of his realm during the king's absence. In Henry's case this meant that a solution had to be found for his conflict with the Capetians. Not only would he need their support to leave from Marseilles, but he also had to make sure that neither the king of France nor his brothers would capitalise on Henry's absence and interfere in Gascony. Consequently, within a week of taking the cross, the English court sent envoys to France to arrange a truce 'for sixteen years or a longer duration'.[60] The proposed length of the truce is worth noting: in the past, truces had run for up to five years, which was just long enough to prepare for another military campaign. Sixteen years, by contrast, was a period which, for the foreseeable future, ruled out a military recovery of Henry's inheritance. In line with the papal initiatives that we have encountered during the 1220s and 1230s, this initiative was not aimed at ending Henry's conflict with the Capetians, but at providing the lull in hostilities necessary for a successful recovery of the Holy Land. Henry III had not abandoned hope of controlling Poitou and Normandy again one day, but this had become a project closely intertwined with, but none the less subject to, his planned campaign in *Outremer*.

Settling his affairs with the Capetians proved a complex undertaking.[61] A deep-seated distrust continued to vex relations, with Gascony the focus. In 1252 and 1253, for instance, Henry complained to Queen Blanche and Alfons of Poitiers that the French crown was supporting rebels in Gascony.[62] Matters were further complicated by Henry's efforts to use his crusade to regain the Plantagenets' lands in France. In fact, when asked by Louis IX to

57 CPR, 1247–58, 158.
58 *Acta capitulorum generalium ordinis praedicatorum*, I: *Ab anno 1220 usque ad annum 1303*, ed. B. M. Reichert, Rome 1898, 48–55.
59 C. T. Maier, *Preaching the crusades: mendicant friars and the cross in the thirteenth century*, Cambridge 1994, 62–79, 111–34.
60 *Royal letters Henry III*, ii, no. 463.
61 CPR, 1247–58, 307.
62 CR, 1251–3, 187–8, 442.

hasten his departure, the king responded that he would do so, once Louis had restored Henry's rights in France.[63] The English court saw the necessity of arranging peace with Louis IX, but this did not mean that the opportunity to settle Henry's claims was easily abandoned. Still, Henry turned down several opportunities for an alliance against Louis IX, and he went to great lengths to accommodate not only Louis, but also the king's brothers. In November 1253, for example, over £7,000 were paid to the count of Toulouse's men who had been wronged by some of Henry's Gascon subjects,[64] and in May 1254 hectic diplomatic efforts were undertaken to find a peaceful solution to recent infringements of the truce.[65] At the same time, Louis IX was not the only ruler with whom peaceful relations had to be established. The king of Navarre, for instance, agreed to a truce concerning Gascony,[66] which proved of considerable benefit when he was later called upon to provide troops for Henry's Gascon campaign.[67] In Britain, the king of England put relations with Scotland onto a firmer footing, when, in 1251, Alexander III of Scotland married Henry's daughter Margaret, and when Henry effectively assumed the role of guardian to the Scottish king,[68] while strong efforts continued to strengthen English rule in Ireland.[69]

The king also strengthened his links with those whose support was to be enlisted for his campaign, and with those who tried to enlist Henry's for theirs. In 1251, for instance, King Ferdinand of Castile sent envoys to England, to convince Henry to fight in Iberia rather than Palestine.[70] Ferdinand had recently captured Seville and was now trying to establish his control over a territory he lacked the manpower and funds to defend effectively.[71] In 1253–4, during negotiations with Ferdinand's successor Alfonso X, a Castilian-led campaign in North Africa was mooted again. The crusade may also hold the key to understanding increasing contacts with Norway.[72] Although there is

---

[63] CPR, 1247–58, 157, 158; Matthew Paris, Chronica maiora, v. 280–1.

[64] CPR, 1247–58, 244, 251.

[65] Ibid. 292.

[66] Ibid. 123.

[67] CR, 1253–4, 288.

[68] Matthew Paris, Chronica maiora, v. 266–7. For the wider background see K. Staniland, 'The nuptials of Alexander III of Scotland and Margaret Plantagenet', Nottingham Medieval Studies xxx (1986), 20–45. See also Chronica de Mailros, 180, and Brown, 'Henry the Peaceable', 48–57.

[69] These were connected primarily to Prince Edward's inheritance on coming of age: Prestwich, Edward I, 10–14; Frame, 'Henry III and Ireland'.

[70] Matthew Paris, Chronica maiora, v. 231–2. The bishop of Morocco, a prominent member of the Castilian court, is attested as being in England in March 1251: CLR, 1245–51, 339. He eventually left by early July: ibid. 363, 364. He was again in England in late 1252: CLR, 1251–60, 79. In 1254 he was one of Alfonso's envoys in ratifying the Treaty of Burgos: Diplomatic documents, no. 270.

[71] B. F. Reilly, The medieval Spains, Cambridge 1993, 138–9.

[72] In 1252 the king's falconer was sent to Norway: CPR, 1247–58, 157. This was complemented by the gift of a new crown: CR, 1251–3, 151, 265. In 1253 the king of the Isle of Man received permission from Henry to travel to Norway: CR, 1251–3, 338.

no conclusive evidence that these were directly connected, it is worth noting that exchanges increased in frequency at about the time when King Haakon and Alfonso agreed on a joint expedition to North Africa.[73] Besides plans for the king's own campaign, other crusaders were received and supported by Henry's court, as, for instance, the Frisian crusaders stranded at Winchelsea in 1254.[74] English diplomacy in preparation for the king's departure thus conformed to a pattern in evidence across the Latin west. It aimed to ensure the territorial integrity of the realm, to secure the expertise required for a successful campaign, and to avoid the shortcomings in infrastructure and logistics which had beset expeditions in the past.

As so often, however, outside forces interfered with Henry's carefully hatched plans, most significantly in Gascony, where an increasingly suspicious aristocracy continued to resist attempts at establishing effective royal control.[75] The events in the province are also useful in highlighting the degree to which the affairs of the Mediterranean influenced and conditioned English royal policy. In 1253 Simon de Montfort's replacement as governor coincided with a rebellion under the leadership of Gaston de Bearn.[76] When looking for support, the rebels found a favourable reception with the new king of Castile, Alfonso X, who viewed this as a welcome opportunity to state his claims to Gascony.[77] Warned that the province would be lost unless he hurried to France, Henry left for Gascony by early August 1253.[78] After initial successes, Henry's progress stalled at La Reole in November.[79] Simultaneously, negotiations began with Alfonso.[80] From then on, the chronology becomes confusing. It was not until February the following year, that Henry made his negotiations public in England.[81] Even then, he still requested troops.[82] It has been suggested that this may have been an attempt to solicit funds from a baronage which had proved reluctant to grant the king the financial aid he needed.[83] The threat of a foreign invasion may have been a

[73] B. Gelsinger, 'A thirteenth-century Castilian–Norwegian alliance', *Medievalia et Humanistica* n.s. x (1981), 55–80; M. Kaufhold, 'Norwegen, das Papsttum und Europa im 13. Jahrhundert: Mechanismen der Integration', *HZ* cclxv (1997), 309–42; J. F. O'Callaghan, *The learned king: the reign of Alfonso X of Castile*, Philadelphia 1993, 163–80; Rodríguez García, 'Henry III'.
[74] *CR, 1253–4*, 130.
[75] R. Studd, 'Reconfiguring the Angevin empire, 1224–1259', in Weiler and Rowlands, *England and Europe*, 31–41; Maddicott, *Simon de Montfort*, 106–24; Powicke, *Henry III*, 208–58; F. B. Marsh, *English rule in Gascony, 1199–1259: with special reference to the towns*, Ann Arbor 1912, 111–51.
[76] Matthew Paris, *Chronica maiora*, v. 368.
[77] Ibid. v. 365–6. This had already caused difficulties during Henry III's minority: Eales, 'The political context', passim, and Carpenter, *Minority of Henry III*, 200–3
[78] Matthew Paris, *Chronica maiora*, v. 378–9, 381, 383.
[79] *Annals of Waverley*, AM ii. 346; *Annals of Tewkesbury*, AM i. 154.
[80] Matthew Paris, *Chronica maiora*, v. 396–400; Baylen, 'John Maunsell'.
[81] Matthew Paris, *Chronica maiora*, lib. add.: chronica maiora, vi. 284–6.
[82] *CR, 1253–4*, 115–16.
[83] Powicke, *Henry III*, 235.

welcome opportunity to press for stronger financial support, and could explain why these negotiations had been kept secret. However, although Henry painted a vivid picture of the threat posed by the Christian and Muslim forces which Alfonso was mustering, and which were said to threaten England as well as Gascony,[84] in January 1254 a parliament refused to accept the king's demands.[85] Even the offer made by Richard of Cornwall, the king's regent, that Magna Carta was to be re-confirmed, had little effect.[86] The fact that, at the time, Henry had accumulated a treasure of 28,000 marks sheds doubts on his claims of penury.[87] That most of the king's treasure had probably been intended for the planned crusade would have carried little weight. The episode was symptomatic of the opposition which Henry encountered in England, and which focused not so much on his undertakings abroad, as on his handling of baronial demands at home.

In the end, no troops were needed, as a peace agreement was reached by March 1254.[88] Alfonso surrendered his claims to Gascony, and ceased to support Gaston and his fellow-rebels.[89] In exchange, Henry III's eldest son, Edward, was to marry the king of Castile's sister,[90] while, in a move reminiscent of Frederick II's release of King Waldemar of Denmark in 1224, the king of England promised to support Alfonso's planned crusade in North Africa.[91] Next to a more friendly standing with Louis IX, this extension of Henry's contacts into the Mediterranean was to be the most important feature of his diplomacy during these years. It is, furthermore, within this wider context of the king's expanding range of contacts in the European south that we ought to consider a project embarked upon during Henry's sojourn in Gascony: the Sicilian Business, or *negotium Sicilie*. Contacted by the pope, he accepted the throne of Sicily on behalf of Prince Edmund.[92] It would be mistaken, though, to view this as putting an end to his crusading plans. No doubt was left about the king's priorities. For instance, immediately after Henry had accepted the Sicilian throne, renewed efforts were made towards the completion of Westminster Abbey before the king 'takes his journey to the Holy Land'.[93] Simultaneously, preparations for the king's campaign in Palestine were hastened and further funds and aids requested from the papal court.[94] Initially, the Sicilian Business was thus little more than a subplot to the planned conquest of Jerusalem, and it was a natural extension of the king's interests in the Mediterranean.

84 *CR, 1253–4*, 109; *CPR, 1247–58*, 362.
85 Matthew Paris, *Chronica maiora*, v. 423–5, 440–1, 447.
86 *Royal letters Henry III*, ii, no. 499.
87 D. A. Carpenter, 'The gold treasure of Henry III', *TCE* i (1983), 61–88 at p. 65.
88 *CPR, 1247–58*, 279–80, 281.
89 *Diplomatic documents*, nos 270, 273.
90 *CPR, 1247–58*, 312, 351.
91 *CR, 1253–4*, 316.
92 *Foedera*, i. 301.
93 *CPR, 1247–58*, 279–80, 281.
94 See also Lloyd, 'Henry III', 112–13.

The outcome of the Gascon campaign was significant in other respects, too. Edward's marriage formed part of a wider picture. Ensuring the continuation of one's dynastic line was a traditional feature of preparing for a crusade. This had been the case with Henry (VII) in 1225, and it was now the case with Edward. Overtures were made by the king of Aragon and the duke of Brabant as well as by Alfonso of Castile. In the end it was the threat posed to Gascony which ensured the success of the Castilian proposal. However, this does not mean that the other proposals had been doomed from the start, nor were political troubles the only difficulties besetting Jaime of Aragon or Henry of Brabant. In October 1251, for instance, Henry III claimed that any delay in negotiations concerning the Aragonese proposal were not his fault, as he had already written to the king, explaining how much money he expected to receive.[95] Considering the habitual penury of the Catalan kingdom in the thirteenth century, the king of Aragon's inability to pay Henry III the sums he demanded might have been as important a factor in determining the ultimate failure of these marriage plans, as Alfonso's interference in Gascony.[96] Also in 1251, the duke of Brabant was asked to wait until Easter 1252 before his marriage proposals could be dealt with. Once more, financial matters were said to pose the biggest problem.[97] Henry's reasons reflect those which, two decades earlier, had driven Frederick II's courtship of Isabella: a need for financial as well as military support. All this also indicates how Henry's priorities had changed. The notorious rivalry between the kings of Aragon and Castile posed the danger of drawing the king of England into yet another conflict.[98] A Brabantine marriage, too, would have pushed Henry into siding with those whose company he had recently sought to avoid: the Avesnes brothers and those on the lookout for support against the countess of Flanders and her Capetian allies.

In many ways the king's response to the proposals from Aragon and Brabant resembled Frederick II's attitude towards Henry III. In preparing for a crusade rights had to be restored, dynastic continuity and the territorial integrity of one's lands had to be ensured. Quite often, this resulted in attempts if not to settle conflicts, at least to find a temporary solution to those issues which would pose a risk to the planned expedition. This principle had underpinned Frederick II's dealings with the king of Denmark in 1224 and with the Lombards in 1227, and it remained a dominant element in Henry III's relations with the rulers of Wales, Scotland, France, Germany, Sicily, Castile and Aragon. In addition, however, this settling of conflicts could be

---

95 CR, 1247–51, 566–7.
96 J. N. Hillgarth, The problem of the Catalan Mediterranean empire, 1229–1337, London 1975, 5. None the less, in May 1253 a marriage between Henry's daughter Beatrice and Jaime II's eldest son was proposed: Foedera, i. 290.
97 CR, 1247–51, 527.
98 J. N. Hillgarth, The Spanish kingdoms, 1250–1516, I: 1250–1410, precarious balance, Oxford 1976, 249–51.

used to stabilise one's own and one's family's position, it could be employed to expand territories and state, defend or strengthen one's claims. These potential gains, though, could be endangered by either openly opposing or too eagerly allying oneself with one's fellow-rulers. Henry III did not openly oppose Louis IX, but sought to use the crusade for a peaceful settlement of his claims. This also had important consequences for his relations with the government of Germany, or that of Conrad IV in Sicily. Henry III's actions differed little from those of his peers and contemporaries.

7

The Sicilian Business, 1254–1263

After 1245 rulers and princes across Europe sought to profit from the Staufens' predicaments:[1] Ferdinand II attempted to take possession of the duchy of Swabia; Louis IX acquired Provence and established Capetian control over Flanders and Hainault. Initially, at least, Henry III did not aim for territorial aggrandisement (with the exception, perhaps, of his grant to the Savoyards in 1246), but for political support. Within a few years of the emperor's death in 1250, however, Henry was to surpass his contemporaries in the range and speed of acquisition, when he and his family went for the biggest prize of all: Sicily, and, in due course, the Holy Roman Empire itself. To some extent the Sicilian Business was a logical continuation of the king's crusading plans, and indicative of a diplomatic approach increasingly focused on the Mediterranean, but it was also driven by competition with and fear of the Capetians.

After Frederick II's death, papal efforts aimed at replacing the Staufen in Sicily as well as Germany and Jerusalem gained in vigour and urgency. The *regno* was offered unsuccessfully to Richard of Cornwall and Charles of Anjou, before Henry III accepted it on behalf of his youngest son Edmund, ten years old at the time, in 1254.[2] Although neither the king nor his son ever set foot in Apulia, its affairs came to dominate English politics. They also developed a diplomatic momentum of their own, and forced actions on the king and his family which, otherwise, they may well have been reluctant to contemplate. Already existing ties with the Mediterranean were strengthened, and renewed impetus was given to Henry's attempts to secure a permanent settlement with Louis IX. When these negotiations ran into difficulties, alternative routes had to be found. This, in turn, led to renewed contacts with the German princes, culminating in the election of Henry's brother Richard as king of the Romans in 1257. The impact of the Sicilian Business on English affairs was equally momentous: when Henry III was forced to hand over the reins of government to a baronial council in 1258, many of the complaints made on that occasion were linked to or originated in his acceptance of the Sicilian throne. At the same time, as we will see, it would be mistaken to judge the initial undertaking by its eventual failure. The project

---

1   A shorter version of this chapter, and with a different emphasis, appeared as 'Henry III and the Sicilian Business: a re-interpretation', *Historical Research* lxxiv (2001), 127–50.
2   *Annales cestrienses*, ed. R. C. Christie (Record Society for the Publication of Original Documents Relating to Lancashire and Cheshire xiv, 1887), 62.

was very much a continuation and extension of the traditional paths of Plantagenet diplomacy, and it responded to pressures and events which had left Henry III little choice.

Negotiations and promises

The Plantagenets had always been the papacy's favourites to replace the Staufen in Sicily.[3] Matthew Paris refers to overtures being made as early as 1250, in the context of Richard of Cornwall's visit to Lyon,[4] with the earliest documentary evidence surviving from August 1252, when Innocent IV contacted Henry III, offering the *regno* to Earl Richard.[5] Little else is known about subsequent negotiations. By November, a papal notary, Albert of Parma, who was later to deal with Charles of Anjou and Henry, is reported as being in England,[6] and by January 1253 Henry thanked the pope for the offer of Sicily.[7] However, dealings with the earl made little progress,[8] and by June 1253 negotiations began with Charles.[9] In the end, Charles found that other areas in Europe offered easier and more promising rewards: in the autumn of 1253 he accepted the county of Hainault.

In December 1253 Albert received authorisation to submit the conditions for an enfeoffment with Sicily to Henry III.[10] What exactly Innocent IV's terms had been we do not know, but they are unlikely to have been different from those submitted to Charles of Anjou.[11] The pope's demands aimed at guaranteeing the safety of papal lands and the separation of imperial territories from the kingdom of Sicily. For instance, Charles had to promise that, in case he or his successors should beget an heiress, she would never marry an emperor or the son of an emperor, or anyone likely to become emperor. Innocent IV viewed the establishment of a new dynasty in Sicily as an opportunity

---

[3] H. Marc-Bonnet, 'Richard de Cornouailles et la couronne de Sicile', in *Mélanges d'histoire du moyen âge à Louis Halphen*, Paris 1951, 483–9; G. Baaken, *Ius imperii ad regnum: Königreich Sizilien, imperium romanum und Römisches Papsttum vom Tode Kaiser Heinrichs VI. bis zu den Verzichtserklärungen Rudolfs von Habsburg*, Cologne–Weimar–Vienna 1993, 387–95; A. Wachtel, 'Die sizilische Thronkandidatur des Prinzen Edmund von England', *DA* iv (1940), 98–178 at pp. 98–106; Rodenberg, *Innozenz IV*, 27–30.

[4] Matthew Paris, *Chronica maiora*, v. 347.

[5] *Foedera*, i. 284.

[6] Matthew Paris, *Chronica maiora*, v. 346.

[7] *CR, 1251–3*, 449.

[8] Matthew Paris, *Chronica maiora*, v. 457.

[9] It should be noted, however, that the *Annales breves wormatienses*, MGH, SS xvii. 76, put the first offer of the Sicilian crown, to Charles of Anjou, in 1248: Wachtel, 'Die sizilische Thronkandidatur', 100–3; *Registres Innocent IV*, nos 6806, 6818; H. Marc-Bonnet, 'Le Saint-Siège et Charles d'Anjou sous Innocent IV et Alexandre IV', *Revue historique* cc (1948), 38–65 at pp. 49–62; Dunbabin, *Charles I of Anjou*, 4–5; Herde, *Karl I*, 34–48.

[10] *Epistolae saeculi XIII*, iii, no. 446.

[11] *Registres Innocent IV*, no. 6819; Baaken, *Ius imperii*, 392–5.

to end the stranglehold into which the union of Sicily and the empire had brought the papal state. In addition, the count of Anjou was requested to pay 1,000 ounces of gold on accepting the kingdom, 10,000 towards the rebuilding of Benevento, a papal enclave in Apulia, an annual tribute of 2,000 ounces and to provide 50 knights in the service of the papacy. These terms aimed at underlining the status of the Sicilian kings as vassals of the Holy See. All in all, papal demands were neither unreasonable nor excessive. What mattered most to Innocent IV at this point was to rid himself of his Staufen foes, and to ensure that the problems be resolved which had beset relations between the rulers of Sicily and the *curia* in the past.

Henry and his court saw little difficulty in agreeing to these terms, and by early March 1254 Albert confirmed Edmund as king of Sicily.[12] It seems, though, as if Henry III had underestimated the speed with which Innocent IV expected him to act. Already in May, when confirming Edmund's enfeoffment, he urged the king to hasten his son's departure.[13] To enable him to do so, the pope promised to contribute 100,000 *livres tournouis* towards Henry's expenses, while also granting an extension of the period during which a tenth for the planned crusade could be collected, as well as a commutation of the king's vow from freeing Jerusalem to conquering Apulia.[14] Innocent, thus, gave all the assistance he could. Henry, however, found himself beset by problems. His attempts at soliciting funds from his English subjects had failed, Gascony had not yet been pacified[15] and he had to see through his son Edward's Castilian marriage.[16] More important, relations with the Capetians had yet to be settled.[17] Despite these difficulties, which made an early departure unlikely, preparations to take possession of the *regno* began, including, for instance, Thomas of Savoy's appointment as prince of Capua.[18] Furthermore, in October 1254 the archbishop of Embrun and the bishop of Hereford were announced as royal envoys to the citizens of Sicily.[19] If Henry saw himself unable to go to Sicily soon or in person, he at least took steps to assert his and his son's authority. Innocent himself, now resident at Naples, also recruited important allies. Most prominent among these were Margrave Berthold of Hohenburg,[20] who had been Manfred's guardian and who had been appointed regent of Sicily by Conrad IV,[21] and Frederick of Antioch.

---

12 *Foedera*, i. 297.
13 Ibid. i. 301, 302.
14 Ibid. i. 301, 303, 304.
15 CPR, *1247–58*, 364.
16 Ibid. 312.
17 Ibid. 311.
18 *Foedera*, i. 308.
19 CPR, *1247–58*, 344.
20 *Foedera*, i. 311.
21 M. Döberl, 'Berthold von Hohenburg', *Deutsche Zeitschrift für Geschichtswissenschaft* xii (1892), 201–78. For Berthold's literary output see F. Neumann, 'Der Markgraf von Hohenburg', *Zeitschrift für deutsches Altertum und deutsche Literatur* lxxxvi (1955–6), 119–60.

The support of Frederick, one of the late emperor's illegitimate sons, and vicar-general of Tuscany and *podestà* of Florence during his father's lifetime,[22] points to the divisions among the Staufen, which the *curia* soon aimed to exploit more fully. It certainly did no harm to the prospects of King Edmund: if even Frederick's own family was willing to support his claim, little reason remained for those loyal to the Staufen to oppose him. Other recruits included men like Richard Filangieri, the nephew of Frederick's governor in Palestine,[23] Richard de Montenero, formerly grand justiciar of Sicily, Peter Ruffus, marshal and governor of Calabria,[24] James de Vulturo, *protoiudicatus* of the principality of Salerno and the Terra Beneventana,[25] and Bartholomew, the constable of Aversa.[26] Edmund's regime thus had the backing of some of the most high-ranking and experienced members of Conrad's administration.[27] During the early months of the project neither Henry III nor Innocent IV seem to have had any doubt concerning the project's eventual success, despite the progress made by Manfred during the autumn and early winter of 1254.[28] By the time of Innocent's death in November, it must have seemed as if Edmund's arrival in Sicily was only a matter of time.[29]

At this stage, the *negotium Sicilie* was still very much part of Henry's crusading plans.[30] As early as 1253, for instance, when Henry III first acknowledged the offer of Sicily to his brother, he also requested that crusade preaching be extended beyond England.[31] Much as the prospect of ruling Sicily must have pleased him, the affairs of the Holy Land still took priority. Even after Henry's involvement in Apulia, planning for his crusade continued. In fact, the pope's offer of commuting Henry's vow from a crusade in Palestine to one against Manfred was not taken up.[32] Rather, the king

---

[22] *Regesta imperii*, nos 2805, 3528–9, 3540, 3551, 3554, 7837, 8360, 8368, 8573, 13562a; C. Sperle, *König Enzo von Sardinien und Friedrich von Antiochia: zwei illegitime Söhne Kaiser Friedrichs II und ihre Rolle in der Verwaltung des Regnum Italiae*, Frankfurt am Main 2001, 253–326, and at pp. 314–17 for his dealings with Innocent IV.

[23] *Regesta imperii*, no. 4644c. Walter of Ocra, on the other hand, remained among Manfred's partisans: Kamp, *Kirche und Monarchie*, 132.

[24] Rodenberg, *Innocenz IV*, 177 n. 4, 186.

[25] *Regesta imperii*, no. 8828.

[26] Ibid. no. 8833.

[27] Among the more interesting coincidences is the appearance of Iohannes Saracenus, nephew of Henry III's erstwhile proctor, as archbishop of Bari from 1259: Kamp, *Kirche und Monarchie*, 596–601.

[28] *Regesta imperii*, nos 4644a–p, 4645.

[29] Note, however, Innocent's warning from November 1254 that, unless the king move speedily, a certain unspecified, but urgent, business would have to be dealt with by someone else: *Foedera*, i. 312. The question remains, though, to what degree this was an attempt to hasten Henry's departure.

[30] Lloyd, 'Henry III', 110–19.

[31] *CR, 1251–3*, 448, 449.

[32] *Foedera*, i. 304. For the context see N. Housley, *The Italian crusades: the papal–Angevin alliance and the crusades against Christian lay powers, 1254–1343*, Oxford 1982, 222–31.

asked to be allowed to campaign with Alfonso in North Africa instead.[33] The planned campaign against the Muslims and the imminent conquest of Sicily existed side by side, and were viewed as mutually complementary. This, in turn, reflected the historical significance of Sicily for the affairs of *Outremer*, as Pope Alexander IV was to point out to Henry III in 1255: the kingdom of Apulia would be an ideal base from which to set out for a conquest of the Holy Land.[34] During the twelfth and thirteenth centuries, most crusades that avoided taking the land route to Palestine had proceeded *via* either Marseilles or Sicily,[35] a tradition which continued well into the fourteenth century: the planned crusade in 1305 against Constantinople, for instance, embarked from Sicily, and during the Council of Vienne the king of Aragon viewed Sicily as the starting point for the final leg of a campaign which was to lead from Granada to the Holy Land.[36] Similarly, later in the thirteenth century, Charles of Anjou was to use the *regno*'s geographical position and naval expertise not only to further his ambitions in Greece, but also to press his claims to the crown of Jerusalem.[37] In short, Henry III was part of a long tradition of rulers to whom Sicily represented an integral element in the overall affairs of Christian *Outremer*.

Equally, Henry III was not the first English king who sought to influence the succession to the Sicilian throne. In 1190, during his crusade, Richard the Lionheart had sought to utilise the political turmoil after William II's death, seized Messina and eventually threw in his lot with those opposing the claims of Frederick II's mother, Constance, to the Sicilian throne.[38] Partly as a result of Richard's involvement, partly due to a variety of dynastic and family links, the affairs of Sicily continued to engage the minds and imagination of Henry III's contemporaries.[39] The *negotium Sicilie* was a logical extension of already existing ties with the Mediterranean. Moreover, the English court must have been aware of papal negotiations with Charles of Anjou.

---

33 *Foedera*, i. 308; R. L. Wolff, 'Mortgage and redemption of an emperor's son: Castile and the Latin empire of Constantinople', *Speculum* xxix (1954), 45–84; Rodríguez García, 'Henry III'.

34 *Les Registres d'Alexandre IV*, ed. C. B. de la Roncière and others, Paris 1895–1959, iv, no. 1543.

35 For the twelfth century see H. Wieruszowski, 'The Norman kingdom of Sicily and the crusades', in her *Politics and culture in medieval Spain and Italy*, Rome 1971, 1–50.

36 S. Schein, *Fideles cruces: the papacy, the west, and the recovery of the Holy Land, 1274–1314*, Oxford 1991, 180, 250.

37 Dunbabin, *Charles I of Anjou*, 225–8; L. Boehm, '*De Karlingis Imperator Karolus, princeps et monarcha totius Europae*: zur Orientpolitik Karls I. Von Anjou', *Historisches Jahrbuch der Görres-Gesellschaft* lxxxviii (1968), 1–35.

38 Gillingham, *Richard I*, 131–7.

39 For a good overview see G. A. Loud, 'Il regno normanno-svevo visto dal regno d'Inghilterra', in G. Musca (ed.), *Il mezzogiorno normanno-svevo visto dall'Europa e dal mondo mediterraneo: atti delle tredicesime giornate normanno-sveve, Bari, 21–24 ottobre 1997*, Bari 1999, 175–95: an English version of this article has been published as 'The kingdom of Sicily and the kingdom of England, 1066–1266', *History* lxxxviii (2003), 540–67.

Although, as we will see, strenuous efforts had been made to settle relations with the Capetians, they met with repeated setbacks. Even the meeting between Louis IX and Henry III in 1254, in the aftermath of the Gascon campaign, was unable to resolve tensions over the Plantagenets' claims to Poitou and Normandy. Preventing an expansion of Capetian power may, thus, have been among the reasons for Henry III's acceptance of Innocent's offer.

Difficulties only ensued with Innocent's death. His successor, Alexander IV, at first strove to resolve the conflict with Manfred peacefully.[40] In fact, the new pope was initially even prepared to accept the Staufens' claims in Sicily, and in January 1255 invited Conrad IV's widow to enter into negotiations on this matter.[41] Talks continued until March 1255, but when these faltered,[42] renewed efforts were made to hasten Henry III's departure for Italy. In March Alexander refused the king's request to commute his vow from crusading in Palestine to a campaign in North Africa, but later offered to commute the vow towards a campaign in Sicily instead.[43] Also, he confirmed Edmund's enfeoffment with Sicily, but insisted on a new set of conditions.[44] Most of these aimed to define more strictly the demands made by Innocent.[45] For instance, Edmund was banned from ever standing for election as emperor. Obligations towards the papacy were extended, and the military service owed to the *curia* was increased from 50 to 300 knights. These new terms probably reflected the need for a stronger military showing: during the early 1250s the papacy had repeatedly faced rebellions in its domains. Most important, either Henry III himself or a suitably provisioned proctor would have to be in Sicily by October 1256. In the meantime, the pope alone could decide upon the granting of lands and privileges in the *regno*. By making Edmund's exercise of regal rights dependent upon his arrival in Sicily, the pope may have hoped that this would provide the necessary incentive for the English court to speed up its preparations. This reflected the military situation in the *regno*, where both Manfred and papal forces had secured victories since the breakdown of negotiations.[46] Furthermore, Innocent's promise to pay 100,000 *livres tournois* was withdrawn. Instead, Henry had to pay the expenses incurred by the papacy, set at about £90,000. This latter point has been viewed as revealing the preposterous nature of the whole project.[47] However, this fails

[40] F. Tenckhoff, *Papst Alexander IV*, Paderborn 1907, 24–75; E. Jordan, *Les Origines de la domination angevine en Italie*, Paris 1909, 94–173.
[41] *Monumenta wittelsbacensia: Urkundenbuch zur Geschichte des Hauses Wittelsbach: erste Abteilung von 1204 bis 1292*, ed. F. M. Wittmann, Munich 1857, no. 57.
[42] *Epistolae saeculi XIII*, iii, nos 380, 382, *Foedera*, i. 315; *Regesta imperii*, no. 8966.
[43] *Foedera*, i. 316, 319.
[44] Ibid. 316–18.
[45] Baaken, *Ius imperii*, 397–8.
[46] A. Karst, *Geschichte Manfreds vom Tode Friedrichs II bis zu seiner Krönung, 1250–1258*, Berlin 1897, 75–83.
[47] Tenckhoff, *Alexander IV*, 39; Wachtel, 'Die sizilische Thronkandidatur', 113–14.

to take into account the specific circumstances under which Henry III and Alexander IV acted. These conditions aimed not at emasculating the king of England financially, but at forcing him to attend to the affairs of Sicily, and to do so soon. In the meantime, the necessary finances had to be secured to maintain the loyalty of those recently won over, and to continue military efforts at overthrowing Manfred's regime. The pope's demands had been born out of necessity, not avarice.

Within a few months of negotiations with the *curia* collapsing, Manfred achieved a number of victories: by spring 1255 he had won control over most of Sicily, and begun his siege of Brindisi;[48] in April a papal army under the leadership of Ottaviano Ubaldini was disastrously beaten.[49] Alexander IV found himself in a situation in which he required military help, and quickly. He could not accept Henry's continuing prevarications. Furthermore, although he made stringent demands on the king's purse, he also lent Henry III whatever assistance he could. Not only did he permit the king of England to commute his vow towards a campaign against Manfred, he also gave permission for the crusading funds already collected to be used for Sicily instead. In addition, the papal grant of a twentieth from the Scottish Church was extended by another three years.[50] Moreover, other crusaders, such as the king of Norway, were requested to commute their vows from fighting in the Holy Land to conquering Sicily.[51] Henry, in short, could count on the *curia*'s economic and diplomatic backing. The demands made of Henry III were many, but the sums requested were not impossible to muster. Sicily was renowned for its riches. Although not too much credence should be given to the sums listed, Matthew Paris's version of Frederick's testament is none the less impressive. In all, the amounts promised to various beneficiaries amounted to 120,000 ounces of gold.[52] Nor should English resources be underestimated. The funds needed were roughly equivalent to the ransom for Richard Lionheart in the 1190s,[53] and could have been collected had it been possible to apply similar means of extra taxation. Even so, by 1259 nearly half of the money required had been paid.[54] Had the reluctance of Henry's English subjects to pay for the king's plans been overcome, and in combination with Edmund's anticipated Sicilian revenues, 135,000 marks seem a less fantastic sum. In their contemporary context Alexander's conditions were harsh but

---

48 *Regesta imperii*, nos 4650d, e.
49 A. Hauss, *Kardinal Oktavian Ubaldini: ein Staatsmann des 13. Jahrhunderts*, Heidelberg 1913, 53–82, 57–61; Karst, *Geschichte Manfreds*, 111–26; Matthew Paris, *Chronica maiora*, v. 497–500.
50 *Foedera*, i. 322.
51 Ibid. i. 319, 320.
52 Matthew Paris, *Chronica maiora*, v. 216.
53 H. Fichtenau, 'Akkon, Zypern und das Lösegeld für Richard Löwenherz', *Archiv für Österreichische Geschichte* cxxv (1966), 11–32; Gillingham *Richard I*, 232–8.
54 Lunt, *Financial relations*, 290.

reasonable; they were designed to solve the most urgent problems facing papal forces in Sicily, and to induce Henry III to keep his promises.

It seemed as if the *curia's* demands had the desired effect. In October 1255 the bishop of Bologna arrived and officially confirmed Edmund as king of Sicily.[55] This coincided with preparations for military action. A visit by Arnold, count of Guines, may point in that direction.[56] This certainly was the case with Henry of Castile, Alfonso X's estranged younger brother, who arrived in England to lead a campaign to Sicily.[57] Henry had considerable military experience, having acted as mercenary leader in North Africa, and he was to play a significant part in the campaigns of both Charles of Anjou and Conradin during the 1260s.[58] In addition, diplomatic contacts were made, including negotiations with the king of France for an English army to pass through his domains.[59] Also contacted were members of leading families in Rome, such as Matthew Annibaldi, the pro-consul of Rome,[60] and potential allies in Lombardy, such as Milan.[61] The Annibaldi were among the leading Guelf forces in Rome, and Milan had been a traditional ally of the *curia*, while also possessing the financial and military resources needed against an increasingly powerful Manfred. Henry III and his court thus worked hard to broaden their basis of support. At the same time, new difficulties arose. The citizens of Asti, with the backing of Charles of Anjou, captured Thomas of Savoy, recently enthroned as prince of Capua, and one of the main pillars of Plantagenet diplomacy in Italy.[62] Thus, Henry found himself deprived of one of his most able and experienced agents. This, and the French court's reluctance to see an English army pass through Capetian lands, caused yet another delay.

To make matters worse, Alexander IV lost patience: he repeatedly complained of the king's slackness, and blamed Henry for the many disasters besetting Christendom in Italy.[63] This was more than mere rhetoric. Since the breakdown of negotiations in April 1255 Manfred had steadily expanded his authority towards central Italy,[64] and by June he effectively controlled the

---

[55] *Annals of Burton*, AM, i. 348–9.

[56] *Foedera*, i. 332.

[57] Matthew Paris, *Chronica maiora*, v. 575–6; CR, 1254–6, 368; CPR, 1247–58, 567.

[58] Rodríguez García, 'Henry III', n. 64; J. P. Trabut-Cussac, 'Don Enrique de Castilla en Angleterre (1256–1259)', *Mélanges de la Casa de Velázquez* ii (1966), 51–8.

[59] Matthew Paris, *Chronica maiora*, v. 515–16.

[60] CPR, 1247–58, 414, 453; M. Thumser, *Rom und der römische Adel in der späten Stauferzeit*, Tübingen 1995, 28–42, and 'Adel und Popolo in Rom um die Mitte des 13. Jahrhunderts', in W. Hartmann (ed.), *Europas Städte zwischen Zwang und Freiheit: die europäische Stadt um die Mitte des 13. Jahrhunderts*, Regensburg 1995, 257–71.

[61] CLR, 1251–60, 321.

[62] Matthew Paris, *Chronica maiora*, v. 564–5; *Diplomatic documents*, no. 281; Cox, *Eagles of Savoy*, 250–64; Dunbabin, *Charles I of Anjou*, 77–9.

[63] *Foedera*, i. 342.

[64] D. Waley, *The papal states in the thirteenth century*, London 1961, 149–62.

Terra di Lavorio, immediately to the south-west of the papal state.[65] Moreover, Conradin confirmed Manfred as his captain and governor of Sicily, thus thwarting papal attempts at splitting the Staufen camp.[66] In addition, several towns within the papal state rebelled against the *curia*. In Rome itself, Brancaleone, a staunch supporter of Frederick II and his sons and recently reinstated as senator, allied himself with Manfred.[67] Alexander IV thus found himself in a situation in which he required military and financial assistance, and naturally looked to England. By September additional grants had been made to alleviate the king's financial difficulties,[68] and the bishop of Worcester was ordered to ensure that Henry III declare a definite date for his arrival in Sicily.[69] The pope needed help, and he needed it soon.

Henry III, however, found himself unable to comply. The barons and clergy had rejected his petitions for funds, and the king was forced to ask for less stringent terms, as he explained to Alexander in 1256: 'For we do not believe that there is any prince ruling anywhere today who could have so much money at hand so suddenly.'[70] Henry therefore asked for better conditions. Some of these were granted in October 1256.[71] It would be mistaken to view Henry's complaints about his financial hardship as the beginning of the end of his Sicilian ambitions. Alexander IV was in a desperate situation, and the English court may have tried to use this to alleviate some of the pressures to which it found itself exposed. The king's complaints may thus have been less a sign of royal frustration, than of bargaining.[72]

This is certainly the impression given by the course of events in 1257. Far from sending an expedition to the Mediterranean, as promised the year before, Henry continued to play for time. In January he wrote to the cardinal of St Maria in Via Lata: due to the opposition he had encountered at a recent parliament, he could not currently pursue the affairs of Apulia. He also blamed his difficulties on the harshness of the conditions to which he had been forced to agree.[73] By April Master Rustand was ordered not to collect any more funds for the Sicilian Business, 'as the king is not sure whether the business of Sicily ought to proceed or not'.[74] In June a group of proctors including Simon de Montfort, Peter of Savoy and John Maunsell were sent to the *curia*,[75] taking with them detailed instructions. They were to ask either for a papal legate to arrange the desired peace with Louis IX, to make a

---

65 *Regesta imperii*, no. 4655e.
66 Ibid. no. 4772
67 Matthew Paris, *Chronica maiora*, v. 662, 699; Waley, *Papal states*, 157, 160.
68 *Foedera*, i. 345.
69 Ibid. i. 347.
70 CR, 1254–6, 404–6.
71 *Epistolae saeculi XIII*, iii, no. 445.
72 CR, 1254–6, 404–6.
73 *Diplomatic documents*, no. 287.
74 CPR, 1247–58, 566.
75 Ibid. 565.

composition with the Church, to ask for an amelioration of conditions, to renounce the said realm or to continue as before.[76] At the same time, Henry declared his willingness to pursue the conquest of Sicily, once a peace with the Capetians had been secured. If Henry III did consider reneging on his promises, he was insincere. While indicating to Alexander that it was possible for him simply to give up on Apulia, he continued contacts with Italy. A letter from Philip of Ravenna, for instance, a papal legate in Italy, implies that negotiations had been conducted with Venice.[77] Furthermore, the king repeatedly promised to send a captain to Sicily and to do so soon.[78] Finally, when announcing Richard's election as king of the Romans to the *curia*, Henry expressed his hopes that the earl would deal with the affair of Sicily in person, probably, we may assume, while he was in Rome to be crowned emperor.[79] The impression thus emerges that Henry III was still planning to conquer his son's realm, but that he saw both an opportunity and a need to mitigate the conditions under which the kingdom had been offered. Alexander IV, however, remained reluctant to comply, and insisted on the fulfilment of the terms agreed in 1255. His situation was made more difficult too, when, in May 1257, Manfred captured Brindisi, one of the last papal outposts in Apulia.[80] More than ever before, drastic and decisive action was needed.

This was to become a recurrent pattern. In early 1258 Herlot, a papal notary, was sent to England.[81] He was authorised to excommunicate the king and his barons, should they not settle their outstanding debts to the Holy See.[82] Henry was successful in his attempts to fight off the worst effects of Herlot's mission, and received an extension for his departure until the autumn.[83] In the meantime, the English court left little doubt about its intentions. The citizens of Teano were assured that the king would soon set sail, as was John of Ebulo, while matters concerning the Muslim colony at Lucera were discussed with Count Thomas of Acerra.[84] Even the Provisions of Oxford, which in the past have so often been described as sounding the death knell for Edmund's Sicilian career,[85] had little immediate impact. Writing to Alexander IV, Henry declared that his barons had agreed to support him in Sicily, once the state of the realm had been reformed. He also used the oppor-

---

[76] Ibid. 567.
[77] *Diplomatic documents*, no. 289.
[78] *CPR, 1247–58*, 592.
[79] *Diplomatic documents*, no. 287.
[80] *Epistolae saeculi XIII*, iii, no. 469.
[81] *Annals of Burton*, AM i. 409.
[82] *Annals of Dunstable*, AM iii. 208. This was a common means of securing financial transactions involving prelates: Werner, 'Prälatenschulden'.
[83] *CR, 1256–9*, 320, 321–2.
[84] *Annals of Burton*, AM i. 398–401.
[85] Treharne, *Baronial plan of reform*, 50. See p. 161 below

tunity to request a further mitigation of terms.[86] It was not until 1261 that Henry blamed the barons for his inability to make true his promises, when he complained that they had broken their pledge to assist him in pursuing the affairs of Sicily and Apulia.[87] Initially, though, there was little reason to suspect baronial sabotage of the king's Mediterranean ambitions. In fact, although Alexander IV initially declared that he was to absolve Henry III from all his promises concerning Sicily,[88] dealings continued as usual.[89] The conclusion of the Treaty of Paris in 1259 was announced as an important step towards an invasion of Sicily,[90] knights from Apulia were received[91] and negotiations continued with the papal court.[92] Various prelates and nobles in the kingdom were contacted,[93] and even in 1262 funds were still being handed out to loyal supporters,[94] while Edmund restated his claim to Urban IV.[95] By that point, however, negotiations with Manfred had broken down, and the pope decided to solve the Staufen problem once and for all.[96] Therefore, negotiations began with Charles of Anjou,[97] and in July 1263 the archbishop of Cosenza was sent to England to free Henry III from any promise he had made regarding the *regno*.[98] Soon after, Charles of Anjou was appointed king of Sicily, and quickly found himself confronted by problems similar to those which had beset Henry III.[99] However, unlike the king of England, he was not dependent on the good will of Louis IX or that of a restive baronage. Also, by being present in Italy, he exercised greater freedom of action and eventually managed to complete what Henry and Edmund had set out to do: to drive the Staufens from Sicily.

86 CR, 1256–9, 325–6.
87 Powicke, *Henry III*, 148–50; H. Ridgway, 'King Henry III's grievances against the council in 1261: a new version and a letter describing political events', *BIHR* lxi (1988), 227–42 at p. 239; *Documents of the baronial movement of reform and rebellion, 1258–67*, ed. R. F. Treharne and E. J. Sanders, Oxford 1973, 211–19; E. F. Jacob, 'Complaints of Henry III against the baronial council in 1261', *EHR* xli (1926), 564–71.
88 Matthew Paris, *Chronica maiora, lib. add: chronica maiora*, vi. 410–16.
89 PRO, SC 1/63.
90 CPR, 1258–66, 52.
91 CLR, 1251–60, 461, 483.
92 CPR, 1258–66, 37, 51.
93 CR, 1259–61, 265–6.
94 *Calendar of entries in the papal registers relating to Great Britain and Ireland: papal letters*, ed. W. H. Bliss, i, London 1893, 382.
95 CR, 1261–4, 113.
96 B. Berg, 'Manfred of Sicily and Urban IV: negotiations of 1262', *Medieval Studies* lv (1993), 111–36; Berger, *Les Origines*, 370–410. The interest still taken by the English court is also evident in a letter written by Henry's proctor, Roger Lovel, concerning recent events from February 1262: *Royal letters Henry III*, ii, no. 569.
97 Wachtel, 'Sizilische Thronkandidatur', 167–70.
98 Kamp, *Kirche und Monarchie*, 849–53; *Epistolae saeculi XIII*, iii, nos 552–3.
99 Dunbabin, *Charles I of Anjou*, 131–5; Herde, *Karl I*, 41–67.

Sicily and England

The English court soon realised that finances were its biggest problem.[100] Recent experiences, such as during the Gascon campaign, must have alerted Henry to the difficulties this would pose. None the less, a parliament was called to Westminster for April 1255,[101] where he requested an aid and the levy of a long-forgotten tallage, *horngelth*. However, when the barons demanded reforms of the realm in exchange, the meeting was postponed.[102] Consequently, more drastic measures had to be taken. During a separate meeting at Reading, Henry asked the prelates to affix their seals to blank charters.[103] Soon after, the bishop of Hereford and Robert Walerand were sent to the *curia*. Presenting the documents to Alexander IV, they suggested that these could be used to force a contribution from the prelates. The names of creditors and the sums 'owed' were inserted, and the bishops and abbots threatened with excommunication should they refuse to pay.[104] The amounts demanded were considerable. St Albans, for instance, was asked to contribute £400,[105] and Oseney 200 marks.[106] Matters were further aggravated by the actions of Rostand, a papal notary. Calling the English abbots and bishops to a meeting at London in October, he confronted the prelates with his demands.[107] The episcopate was further alienated by the fact that the English Church already contributed to the king's planned crusade.[108] In early 1256, however, new demands were made, including a tenth, the usufruct of vacant benefices, a universal obligation to pay for up to 150,000 marks-worth of loans, half of the income from non-resident benefices and the goods of those dying intestate.[109] Both magnates and prelates objected.[110] None the less, some progress was made. According to Matthew Paris, the barons declared their willingness to co-operate, once the king had confirmed Magna Carta.[111] This resulted in some progress. During the Easter parliament of 1257 the prelates agreed to a one-off aid of 52,000 marks, in exchange for the king's promise that he would observe Magna Carta.[112] It needed two years of repeated meetings, and considerable papal pressure, before the barons and clergy were willing to contribute. In particular among the prelates, who had

100 Lunt, *Financial relations*, 263–90.
101 Matthew Paris, *Chronica maiora*, v. 493.
102 *Annals of Burton*, AM i. 336.
103 *Annals of Oseney*, AM iv. 109–10.
104 Matthew Paris, *Chronica maiora*, v. 510–13.
105 Ibid. v. 525.
106 *Annals of Oseney*, AM iv. 110.
107 Matthew Paris, *Chronica maiora*, v. 532.
108 CR, 1254–6, 380–1.
109 *Annals of Oseney*, AM iv. 114–15. See also *Foedera*, i. 344–6.
110 *Annals of Dunstable*, AM iii. 200.
111 Matthew Paris, *Chronica maiora*, v. 540–1.
112 Ibid. v. 623–4.

to bear the brunt of obligations and contributions, hostility was ripe. In 1256, for instance, Henry had to command the barons of Dover to prevent any cleric from leaving the country for Rome, unless they had first sworn to undertake nothing to the detriment of the Sicilian affair.[113] Similarly, little enthusiasm could be aroused among the barons. Alexander's offer that crusading vows could be fulfilled by joining the king's campaign against Manfred met with only a lukewarm reception.[114] If Henry was enthusiastic about his prospects in Sicily, his subjects clearly were not.

Their reluctance to support their king was, however, neither unanimous, nor directed primarily at the *negotium Sicilie*. The affairs of Apulia were a symptom, not the cause, of Henry's fraught relations with his barons, and money was only one among many grievances. This is exemplified by a set of complaints put before the king between 1256 and 1258.[115] Among them was the destruction of England by itinerant judges and various prises and oppressions, as well as the king's and the kingdom's poverty. More important were complaints about the king's administration of justice, a point that was made whenever the observance of Magna Carta was invoked. The criticism allegedly made by Richard of Cornwall points in a similar direction: the Sicilian Business had been embarked upon without his or the barons' counsel.[116] The complaints against the *negotium Sicilie* formed part of a wider and more general dissatisfaction with the way Henry III governed England. The issue was not that the king wanted to conquer Sicily, but that he had embarked upon such an expensive, potentially risky and far-reaching endeavour without consulting those whom he expected to pay for it, and whom he expected to fight for him.

None the less, one should beware of putting too much trust in reports of universal opposition towards the Sicilian Business. Even Matthew Paris, among the most persistent critics of the king's plan, had to admit that no unified opposition could be mustered.[117] Even some members of the clergy came to assist the king. In October 1256, for instance, the abbot of Westminster and the bishop-elect of Salisbury are said to have acted as Henry's proctors in Rome.[118] The abbot of Westminster, interestingly, had to swear an oath that he would not undertake anything detrimental to his community while at the *curia*, probably in connection with business he had to conduct

---

113 CR, 1254–6, 395.
114 Matthew Paris, Chronica maiora, v. 521–2; Papal letters, 329.
115 The Annals of Dunstable, AM iii. 200, give a short summary of these points under 1256. A more extended version is given by the Annals of Burton, AM i. 387–8, under the same year. There, however, reference is made to the absence of Richard of Cornwall, probably referring to his election as king of the Romans, which would put proceedings into 1257. Matthew Paris, writing closest to events, lists them under 1258: Chronica maiora, v. 680–1. Different conventions of dating years have, of course, also to be taken into account.
116 Matthew Paris, Chronica maiora, v. 621.
117 Ibid. v. 527.
118 Epistolae saeculi XIII, iii, no. 445.

concerning Sicily.[119] Similarly, Henry could count on a number of his barons, such as the earls of Leicester, Gloucester and Warenne. Even Richard of Cornwall, despite some apprehension,[120] came round to assist the king in his project. Although opposition to the Sicilian Business existed, it was divided, with a considerable number of prelates and magnates – however reluctantly – supporting the king.

The most fervent criticism Richard of Cornwall is said to have made was directed at the king's decision to embark on the Sicilian affair without his barons' counsel. Henry certainly did not call a parliament or a larger assembly of magnates to discuss the matter, and he relied heavily on his foreign relatives and court officials for advice. In November 1255, for instance, the witnesses to a memorandum that all provisions concerning Sicily had been made with the king's assent and in his council, included the bishop of Hereford, the bishop-elect of Winchester, Godfrey de Lusignan, the earls of Hereford and Warenne, John Maunsell, Philip Lovel, Ralph FitzNicholas and Henry of Bath.[121] Pierre de Aigueblanche, bishop of Hereford, had some experience in Italian affairs, having arranged the 1246 enfeoffment of Amadeus of Savoy, and continued to play a leading role in the Sicilian business. In addition he was, like William de Valence, the elect of Winchester, and Godfrey de Lusignan one of the king's foreign relatives.[122] The earls of Gloucester and Warenne were the only representatives of the English magnates, with Richard de Clare soon to take a more active role in the king's affairs. John Maunsell was one of Henry's most trusted advisors and the closest he had to a chief diplomat, while Philip Lovel was Henry's treasurer. In 1235 Ralph FitzNicholas had accompanied Isabella to Germany, and had represented the king and his barons at Lyon in 1245. The council, on this occasion, thus included a (small) number of barons, but mostly the king's relatives and officials. A similar pattern can be observed with regard to those who later came to be involved in the Sicilian Business. These included, at various stages, Peter of Savoy,[123] Peter Chaceporc,[124] Robert Walerand, the chancellor Henry de Wengham[125] and Simon de Montfort.[126] Most of these were either the king's officials, or, like Simon de Montfort, Peter of Savoy and

---

[119] Foedera, i. 344.

[120] He was absent from the Easter 1255 parliament: Royal letters Henry III, ii, no. 502. This is not quite the same as Matthew Paris's claim that the earl had remained neutral during proceedings: Chronica maiora, v. 514. Later that year, when asked for a loan by the pope, he refused, as he could not disseize a superior, and his brother was equally unsuccessful: ibid. v. 520–1, 524. It would be mistaken, though, to view this as a sign of hostility. By October the earl had already lent his brother nearly 25,000 marks: Denholm-Young, Richard of Cornwall, 159–60.

[121] CR, 1254–6, 240.

[122] CR, 1256–9, 462–3.

[123] CR, 1254–6, 194–5.

[124] CPR, 1247–58, 344.

[125] Royal letters Henry III, ii, no. 508.

[126] CPR, 1247–58, 567.

Peter Chaceporc, foreign lords who also held lands in England. This may have been appropriate inasmuch as those were the people who could provide either the expertise or the loyalty necessary to prepare a project like the conquest of Sicily.[127] This fell, however, short of the broad consultation envisaged by Magna Carta, and it did little to help an undertaking which could only be concluded successfully with the backing of the king's subjects. More important, it relied on men which were increasingly perceived as at the very root of the problems besetting England.

All this came to the fore in 1258 with the Provisions of Oxford. David Carpenter has argued convincingly that one reason for events during the Oxford parliament was increasing exasperation with the king's Lusignan relatives.[128] However, we also need to take into account that during spring and summer 1258 England was beset by famine, war and the threat of interdict.[129] That is, the provisions were formulated at a time when various crises had come to a head and combined to create a climate of fear, anger and disillusion. The two parliaments called that year, first at Westminster and then at Oxford, were primarily concerned with averting the king's excommunication.[130] How serious that threat was remains a matter of conjecture. The king himself certainly seems to have viewed it with some apprehension, and Matthew Paris reports that Simon Passelewe was sent to various abbeys to solicit additional funds to meet the legate's demands.[131] In combination with Henry III's failure to keep his repeated promises to observe Magna Carta, his obstruction of justice in favour of his Lusignan half-brothers and the political reserves besetting England as a result, this may have contributed to a feeling that urgent measures had to be taken. Moreover, relations with Scotland had entered a period of renewed instability, while in Wales an insurrection led by Llywelyn ap Gruffudd since 1256 had left English control in a shambles.[132] After all, one of the items on the agenda of the Oxford Parliament had been to muster troops for a Welsh campaign. The baronial rebellion put an end to the Sicilian Business, but its demise was accidental rather than intentional. The problem his barons had with the king was not that he sought to get the Sicilian throne for his son, but how he went about getting it.

127 Powicke, *Henry III*, 257; Howell, *Eleanor of Provence*, 131–4.
128 D. A. Carpenter, 'What happened in 1258?', in J. Gillingham and J. C. Holt (eds), *War and government in the Middle Ages: essays in honour of J. O. Prestwich*, Woodbridge 1984, 106–19.
129 *Chronica buriensis, 1212–1301*, ed. A. Gransden, London 1964, 22; H. M. Cam and E. F. Jacob, 'Notes on an English Cluniac chronicle', *EHR* xliv (1929), 94–104 at p. 100; Clanchy, *England and its rulers*, 263.
130 *Annals of Dunstable*, AM iii. 208–9.
131 Matthew Paris, *Chronica maiora*, v. 682–8.
132 Liebermann, 'Annals of Lewes Priory', 89. Davies, *Age of conquest*, 309ff.; J. B. Smith, *Llywelyn ap Gruffudd, prince of Wales*, Cardiff 1998, 90–108.

The European connection

Henry III had been unable to reach a permanent settlement with Louis IX.[133] Without that, getting an army to Sicily would be expensive and difficult. Within two days of receiving Alexander's confirmation of his grant to Edmund, Simon de Montfort and Peter of Savoy were therefore sent to negotiate an extension of the existing truce.[134] In fact, the unsettled state of affairs with the Capetians was at least once cited to explain a delay in the king's departure for Sicily.[135] The Plantagenets' relations with the Capetians were, however, of concern to others as well. Alfonso of Castile, for instance, sent envoys to facilitate a peace agreement.[136] To him peace between Henry and Louis must have been essential for his planned African campaign. However, all these efforts came to nothing. For 1256, the *Chronica maiora* reports a *parliamentum* at Paris. Representing Henry III, John Maunsell requested a safe conduct for an English army to pass through France on its way to Sicily, but the petition was refused.[137] That Henry's envoy also pressed for a restitution of Normandy and Poitou will have done little to assuage the suspicions of Louis IX and his barons.[138] Fears as to the effect this might have on the Sicilian Business are highlighted by a letter from Henry III to his proctor at the *curia* from spring 1256, in which he warned of French conspiracies, which, if successful, could jeopardise the Sicilian Business.[139] Like the crusade, the conquest of Sicily gave an opportunity to raise the issue of the king's inheritance yet again. At the same time, exactly because this issue had not yet been resolved, it began to threaten the king's crusade, and his son's chances of becoming ruler of Sicily.

Partly in response to his lack of success in France, Henry III tried to strengthen links with William of Holland. Once the Sicilian venture had been embarked upon, missions to and from the empire increased in frequency. In February 1255 Jean de Avesnes sent two envoys to the English court,[140] with one of his agents still in England by June,[141] and another arriving in October.[142] In November the dukes of Luxemburg and Limburg came to England,[143] both among William's leading supporters.[144] This time,

---

133 *CR, 1254–6*, 412, 424.
134 *CPR, 1247–58*, 411; Matthew Paris, *Chronica maiora*, v. 515–16.
135 *CR 1256–9*, 136–7. See Matthew Paris, *Chronica maiora*, v. 680–1, for the use of the Capetian problem by those opposed to the *negotium*.
136 *CR, 1254–6*, 194–5.
137 Matthew Paris, *Chronica maiora*, v. 547–8.
138 Ibid. v. 516.
139 *CR, 1254–6*, 408.
140 *Diplomatic documents*, no. 277.
141 *CLR, 1251–60*, 228.
142 Ibid. 244.
143 Ibid. 253.
144 Matthew Paris, *Chronica maiora, lib. add.: chronica maiora*, vi. 252–5.

however, German overtures were returned. In August 1255, for the first time in almost ten years, Henry III sent an envoy to Germany,[145] which was followed, in October, by the mission of Prior John of Newburgh.[146] The exact purpose of these embassies remains obscure. It would seem plausible, though, that the affairs of Sicily featured in negotiations. After William's death, for instance, one of the reasons given for Plantagenet involvement in German affairs was that only a king favourably disposed to Henry's interests, and not exposed to pressure from Louis IX, could safeguard success in Sicily.[147] Another consideration may have been the need to isolate the Staufen in Sicily from those in the empire. It is hard to think of an outcome which could have been more harmful to Henry's Mediterranean ambitions than the election of Conrad IV's son Conradin as king of the Romans and emperor-to-be.[148] More important, these contacts began just as Alexander IV voiced his determination to crown William emperor,[149] and Henry would have wanted to ensure that William did not follow in the steps of Otto IV and lay claim to Sicily. Whatever the king of England's expectations may have been, however, they were thwarted when William was killed in January 1256.

Henry III immediately set out to influence the imminent election of a new king.[150] In the end, William was to be succeeded by Richard of Cornwall, a fact that has influenced most studies of English involvement in Germany.[151] Initially, though, the earl had not even been among the candidates.[152] It was not until the candidacies of the count of Henneberg,[153] Margrave Otto of Brandenburg[154] and the king of Bohemia had failed[155] that Richard entered the field.[156] His candidacy was an act of last resort, with the earliest evidence for it surviving from late November 1256.[157] Until then, the English court had been content with trying to influence the outcome of the election, rather than supporting a particular candidate. A first step was taken in February

---

145 *CLR, 1251–60,* 238.

146 Ibid. 245; Matthew Paris, *Chronica maiora,* v. 437.

147 *CR, 1254–6,* 408–9.

148 Matthew Paris, *Chronica maiora,* v. 493

149 *Baumgartenberger Formelbuch: eine Quelle zur Geschichte des XIII. Jahrhunderts vornehmlich der Zeiten Rudolfs von Habsburg,* ed. H. Baerwald, Vienna 1866, no. 46.

150 Wachtel, 'Die sizilische Thronkandidatur', 149–65.

151 C. C. Bayley, 'The diplomatic preliminaries of the Double Election of 1257 in Germany', *EHR* lxii (1947), 457–83.

152 M. Groten, 'Konrad von Hochstaden und die Wahl Richards von Cornwall', in H. Vollrath and S. Weinfurter (eds), *Köln: Stadt und Bistum in Kirche und Reich des Mittelalters: Festschrift Odilo Engels,* Cologne–Weimar–Vienna 1993, 483–510.

153 J. Siebert, 'Graf Hermann von Henneberg als Bewerber um die deutsche Königskrone', *Zeitschrift für deutsche Philologie* lvii (1932), 215–23.

154 *Chronica principum Saxoniae ampliata,* MGH, SS xxx, i. 30.

155 *Pokračowatelé Kosmowi,* in *Fontes rerum bohemicarum,* II: *Cosmae chronicon boemorum cum continuatoribus,* ed. J. Emler, Prague 1874, 294; *Kronika Pulkavova,* in *Fontes rerum bohemicarum,* v, ed. J. Emler and J. Gebauer, Prague 1893, 148.

156 Groten, 'Konrad von Hochstaden', 491.

157 *Constitutiones, 1198–1272,* no. 379.

1256, when William Bonquer was accredited as Henry III's envoy to the *curia*.[158] In March and April he received a commission, ordering him to request papal support. Henry promised to pay his remaining debts, and either to go himself or to send a representative to Apulia soon. That would not be possible, however, unless favourable conditions had first been created in the empire. Alexander IV was therefore asked to ensure that no king of the Romans be elected who would pose a threat to the Sicilian Business, and to send a legate to Germany to oversee the matter.[159] The pope, though, was reluctant to comply, and merely wrote to the archbishop of Mainz to insist that no Staufen be elected king.[160] The English court thus had to take matters into its own hands. In June 1256 Robert Walerand and Richard de Clare were sent 'to all the princes of Almain'.[161] That this mission consisted of two such prominent members of Henry's court certainly testified to the importance attached to its outcome. It would, however, be mistaken to view this as an early indication of Richard's candidacy.[162] Robert Walerand, the king's steward, was among the driving forces behind the Sicilian Business,[163] and Richard de Clare, the earl of Gloucester, was one of the king's most trusted advisors, and repeatedly involved in the affairs of the *regno*.[164] At this stage, the English court was concerned with ensuring the necessary diplomatic contacts for a successful crossing to Sicily, and not with gaining yet another appanage for a Plantagenet prince. Any German prince would do, as long as he was not hostile to Henry's ambitions in the Mediterranean.

The king's court sought to enlist as broad a range of support as possible. John de Avesnes became a regular and richly rewarded visitor to the English court. In April he received part of his annual fee of now £200,[165] which was collected by his brother Baldwin and by John de Castello.[166] The latter seems to have returned by the end of June, shortly after the English mission had been announced to Germany.[167] Henry's court was trying to ensure the support and assistance of those close to the deceased king to further its interests in the election of William's successor. That it ignored traditional allies, such as the duke of Brunswick, may be connected with the fact that they were not among the electors, as was probably known in England.[168] Henry's primary concern in his dealings with Germany was to safeguard his Apulian

---

158 CPR, 1247–58, 462.
159 CR, 1254–6, 408–9.
160 *Regesta imperii*, nos 4289a, 9068.
161 CPR, 1247–58, 481.
162 Groten, 'Konrad von Hochstaden', passim.
163 Matthew Paris, *Chronica maiora*, v. 511, 521; CPR, 1247–58, 344.
164 CLR, 1251–60, 455–6.
165 Ibid. 279; CPR, 1247–58, 461.
166 CLR, 1251–60, 280.
167 Ibid. 307; CPR, 1247–58, 413.
168 Matthew Paris, *Chronica maiora*, v. 604.

ambitions.[169] This, in turn, is indicative of the shift in Henry's diplomatic goals in dealing with Germany. There was a degree of continuity: the king of England sought to reactivate relations with William of Holland, just as relations with the Capetians had reached a dead end. But there also was an important difference: the reason underpinning the sudden interest in German affairs was not a military recovery of the Poitou and Normandy. Rather, friendly relations with the ruler of Germany were a means of protecting Henry's new interests in the Mediterranean, and ensuring that he would be able to pursue his ambitions there. The hostility Henry encountered from the Capetians was certainly the cause of his involvement in German affairs, but they were no longer the object of the alliance he sought to forge.

In the end, none of those approached seemed willing or able to become king. Faced with a prolonged stalemate which would have delayed the king's departure for Sicily even further, Henry and his court took decisive action. In November 1256 Henry, the count palatine of the Rhineland and the duke of Bavaria, promised to elect Richard of Cornwall as king of the Romans, with the archbishop of Cologne following suit in December, and that of Mainz a few weeks after that.[170] Henry soon tried to use his brother's election for the affairs of Apulia. During the 1256 Christmas parliament at Westminster Richard's elevation was employed in an attempt to woo the English barons.[171] Envoys from Germany arrived and brought news that Richard had been elected king of the Romans.[172] When offered the crown, the earl gave the required display of humility,[173] and refused. Eventually, he was swayed by advice, which was directed as much at him as at the assembled nobles and clergy: he was exhorted not to follow the example of Robert Curthose, who had refused the crown of Jerusalem. For this act of pride God punished him, and he was pursued by misfortunes ever after. Richard had been singled out by divine favour, and it would be presumptuous to act contrary to His will.[174] If this was true for the earl of Cornwall becoming king of the Romans, it must have been true also for Henry's son becoming king of Sicily. Henry continued to exploit the parallel. A parliament was called to coincide with the earl's

---

169 This caused, of course, problems, one of the promises made by Richard's proctors having been that he would safeguard Conradin's rights in Sicily: *Constitutiones, 1198–1272*, no. 381. The Apulian connection may also be underlined by the fact that one of the witnesses to the agreement between Richard's proctors and Conradin's guardian, the count palatine, was an otherwise unidentifiable 'Kertefordus de Apulia': ibid. no. 379.

170 Ibid. nos 377–80, 383; R. Reisinger, *Die römisch-deutschen Könige und ihre Wähler, 1198–1273*, Aalen 1977, 71–84.

171 Matthew Paris, *Chronica maiora*, v. 601–3; H.-E. Hilpert 'Richard of Cornwall's candidature for the German throne and the Christmas 1256 parliament at Westminster', *JMH* vi (1980), 195–8.

172 *CLR, 1251–60*, 347.

173 Matthew Paris seems to describe the *topos* of reluctant kingship: B. K. U. Weiler, 'The *rex renitens* and the medieval ideal of kingship, c. 950–c.1250', *Viator* xxxi (2000), 1–42.

174 Matthew Paris, *Chronica maiora*, v. 603; Weiler, 'Matthew Paris'.

departure for Germany,[175] and was combined with Edmund's formal coronation as king of Sicily.[176] Richard, too, continued to support his brother's
projects. Once in Germany, he wrote to Prince Edward,[177] the archbishop of
Messina,[178] the mayor and citizens of London[179] and the bishop of Lincoln,[180]
extolling his great successes, his warm reception and the ease with which he
overcame his enemies. As these letters are to be found in various chronicles,
they probably had been intended for a wider circulation. They painted a
glorious picture of the earl's successes and may have been aimed not only at
calming fears concerning the risks of the Sicilian Business, but also at elic-
iting much-needed enthusiasm. More important, they conveyed the message
that opposition could easily be overcome, once a king appeared in person.

The earl of Cornwall's success in the empire also initiated swift progress in
relations with Louis IX. Even before Richard left for Germany, contacts with
the Capetians had been renewed.[181] This eventually resulted in a meeting
between English, French and German proctors at Cambrai in November
1258,[182] laying the foundations for what was to become the Treaty of Paris.[183]
The agreement set to rest the conflict over Normandy, Anjou and Poitou,
with Henry surrendering his claims, and doing homage for Gascony. This
paved the way for Plantagenet ambitions in the Mediterranean. One clause
stipulated that Louis IX was to provide Henry III either with 500 knights for
two years or with 1,000 for one.[184] In a separate document, Richard also
suggested an alliance with Louis.[185] This, at last, eased, diplomatically,
Henry's planned conquest of Apulia. It would be mistaken, however, to view
the Treaty of Paris as a one-sided concession on Henry's part. Although Louis
had gained acceptance of Capetian rule in what had once been Henry III's
inheritance, he was now faced with the prospect of Plantagenet rule in
Germany and Sicily. Moreover, in 1258–9 it looked as if Richard were on his
way to being crowned emperor and would thus be able to establish his
authority across the empire.[186] The Treaty of Paris was as much an acknowl-

---

[175] Matthew Paris, *Chronica maiora*, v. 621–3.
[176] *John of Wallingford*, MGH, SS xxviii, 510.
[177] *Annals of Burton*, AM i. 392–4.
[178] Ibid. 391–2.
[179] *De antiquis legibus*, 26–9.
[180] Liebermann, 'Zur Geschichte', 220.
[181] CPR, *1247–58*, 549.
[182] Matthew Paris, *Chronica maiora*, v. 720–1; *Annals of Burton*, AM i. 461.
[183] P. Chaplais, 'The making of the Treaty of Paris and the royal style', *EHR* lxvii (1952),
235–53; Powicke, *King Henry III*, 247–52; I. J. Sanders, 'The texts of the Treaty of Paris,
1259', *EHR* lxvi (1951), 81–97; van Eickels, *Vom inszenierten Konsens*, 183–228; Cuttino,
English medieval diplomacy, 54–83.
[184] This seems to have been part of negotiations from an early stage: Henry to Alexander
IV, 30 July 1258, CR, *1256–9*, 325–6.
[185] *Acta imperii inedita*, no. 564.
[186] *Les Actes pontificaux originaux des Archives nationales de Paris*, I: *1198–1261*, ed.
B. Barbiche, Vatican City 1975, no. 1001.

edgement by Henry III that there was little hope of ever regaining Normandy or Poitou, as it was an attempt by Louis IX to avoid being placed between two hostile neighbours.[187]

The Treaty of Paris symbolised the shift in Henry's attentions, away from the Angevin empire and towards the Mediterranean. In addition, it signified the extent to which both Henry III and Richard were now plagued by the problems which in the past had beset Frederick II in his dealings with the Capetians. It was impossible to establish effective overlordship in either Sicily or the empire, if a source of support remained for rival candidates and claimants. Just as Otto IV had been defeated by the Capetians' support for Frederick II, as Frederick had tried so hard to ensure that neither Henry (VII) nor the anti-kings elected after the council of Lyon would find support from Louis IX, so Henry III, too, depended on Louis's political, military and diplomatic backing for the fulfilment of his ambitions.

Richard's election had repercussions not only for the Plantagenets' relations with the Capetians, but also for those with the Iberian Peninsula. After all, the earl of Cornwall was not the only one to be elected king of the Romans. In April 1257 the archbishop of Trier, acting on behalf of the duke of Saxony and the margraves of Brandenburg, had chosen Alfonso X of Castile.[188] Even earlier, in June 1256, Alfonso's proctors had agreed with the commune of Pisa that they would elect him emperor.[189] Whether the English court was aware of this remains an open question. Matthew Paris, for one, pleaded ignorance and accused the Germans of having kept secret Alfonso's candidacy.[190] Although Alfonso later complained that Richard had ignored his earlier claim, he steered clear of accusing Henry of thwarting his imperial ambitions.[191] At the same time, throughout 1256 envoys had been sent to or received from Castile,[192] and in late January 1257 English envoys were sent to Iberia, Gascony, Germany and Gotland.[193] As this happened so shortly after

---

187 Louis acted in preparation for his second crusade, and a similar agreement had been concluded with the king of Aragon: *Layettes*, nos 4439–40, 4411–12, 4433–5; Jordan, *Louis IX*, 199–200; O. Engels, 'Der Vertrag von Corbeil (1258)', *Spanische Forschungen der Görresgesellschaft: erste Reihe: Gesammelte Aufsätze zur Kulturgeschichte Spaniens* xix (1962), 114–46. I am grateful to Chris Given-Wilson for suggesting this link.

188 *Annales wormatienses*, MGH, SS xvii. 59; R. Holbach, 'Die Regierungszeit des Trierer Erzbischofs Arnold II. von Isenburg: ein Beitrag zur Geschichte von Reich, Territorium und Kirche um die Mitte des 13. Jahrhunderts', *Rheinische Vierteljahresblätter* cxlvii (1983), 1–66.

189 *Constitutiones, 1198–1272*, nos 392–5; A. Busson, *Die Doppelwahl des Jahres 1257 und das römische Königthum Alfons X. von Castilien*, Münster 1866; C. J. Socarras, *Alfonso X of Castile: a study of imperialistic frustration*, Barcelona 1976; O'Callaghan, *The learned king*, 198–213.

190 Matthew Paris, *Chronica maiora*, v. 657.

191 CR, *1256–9*, 314–15; CR, *1258–61*, 167; CR, *1261–4*, 172–3.

192 CLR, *1251–60*, 280; CR, *1254–6*, 313, 318.

193 CR, *1256–9*, 26; CPR, *1247–58*, 539.

Richard's election, one may assume that it was one of the items of news disseminated. None the less, there is little evidence to suggest that any of this responded to Alfonso's earlier moves. In late January 1257 Henry III thanked the bishop of Hereford for his efforts in arranging a treaty with Alfonso, and mentioned, more in passing, Richard's election.[194] Henry even provided a vessel for a Castilian envoy to Norway.[195] Simultaneously, negotiations continued for the planned African crusade.[196] There were, thus, sufficiently regular contacts to assume that the English court might have heard of Alfonso's ambitions. However, it has to be taken into account that Alfonso himself did not publicise his new-found dignity. He did not begin to issue grants for Germany until September 1257,[197] and his contacts in the empire were initially confined to Pisa and Marseilles.[198] Furthermore, Alfonso may have had good reason to keep his ambitions secret from the English court: the treaty with Pisa guaranteed the commune's rights in Sicily, should Alfonso, his son or their representative, conquer the *regno*.[199] To what extent this reflected Castilian intentions remains, however, unclear. Alfonso had little to gain from alienating Henry. Pisa, on the other hand, continued to pose a threat. In 1258, for instance, several of his Sicilian subjects warned Edmund that Genoa and Pisa were conspiring to conquer the island.[200] Should Henry III have been aware of this, it may have given added urgency to English diplomacy in Germany, and may hold the key to understanding Henry's seeming disregard for his Castilian in-laws.

Despite the temporary cooling in relations with Alfonso, Henry none the less tried to avoid being drawn into the internal squabbles of Iberia. Several offers made by Alfonso's estranged father-in-law,[201] Jaime of Aragon, to forge closer links were turned down. At various points their conflict threatened to involve both Capetians and Plantagenets. In early 1255, for instance, Alfonso asked Henry that his Gascon subjects assist him against his Aragonese foe.[202] Although there is no record of Henry complying, he also refused to enter into an alliance with Jaime. In December 1255, for example, Henry thanked the king of Aragon for his – otherwise unspecified – offer, and promised to send an envoy by next Pentecost.[203] Little seems to have come of this, and the king of England remained reluctant to abandon Alfonso. In fact, in April 1256 Henry III suggested yet another marriage to Alfonso, this time

---

[194] *CR, 1256–9*, 118–20.
[195] *CR, 1254–6*, 360.
[196] *Foedera*, i. 343; *CR, 1254–6*, 389–91.
[197] *Regesta imperii*, no. 5489; I. Schwab, 'Kanzlei und Urkundenwesen König Alfons X. von Kastilien für das Reich', *AfD* xxxii (1986), 569–616.
[198] *Acta imperii selecta*, no. 678.
[199] *Constitutiones, 1198–1272*, no. 394; Lloyd, 'Henry III', 114 n. 88.
[200] *Diplomatic documents*, no. 301.
[201] O'Callaghan, *The learned king*, 152–7; Bisson, *Medieval crown of Aragon*, 67–8.
[202] *Diplomatic documents*, no. 280.
[203] *Royal letters Henry III*, ii, no. 504.

between Alfonso's brother and one of Henry's daughters.[204] In June 1257, after Richard's election had brought into the open his conflict with Alfonso, another Aragonese embassy was received. However, Henry III insisted that he was not willing to break any of the clauses agreed upon in his truce with Alfonso.[205] Henry saw little reason to abandon his alliance with Alfonso. We cannot be sure to what extent Henry III wilfully disregarded Alfonso's imperial aspirations, or whether he even knew about them. If he took a calculated gamble, it certainly paid off. Alfonso no longer stated claims to Gascony, and with the Treaty of Paris, the prospect of the king of Castile winning support from Louis had also become much less likely.

In many ways the Sicilian Business developed further an already existing trend in Henry's diplomacy: its reorientation towards the south. This did not stop at creating a permanent settlement with the Capetians or safeguarding relations with Castile. The need to protect Plantagenet claims in Apulia led to a quest for allies.[206] In June 1256, for instance, a clerk from the queen of Cyprus arrived in England,[207] with negotiations soon centring on a planned double marriage between Edmund and Queen Plaisance, and between Henry's daughter Beatrice and the infant king of Cyprus.[208] An alliance with the Lusignan rulers of Cyprus, who were, after all, hereditary regents of Jerusalem, would have profited not only Henry's affairs in the Mediterranean, but also his crusade.[209] This was not dissimilar to Frederick II's policies or the actions of Charles of Anjou after he had seized the *regno*, and which included a claim to the kingship of Jerusalem, and a desire to rule most of the eastern Mediterranean.[210]

In the end, the marriage alliance with the Cypriot Lusignans failed to materialise. At the same time, it had been only one among several projects pursued by Henry's court. Also in 1256, the archbishop of Tarentaise and Master Rustand received plenary powers to arrange a marriage for Edmund.[211] That these marriage plans were directed at the *regno* is suggested by the presence of an Apulian knight in England at that time,[212] while the identity of the prospective spouse is revealed in a letter from Master Rustand to

---

204 *Foedera*, i. 340.
205 *CR, 1254–6*, 135–6.
206 Lloyd, 'Henry III', 113–16.
207 *CLR, 1251–60*, 319; *Foedera*, i. 341.
208 *CR, 1254–6*, 445–6.
209 Edbury, *Kingdom of Cyprus*, 75–100. Lloyd, 'Henry III', 115, is perhaps going too far in assuming that Edmund could actually have exercised the regency on behalf of his intended stepson/brother-in-law (quite apart from the canonical implications that this might have had). He himself was only ten years old at the time.
210 Jacoby, 'La Dimensione imperiale oltremare', 31–5; Dunbabin, *Charles I of Anjou*, 114–26.
211 *Diplomatic documents*, no. 282.
212 *CR, 1254–6*, 313.

Henry III, in which he repeated the advice of an unnamed cardinal, that a marriage between Edmund and one of Manfred's daughters could salvage Henry III's prospects.[213] In the end, this union, too, failed to materialise. None the less, the episode helps to illustrate both the divisions within the papal *curia* at the time, and that many still thought Henry capable of providing the leadership necessary to replace Manfred as king of Sicily.[214]

As far as Edmund's chances for success are concerned, it is important to distinguish between the years before and after 1258. It was not until that date that Manfred was able to seize the throne of Sicily himself, and had Henry or Edmund been able to appear in person, matters may well have turned out differently. In 1254 Edmund would not have had to fight for recognition of his claims against an already established rival. Furthermore, his supporters included some of the most prominent administrators and political figures of Sicily, as well as members of Frederick's family. The project only ran into difficulties when Henry failed to provide the leadership and protection which his supporters had come to expect. The difficulties which Henry had to over-come were political rather than military, and the project failed not because Henry III and his council had been unable to build up the necessary support abroad, but because they had been unable to convince those who really mattered: the king's English subjects.

Neither Henry's ambitions, nor the tools with which he sought to realise them differed greatly from those used by his peers and contemporaries. He may have outdone his fellow-rulers as regards the size of the gains made, but he still acted within parameters common to them all. Most notably, Freder-ick's death failed to bring with it full victory for the *curia*. Rather, the lay princes of Latin Europe were those who profited most from the collapse of the Staufen empire. This was a phenomenon by no means limited to rulers from outside the *imperium*. In the empire, Ottokar of Bohemia, for instance, was able to seize the duchies of Styria, Carinthia and Austria, giving him control over a territory roughly the size of England;[215] in the Rhineland, Conrad of Hochstaden, the archbishop of Cologne, sought to perform functions previ-ously associated with the emperor, and soon competed with the Rhenish League of cities, initially formed to safeguard imperial rights and communal freedoms.[216] This, in turn, should also warn against too simplistic an interpre-

---

[213] *Diplomatic documents*, no. 283.

[214] Manfred himself seems to have been worried about this. In March 1256 the bishop of Rochester warned that assassins were being dispatched to England from Apulia: *Royal letters Henry III*, ii, no. 508; H.M. Schaller, 'König Manfred und die Assassinen', *DA* xxi (1965), 173–93.

[215] *Codex diplomaticus et epistolaris regni Bohemiae*, ed. J. Sebanek and S. Duskova, v/1, Prague 1974, no. 345.

[216] Kettering, 'Die Territorialpolitik'; K. L. Menzel, *Geschichte des Rheinischen Städtebundes im 13. Jahrhundert*, Hanover 1871; A. Buschmann, 'Der Rheinische Bund von 1254–1257: Landfriede, Städte, Fürsten und Reichsverfassung im 13. Jahrhundert', in H. Maurer (ed.), *Kommunale Bündnisse Oberitaliens und Oberdeutschlands im Vergleich*, Sigmaringen 1987,

tation. Frequently, rulers and princes responded to developments which posed a threat to their territories too. Charles of Anjou's activities in Flanders, for instance, constituted a response to a plea for help from one of the Capetians' allies and dependants. Had Louis not intervened on behalf of the Dampierre brothers, he would have failed in one of his most noble duties as king, with repercussions well beyond the initial dispute itself. In the absence of strong royal authority, it fell to powers in the locality to exercise royal or imperial functions. This is not to deny that territorial aggrandisement was one of the objectives achieved by these actions, but it would be mistaken to view it as their sole driving motivation.

Political difficulties among neighbours were not, however, the only motivation we need to consider. Most recently, Jose Manuel Rodríguez García has pointed to the connection between Alfonso X's pursuit of the imperial crown, and his crusading endeavours.[217] Although the office of emperor was not viewed as intrinsically linked to the recovery of the Holy Land until the late thirteenth century,[218] there always had been a close association between the Staufen and the Holy Land. Controlling the empire gave those who held it the prestige, as well as the political and economic clout to pursue the liberation of Jerusalem. Similarly, although Henry III's acceptance of Sicily was in part driven by competition with the Capetians, it was initially viewed as contributing towards either a campaign in North Africa, or the recovery of Jerusalem. A ruler's moral obligation sometimes transcended the narrow confines of territorial and dynastic interests, and Henry III, like many of his contemporaries, felt that they had to take on at least some of Frederick's functions. In doing so, the king of England and his family soon faced the very challenges and difficulties which in the past had so frequently frustrated their own efforts at forging stronger links with Frederick II and the Staufen. Nowhere is this more evident than in the German career of the king's brother, Richard of Cornwall.

167–212; M. Kaufhold, *Deutsches Interregnum und europäische Politik: Konfliktlösungen und Entscheidungsstrukturen, 1230–1280*, Hanover 2000, 168–215.
217 Rodríguez García, 'Henry III'.
218 Weiler, '*Negotium*'.

8

The Reign of King Richard, 1257–1272

In January 1257 Richard of Cornwall was elected king of the Romans. Henry III had at last found a ruler of Germany sympathetic towards his interests. Recovering Normandy or Poitou was, however, no longer a priority, and the earl's candidacy had been pursued not as a means of reclaiming Henry's inheritance, but of facilitating his conquest of Sicily. Richard's reign furthermore highlights some of the challenges and problems which in the past had beset Frederick II or Henry (VII). As in the case of his brother's affairs in Sicily, the moment Richard took control of Germany, and the moment he had declared his ambition to be crowned emperor, he pursued the very policies which, in the past, had so frequently frustrated the king of England's efforts. This continuity in policies was partly due to the advisors on whom Richard had to rely, but it also reveals fundamental features in the political and governmental structure of the empire.[1]

Securing the throne, 1257–9

Richard was no newcomer to imperial politics. He had been chosen to represent Henry III at Vaucouleurs in 1236 and 1237,[2] and he unsuccessfully sought to mediate between Frederick and Gregory IX in 1241.[3] Moreover, both emperor and pope had looked to him for support.[4] To his German supporters he could thus offer what none of the other claimants could – a career untainted by the internal rivalries of German politics. In addition, unlike Alfonso of Castile, he was not tied up by the affairs of a realm he had to govern already, and was free to take personal control of his kingdom. More important, he possessed the financial means to do so – he was, after all, one of the richest men of his time. Finally, his election permitted some of his allies to return from a period of political exile. To Louis, count palatine of the Rhineland and duke of Bavaria and guardian of Frederick II's grandson Conradin, supporting Richard offered an opportunity to end the political

---

[1]   The best coverage of Richard's early reign remains J. F. Bappert, *Richard von Cornwall seit seiner Wahl zum deutschen König, 1258–1272*, Bonn 1905, 3–36. Parts of this chapter have appeared as 'Image and "reality" in Richard of Cornwall's German career', *EHR* cxiii (1998), 1111–42.
[2]   Matthew Paris, *Chronica maiora*, iii. 393.
[3]   Ibid. iii. 471–2; iv. 145–8.
[4]   Ibid. iv. 569–75, 577–8; v. 111–12, 117–18, 201.

isolation into which he had been brought by his wife's execution. In the case of Conrad of Hochstaden, the archbishop of Cologne, it offered the chance to reassert his once dominant position in Germany, which he had lost when, from 1255 onwards, he and William of Holland clashed repeatedly, culminating in a bungled attempt at assassinating the king and a papal legate.[5] Conrad was excommunicated for his part in the affair, and one of the promises Richard had to make to win the prelate's vote was that he would restore peace between legate and archbishop.

In pursuing his election, Richard took a course markedly different from that of his brother in Sicily. He did not declare his intentions until a sufficiently strong basis of indigenous support had been secured. This reflected a political system in Germany which was fundamentally different from that of Sicily. No candidate had emerged as clear front-runner to fill the vacuum left by William, and there was no feudal overlord in whose right it was to select a king. It was up to the princes of the empire to choose their ruler, not to the pope to appoint one. A first step towards winning the necessary support had been made in November 1256, when Jean de Avesnes and the bishop of Cambrai, acting as Richard's proctors, concluded a treaty with Louis.[6] Although Richard had to promise that he would not hinder the claims of Frederick II's grandson Conradin to the kingdoms of Sicily and Jerusalem or to the duchy of Swabia, he never confirmed Conradin's rights. In December, Conrad of Hochstaden, the archbishop of Cologne, agreed to vote for Richard,[7] with the archbishop of Mainz being promised another 8,000 marks if he declared himself for him.[8] That the earl paid large sums of money – nearly £20,000 in all – to his electors has frequently been commented upon.[9] However, offering financial rewards was not at all unusual in thirteenth-century Germany. In fact, Richard's generosity pales in comparison with that of later candidates,[10] and it was only during the political unrest after his death that the sums paid became an issue.[11] The earl was supported by three of the most powerful princes of the empire. More important, unlike Alfonso, whose claims rested on his proclamation by Pisa and Marseilles, the earl was to be elected by princes who had traditionally been associated with the right to elect a king.

5   *Regesta imperii*, no. 5213a.
6   *Constitutiones, 1198–1272*, nos 379–80.
7   Ibid. no. 383.
8   *Thomas Wyke's chronicle*, AM iv. 113.
9   *Emonis et Menkonis werumensium chronica*, MGH, SS xxiii. 546; *Balduini ninovensis chronicon*, MGH, SS xxv. 544; *Catalogus archiepiscoporum coloniensum*, MGH, SS xxiv. 356; *Annales hamburgenses*, MGH, SS xvi. 383–4.
10 H. Stehkämper, 'Geld bei deutschen Königswahlen des 13 Jahrhunderts', in J. Schneider (ed.), *Wirtschaftskräfte und Wirtschaftswege: Festschrift Hermann Kellenbenz*, Stuttgart 1978, i. 83–115 at pp. 92, 96, 106; O. Redlich, 'Die Anfänge König Rudolfs I', MIÖG x (1889), 341–418 at p. 413 n. 2.
11 Weiler, 'Image and "reality" ', 1126–8.

In addition to securing the necessary votes, soundings were taken as to the situation in Germany. In January 1257 the earl of Gloucester, whom Henry III had dispatched to the empire in 1256, travelled to the Rhineland once again, this time acting as Richard's emissary.[12] Although his report was positive, Richard still delayed his departure until the Easter parliament, when the archbishop of Cologne arrived in England to report that Richard had formally been elected on 8 January 1257.[13] Significantly, the earl did not set sail until after he had concluded a formal treaty of friendship with Henry III.[14] To some extent, Richard's election constituted the culmination of Henry's diplomatic efforts concerning the empire, and places Richard's career firmly within the context of the Sicilian Business as well as – at least in the eyes of Louis IX – the king's claims to Poitou and Normandy. At the same time, the parameters within which these relations were conducted had changed, and to some extent this treaty had outlived its usefulness the moment it was signed. For as much as Henry had realised that he would be unable to pursue his Mediterranean ambitions without first settling his relations with the Capetians, so Richard, too, was soon to find out why Frederick II had shunned an alliance with Henry III.

The earl's entourage was kept small. The safe-conducts issued list no more than fifty names.[15] The composition of this mission was, moreover, far from high-ranking, with John de Warenne, earl of Salisbury, and the bishop-elect of Coventry as the most prominent names. Furthermore, most of them had received safe-conducts which were valid only until Michaelmas 1257, which suggests that they had never been intended to remain in Germany for long.[16] The earl's visit was certainly not planned to initiate an armed conquest. Richard's progress through Germany had to be effortless in order to be successful. By the time of Richard's departure in early May, Alfonso's rival candidacy was known in England as well as in Germany and at the *curia*.[17] Therefore, Richard had to convince his brother's English subjects, whose support both kings needed, those in Germany who were still undecided in their allegiance, and ultimately the pope, with whom rested the decision whom to crown emperor, that he was the only legitimate claimant. The more

---

[12] *Constitutiones, 1198–1272*, no. 386; Matthew Paris, *Chronica maiora*, v. 604, 622; *CR, 1256–9*, 124.

[13] Matthew Paris, *Chronica maiora*, v. 624–6; *Diplomatic documents*, no. 297; *CR, 1256–9*, 53; *CPR, 1247–58*, 548.

[14] *CPR, 1247–58*, 128.

[15] Denholm-Young, *Richard of Cornwall*, 90–2.

[16] This takes the sting out of Matthew Paris's comment that Richard's English knights were sent home because the Germans did not want to be ruled by foreigners: *Chronica maiora*, v. 653. These comments were related to English politics rather than German realities: *Gesta treverorum continuata*, MGH, SS xxiv. 412–13; A. Wolf, 'The family of dynasties in medieval Europe: dynasties, kingdoms and Tochterstämme', *Studies in Medieval and Renaissance History* xii (1991), 183–260.

[17] Matthew Paris, *Chronica maiora*, v. 657.

easily opposition could be overcome, the more strikingly would the hollow-
ness of Alfonso's claims be revealed. That this was a consideration is underlined by Richard's letters, all of which emphasised the ease with which he
found himself accepted.[18] This also forms the background to statements like
the one in which Richard described the archbishop of Mainz's martial
exploits. His wish that England, too, would have such war-like prelates[19] was
less an expression of naïveté, than an illustration of the strength and power of
his supporters. We have to read Richard's actions and the way he described
them with his intended audience in mind. That certainly included the
princes, prelates and burghers of Germany, but also – and perhaps more
important at this stage – those who had to fund this campaign and who ultimately had to legitimise his claim: his English peers and the papacy.[20]

   This is not to say that the earl lacked military or political muscle in
Germany. To begin with, Richard could count on the backing of his electors.
The archbishop of Cologne, for instance, had begun to lay siege to Boppard,
which supported Alfonso, well before the earl's arrival. The earl thus relied
on a mixture of symbolic gestures and force to press his claims. While those
backing Richard were rewarded with grants – 'so long as they be of good
behaviour' [21] – troops were deployed against his enemies.[22] The *Annales
wormatienses* testify to the effectiveness of this approach: while plunder and
warfare beset those opposing his regime, those supporting it were rewarded
with lavish grants and privileges.[23] Few of his opponents found it possible to
resist for long, and by the autumn of 1258 most of them had surrendered.[24] By
the beginning of 1259 Richard had won control over the political and
economic heartland of Germany. Despite his tendency to exaggerate, the earl
could now rightly claim, as he had previously done in October 1257, that he
controlled the Rhine all the way to the Alps.[25] At the same time, Richard
was not blind to the difficulties still facing him. Most of those supporting him
came themselves from the Rhineland, and, at this stage, he had few
supporters in the south of Germany, in the east or north.[26] Richard still faced

---

18 Liebermann, 'Zur Geschichte', 220; K. Hampe, 'Ungedruckte Briefe zur Geschichte
König Richards von Cornwall aus der Sammlung Richards von Pofi', NA xxx (1905),
685–6.
19 *Annals of Burton*, AM i. 392–4.
20 See also Weiler, 'Matthew Paris', 78–9.
21 CPR, 1247–58, 553, in a privilege from 11 May 1257 to the citizens of Lübeck. See also
Codex diplomaticus lubecensis, in *Lübeckisches Urkundenbuch*, Lübeck 1843–1905, i, nos 78,
80.
22 Liebermann, 'Zur Geschichte', 220.
23 *Annales wormatienses*, MGH, SS xvii. 59–60.
24 Ibid. 59, 60, 62; *Die Gerichtsstandsprivilegien der deutschen Könige und Kaiser*, ed.
F. Battenberg, Cologne–Vienna 1983, no. 52.
25 Liebermann, 'Zu Kaiser Friedrich II', 220.
26 A grant to Aachen, for instance, made on the occasion of his coronation (17 May
1257), included the archbishops of Mainz and Cologne, the bishops of Cambrai,
Maastricht, Münster, Paderborn, the bishop-elect of Liège, the duke of Limburg, the counts

the task of expanding his authority beyond those areas controlled by his close allies.

To accomplish this task, Richard had to prove that he was, indeed, a non-partisan choice for king. His early charters thus list many of William's former supporters among their witnesses and recipients, but also include a number of imperial knights and nobles once active in the service of Frederick II and his sons.[27] The staff of Richard's chancery, as well as many of his officials, had been active under William, Conrad and Frederick. His chamberlain, for instance, was Philip of Falkenstein,[28] previously Conrad IV's steward, while Philip's uncle had held the same post under Frederick II, with other members of his family prominent in William's government.[29] Bishop Nicholas of Cambrai acted as chancellor (an office he had held under William of Holland), and John de Avesnes as seneschal.[30] Most significant, however, was the appearance of Arnold of Holland, provost of Wetzlar, in Richard's entourage. He had been prothonotary under William, and soon became Richard's chief diplomat: he acted as Richard's proctor in negotiating the Treaty of Paris, and represented him at the *curia*.[31] He also accompanied the earl to England, thus providing him with the necessary expertise needed for the king's business even while abroad.[32] From the beginning, Richard had thus been surrounded by men who would ensure a smooth transition for the new regime and the continuity of effective imperial government, and whose choice bridged the political divides of Germany. In addition, the support Richard had initially received from the count palatine also gave him legitimacy in the eyes of those once loyal to the Staufen. This, in turn, may explain Richard's repeated assurances that he would not interfere with Conradin's claims to Sicily, Swabia and Jerusalem.[33] None the less, all this

of Guelders, Holland, Kleve, Lützelenburg, Jülich, Loos, Berg and Bar. Noteworthy is the absence not only of those supporting Alfonso – the archbishop of Trier, the dukes of Saxony and Brabant, and the margraves of Brandenburg – but also of those one would expect in Richard's entourage, such as the duke of Brunswick or the count Palatine: *Urkundenbuch Niederrheins*, ii, no. 99.

[27] Ennen and Eckertz, *Quellen Köln*, ii, no. 372; K. Bosl, *Die Reichsministerialität der Salier und Staufer*, Stuttgart 1950–1, ii. 371; E. Jacob, *Untersuchungen über Herkunft und Aufstieg des Reichsministerialengeschlechts Bolanden*, Giessen 1936, 34–5.

[28] *Regesta imperii*, no. 5301.

[29] Jacob, *Untersuchungen*, 32–5.

[30] Matthew Paris, *Chronica maiora*, v. 641; *Regesta imperii*, no. 5309. However, Denholm-Young, *Richard of Cornwall*, 93 n. 1, citing Bappert, *Richard von Cornwall*, 11 n. 3, who in turn cites Ficker, 'Die Reichshofbeamten', 482, 516–17, points out that no charter evidence survives to corroborate Matthew's statement, and that it was indeed Werner of Bolanden who acted as seneschal. Matthew may have been confused by the eminent role which John continued to play, and John's death in 1258 may further complicate matters.

[31] *Acta imperii inedita*, i, nos 563–4; *Regesta imperii*, nos 4885e, 5005, 5187, 5258; *Foedera*, 384.

[32] *CChR, 1257–1300*, 24–5; *CR, 1259–61*, 399; *CPR, 1258–66*, 496.

[33] *Constitutiones, 1198–1272*, no. 386.

could only be a first step. Richard still had to convince his subjects not only that he claimed the title of a king, but also that he was able to act like one.

Where possible, Richard tried to ease the way towards acceptance of his authority. Worms, for instance, was offered 1,000 marks and the confirmation of its privileges when it surrendered.[34] This proved to be the right approach. Richard was soon acknowledged even in the Staufens' heartland, with privileges surviving for Nuremberg in Franconia and the abbey of Maulbronn in Swabia.[35] At the same time, once Richard had established his authority in an area, he exercised it fully.[36] The burgrave of Landskron, for example, after having his claims to the imperial castle of Landskron confirmed in 1257, was ordered to provide troops for the siege of Worms in 1258.[37] Accepting Richard as king also meant accepting that he would exercise his royal rights and privileges. Where feasible, the king also tried to expand imperial territory. A number of privileges survive from Richard's reign, confirming or granting towns and abbeys imperial privileges or taking them under imperial protection.[38] This meant that they were taken out of the control of local nobles or princes, and into that of the empire, granting them an increase not only in status, but also in political and commercial freedom. In exchange, Richard was able to count on strong support from some of the Rhenish cities when relations between him and their former lords deteriorated.[39] Lacking a territorial basis in Germany, Richard had to rely on these imperial enclaves to provide him with the necessary support. Furthermore, Matthew Paris reports that Richard tried to take back towns into his protection which had been pawned by his predecessors,[40] a claim which is backed up by some circumstantial evidence.[41]

---

34 *Annales wormatienses*, MGH, SS xvii. 60–2.

35 *Nürnberger Urkundenbuch*, Nuremberg 1959, no. 374; *Wirtembergisches Urkundenbuch*, Stuttgart 1849–1913, v, no. 1447.

36 *Acta imperii selecta*, no. 378

37 *Urkundenbuch zur mittelrheinischen Territorien*, nos 1401, 1451.

38 Ibid. no. 1402; *Acta imperii selecta*, no. 382; *Urkundenbuch der Abtei Heisterbach*, ed. F. Schmitz, Bonn 1908, no. 144.

39 Cologne provides a particularly good example: E. Ennen, 'Erzbischof und Stadtgemeinde in Köln bis zur Schlacht von Worringen', in F. Petri (ed.), *Bischofs- und Kathedralgeschichte des Mittelalters und der frühen Neuzeit*, Cologne–Vienna 1976, 27–46, repr. in her *Gesammelte Abhandlungen*, Bonn 1977, 388–404; U. Höroldt, *Studien zur politischen Stellung des Kölner Domkapitels zwischen Erzbischof, Stadt Köln und Territorialgewalten, 1198–1332: Untersuchungen und Personallisten*, Siegburg 1994, 153–92; M. Groten, *Köln im 13. Jahrhundert: gesellschaftlicher Wandel und Verfassungsentwicklung*, Cologne–Weimar–Vienna 1995, passim. This had considerable consequences for Richard's standing within the town: Gotfrid Hagen, *Dat Boich van der stede Colne*, ed. C. Schröder and A. Birlinger, in *Die Chroniken der deutschen Städte vom 14. bis ins 16. Jahrhundert*, XII/1: *Die Chroniken der niederrheinischen Städte: Cöln*, Leipzig 1875, lines 687–756, pp. 41–3. I am grateful to Len Scales for this reference.

40 Matthew Paris, *Chronica maiora*, v. 695–8.

41 In 1260, for example, Richard guaranteed to pay off the debt for which Hagenau had formerly been consigned as security: *Regesta imperii*, no. 5377.

Richard's government has received a largely negative press from modern historians.[42] Most recently, Joseph Huffman has reiterated the belief that Richard 'dispensed with what little authority was left in Germany'.[43] The surviving evidence, however, suggests a more complex picture. Andreas Schlunk has highlighted considerable fluctuations in the extent of the imperial domain during the period 1245–73.[44] It would be naïve to assume that Richard's prolonged absence, and in particular the political weakness displayed during the 1260s, did not allow for appropriations of imperial lands and rights by local lords. This was not, however, the result of a conscious policy on the king's part. Quite to the contrary: the issues of his chancery point to a marked refusal to part with what remained of the imperial domain. Richard's first major privilege, issued on 22 May 1257, shortly after his coronation, to the citizens of Aachen, for instance, was an almost exact copy of an earlier grant by Frederick II.[45] The preservation and, to some extent, enlargement of the royal domain remained the principle underlying Richard's grants,[46] and little was given away that had not been lost already.[47] Historians have voiced much concern regarding, for example, Richard's privileges for the citizens of Cologne.[48] Following the grants made by William,[49] the earl promised not to lead armed men into the city, except for his entourage who would be armed modestly; no diets were to be held, nor castles or fortifications built. This has been viewed as a sell-out of imperial rights,[50] but by 1257 Cologne had already ceased to be a major venue for imperial diets or sojourns. Conrad IV had been there only twice, Henry (VII) once and even Frederick

---

[42] Kempf, *Geschichte des deutschen Reiches*, 202–4; A. Gerlich, 'Rheinische Kurfürsten und deutsches Königtum im Interregnum', in *Geschichtliche Landeskunde*, III/2: *Festschrift Bärmann* (1967), 44–126 at p. 107; Denholm-Young, *Richard of Cornwall*, 114. For a more positive assessment see G. C. Gebauer, *Leben und denckwürdige Thaten Herrn Richards, Erwählten Römischen Kaysers, Grafens von Cornwall und Poitou*, Leipzig 1744, 456–72; F. Trautz, 'Richard von Cornwall', *Jahrbuch des Vereins für Geschichte von Stadt und Kreis Kaiserslautern* vii (1969), 27–59 at pp. 56–7; Weiler, 'Image and "reality" '. See also F. Schwind, *Die Landvogtei in der Wetterau: Studien zu Herrschaft und Politik der staufischen und spätmittelalterlichen Könige*, Marburg 1972, 92–4.

[43] Huffman, *Social politics*, 291–2.

[44] A. C. Schlunk, *Königsmacht und Krongut: die Machtgrundlage des deutschen Königtums im 13. Jahrhundert und eine neue historische Methode*, Stuttgart 1988.

[45] *Urkundenbuch Niederrhein*, ii, no. 438. Other examples include Fischbeck, St Gisela and Maastricht: *Acta imperii inedita*, i, no. 572; *Acta imperii selecta*, nos 385–7; *Annales hamburgenses*, MGH, SS xvi. 384; *Urkundenbuch des Stiftes Fischbeck*, I: *955–1470*, ed. H. Lathwesen and B. Poschmann, Rinteln 1978, no. 36.

[46] *Codex diplomaticus moenofrancofurtanus*, in *Urkundenbuch der Reichsstadt Frankfurt*, ed. J. F. Böhmer and F. Lau, Frankfurt 1901–5, i, no. 217. Richard guaranteed that none of the imperial cities in the Wetterau region would be alienated from the royal domain.

[47] Bappert, *Richard von Cornwall*, 13.

[48] *Urkundenbuch Niederrhein*, ii, no. 438; *Die Gerichtsstandsprivilegien*, i, no. 51.

[49] *Regesta imperii*, no. 4980.

[50] G. Rauch, *Die Bündnisse deutscher Herrscher mit Reichsangehörigen vom Regierungsantritt Friedrich Barbarossas bis zum Tod Rudolfs von Habsburg*, Aalen 1966, 125.

II just three times.[51] Richard himself went three times. The exception was William of Holland who issued charters at Cologne on nine different occasions.[52] New privileges were issued on a limited scale and with limited value. The Teutonic Knights, for example, were freed of all tolls for wine and other goods which they shipped along the Rhine.[53] Similarly, the citizens of Aachen received permission to use the royal baths.[54] We may assume that, even in 1257, the royal domain was still substantial enough not to make this a wasteful squandering of scarce resources.

Securing the German throne was not, however, something which could be accomplished in Germany alone. Alfonso had to be entirely overcome before Richard could feel secure. Worms and Speyer, for instance, had only been willing to open their gates because the king of Castile had failed to come to Germany.[55] Theirs was not an isolated case. Friedberg, Wetzlar and Frankfurt were promised that they would never be alienated from the empire, but Richard also conceded that, should the pope recognise another king, they were free to switch allegiance.[56] As long as there was a rival candidate around whom opponents could rally, the foundations of Richard's kingship remained dangerously weak.

This added urgency to Richard's efforts to be crowned emperor, which would have given full acknowledgement to his claims. This was certainly what past precedent suggested: Innocent III did not crown Otto emperor until after Philip had been killed, Frederick II was not crowned until after Otto's death and William of Holland could only pursue his imperial coronation after Conrad IV had died. Being crowned emperor meant that one's opponents had been overcome.

Before Richard could claim the imperial title, however, relations with the Capetians had to be settled. Although relations between the kings of England and France had improved during the 1250s, they were far from friendly. In fact, as we have seen, one of the chief worries prompting Henry III's involvement in the affairs of Germany in 1256 had been fears that the Capetians might seek to thwart his ambitions in Sicily. Equally, the king of France eyed Henry III's activities in Germany with suspicion. Matthew Paris, for instance, reported that Louis IX reacted to Richard's election by fortifying

---

51 Numbers based on royal itineraries as presented in *Zeit der Staufer*, III (maps).
52 Numbers based on entries in *Regesta imperii*.
53 *Acta imperii inedita*, i, no. 560. Similarly, a privilege for the abbey of Camp was limited to freedom from tolls at the imperial toll station of Kaiserswerth: H. Cardauns, 'Fünf Kaiserurkunden', *Forschungen zur deutschen Geschichte* xii (1872), 453–6, no. 4; S. Lorenz, *Kaiserswerth im Mittelalter: Genese, Struktur und Organisation königlicher Herrschaft am Niederrhein*, Düsseldorf 1993, 70–82.
54 *Regesten Aachen*, i, no. 174.
55 *Annales wormatienses*, MGH, SS xvii. 59.
56 *Urkundenbuch der Stadt Friedberg: erster Band, 1216–1410*, ed. M. Foltz, Marburg 1904, nos 35–6; *Regesta imperii*, nos 5318, 5322, 14809; *Urkundenbuch Frankfurt*, i, no. 217.

castles in Normandy.[57] Furthermore, the chronicler continued, Louis decided to capture Richard's messengers and to undermine his support in Germany, so as to prevent the earl from invading the kingdom of France.[58] Clearly, relations between Capetians and Plantagenets had not yet settled sufficiently for a king of France to believe that having an English prince ruling Germany would not result in an attack on his domains. This had consequences beyond Louis interrupting lines of communication between Henry and Richard. Matthew's statement that the king of France sought to undermine the earl's support in Germany thus merits some consideration. Although no clear link can be established between Alfonso and the Capetians, sufficient circumstantial evidence survives to suggest that he was at least perceived as someone likely to count on Louis's backing. Moreover, relations had previously been cordial: in 1255 plans had been mooted for a marriage between Louis's eldest son and a Castilian princess, while in May 1256 a Castilian embassy had arrived in Paris to discuss matters pertaining to the election of a new emperor.[59] The king of Castile could thus reasonably expect his candidacy to be viewed more favourably by Louis IX than that of the king of England's brother who, moreover, had not yet abandoned his title of count of Poitou. In addition, most of Alfonso's followers outside Italy came from the empire's western borders, and were either vassals or dependants of the Capetians. In September 1257, for instance, Albert de la Tour received Arles and Vienne.[60] More important, in October Alfonso appointed the duke of Brabant as his imperial vicar.[61] The duke had already proven himself a reliable ally to Louis IX, exemplified not least by the marriage of Alfons of Poitou into the ducal dynasty. Similarly, in September 1258 Alfonso received homage from the duke of Burgundy,[62] and in November Count Guido of Flanders, who had established his claims with the help of Charles of Anjou, accepted Alfonso as king.[63] If nothing else, the king of Castile forged strong links with those who in the past had been most loyal to the king of France and his family. This, in turn, posed considerable difficulties for Richard. To overcome his Castilian opponent in Germany, he needed recognition from the pope, and his coronation as emperor. That, however, was unlikely to be granted while the Capetians viewed his candidacy as a threat. Consequently, Richard had to show that he did not plan any hostile actions against the Capetians.

Richard demonstrated his good intentions by tackling the still simmering conflict over the Flemish inheritance. Should John de Avesnes have hoped that his pre-eminent role in securing Richard's election – he had acted as one

---

[57] Matthew Paris, *Chronica maiora*, v. 626.

[58] Ibid. v. 605, 657.

[59] G. Daumet, *Mémoire sur les relations de la France et de la Castille de 1255 à 1320*, Paris [1913], 1–12.

[60] *Regesta imperii*, no. 5489.

[61] Ibid. no. 5493.

[62] Ibid. nos 5496–7.

[63] Ibid. no. 5500.

of Richard's proctors with the archbishop of Cologne – would lead to support for his claims in Flanders, he was to be disappointed. In September 1256 John had been forced to accept Louis's arbitration confirming his loss of Flanders and Namur,[64] and in November 1257 he and his brother Baldwin renewed their acceptance of this agreement.[65] Furthermore, in spring 1258 the earl himself promised the countess that he would strive to revoke William's sentence, which had deprived her of all imperial fiefs, but did so under the condition that she would offer personal homage.[66] However, this did not prevent Richard from confirming the duke of Luxemburg in his recent conquest of Namur, claimed by Margaret of Flanders.[67] None the less, the earl stayed clear of openly assisting the Avesnes brothers in actions which would further alienate Louis IX.[68] Thus, the way was paved for negotiations with the king of France, while also undermining the position of Alfonso of Castile. In this context it is perhaps worth reminding ourselves that many of Alfonso's supporters had initially looked towards the Capetians as a means of protecting themselves against William of Holland and his allies. The fact that these very men, and John de Avesnes in particular, had played such a prominent role in bringing about Richard's candidacy would have left them little choice but to side with the king of Castile. This, in turn, meant that, to secure his throne, Richard had to some extent at least to distance himself from the very people who had secured him his election.

Like his brother Richard, Henry III, too, had little interest in a renewed outbreak of hostilities, and stepped up his efforts at finding a permanent settlement almost immediately after Richard's coronation at Aachen.[69] Ultimately, as we have seen, this was to result in Henry's agreeing the Treaty of Paris. Richard ratified the settlement as earl of Cornwall, but also aimed to emphasise his special status, and suggested that he and Louis IX enter a separate agreement. In the spirit of the Treaty of Catania, the two rulers were to promise each other their mutual support, friendship and assistance. To underline his position even further, Richard was not represented by his brother's proctors, but by his own imperial prothonotary. Although no evidence

---

64 Ibid. nos 11756–8.
65 *Thesaurus novus anecdotorum*, i, ii, ed. E. Martène and U. Durand, Paris 1717, repr. New York 1968, i. 1092; *Regesta imperii*, nos 11797–8.
66 *Regesta imperii*, no. 5343; BN, Mélanges de Colbert, 378, 502. I am grateful to Dr Ingo Schwab who provided me with his transcripts of this document, as well as of similar proceedings in 1260 (Mélanges Colbert, 378, 503) and 1262 (Mélanges Colbert, 378, 504); and for his discussion on the role the 1258 document played in preparing the Treaty of Paris.
67 *Urkunden- und Quellenbuch zur Geschichte der altluxemburgischen Territorien bis zur burgundischen Zeit*, ed. C. Wampach, Luxemburg, 1935–55, iii, no. 250.
68 For the difficulties and problems facing Richard on the western borders of Germany see A. Joris, 'La Visite à Huy de Richard de Cornouailles, roi des Romains (29 décembre 1258)', in his *Villes: affaires-mentalites: autour du pays mosun*, Brussels 1993, 457–66. I am grateful to John Maddicott for this reference.
69 *Foedera*, 358.

survives that this proposed agreement was concluded, Richard had settled his relations with France, and could now more confidently approach the pope.[70]

Imperial ambitions and English rebels, 1259–68

Immediately after his coronation, Richard, promising to expel rebels and ensure that law and justice be upheld, announced to the citizens of Rome that he wished to become emperor.[71] Richard's plans received a favourable reception from members of the papal *curia*. This support can not have come easily. After all, by backing Plantagenet candidates for both the imperial throne and that of Sicily, the papacy would have created the very situation it had striven so hard to prevent – the same dynasty ruling lands to the north and south of the papal states. It seems, though, that in 1257 many believed the possible advantages to outweigh potential risks. Letters from a number of cardinals survive, either urging Richard to come to Rome quickly, or pressing Alexander IV to lend the earl his support.[72] Richard, too, prepared to recruit supporters. Contacts were made with the patriarch of Aquileia,[73] Azzo of Este,[74] Uberto Pallavacini[75] and Thomas of Savoy.[76] The earl left little doubt as to his intentions, and, as in the case of his German election, he tried to prepare the ground politically and diplomatically before venturing south.

Initially, Richard made swift progress,[77] and in April 1259 Alexander IV promised to send a legate to Germany to exhort the princes to adhere to Richard.[78] In fact, a papal letter survives in which the duke of Burgundy – previously one of Alfonso's partisans – is admonished to assist Richard, king of the Romans, *in imperatorem promovendo*, 'who is [yet] to be made emperor'.[79] Similarly, the archbishop of Cologne was praised for the support shown to Richard and exhorted to continue doing so.[80] Although this fell

---

[70] Hampe, 'Ungedruckte Briefe', 673–90 at pp. 685–6; *Annals of Burton*, AM i. 469–70.

[71] Hampe, 'Ungedruckte Briefe', 685–6.

[72] *Acta imperii inedita*, i, nos 741–4.

[73] Ibid. i, no. 742.

[74] Ibid. i, no. 567.

[75] Ibid. ii, no. 82.

[76] Ibid. i, no. 562; *Regesta imperii*, no. 5342. A fourteenth-century German chronicler reports that Richard had granted Asti and Turin to the pope. This would have contravened Richard's general attitude towards the Savoyards, but, should the report be accurate, it may have formed part of the settlement for Thomas's release from captivity in 1257: *Liber de rebus memorialibus sive Chronicon Henrici de Hervordia*, ed. A. Potthast, Göttingen 1859, 195.

[77] Busson, *Die Doppelwahl*, 46–58; H. Otto, 'Alexander IV. und der deutsche Thronstreit', MIÖG xix (1898), 75–91.

[78] *Annals of Burton*, AM i. 469–70; *Das Baumgartner Formelbuch: eine Quelle zur Geschichte des XIII. Jahrhunderts vornehmlich der Zeiten Rudolfs von Habsburg*, ed. H. Baerwald, Vienna 1866, no. 9.

[79] *Actes pontificaux*, no. 1001; *Flores historiarum*, ed. H. R. Luard (RS, 1890), ii. 427–8.

[80] *Baumgartner Formelbuch*, no. 11.

short of a certain promise that Alexander would crown the earl emperor, it none the less suggested very strongly that Richard would be able to count on the *curia's* backing. In 1260, therefore, the earl is said to have left for Germany to plan his coronation as emperor.[81] A visit to Rome was certainly planned: in October 1259 Richard, 'going to the court of Rome on the affairs of himself, the king and the realm' had been allowed to tallage his manors and boroughs in England.[82] Furthermore, in September 1260, Richard wrote to the citizens of Bologna to announce his imminent arrival.[83] This coincided with intense diplomatic activity aimed at the king of France. Before the earl left England, envoys arrived from Louis IX,[84] and contacts continued during Henry III's sojourn on the mainland later that year.[85] Henry III even felt confident enough to ask Louis IX for money to repay a loan he had received from Richard.[86] That the king of England could ask his Capetian counterpart to support the earl's planned coronation as emperor signifies both the changing nature of Anglo-French relations, and the importance of peaceful relations with the Capetians for Richard's imperial project. However, nothing was to come of the proposed journey. In mid-June the earl left for the continent,[87] but returned in October, largely due to the situation in England. During a parliament earlier that month, Henry of Almain, Richard's eldest son, had begun to act as Simon de Montfort's proctor, in opposition to Henry III. Various initially competing factions began to work together, pressing their claims against the king.[88] This state of affairs was alarming enough to prompt Richard's immediate return. Not for the last time, political developments in England interfered with the earl's ambitions in Germany.

The full effects of Richard's continuing entanglement in English politics were not to be known until some years later. In the meantime he was elected senator of Rome in spring 1261,[89] and was urged by various cardinals to come quickly to receive his crown.[90] In April 1262, however, Urban IV declared a change in papal policy, and announced that he was unable to favour either him or Alfonso.[91] The pope's decision had not been hasty or rushed. For some time, Richard's failure to come to Rome had caused unease.[92] If a date can be fixed to pin down this shift in attitude, it was probably the council held in

---

81 *Flores,* ii. 452.
82 *CPR, 1258–66,* 57.
83 *Regesta imperii,* no. 5382.
84 *CPR, 1258–66,* 119.
85 *CR, 1259–61,* 167.
86 *CPR, 1258–66,* 74.
87 *Flores,* ii. 452.
88 Maddicott, *Simon de Montfort,* 192–203.
89 Liebermann, 'Zur Geschichte', 222. See also F. R. Lewis, 'The election of Richard of Cornwall as senator of Rome in 1261', *EHR* li (1937), 657–62.
90 Hampe, 'Ungedruckte Briefe', 687.
91 Ibid. 689–90.
92 Ibid. 688; *Diplomatic documents,* no. 340.

1261, dealing, among other things, with the German double election.[93] From then on Pope Urban IV avoided committing himself. By August 1263 he announced that both Alfonso and Richard were from now on to be addressed as elected kings of the Romans,[94] that is, they both held an equal claim to becoming emperor, at least until a papal investigation into their claims had reported its findings. That investigation was, however, never concluded: in 1264, Richard, held captive by Simon de Montfort, was unable to authorise his proctors at the *curia*, and proceedings had to be delayed; then Urban IV died, just when he was ready to announce his decision;[95] his successor, Clement IV, declared that he first had to consult the records, and gave 1 June 1269 as the date for his final decision, but died in November 1268. Although a new pontiff was elected in September 1271, he was not enthroned until late March 1272, just a few days before Richard's death. Much of the image of the years 1250–73 as a period of political anarchy, unrestrained by the authority of a king, rests on the inability of either Alfonso or Richard to secure an imperial coronation. However, by 1272, when Richard died, the papal throne had been vacant for nearly three years, while Richard's opponents had either been overcome or killed. Richard and many of his contemporaries still expected him to become emperor.

Urban's change of mind was only in part connected to Richard's rule in Germany. To appreciate fully why he refused to endorse either candidate we need to consider the situation in Christendom in general, and along the Mediterranean in particular. 1260–1 were years of crisis. Constantinople had fallen to the Palaiologoi; a Mongol invasion was feared;[96] affairs in the Holy Land had taken yet another turn for the worse;[97] while waves of flagellants swept across northern Italy.[98] Manfred still ruled Sicily, and even began to widen his circle of contacts to include the Muslim rulers of Egypt,[99] and he increasingly found support in the west.[100] Under these circumstances, the *curia* needed two things: powerful protectors, and a political climate conducive to joint action against the various threats facing Latin Christendom. During the early 1260s neither the earl of Cornwall nor the king of Castile would have been able to provide the former, and their continuing rivalry was in danger of jeopardising the latter. Furthermore, initially at least, Urban's decision may have been an attempt to force either Richard or Alfonso first to prove that they were emperors-elect in name as well as deed, and, secondly,

93 *Alberti milioli notarii regini liber*, MGH, SS xxi. 366.
94 *Epistolae saeculi XIII*, iii, nos 558, 561.
95 Ibid. iii, nos 631, 653.
96 J. Richard, 'The Mongols and the Franks', *Journal of Asian History* iii (1969), 45–57; *Continuatio William of Newburgh*, in *Chronicles of Stephen, Henry and Richard*, 539.
97 P. Jackson, 'The crisis in the Holy Land, 1260', *EHR* xcv (1980), 481–513.
98 G. Dickson, 'The flagellants of 1260 and the crusades', *JMH* xv (1989), 227–67.
99 *The memoirs of a Syrian prince: Abu'l-Fida'*, *sultan of Hamah (672–732/1273–1331)*, ed. P. M. Holt, Wiesbaden 1983, 31–2.
100 Berg, 'Manfred', 111–36; *Epistolae saeculi XIII*, iii, no. 519.

to do so by offering the papacy the support it needed. Only when Richard became ever more deeply entangled in the affairs of England, and when Alfonso, too, began to face opposition from his nobles, did the *curia* seriously begin to look for an alternative candidate to replace both.

Richard's success in Germany rested upon the revenues of his English estates. They allowed him to recruit and reward followers, hire troops and buy back or acquire imperial lands. Consequently, any disturbance in England would limit his ability to rule the empire, and the earl could thus not avoid involving himself in the affairs of his brother's realm. Somewhat ironically, perhaps, Richard had been able to take the German throne because of his role in England, but over time it was this very role which endangered his kingship of the Romans. The complexity of his situation is indicated by an exchange between the king and his brother in November 1258, when Henry requested that Richard endorse the Provisions of Oxford: despite being king of the Romans, Richard remained a baron of England, and, as such, had to comply with its laws.[101] Matthew Paris claims that the earl's German entourage was bewildered by the treatment he received, and that they consequently disregarded his authority.[102] In this, he may have been exaggerating. However, the king of the Romans continued to be hindered by the fact that he was also earl of Cornwall, and this provides the background for the *curia's* cooling enthusiasm.

By 1263, when Urban IV finally ended papal support for Richard, the political crisis in England had escalated further. In June the bishop of Hereford had been dragged from his cathedral and incarcerated by Simon de Montfort's partisans. Soon after, the estates of Henry's seneschal were plundered, and baronial forces came to occupy much of the south-east.[103] Although the earl undertook several attempts at mediating between Simon and Henry,[104] his efforts met with little success, and he was even reprimanded for his failure by the pope: in September Urban IV ordered Richard to come to the king's defence. Harsh words were used: although the earl had not caused the recent violence, he none the less condoned it.[105] Despite the fact that royal control was eventually restored, Richard's position had been weakened.

Furthermore, this was not the only poor performance given by Richard. When exhorting the earl to come to his brother's assistance in 1263, Urban IV also referred to German knights who had come to fight Henry III. A clue to their provenance may be given by a separate warning, which Urban issued to the archbishop of Cologne, who was ordered to comply with any decision a

---

101 CR, 1256–9, 460; *Royal letters Henry III*, ii, no. 520.
102 Matthew Paris, *Chronica maiora*, v. 736–7.
103 Maddicott, *Simon de Montfort*, 225–39.
104 *Royal letters Henry III*, ii, nos 604–7.
105 *Papal letters*, 402.

recently dispatched papal legate would make regarding England.[106] Archbishop Engelbert II also posed the biggest challenge so far to Richard's authority in Germany, when he began to support Frederick II's grandson Conradin. In May 1262 Conradin held a diet at Ulm claiming the duchy of Swabia as his inheritance,[107] and was soon supported by several nobles and towns in Swabia.[108] More important, the count palatine came to his assistance. From then on events moved quickly: in early June Urban IV thanked the king of Bohemia for giving warning about plans to elect Conradin as anti-king.[109] Richard, too, reacted promptly, and set out for Germany in June 1262. Lacking military resources – it seems that he had relied on Henry III to provide troops, which, however, were not forthcoming [110] – he took to alliances and symbolic gestures instead. While Richard was at Aachen in August, for instance, he confirmed King Ottokar of Bohemia in his – disputed – possession of Austria, thus demonstrating in whose power it was to grant or receive imperial lands.[111] The same day, a memorandum was issued listing the imperial insignia Richard had presented to St Mary's at Aachen,[112] aimed to emphasise Richard's position as properly crowned and consecrated king. Moreover, he scored a major success when he negotiated a truce between the duke of Brabant and one of his local opponents.[113] Thus, the last and most important of Alfonso's partisans was won over. In October Richard reached Alsace.[114] Old supporters were won back,[115] and even the count palatine was brought temporarily to heel.[116] Although no military encounter followed, this had been enough to thwart Conradin's ambitions, and he remained confined to parts of Swabia and the domains of the duke of Bavaria.

---

[106] Ibid. 396–8.

[107] *Notae historicae sangallenses*, MGH, SS i. 71.

[108] *Regesta imperii*, no. 4791; L. Weiland, 'Sieben Kaiserurkunden', *Forschungen zur deutschen Geschichte* xviii (1878), 204–10 at p. 210. H. Maurer, 'Die Anfänge der Stadt Tiengen und das politische Kräftespiel am Hochrhein um die Mitte des 13 Jahrhunderts', *Alemannisches Jahrbuch* (1964–5), 119–58 at p. 141.

[109] *Epistolae saeculi XIII*, iii, no. 520.

[110] *CR, 1261–4*, 175–6.

[111] *Codex diplomaticus Bohemiae*, no. 345.

[112] *Regesten Aachen*, i, no. 174; A. Huyskens, 'Der Plan des Königs Richard von Cornwallis zur Niederlegung eines deutschen Krönungsschatzes in Aachen', *Annalen des Historischen Vereins für den Niederrhein* cxv (1929), 180–204 at pp. 202–4, and 'Noch einmal der Krönungsschatz Königs Richard von Cornwallis', *Annalen des Historischen Vereins für den Niederrhein* cxviii (1931), 136–43; A. di Miranda, *Richard von Cornwallis und sein Verhältnis zur Krönungsstadt Aachen*, Bonn 1880; J. Petersohn, 'Über monarchische Insignien und ihre Funktion im mittelalterlichen Reich', *HZ* cclxvi (1998), 47–96.

[113] *Regesta imperii*, no. 14811e.

[114] Ibid. nos 5409–16.

[115] *Urkundenbuch der Stadt Strassburg*, ed. W. Wiegand, Strasbourg 1879–1900, i, no. 507; *Regesta imperii*, nos 5408, 5413.

[116] *Regesta imperii*, no. 5402. By 1265 he was already siding with Conradin again: *Monumenta boica*, xxx, Munich 1834, no. 804.

Although this may have sufficed to safeguard Richard's claims in Germany, it was not enough to win over the pope.

All this makes Urban's cooling enthusiasm seem less surprising. In a way, the pope was vindicated, for, despite his best efforts, Richard had to become embroiled in English affairs. In 1264 the earl was involved in negotiating the Mise of Amiens,[117] and he acted as regent during the king's absence in France. When this last attempt at a peaceful settlement failed, the king and his barons went to war and in May 1264 the two kings and their sons were taken prisoner by Simon de Montfort after the battle of Lewes. This marked the nadir of Richard's relations with the *curia*.[118] What saved his kingship was that Alfonso was in no better situation.[119] At the time it may have seemed, however, as if neither would be able to make it to Rome to receive the imperial crown: in 1265 Clement IV wrote to the archbishop of Seville, urging him to induce Alfonso to withdraw his candidacy. Clement declared that he did not ask this because he preferred Richard. Rather, a third and more powerful candidate was to be appointed.[120] It was only the royal victory at Evesham in 1265 that prevented Richard's immediate demise. His position was, however weakened, and he remained unable to see to his imperial affairs.[121] The pope in Rome and his legates in Germany continued to ignore him.[122] Thus, Richard's visit to Germany in 1268 was probably also undertaken with the aim of proving to the *curia* that he still marshalled the support necessary to become emperor.

Despite Richard's weakening standing with the *curia*, his position in the empire was still strong enough to survive various challenges. Despite lacking a strong military entourage in 1262, Richard had been able to overcome Conradin's supporters with relative ease. Similarly, in 1266, when rumours spread about the impending election of another anti-king,[123] it was not even necessary for Richard to appear in person. His captivity appears to have had limited political impact. For instance, some charters survive in which those issuing grants date their privileges as having been given *regnante Romanorum rege Richardo*, 'when Richard, king of the Romans, reigned', long after news of his defeat at Lewes must have reached Germany.[124] Similarly, in late June 1264, four weeks after the event, a peace was agreed between the archbishop of Mainz and the count palatine, which still looked to Richard as the

---

117 *Royal letters Henry III*, ii, no. 608.
118 *Epistolae saeculi XIII*, iii, no. 631.
119 O'Callaghan, *The learned king*, 182–94.
120 *Thesaurus novus*, ii. 137–8.
121 *Acta imperii selecta*, no. 384; *Chronica de Mailros*, 196. M. Page, 'Cornwall, Earl Richard and the Barons' War', EHR cxv (2000), 21–38.
122 *Regesta imperii*, nos 10617a–10624; H. Ollendiek, *Die päpstlichen Legaten im deutschen Reichsgebiet von 1261 bis zum Ende des Interregnums*, Fribourg 1976, 176–9.
123 *Constitutiones, 1198–1272*, no. 406; *Epistolae saeculi XIII*, iii, no. 657.
124 *Westfälisches Urkundenbuch*, Münster 1847–1977, iv, no. 1035 [25 June 1265].

ultimate source of authority within the empire.[125] Only the count palatine and duke of Bavaria seems to have been willing to take advantage of Richard's prolonged absence.[126] Even he, however, came to recognise Richard again in 1269.[127] Although there was a decline in the frequency with which Richard issued charters during the 1260s, business still continued as usual. He retained the company of his imperial chancellor, he was met and consulted by envoys from Germany.[128] Privileges were still issued and conflicts settled.[129] The earl's prospects of being made emperor may have become bleak, but he still faced little serious opposition in Germany.

Triumph, 1268–72

By the time of Richard's fourth visit to Germany in August 1268, his opponents were either dead, or they were beset by domestic problems and thus unable to pursue their imperial ambitions.[130] Most princes initially hostile had come round to either requesting his help or quietly accepting him. Those still opposed to Richard's regime lacked a focal point around which to rally. The earl of Cornwall was thus free to exercise his authority, at a point that coincided with the final phase of papal deliberations on who was to become emperor. As soon as he arrived, Richard underlined the breadth of his success. The inheritance of Brabant was settled, and first contacts were made with the towns and princes of Italy.[131] In the context of Germany, the most significant manifestations of Richard's new freedom of action were his marriage to Beatrice of Falkenburg, and the Diet of Worms of 1269.[132]

Beatrice was the daughter of an important lord in the Rhineland.[133] Renowned for her beauty, she also provided a link with a powerful family in Richard's heartland (her uncle being the archbishop of Cologne). The political dimension is emphasised by Thomas Wykes: fighting the Germans'

---

[125] *Constitutiones, 1198–1272*, no. 442.
[126] Ibid. no. 464.
[127] *Regesta imperii*, no. 5455a.
[128] *Acta imperii inedita*, i, no. 570; *Royal letters Henry III*, ii, no. 550; *CPR, 1258–66*, 496.
[129] *Regesta imperii*, nos 5427–8, 5483; *Urkundenbuch altluxemburgische Territorien*, iii, nos 472–3; *Regesten Aachen*, i, no. 213; *Mecklenburgisches Urkundenbuch*, Schwerin 1863–1977, ii. 824; *Acta imperii inedita*, i, no. 576.
[130] Conradin had been executed at Naples in 1268: *Bartholomaei de Neocastro historia Siculi*, ed. G. Paladino, RIS xiii/3, Bologna 1921–2, 7–10; F. Geldner, 'Konradin und das alte deutsche Königtum: Opfer der hohenstaufischen Italienpolitik?', *Zeitschrift für bayerische Landesgeschichte* xxxii (1969), 495–524; A. Nitschke, 'Konradin und Clemens IV', *Quellen und Forschungen aus italienischen Archiven und Bibliotheken* xxxviii (1958), 268–77.
[131] *Regesta imperii*, no. 5454
[132] *Annales wormatienses*, MGH, SS xvii. 68; F. Pfeiffer, *Rheinische Transitzölle im Mittelalter*, Berlin 1997, 399–404.
[133] F. R. Lewis, 'Beatrice of Falkenburg, the third wife of Richard of Cornwall', *EHR* lii (1937), 279–282; *Annals of Oseney*, AM iv. 224.

'furious insanity', the earl first tackled the manifold extortions forced upon travellers and merchants along the Rhine. Richard called a meeting to Worms, where these tolls were banned. For this he was widely praised by the Germans. Afterwards, foreseeing that this would tie him closer to his subjects, he married Beatrice of Falkenburg.[134] Richard thus not only forged dynastic links, but also exercised a king's most solemn duty: the upholding of peace and justice. By marrying a German wife, Richard emphasised his intention to be more than an absentee king, while the measures taken at Worms proved that he had the means and the authority to rule as well as to reign.

The diet's pronouncements do not survive, but on 20 April Richard issued a decree referring to the meeting. He declared that, after having received complaints from the consuls of Worms about a toll called *Ungelt* (a duty levied on goods which were to be transported or traded), he had called a meeting, where the archbishops of Mainz and Trier, the bishops of Worms and Speyer, princes, magnates and counts had sworn not to extort the toll in future.[135] Abolishing an unpopular tax was not, however, the diet's only purpose: a general peace was also declared.[136] This was the first attempt by a king since 1235 to establish a general peace, not just for a specific region, but across Germany as a whole. Although the Worms diet had been attended only by a limited number of clergy and nobles, mostly from the Lower Rhineland, Richard did not believe this to be sufficient. He ordered the citizens of Strasbourg to follow the example set by others, and abolish *Ungelt* within eight days, if they wanted to be part of the general peace declared at Worms.[137] That the implicit use of force was no empty threat is suggested by a letter from the bishop of Mainz to the citizens of Oppenheim from August 1269, when he ordered them to equip a warship to be used against disturbers of the peace agreed at Worms.[138]

By then, even those who were initially opposed to Richard's candidacy came to seek his support and recognition. We have already seen how the rulers of Flanders and Brabant abandoned Alfonso for Richard. A similar case can be made for several towns, initially hostile towards him. This is perhaps best exemplified by the *Annales wormatienses*, one of the few narrative sources that concerns itself with Richard beyond the event of his election. For 1257 a gleefully hostile account is given. Richard is considered to be an impostor and usurper – 'pro rege se gerebat' ('he acted as if he were king').[139] His activities in the Rhineland are described as those of a tyrant: his opponents were

---

134 *Wyke's chronicle*, AM iv. 222–5.
135 *Constitutiones, 1198–1272*, nos 389–90.
136 *Annales wormatienses*, MGH, SS xvii. 68.
137 *Constitutiones, 1198–1272*, no. 391; C. Rotthoff, 'Die politische Rolle der Landfrieden zwischen Maas und Rhein von der Mitte des 13. Jahrhunderts bis zum Auslaufen des Bacharacher Landfriedens Ludwigs des Bayern', *Rheinische Vierteljahresschrift* xlv (1981), 75–111.
138 *Constitutiones, 1198–1272*, no. 446.
139 *Annales wormatienses*, MGH, SS xvii. 59–60.

oppressed by continuous warfare, while his supporters received privileges and liberties. By the time of the earl's entry into Worms, however, the chronicler's stance had softened.[140] No more doubt is voiced concerning Richard's legitimacy as king. *Richardus rex* entered Worms.[141] In 1260 the king was involved in settling a conflict between the town and neighbouring *ministeriales*, and was addressed as *rex*.[142] The annals are the only German chronicle mentioning the diet of Worms in 1269. In comparison to Thomas Wykes's account of the same meeting, the entry in the *Annales* is sober and restrained. They state only that the king in the presence of various prelates and nobles had abolished the much disliked *Ungelt*, and that a general peace had been sworn. Still, the change in attitude remains clear. By no means was his reign a mere interlude. In fact, in many respects Richard laid the foundations for the attempted renewal of imperial power during the reign of his successor, Rudolf of Habsburg.[143]

Once again, affairs in England forced Richard to return. The kingdom, only partially pacified after 1265, experienced continuing unrest. Pockets of resistance remained in the north, and the royal court was torn by a feud between the earl of Gloucester and the Lord Edward, while English rule in North Wales collapsed.[144] Richard was called upon to arbitrate. His earlier friendly relations with the rulers of Wales – in 1240 Llywelyn's uncle had accompanied the earl on his crusade,[145] while Llywelyn himself had sent one of his envoys to meet Richard just prior to his departure for Germany in 1257 – made him acceptable to both parties. After the conflict was laid to rest, Richard acted as one of Edward's proctors during his crusade,[146] and in 1271 as regent of England on his brother's behalf.[147] There is no indication, though, that the earl thought his absence from Germany to be permanent.[148] Quite to the contrary: there was no slackening in the issue of royal grants for Germany.[149] Moreover, the summer of 1271 saw renewed efforts by Henry III to repay debts owed to his brother,[150] which in previous years had been an indication of the earl's imminent departure. Also in February 1271 Henry III urged his son to return from crusade. Among the reasons given was that

---

[140] Ibid. 60.
[141] Ibid. 60–2.
[142] Ibid. 65.
[143] Hilpert, *Kaiser- und Papstbriefe*, 120–31.
[144] *Brut y tywysogyon or the Chronicle of the princes, Peniarth MS 20 version*, ed. and trans. T. Jones, Cardiff 1952, 114–15; *Litterae Walliae preserved in Liber A in the Public Record Office*, ed. J. G. Edwards, Cardiff 1940, no. 1.
[145] *Chronicon de Lanercost*, 48.
[146] *CPR, 1266–72*, 468, 508, 509.
[147] Ibid. 592.
[148] This contradicts the traditional view of Richard's kingship, which assumes that, with his return in 1269, his ambitions had lapsed. See, most recently, Huffman, *Social politics*.
[149] *Regesta imperii*, nos 5476–83; *Monumenta boica*, xxx, no. 823; *Urkundenbuch Mittelrheinische Territorien*, ii, nos 611, 618.
[150] *CLR, 1267–72*, nos 1500–1; *CPR, 1266–72*, 534, 543–4, 545–6.

Richard would soon be able to set sail for Rome to be crowned emperor.[151] The king was not alone in this belief. A number of chroniclers from outside England associated the visit of Richard's son Henry to Viterbo in 1271 with demands that Richard be crowned emperor.[152] Similarly, in a contract between the burgrave of Landskron and a local noblewoman from December 1270, reference is made to their undertaking having to be confirmed by King Richard, who was expected to arrive soon.[153] This sojourn would have coincided with the election of a new pope, and it is perhaps safe to assume that it was above all the cardinals' inability to choose a new pontiff which delayed Richard's departure. More important, by 1271 there was little doubt that he had recovered some of the ground lost during his involvement in the baronial wars, and could reasonably expect to have his claims finally recognised by the pope.

By no means had Richard proved himself able to fill the vacuum created by Frederick II's death. Neither, however, was his reign the disaster it has so often been portrayed. In fact, many of the earl's actions and undertakings reflected structural features which had similarly guided those of Frederick II, and which were to direct those of his successor and erstwhile supporter, Rudolf of Habsburg. All that was different with Richard was that the limitations of imperial authority had become much more visible than they had been before.

England and Germany, 1257–72

In the end, Richard's election and coronation gave Henry III what he always wanted: a formal treaty of friendship with the ruler of Germany and Italy. We should therefore not underestimate the significance of the treaty concluded between Richard and his brother prior to the earl's departure for Germany in 1257. Richard's career thus cannot be separated from his brother's Sicilian ambitions. His candidacy for the German throne had initially been little more than a means to an end. It was to ensure that no ruler of Germany would hinder the Plantagenets' aspirations in the Mediterranean. Ultimately, it proved more successful than his brother's Apulian venture, and by 1265 it was the sole remnant of Henry III's once grandiose ambitions. The final point to consider therefore is its impact on relations between the English royal court and the princes of the empire. Naturally, the majority of contacts centred on the new emperor-elect, but we will also have to assess the effect of this on the traditional partners, such as the dukes of Brunswick and Brabant.

---

151 CR, 1268–72, 397–8.
152 *Chronique Latin de Guillaume de Nangis de 1113 à 1300 avec les continuations de cette chronique de 1300 à 1368*, ed. H. Geraud, Paris 1843, 241; *Gestes des Chiprois*, 172–7.
153 *Quellen zur Geschichte der Herrschaft Landskron an der Ahr*, ed. T. Zimmer, Bonn 1966, i, no. 101.

Furthermore, as we have seen, Richard could not pursue his German career without his English resources. How then, did this affect his standing in England?

Most English chroniclers took an ambivalent view of Richard's adventure. The *Annals of Burton*, for instance, listing the arguments made by the barons against the Sicilian Business, included Richard's absence as among the evils besetting the realm. The kingdom was deprived of counsel, funds and men.[154] Matthew Paris, too, viewed Richard's departure with unease. Although he gleefully reported the earl's successes, he also complained that he was plundering England to satisfy the Germans' greed.[155] It is difficult to verify this from the surviving evidence. Although Henry III assisted Richard, he did not load him with riches. The grants made on his behalf did not strain the English royal purse. In fact, they fell well short of the efforts undertaken, for instance, in the context of the Sicilian Business. This can, of course, come as no surprise. For one, it helps to underline the priority still enjoyed by the planned conquest of Apulia. Beset by the papacy and facing a reluctant baronage, Henry was, moreover, in no position to make generous grants. Secondly, when elected, Richard could already count himself amongst the richest men in Europe. Matthew Paris is probably exaggerating when he estimates the earl's treasure at £70,000,[156] but the fact remains that the earl needed little financial help from his brother. Most grants thus took the form of safeguarding Richard's claims, or of awarding privileges which cost the king little. In 1257, for instance, Richard was freed of the customary feudal service in Wales,[157] and in 1259 he received venison from the king's estates, and was allowed to tallage lands formerly part of the royal demesne.[158] It was not until 1260 that any major financial contributions were made, when Henry III considered pawning his insignia to repay a loan made by his brother.[159] Even after 1265, when financial grants were awarded on a more regular basis, they normally took the form of repaying accumulated debts more quickly.[160] Rather than depending on his brother's handouts, Richard was in fact using his German resources to alleviate shortages in England. In 1258, for instance, Matthew Paris reports that the earl dispatched fifty ships with provisions to combat the famine threatening England.[161] Furthermore,

---

154 *Annals of Burton*, AM i. 387.
155 Matthew Paris, *Chronica maiora*, v. 629–30, 660–1. There may be some truth in this: in 1257 the *Annals of Dunstaple* report that, due to an unexpected shortage of cash, Richard ordered his woods in England to be sold: AM iii. 206.
156 Matthew Paris, *Chronica maiora*, v. 630.
157 CPR, 1247–58, 571.
158 CPR, 1258–66, 57; CR, 1256–9, 291.
159 CPR, 1258–66, 74.
160 CR, 1264–8, 463, 470–1. Richard also received wardships (CR, 1268–72, 29) and receipts of judicial eyres in Cornwall (CPR, 1266–72, 244). Richard's officials, too, were promised some financial support: CPR, 1258–66, 141.
161 Matthew Paris, *Chronica maiora*, v. 673.

some indication survives that, during the baronial wars, German mercenaries fought alongside Henry III and his brother.[162]

As far as Richard's wise counsel was concerned, its absence seems not to have been overly missed. The earl was frequently vilified for his hostile stance on the Provisions of Oxford: several chroniclers blamed Richard for the movement's failure.[163] It was, in fact, the king who mostly relied on the earl's advice. In 1260 Richard was entrusted with the defence of the realm,[164] and in 1264 he acted as Henry's regent in England.[165] Prior to the baronial takeover in 1258, English envoys to Germany were attested with some frequency.[166] The earl himself inquired about the king's affairs,[167] and even during his absence Richard's officials solicited grants and privileges. In September 1257, for instance, Roger de Stanes was pardoned for homicide, at the instance of the king of the Romans,[168] and in 1258, at Richard's request, a London merchant was allowed to import wine.[169]

When in England, Richard regularly witnessed Henry's grants,[170] and was involved in averting the worst results of both the king's and Simon de Montforts' intransigence. Due to the very nature of his kingship, Richard had little interest in exacerbating an already volatile situation. Consequently, he spent most of his time arbitrating and negotiating, between Simon and Henry, between his son and the kings' supporters, and between the Lord Edward and the earl of Gloucester.[171] When his efforts came to naught, he had little choice but to assist his brother, rather than Simon and the barons, effectively taking a stance not unlike that of Louis IX who, in 1264, had condemned the Provisions of Oxford and demanded that the barons submit to the authority of their king. In this context, it may also be worth noting the emphasis Richard placed on his difference in status. During his regency in 1264, for instance, the earl dated even official English correspondence by his regnal years.[172] After the battle of Lewes this was to provide the opportunity for some mockery by the victorious rebels. The 'Song against the king of Almain' gives a detailed description of how the earl sought refuge in a nearby windmill, hiding from the barons amongst sacks of flour.[173] The Melrose

---

162 'The song against the king of Almain', in *Political songs of England from the reign of John to that of Edward II*, ed. T. Wright (Camden, 1839), repr. with new introduction by P. Coss, Cambridge 1996, 69–71.
163 *Flores*, ii. 447; *Chronicon de bello*, MGH, SS xviii. 554.
164 CR, 1259–61, 285.
165 PRO, SC 1/8, no. 5.
166 CR, 1256–9, 58, 65, 405, 425; CLR, 1267–72, no. 2300a; CPR, 1247–58, 606, 625.
167 *Royal letters Henry III*, ii, no. 528.
168 CPR, 1247–58, 578.
169 Ibid. 618.
170 PRO, C 53/50, mem. 3; C 53/51, mem. 3; C 53/53, mem. 4.
171 CPR, 1258–66, 79; CR, 1261–4, 126; S. D. Lloyd, 'Gilbert de Clare, Richard of Cornwall and the Lord Edward's crusade', *Nottingham Medieval Studies* xxix (1985), 46–66.
172 PRO, SC 1/8, nos 5–6.
173 *Political songs of England*, 169–70

chronicle elaborated on this: having traced Richard, the barons deliberated at great length and ostentatiously debated what to call him – feisty miller or by his official title *romanorum rex et semper augustus*.[174] Richard, in short, continued to play a significant part in the affairs of England, and unsurprisingly so. At the same time, his kingship found a mixed reception in England, and was in part at least overshadowed by his role in the barons' wars.

It hardly comes as a surprise that most of Henry III's contacts with Germany were arranged via Richard of Cornwall. The earl relied on his brother to provide the necessary backing in his attempts at winning support there. Thus, the citizens of Lübeck were granted trading privileges 'as long as they be of good behaviour to the said Richard',[175] and those of Groningen received theirs during the earl's life-time,[176] while the merchants of Brabant were assured that they could trade safely in England, despite any contention that might exist with the duke.[177] The earl's sojourns in Germany were often preceded by English grants to his imperial subjects. Thus, in 1260, a day before Richard's second departure, Henry III confirmed the privileges of those Germans who owned the *Gildehalla teutonicorum* in London.[178] Similarly, in 1262, grants were made to several north German towns,[179] just as safe-conducts were issued for the earl's entourage.[180] Although Henry was unable to provide generous military or financial help, he assisted his brother in rewarding those on whose support Richard depended in Germany. This may explain plans to marry Edmund Crouchback to one of the daughters of Guido of Flanders in 1261.[181] After all, Guido had originally been among Alfonso's partisans, and Richard's promise to restore the countess's claims to imperial Flanders made but slow progress. Among those who were brought back into the range of English diplomacy by Richard's elevation was the archbishop of Cologne. Notably absent from Henry's diplomacy in Germany since his consecration, Conrad of Hochstaden led the delegation which in 1257 came to escort Richard to Germany.[182] This resulted in the knighting of various men of Cologne by the king, and a number of grants to members of the archbishop's entourage.[183] Furthermore, as Cologne Cathedral had been destroyed by fire in 1248, a mandate was issued allowing the archbishop's

---

[174] *Chronica de Mailros*, 196.
[175] *CPR, 1247–58*, 553.
[176] *CChR, 1257–1300*, 10.
[177] *CR, 1256–9*, 56.
[178] *CPR, 1258–66*, 77.
[179] *Hansisches Urkundenbuch*, ed. K. Höhlbaum, Halle 1876–1907, i, nos 575–6.
[180] *CPR, 1258–66*, 216, 218; *CR, 1261–4*, 129.
[181] *Royal letters Henry III*, ii, no. 564. Similar reasons may have guided the marriage between Henry of Almain, Richard's eldest son, and Constance de Bearn: R. Studd, 'The marriage of Henry of Almain and Constance of Bearn', *TCE* iii (1989), 161–79.
[182] Matthew Paris, *Chronica maiora*, v. 627.
[183] *Diplomatic documents*, no. 297; *CR, 1256–9*, 53; *CPR, 1247–58*, 548.

commissioners to collect funds in England for its rebuilding.[184] With that, however, Conrad's role ended. In March 1258 a merchant from Cologne, who had been sent at the bishop's behest, received two robes,[185] but no evidence for further dealings survives. Contacts between the English court and Germany were dominated by Richard's needs, and as relations between the earl and Conrad's successor deteriorated, so did those between the king of England and the Rhenish prelate.

It would seem at first as if the duke of Brunswick remained conspicuously absent from the list of Richard's supporters. He was not present at the earl's coronation, nor did he witness his charters or provide him with troops. He also stands out as the only German prince who continued to deal directly with the English royal court. At the same time, the duke's lack of involvement in imperial affairs was not untypical: none of the north German princes took an active part in imperial politics.[186] The duke of Saxony and the margrave of Brandenburg, for instance, did not even attend the meeting at which Alfonso was elected king. The duke's apathy does therefore not necessarily indicate hostility towards Richard. In fact, circumstantial evidence suggests an early acceptance of Richard's authority. In 1260 the duke was part of a *Landfrieden* covering parts of Westphalia.[187] The participants agreed to seek royal consent and confirmation for their agreement. This was highly unusual for a mere local *Landfrieden*. No similar clause can be found in comparable agreements for Hainault (1200), Brixen (1226) or the *Pax Bavarica* (1244).[188] By implication, the duke was not opposed to accepting Richard as king. Furthermore, in 1270 Richard enfeoffed Duke Albrecht of Brunswick with lands recently sold by the count of Dassel, but pertaining to the empire. It seems that the duke had taken the initiative.[189] A formal declaration of fealty may not have been deemed necessary, as duke and king had probably met on an earlier occasion. In 1262 Henry III had made a grant on the occasion of the duke's marriage with a sister of the margrave of Montferrat,[190] and the couple were expected in England by Easter 1263.[191] When they eventually arrived in the autumn of 1266, they received lavish gifts, and initiated various grants for German merchants.[192] Considering

---

184 *CPR, 1247–58*, 591.

185 *CR, 1256–9*, 207.

186 H. Steinbach, *Die Reichsgewalt und Niederdeutschland in nachstaufischer Zeit*, Stuttgart 1968, 50–66.

187 *Urkundenbuch Niederrhein*, ii, no. 489.

188 *Constitutiones, 1198–1272*, nos 425–7.

189 *Urkundenbuch zur Geschichte der Herzöge von Braunschweig und Lüneburg und ihrer Lande*, ed. H. Sudendorf, Hanover 1859–83, i, nos 70–1. This would explain the presence of envoys from Brunswick at the English court in 1270: *CLR, 1267–72*, nos 1272, 1312.

190 *CR, 1261–4*, 170.

191 Ibid. 176.

192 *CR, 1264–8*, 263–4; *CPR, 1266–72*, 5; *Sächsiche Weltchronik und ihre Fortsetzungen*, MGH, Deutsche Chroniken 2, 296–7.

Henry III's close relationship with his brother during these years, it seems unlikely that he would have received someone openly hostile towards him.

Like his brother, Richard had to some extent been plagued by circumstances beyond his control. This was largely due to the situation in England, aggravated by the lack of an indigenous power base in Germany. Still, the degree of continuity with the governments of William and Frederick was remarkable. Like the late emperor, Richard soon realised that it would be impossible to establish effective governance in the empire without having first secured friendly relations with the Capetians. By 1259 he had not only surrendered all claims to Poitou and Normandy, but even suggested that he and the king of France enter into an agreement which in many ways echoed the Treaty of Catania. This continuity was equally evident in Richard's internal governance of Germany, and was due as much to the personnel of his administration as to the challenges he faced. To govern Germany was a matter of negotiating and arbitrating, of settling conflicts and of an even-handed administration of patronage, rather than of using military power or of utilising fiscal and juridical mechanisms. It called for very different talents from those his brother required in England or Sicily.

This, in turn, gives us the opportunity to reflect on some basic features of imperial lordship in the thirteenth century. Like Frederick II, Richard realised that his lordship would be weak as long as an alternative source of patronage existed, or as soon as one appeared. This had been the driving force behind the emperor's friendly overtures to the Capetians, and it was the reason which forced Richard to put pressure on the Avesnes brothers, and to forsake his Norman and Poitevin inheritance. Secondly, imperial lordship depended on a broad base of support in order to be effective, and this included the former adherents of erstwhile rivals. Otto IV, Frederick, William of Holland as well as Richard of Cornwall all sought to include those in their governance who had once resisted them. After all, it was paramount for imperial lordship to be effective to ensure that no alternative source of patronage emerged or was called for. It was, furthermore, an intensely personal form of kingship, especially for those like Richard or Alfonso who did not have an established power base within the empire. Frederick II, for instance, had been able to draw on the services of men who had a long tradition of loyalty to the Staufen dynasty, and he could utilise both the resources of the empire and those of his own family. He also had the prestige and the papal backing which enabled him to exercise some sort of control over Germany even when he was not there in person. Richard, by contrast, was dependent on his English resources and on his ability to demonstrate his ability to rule in person: in fact, one of the conditions Conrad of Hochstaden had made for his support was that Richard would come to Germany by a specified date. Ultimately, it was the fact that he, unlike Alfonso, actually appeared in Germany in person which secured him the success he had in 1257–9, but it was also his inability to disentangle himself from the affairs of England which prevented him from making full use of this early advantage. It was during the recurrent crises in England that some of his German subjects contemplated electing an anti-king, but this threat was easily overcome once the earl arrived in Germany. This personal dimension of lordship was particularly pronounced in the empire, but it had been evident elsewhere, too: after all, Henry's Sicilian adventure failed ultimately because his supporters and followers had lost hope that he or Edmund would ever set foot in Sicily. Last, but not least, the concerns of an emperor extended well beyond his empire. By the mid-thirteenth century, the idea that an emperor's duties extended to the defence of Christendom at large had begun to emerge, and it was formulated by the time of the Second Council of Lyon in 1274.[193] Even before then, however, a concern for the affairs of Christendom as a whole had been utilised, for instance, by Frederick II and his chancery in their war of propaganda against the *curia*, and it also seems to have played its part in deliberations as to how to deal with the German Double Election of 1257. All this should therefore militate against too simplified a view of medieval politics, which fails to place a ruler's actions in relation not only to the expectations and undertakings of his subjects, but also those of his peers and rivals.

---

193 Weiler, '*Negotium*'.

Conclusion: Politics and Diplomacy in Thirteenth-Century Europe

For most of Henry III's reign, relations with the Staufen empire were a means rather than an end. Frederick II certainly mattered, but he did so because of the direct or indirect support he might be able (or refuse) to lend the king of England. Up to about 1250, most of the king's initiatives were thus aimed at preventing closer ties between Staufen and Capetians, or at winning the emperor's backing, or at least that of his subjects, for an armed expedition across the Channel. This only changed after Frederick had died. From about 1250 onwards, Henry was preoccupied with his planned crusade, and even the Sicilian Business was initially pursued as a project subsidiary to rather than in place of the former. In fact, to some extent, Alfonso X – threatening, as he did, Plantagenet possession of Gascony, and forcing attempts at a reorientation of the king's crusade – was of far greater significance than Frederick's heirs or William of Holland. It was only with the Sicilian Business proving itself to be a much more difficult undertaking than originally envisaged that Henry III's interests returned to the Staufen empire. Ultimately, this even came to supersede the objective which had guided so many of Henry's diplomatic initiatives until then: by 1258–9 the king of England was prepared to surrender his family's claims to Normandy and Poitou in order to safeguard what he and his brother had gained (or hoped to gain) in Germany and the Mediterranean.

Anglo-imperial relations were not, however, limited to dealings between king and emperor. The archbishop of Cologne, the dukes of Brunswick, Austria and Brabant, and the counts of Savoy, played an equally significant role, especially during the early years of Henry's reign, and they were often much more willing than the emperor to enter into dealings with Henry III. This only changed in 1235, with Isabella's marriage. This did not, of course, put an end to Henry's relations with the imperial princes. New ties were forged – as with the king's Savoyard relatives – or old ones strengthened if and when the need arose, as in the context of the Council of Lyon. None the less, what ultimately mattered was the stance Frederick himself was going to take, and Henry either sought to influence the emperor himself, or muster the backing of those who might be able to intervene successfully on his behalf. Henry's contacts were largely chosen for their (real or imagined) ability to serve as allies against the Capetians. Once they proved unable to meet these expectations, or if someone appeared who was more likely to come to the king's aid, alliances could change, and do so rapidly. The archbishop of Cologne and the duke of Brunswick, for instance, disappear from

English records the moment relations with Frederick had been put on firmer grounding in 1235. The king's diplomacy towards the empire was driven by a clear awareness of what was to be achieved, and of who was likely to help achieve it.

As far as the king's partners in the empire were concerned, and the expectations they held of him, we must distinguish between the emperor and his princely subjects. To Frederick II, until 1235 at least, Henry III was a nuisance at best. From the marriage with Isabella onwards we can, however, observe a subtle shift in his attitude towards the Plantagenets. Although the emperor never abandoned his Capetian allies, Henry III none the less mattered – and was courted – as someone who could provide funds, men and political support in Lombardy and, from 1239 onwards, back the emperor at the papal court. The high point of this relationship was reached in 1245, when Frederick called on the king to act as his proctor at Lyon. Although Henry's efforts failed, the hope that he might successfully intervene with the *curia* continued to influence relations between the two until Frederick's death.

As far as the princes and prelates of the empire were concerned, Henry III was important as a source of patronage and prestige. In 1225, for example, Archbishop Engelbert I had as much to gain from the proposed marriage as the king of England. It provided an opportunity to assert his and his regency's independence of the imperial court, and to strengthen the position of his see in economic and political dealings with England and in relation to other imperial princes. The dukes of Austria and Brunswick equally looked to Henry III as someone who might provide them with lands, privileges and prestige. Even in 1225, however, the king of England was at best an additional, never a rival source of patronage, and few princes would have risked their standing with the emperor to gain the backing of Henry III. This began to change after Frederick's second excommunication in 1239, and even more so after his deposition in 1245. With the empire beset by internal disputes, and neither Frederick nor his opponents capable of exercising full control over its constituent parts, princes and prelates were beginning to look for support and assistance elsewhere. The countess of Flanders relied on Louis IX, the counts of Savoy sought to utilise their family links with the king of England, and even when the citizens of Pisa and Marseilles elected Alfonso X as emperor, this was initially little more than an attempt to secure external help against their Genoese rivals and Charles of Anjou. These approaches aimed first and foremost to secure the patronage of someone capable of filling the power vacuum created by the absence of an emperor.

Initially, Henry III was thus only one among several non-imperial rulers approached, and, until 1256, the English court went to considerable lengths to avoid being drawn into the internal affairs of the empire. This changed when the king promoted his brother Richard's candidacy for the imperial throne. The earl of Cornwall's imperial career marked the temporary return to power and influence of the archbishop of Cologne. It also reflected a phenomenon which had been in evidence since 1246, that is, the inability of the imperial elites to perform the functions of emperor on their own, and the need to rely on those from outside the conflicting networks of political and family loyalties which characterised imperial politics to do so. At the same time, Richard's election and coronation also marked a fundamental shift in Anglo-imperial relations. For at no point during the previous forty years had Henry III contemplated involving himself directly in the choice of who was to be emperor or emperor-elect. In fact, all the surviving information points in the opposite direction: there is no evidence that he supported plans for electing an anti-king in 1227–9, and when Henry (VII) rebelled against his father, he looked to the Italian cities and the Capetians for support, not to the king of England. Rather, the Sicilian Business required (and mirrored) a fundamental reorientation of Plantagenet diplomacy. It was, however, an equally remarkable step for the German princes who chose Richard. There was, after all, a marked difference between approaching the English royal court for privileges or rents, and choosing a Plantagenet prince as one's ruler. In Richard someone was for the first time chosen as emperor-elect who had absolutely no dynastic claim to the imperial throne and who was – unlike Henry Raspe or William – from outside the empire itself.

The way Henry III interacted with the Staufen and their subjects reveals a pattern in evidence across the medieval west. To him and his fellow-rulers the empire mattered as a source of potential political and military backing, but the affairs of the Staufens also posed considerable challenges. All too often, Henry and his peers were forced to pursue a careful balancing act, seeking to alienate neither pope nor emperor, but also to further their own ambitions in the process. For Louis IX this meant that he brought most of imperial Burgundy under Capetian control, as well as parts of Flanders, while Fernando of Castile and his son Alfonso had initially sought possession of Swabia, before Alfonso claimed the imperial throne itself. Similarly, Henry III tried to exploit the services he had previously done Frederick to win the emperor's backing in Poitou, and he aided his wife's relatives in securing their position in northern Italy and along the Alps. Neither Henry nor his peers embarked on a conscientious strategy of expansion the moment Frederick fell out with the pope. Rather, they sought to mediate and arbitrate: at Lyon the representatives of Louis IX, who had recently taken the cross, argued most fervently in favour of Frederick; Henry III's proctors had been authorised by the emperor to act on his behalf; while Fernando of Castile had dispatched the abbot of Sahagún to urge a compromise. At the same time, this provided an opportunity to settle long-held claims, or to resolve political issues which in the past had threatened the security of a ruler's own lands and domains. Moreover, from 1250 onwards at the latest, with Frederick dead, a dangerous vacuum began to develop at the heart of the Staufen empire. None of the monarchs in question, it should be noted, aimed to fill this void as such. However, they found themselves increasingly forced to exercise functions previously associated with the emperor, as evident, for instance, in Louis IX's role as arbitrator in Flanders and across some of the French-speaking parts of the empire from 1250 onwards. Equally, Alfonso of Castile had not actively sought the imperial throne, but when the communes of Marseilles and Pisa offered it to him, this proved too good an opportunity to miss. Henry III's Sicilian affair followed a similar pattern, and at first was little more than an attempt to forestall Capetian expansion into the Mediterranean, and the same applied to Richard's German career. None of them had planned to build an empire.

Neither the scope nor the direction of Henry's ambitions was thus unusual, and neither was his ultimate failure. Alfonso X, for example, suffered a similar fate, with his imperial ambitions in ruin, when he faced the combined threat of a revolt by the Mudéjar of Castile, a Muslim invasion from North Africa and a rebellion by his native aristocracy. Similarly, Haakon of Norway was to prove unable to fulfil the promises evident in the 1240s, with his family among the prospective successors to the Staufen. If we want to understand the king of England's ultimate failure, it is perhaps more important to look at his affairs at home, rather than his ambitions abroad.

Much of the opposition or reluctance the king encountered had less to do with the specific project he aimed to pursue, than with a range of domestic political grievances. The question of Isabella's dowry, for instance, contributed to the confirmation of Magna Carta in 1237, but this was only the case because the king's financial travails enabled his barons and clergy to press more strongly their case for political reform. Equally, the Sicilian Business certainly featured among the complaints made in 1258, but it did so because it highlighted resentment concerning the king's governance (he had failed to take the counsel of his barons, and relied overly on his alien relatives and officials), and not so much because of the project itself (some of the leading figures behind the Provisions had, after all, been instrumental in pursuing the *negotium Sicilie*). We should therefore avoid confusing baronial opposition to Henry's unwillingness to take their advice and counsel with a principled antagonism to the king's engagement with the politics of the Latin west. After all, most English magnates – by way of family ties, ethos, culture and function – themselves possessed manifold ties with mainland Europe, and shared with their king both the framework within and the ethical norms according to which they acted. All too frequently, their hostility towards the king's plans was rooted not in doubt as to the feasibility of his plans, but in the realisation that this was the best means they had of voicing their complaints.

The wider framework

Let us now turn to the wider framework within which the king acted, and let us begin by considering the papal court. The *curia* mattered as a player in its own right, but also as an institution which was essential in defining the broader context within which international relations could be conducted. This dual role is most clearly evident in the papal–imperial conflict. The Staufens' relations with the *curia* were, however, complex, and should not be viewed exclusively from the vantage point of the emperor's excommunications in 1227 and in 1239, or his deposition in 1245.

Papal diplomacy, too, was subject to fluctuations. These reflected the fact that the pope, like any secular leader, could not act alone or in isolation. We have seen – most visibly in the case of Frederick II's excommunication, but also with regard to the Sicilian Business and Richard's attempts to be made emperor – how members of the papal court voiced their doubts about specific initiatives, and how they tried to counteract them. More importantly, in order for Frederick's excommunications or his deposition to be effective, the support of Frederick's fellow-princes as well as that of the secular aristocracy of Germany had to be enlisted. This was a matter of finding recruits to fill the imperial throne, but also – and perhaps more important – of soliciting the financial and political backing of the monarchs of the Latin west. The *curia* depended on payments from the Church's members to finance its wars – a matter of increasing significance in England – and on lay rulers to provide it with armed protection – as with Frederick's march on Lyon in 1247 – and to fight the Staufen and their partisans – as in the case of the duke of Brabant from 1247 onwards. This means that, partly due to the very nature of the *curia's* universal role, its affairs and ambitions impinged on the conduct of thirteenth-century diplomacy on every level.

The political actions of successive popes had an equally significant impact on Henry III. In 1216 his tenuous grip on the throne had been maintained by a regency council which included the papal legate, and he frequently sought to muster the support of his – nominal – liege lord when seeking to recover the Plantagenets' continental possessions. Equally significant were, however, the expectations which various pontiffs had of their English vassals. From about 1239 onwards, papal requests for money began to play an increasingly prominent role in the politics of England as well as France. Naturally, we should not ignore the difficulties facing the *curia* in forcing its will upon the Church's members. The ecclesiastical history of thirteenth-century England is full of complaints about papal demands, open or veiled resistance to them, and various attempts by secular and religious clergy alike to avoid meeting them, watering down demands or subjecting the necessary agreement to a lengthy series of delays and postponements. This, in turn, had repercussions both for the projects funded by the papal court and for the general standing and prestige of successive popes with those whose funds and willing collaboration they needed. Like any medieval ruler, so the popes, too, faced a sometimes striking dichotomy between what they believed it was their right to demand from their subjects, and what their subjects were willing to grant.

The *curia's* role was further complicated by the fact that both the papal–imperial conflict and the way in which king and pontiff sought to justify their actions introduced yet another legitimising discourse. That is, the freedom of the papal states, the honour of King Henry and the rights of Emperor Frederick were important, but became increasingly entwined with another set of values: the crusades. A campaign in aid of the Holy Land (although feasibly to be fought elsewhere and not necessarily against Muslims alone) was both an ideal, the realisation of which could be used to evaluate political actions, and an undertaking, which was subject to the concerns and needs of thirteenth-century *Realpolitik*. In the eyes of successive popes, showing concern for Christian *Outremer* was a means by which political legitimacy could be ascertained, while undertaking actions detrimental to Christians in Palestine justified invoking the full arsenal of sanctions available to the thirteenth-century papacy. In practice this could mean, for instance, that Henry III was not able to count on the *curia*'s unconditional backing when seeking to reclaim Poitou in 1224–5 or that Frederick II was urged to agree to a marriage in 1235 which potentially risked his relationship with the Capetians.

This concept was, however, as binding on the papal court as it was on those against whom it was invoked. When Innocent IV justified Frederick II's deposition at the Council of Lyon with reference to the damage the emperor had done to Christian Palestine, he applied this principle. As a result, the imperial as well as the papal chancery sought to enlist the support of Frederick's fellow-monarchs with reference to the advantages their support might bring to the affairs of the Holy Land. Similarly, Henry III, Louis IX and the king of Hungary frequently phrased their appeals to the warring parties in terms which emphasised the needs of *Outremer*. The needs of the Holy Land provided a generally accepted framework within which to conduct political relations. At the same time, they also brought with them the expectation that action would be taken to turn this ideal into reality. Frederick II, Henry III, Alfonso X and Louis IX all faced similar challenges the moment they declared their intention: they had to secure their line of dynastic succession, the smooth running of the realm in their absence and the settlement of disputes and rivalries with their neighbours and peers. In many cases this provided an opportunity to state claims which otherwise might have been more difficult to enforce, but which could be justified because of the benefit which ultimately would accrue from them for the affairs of Christian *Outremer*. The taking of the cross thus frequently resulted in attempts at strengthening royal control both within one's own realm and over adjoining regions. At the same time, it also provided one's peers with an opportunity to press for concessions, as evident, for instance, in the hectic marriage diplomacy surrounding Henry (VII) in 1225, or Henry III's progeny after 1250. The needs of the Holy Land were a powerful weapon, but one which could not be wielded lightly.

Among Henry's contemporaries Louis IX was probably the one most successful in using the crusades to his political advantage. Combining the ability to make good use of the prestige accrued from actually setting out for the east, and pursuing ruthlessly the political preparations for this campaign,

Louis and his family took control of Toulouse, Provence and the county of Flanders, and began to exert unprecedented influence in the affairs of imperial Burgundy. This, in turn, introduces the final factor in thirteenth-century 'international relations', the one without which the actions of neither Frederick nor Henry can be fully understood: the Capetians. In Henry III's case, they mattered as the object of his political alliances. Frederick's relations with the Capetians, by contrast, were based on dependence, not rivalry. Without their financial and military assistance, he would have stood little chance of ever assuming the throne. Even Louis VIII's actions in Languedoc could test, but never undermine, his loyalty. To a large extent this was born of necessity. In fact, it may be indicative that Frederick only began to forge closer ties with the king of England in 1235, when he had reached the apogee of his standing within Latin Europe. Even then, this was immediately followed by an active search for a settlement between Henry III and Louis IX. The reluctance of Louis IX's regents to take sides against Frederick had thwarted papal attempts to install an anti-king during the emperor's first excommunication, and after 1239 much depended on Louis's continuing intercession. More important, as Frederick's own career had taught, it was possible to claim the imperial throne without Capetian backing, but it was a much more difficult task to keep it despite them.

The Capetians did not, however, suddenly emerge as a major player, nor was their rise to prominence the result of conscientious planning. Rather, it was caused by chance, and by the weakness of others. Henry III's continuing inability to muster the full military and financial backing of his English subjects contributed as much to the strength of Louis IX as did Frederick II's increasingly fraught relations with the papacy. Equally important, however, was the complex political structure of the Staufens' domains. The greatest threat to the authority of an emperor (or emperor-elect) remained an alternative source of patronage. The Capetians, in turn, were those most frequently approached by prospective candidates. This, again, explains why Henry III and Richard of Cornwall, once they faced a situation similar to that encountered by Frederick II, sought to apply similar solutions. In the case of Henry III, the need to organise his crusade, and later to ship men to Sicily, initiated renewed efforts to find a lasting settlement of his claims in France. Equally striking are the parallels between Richard and his Staufen predecessor. In Alfonso X the earl of Cornwall did face a rival who, at least initially, had been able to count upon the indirect support of the king of France. Even before Richard set out to assume his new throne, we thus find him negotiating with the king of France, and pressing for the settlement which was to result in the Treaty of Paris. In fact, he even suggested entering into an agreement not unlike the Treaty of Catania concluded between Frederick II and Louis VIII fifty years earlier. Richard, too, was unable to maintain his hold on the German throne without assuring himself at least of the neutrality of Louis IX. As in many other aspects of his reign and rule, Richard truly was the heir of Frederick II.

The tools and mechanisms of diplomacy in the thirteenth century

What, however were the means, tools and processes by which thirteenth-century rulers could interact with each other, and with which they both formed and made use of the political framework we have just discussed?

On a most elementary level, the chief tools available to Henry and his peers were treaties, which might be defined as written agreements outlining principles in accordance with which concord between two parties might be established, or ought to function. A formal treaty was therefore the ultimate goal of many of the missions dispatched during this period. A treaty provided a legally defined bond, which obliged all the parties involved in equal measure to see to its enforcement.

In addition to treaties, Henry III and his contemporaries had access to a range of less formal means. These could, for instance, involve ties of patronage or even friendship between one ruler and a member of another's court or aristocracy. For example, Henry III sought to utilise the patronage he had meted out to Peter de Vinea since 1235 to further his plans for an alliance with Frederick II in preparation for the 1242–3 campaign. We can similarly trace regular payments to several individuals closely linked to the duke of Brabant or the archbishop of Cologne, with – we may assume – similar expectations of future support. Equally, Frederick sought to strengthen contacts he had already made with men such as Peter des Roches or Richard of Cornwall, and on occasion he approached them rather than the king himself. Such contacts opened up new channels of influence, and were resorted to most frequently when relations had previously been less than cordial or when the request voiced was in need of backing from those who had a ruler's ear, or who might otherwise be able to exercise influence over him. Peter des Roches, for instance, was able to use his good standing with both Frederick II and Henry III to help facilitate the first direct contact between emperor and king since 1216. Equally, when Frederick was in need of support from Henry III after 1239, he approached not the king, but Earl Richard and the English barons.

This reliance on informal contacts reflected both common political practice and the specific challenges facing medieval diplomatic exchanges. The use of intercessors, of those close to the one whose favour, support or backing had to be gained, formed an integral element within the political practice of twelfth- and thirteenth-century Europe. This meant that those most familiar with the specific concerns of the party approached might be able to put forth a proposal in terms which might hold greater sway. This did not necessarily mean that such approaches were always successful – in fact, we only need to consider Henry III's failed arbitration attempts at Lyon to see that this was not always the case. Equally, officials or proctors frequently expected that their patrons would, in turn, aid them, and this could cause some embarrassment, as, for instance, with the disputed election at Liege in 1238. Nor did royal patrons always aid their agents, as Petrus Saracenus found out in

1238–9. Similarly, previous patronage did not always bring with it future support. After all, one of the most noticeable names missing from the list of Prince Edmund's supporters in Sicily was that of Walter of Ocra, who had been the regular recipient of funds from the English court during the 1230s and 1240s. None the less, such connections provided a useful channel of communication which complemented more formalised lines of exchange and which allowed for sensitive issues to be explored, informal approaches to be made and matters of mutual concern to be discussed.

Therefore, even undertakings like the pilgrimage by the duke of Limburg to Canterbury in the 1230s, or the grant allowing the chapter of Cologne Cathedral to carry their relics through England on a fundraising tour for the rebuilding of their church in 1257, might be viewed within the broader context of contemporary diplomatic exchanges. The same applies to economic contacts. We certainly should avoid viewing each and every trading privilege as indicative of wider political manoeuvres. None the less, such grants were made more frequently when the lord of a particular region or town was being courted. Equally, deteriorating political relations might result in trading privileges being curtailed or ignored, as with merchants from Holland and Flanders in the early 1250s, or as implicit in some of the privileges issued by Henry III's chancery in preparation for Earl Richard's journey to Germany in 1257. Moreover, if we remind ourselves that many – in the widest possible sense – diplomatic links were as much concerned with finding friends and allies, as with the provision of information and news, the full significance of trading contacts becomes apparent.

Not every mission had to achieve its proclaimed goal in order to be successful. In 1225, for instance, the success of Walter of Carlisle's embassy to Cologne should not be measured against its declared aim – a double marriage between Henry III and the duke of Austria's daughter, and Henry (VII) and Isabella Plantagenet – but rather with regard to the wider political context within which it occurred. That is, the aim of Walter's embassy was not necessarily to arrange an Anglo-imperial alliance, but to prevent a cementing of the Capetian–Staufen entente as expressed in the Treaty of Catania and in plans for a Staufen–Capetian marriage. In the end, this objective was only partly accomplished, inasmuch as there certainly was no Capetian–Staufen marriage, but – partly due to the assassination of Engelbert of Cologne – Henry (VII)'s regency still confirmed the Treaty of Catania. Similarly, many of Frederick II's pleas for assistance during the 1240s were not necessarily aimed at gaining the full support of his fellow-kings, but rather at undermining papal efforts to raise funds. Failure could, in fact, be the desired outcome of diplomatic initiatives. In 1236 and 1237, for instance, Frederick II's proposed conference at Vaucouleurs held out the prospect that Henry III might be forced to agree to a settlement which it was in his best interest to avoid. Moreover, the proposals submitted to Blanche of Castile during the early 1230s concerning a settlement of Henry III's claims in Poitou and Normandy, it would seem, included a failure of these negotiations among their possible outcomes. Diplomatic initiatives need to be viewed within the wider context of the political aims, ambitions and hopes of those who pursued them, and, not infrequently, the ultimate aim of many missions was quite different from the one they were officially sent to accomplish.

All this should warn us against too simplistic a view of how medieval diplomacy was conducted, or what international relations meant in a thirteenth-century context. Henry III, his partners, rivals, peers and subjects had at their disposal a range of mechanisms, institutions and procedures by means of which to arrange contacts, gather information, pursue alliances or thwart the moves of others. Diplomatic exchanges were by no means limited to formal treaties and alliances, but included family and commercial links, patronage, friendship or pilgrimage. In fact, the degree of flexibility with which these tools were handled remains one of the most remarkable features of this investigation. That diplomacy and 'international' relations in the thirteenth century do not resemble their modern equivalents does not mean that they did not exist or that they were not practised.

To return to Henry III. What do his relations with the empire tell us about his wider political plans, hopes and ambitions? Any answer to this question will have to be preliminary. Not only are we dealing with only a small part of Henry's activities, but matters are also not helped by the fact that too much of Henry's reign remains *terra incognita*. We still lack a more detailed investigation of his financial administration beyond the work done by Robert Stacey for the years up to 1244, or by David Carpenter for the early 1250s;[1] there is, as yet, no analysis of the personnel and workings of the exchequer or chancery; even less work has been done on the political culture of thirteenth-century England, Henry's religious patronage or the cult of the saints;[2] Henry III's dealings with his British neighbours are only beginning to be explored;[3] and, apart from Simon Lloyd's work on Henry's involvement in the crusading movement,[4] we know very little about his wider diplomatic initiatives: there is, as yet, no study of his dealings with the Capetians or the rulers of Iberia. In short, the present book can attempt to fill some of these gaps, but it raises as many questions as it has sought to answer.

With these qualifications in mind, the king who emerges from this investigation presents a very different picture from the one we normally encounter in his domestic undertakings, but one who grappled with similar problems.

---

1 Stacey, *Politics, policy and finance*; Carpenter, 'The gold treasure'.
2 N. Vincent, *The holy blood: King Henry III and the Westminster blood relic*, Cambridge 2001, is the notable exception.
3 The first detailed modern investigation of his dealings with Scotland was published in 2002: Brown, 'Henry the Peaceable?'. For Henry III and Wales see H. Pryce, 'Negotiating anglo-Welsh relations: Llewelyn the Great and Henry III' in Weiler and Rowlands, *England and Europe*, 13–30.
4 Lloyd, *English society*.

Just as King John and Magna Carta dominated Henry's English affairs, so the loss of Normandy dominated his activities on the mainland. As at home, he faced a situation which was none of his own making, for which he could take no responsibility, and where only a limited range of options was available to him. The ones he chose in the end tended to be conservative, but they were pursued with an acute awareness of what was possible. Henry was not reckless, and showed little bravado. He may have admired Richard the Lionheart, but he had none of his uncle's predilection for reckless risk-taking. However, in Henry's case, caution did not produce the rewards he may have expected. This was largely due to the way he pursued his affairs in mainland Europe, and his unwillingness to engage fully in his decisions those men who were to man and finance his expeditions: the English barons. Many of Henry III's undertakings failed because of how he pursued them, not because he pursued them. Whereas abroad, from about 1245 onwards, he was able to explore new means of achieving his goals, and show a willingness to respond quickly to changing circumstances, at home he continued to avoid addressing the issues and problems he had inherited from his father, adopting a policy which demonstrated an awareness of King John's failure, but a reluctance to depart from the very tenets which had brought about that failure. In this respect, Henry III truly was his father's son.

Neither the actions of Henry III nor those of Frederick II can be viewed in isolation. They shared with their contemporaries the values, tools and mechanisms by which, and the framework within which they acted, and the ethical norms according to which they were judged. They responded to common pressures and concerns, and they did so in a manner easily understood and appropriated by their peers, neighbours and rivals. Only if this background is ignored do Henry's actions abroad appear as foolish and incompetent. Historians of thirteenth-century England can ignore her European connection, but they do so at their own grave peril.

Bibliography

Unpublished primary sources

London, The National Archives
Public Record Office
C 53 charter rolls
SC ancient correspondence
E 372 pipe rolls

Printed primary sources

Aachener Urkunden, 1101–1250, ed. E. Meuthen, Bonn 1972

Acta aragonensia: Quellen zur deutschen, italienischen, französischen, spanischen, zur Kirchen- und Kulturgeschichte: aus der diplomatischen Korrespondenz Jaymes II (1291–1327), ed. H. Finke, Munich 1908–33

Acta capitulorum generalium ordinis praedicatorum, I: Ab anno 1220 usque ad annum 1303, ed. B. M. Reichert, Rome 1898

Acta imperii inedita saeculi XIII et XIV: Urkunden und Briefe zur Geschichte des Kaiserreichs und des Königreichs Sizilien, ed. E. Winkelmann, Innsbruck 1880–5

Acta imperii selecta: Urkunden der Deutscher Könige und Kaiser, 928–1398, mit einem Anhange von Reichssachen, ed. J. F. Böhmer, Innsbruck 1870

Actes et lettres de Charles I roi de Sicile concernant la France (1257–1284), ed. A. de Boüard, Paris 1926

Les Actes pontificaux originaux des Archives Nationales de Paris, I: 1198–1261, ed. B. Barbiche, Vatican City 1975

Alberti milioli notarii regini liber, MGH, SS xxxi, Hanover 1903

Alberti stadensis chronica, MGH, SS xvi, Hanover 1869

Albrici abbatis Trium Fontium chronica (excerpts), MGH, SS xxiii, Hanover 1874

Alsatia aevi merovingici, carolingici, saxonici, salici, suevici diplomatica, ed. J. D. Schoepflin, Mannheim 1772–5

Andrae Danduli ducis venetiarum chronica per extensum descripta, ed. E. Pastorello, RIS xii/1, Bologna 1938

Annales aquicinctini, MGH, SS xvi, Hanover 1869

Annales argentinenses Ellenhardi, MGH, SS xvii, Hanover 1861

Annales augustani minores, MGH, SS x, Hanover 1852

Annales bergomates, MGH, SS xviii, Hanover 1863

Annales blandinienses, MGH, SS v, Hanover 1844

Annales breves wormatienses, MGH, SS xvii, Hanover 1861

Annales capituli cracovienses, MGH, SS xix, Hanover 1866

Annales cestrienses, ed. R. C. Christie (Record Society for the Publication of Original Documents Relating to Lancashire and Cheshire xiv, 1887)

Annales civitatis vincentiae, ed. G. Soranzo, RIS viii/5, Bologna 1921

Annales cremonenses, MGH, SS xviii, Hanover 1863

Annales elwangenses, MGH, SS x, Hanover 1852

Annales ensdorfenses, MGH, SS x, Hanover 1852

Annales erphordenses fratrum praedicatorum, in *Monumenta erphesfurtensia saec. XII, XIII, XIV*, ed. O. Holder-Egger, MGH, SS sep.ed., Hanover–Leipzig 1899

Annales floreffienses, MGH, SS xvi, Hanover 1869

Annales hamburgenses, MGH, SS xvi, Hanover 1858

Annales hamburgenses maiores, MGH, SS xxiv, Hanover 1879

Annales ianuenses , MGH, SS xviii, Hanover 1863

Annales laubiensum continuatio, MGH, SS iv, Hanover 1841

Annales londonienses, in *Chronicles of the reigns of Edward I and Edward II*, ed. W. Stubbs (RS, 1882–3), i. 1–252

Annales mantuani, MGH, SS xix, Hanover 1866

Annales marbacenses qui dicuntur, ed. H. Bloch, MGH, SS rer. Germ. sep.ed., Hanover–Leipzig 1907

Annales marchianenses, MGH, SS xvi, Hanover 1869

Annales mediolanenses brevissimi, MGH, SS xviii, Hanover 1863

Annales moguntini, MGH, SS xvii, Hanover 1861

Annales monastici, ed. H. R. Luard (RS, 1864–9)

Annales mosomagenses, MGH, SS iii, Hanover 1839

Annales neresheimenses, MGH, SS x, Hanover 1852

Annales ottenburani minores, MGH, SS xvii, Hanover 1861

Annales parchenses, MGH, SS xvi, Hanover 1869

Annales parmenses maiores, MGH, SS xviii, Hanover 1863

Annales placentini gibellini, MGH, SS xviii, Hanover 1863

Annales placentini guelfi, MGH, SS xviii, Hanover 1863

Annales pragenses, MGH, SS iii, Hanover 1839

Annales S Rudberti salisburgenses, MGH, SS ix, Hanover 1851

Annales saxonici, MGH, SS xvi, Hanover 1869

Annales scheftlarienses maiores, MGH, SS xvii, Hanover 1861

Annales scheftlarienses minores, MGH, SS xvii, Hanover 1861

Annales spirenses, MGH, SS xvii, Hanover 1861

Annales veterocellenses, MGH, SS xvi, Hanover 1869

Annales wormatienses, MGH, SS xvii, Hanover 1861

Annales zwifeltenses maiores, MGH, SS x, Hanover 1852

Annals of Bermondsey, ed. H. R. Luard, AM iii, London 1866, 421–88

Annals of Burton, ed. H. R. Luard, AM i, London 1864, 183–500

Annals of Dunstable, ed. H. R. Luard, AM iii, London 1866, 3–408

Annals of Margam, ed. H. R. Luard, AM i, London 1864, 1–40

Annals of Oseney, ed. H. R. Luard, AM iv, London 1869, 3–355

Annals of Southwark, MGH, SS xxvii, Hanover 1885.

'The annals of Southwark and Merton', ed. M. Tyson, *Surrey Archaeological Collections* xxvi (1925), 24–57

Annals of Tewkesbury, ed. H. R. Luard, AM i, London 1864, 43–182

Annals of Waverley, ed. H. R. Luard, AM ii, London 1865, 129–412

Annals of Winchester, ed. H. R. Luard, AM ii, London 1865, 3–128

Annals of Worcester ed. H. R. Luard, AM iv, London 1869, 355–562

Anonymus, 'Quatre Pièces relatives à l'Ordre Teutonique en orient', *Archives de l'orient latin* ii (1884), 164–9

Arab historians of the crusades, ed. and trans F. Gabrieli, English trans. E. J. Costello, London 1969

Arnoldi abbatis lubecensis chronica, MGH, SS xxi, Hanover 1870

Ayyuibids, Mamlukes and crusaders: selections from the Tarikh al-Duwal wa'l-Muluk of Ibn al-Furat, ed. M. C. Lyons, U. Lyons and J. S. C. Riley-Smith, Cambridge 1971

Balduini ninovensis chronicon, MGH, SS xxv, Hanover 1880

Bartholomaei de Neocastro historia Siculi, ed. G. Paladino, RIS xiii/3, Bologna 1921–2

Bartholomaei scribae annales, MGH, SS xviii, Hanover 1863

Battenberg, F., *Die Gerichtsstandsprivilegien der deutschen Könige und Kaiser*, Cologne–Vienna 1983

Baumgartenberger Formelbuch: eine Quelle zur Geschichte des XIII. Jahrhunderts vornehmlich der Zeiten Rudolfs von Habsburg, ed. H. Baerwald, Vienna 1866

Bellum Walterianum, MGH, SS xvii, Hanover 1861

Die Berichte der Generalprokuratoren des Deutschen Ordens an die Kurie, ed. K. Forstreuter, Göttingen 1961–76

Bond, E. A., 'Historiola de pietate regis Henrici III', *Archaeological Journal* xvii (1860), 317–19

Braunschweigische Reimchronik, ed. L. Weiland, MGH, SS vern. ling. ii, Hanover 1878

Bremisches Urkundenbuch, ed. D. R. Ehmck and W. von Bippen, Bremen 1873–1943

Das Brief- und Memorialbuch des Albert Behaim, ed. T. Frenz and P. Herde, MGH, Briefe des späten Mittelalters, i, Munich 2000

Briefsteller und Formelbücher des 11.–14. Jahrhunderts aus bayerischen Bibliotheken, ed. L. Rodinger, Munich 1863–4

Brut y tywysogyon or the Chronicle of the princes, Peniarth MS 20 version, ed. and trans. T. Jones, Cardiff 1952

Burchardi et Cuonradi urspergensis chronicon: continuatio, MGH, SS xvi (1859)

Calendar of charter rolls preserved in the Public Record Office, London 1903–27

Calendar of entries in the papal registers relating to Great Britain and Ireland: papal letters, ed. W. H. Bliss, i, London 1893

Calendar of the liberate rolls preserved in the Public Record Office: Henry III, London 1916–64

Calendar of patent rolls of the reign of Henry III preserved in the Public Record Office, London 1901–13

Cam, H. M. and E. F. Jacob, 'Notes on an English Cluniac chronicle', *EHR* xliv (1929), 94–104

Cardauns, H., 'Fünf Kaiserurkunden', *Forschungen zur deutschen Geschichte* xii (1872), 453–6

Casum S Galli continuatio III, MGH, SS ii, Hanover 1829

Catalogus archiepiscoporum coloniensum, MGH, SS xxiv, Hanover 1879

Chronica buriensis, 1212–1301: the chronicle of Bury St Edmunds, ed. A. Gransden, London 1964

Chronica Johannis de Oxenedis, ed. H. Ellis (RS, 1859)

Chronica latina regum Castellae, in *Chronica Hispana saeculi XIII*, ed. L. C. Brea, J. A. Estévez Sola and R. C. Herrero (Corpus Christianorum Continuatio Medieualis lxxiii), Turnhout 1997

Chronica Magistri Guillelmi de Podio Laurentii, ed. J. Duvernoy, Paris 1976, repr. Toulouse 1996

Chronica Magistri Rogeri de Houdene, ed. William Stubbs (RS, 1868–71)

Chronica de Mailros, ed. J. Stevenson, Edinburgh 1835

Chronica pontificum et imperatorum mantuana, MGH, SS xxiv, Hanover 1879

Chronica principum Saxoniae ampliata, MGH, SS xxx, Hanover 1896–Stuttgart 1934

Chronica regia coloniensis, ed. G. Waitz, MGH, SS sep.ed., Hanover 1880

Chronica regia coloniensis continuatio S Pantaleonis v, in *Chronica regia coloniensis*.

Chronica reinhardsbrunnensis, MGH, SS xxiv, Hanover 1879

Chronicae magni presbyteri continuatio reicherspergenses continuatio, MGH, SS xvii, Hanover 1861

The chronicle of Walter of Guisborough, previously edited as the chronicle of Walter of Hemingford or Hemingburgh, ed. H. Rothwell (Camden, 1957)

Chronicles of the reigns of Stephen, Henry II and Richard I, ed. R. Howlett (RS, 1884–8)

Chronicon de bello, MGH, SS xxviii, Hanover 1888, 554

Chronicon imaginis mundi, Monumenta Historiae Patriae Scriptores v, Turin 1848

Chronicon de Lanercost, 1201–1346, ed. J. Stevenson, Edinburgh 1839

Chronicon marchiae tarvisinae et lombardiae, ed. L. A. Bottegli, RIS viii/3, iii, Citta di Castello 1914–16

Chronicon St Martini Turonensi, MGH, SS xxvi, Hanover 1882

Chronicon wormatiense saeculi XIII, in *Quellen zur Geschichte der Stadt Worms*, ed. H. Boos, Berlin 1886–93, ii. 143–99

Chronique latin de Guillaume de Nangis de 1113 à 1300 avec les continuations de cette chronique de 1300 à 1368, ed. H. Geraud, Paris 1843

Close rolls of the reign of Henry III preserved in the Public Record Office, London 1902–38

Close rolls (supplementary, of the reign of Henry III, 1244–1266), ed. A. Morton, London 1975

Codex diplomaticus dominii temporalis sancti sedis, ed. A. Theiner, Rome 1861–2

Codex diplomaticus et epistolaris regni Bohemiae, ed. J. Sebanel and S. Duskova, Prague 1974–

Codex diplomaticus lubecensis, in *Lübeckisches Urkundenbuch*, Lübeck 1843–1905

Codex diplomaticus Nassoicus, ed. W. Sauer and K. Menzel, Wiesbaden 1885–7

Constitutiones et acta publica imperatorum et regum, II: 1198–1272, ed. L. Weiland, MGH, Legum Sectio iv, Hanover 1896

Constitutiones et acta publica imperatorum et regum, 1273–1298, ed. J. Schwalm, MGH, Leges iv/3, Hanover 1904–6

Continuatio Burchardi et Cuonradi urspergensis chronici, MGH, SS xxiii, Hanover 1874, 380–3

Continuatio garstensis, MGH, SS ix, Hanover 1851

Continuatio lambacensis, MGH, SS ix, Hanover 1851

Continuatio Laurentii de Leodio gesta, MGH, SS x, Hanover 1852

Continuatio mellicenses, MGH, SS ix, Hanover 1851

Continuatio sancrucensis II, MGH, SS ix, Hanover 1851

Continuatio William of Newburgh, in *Chronicles of Stephen, Henry and Richard*

Continuatio zwetlensis III, MGH, SS ix, Hanover 1851

Continuation de Guillaume de Tyre dite du manuscrit de Rothelin, in *Receuil des historiens des croisades: historiens occidentaux*, ii, Paris 1859

Correspondance administrative d'Alfonse de Poitiers, ed. A. Molinier, Paris 1894–1900

Councils and synods with other documents relating to the English Church, II/1: *1205–65*, ed. F. M. Powicke and C. R. Cheney, Oxford 1964

Cronica di Antonio Godi Vincentino, ed. G. Soranzo, RIS viii/2, Citta di Castello 1908

Crusader Syria in the thirteenth century: the Rothelin continuation of the history of William of Tyre with part of the Eracles or Acre text, trans. J. Shirley, Aldershot 1999

De antiquis legibus liber: cronica maiorum et vicecomitum Londoniarum, ed. T. Stapleton (Camden, 1846)

Decrees of the ecumenical councils, ed. and trans. N. P. Tanner, London–Washington, DC 1990

Delaborde, H.-F., 'Lettre des chrétiens de Terre-Sainte à Charles d'Anjou (22 avril 1260)', *Revue de l'orient latin* ii (1894), 206–15

Diplomatic documents preserved in the Public Record Office, 1101–1272, ed. P. Chaplais, London 1964

Documenti sulle relazioni tra la casa di Savoia e la Santa Sede nel medio evo (1066–1268), ed. P. Fontana, Turin 1939

Documents of the baronial movement of reform and rebellion, 1258–67, ed. R. F. Treharne and I. J. Sanders, Oxford 1973

Dörrie, H., 'Drei Texte zur Geschichte der Ungarn und Mongolen', *Nachrichten der Akademie der Wissenschaften zu Göttingen (Philosophisch-Historische Klasse)* (1956), 125–202

Ellenhardi chronicon, MGH, SS xvii, Hanover 1861

Elsässische Urkunden vornehmlich des 13. Jahrhunderts, ed. A. Hessel, Strasbourg 1915

Emonis et Menkonis werumensium chronica, MGH, SS xxiii, Hanover 1874

English episcopal acta, IX: Winchester, 1205–1238, ed. N. Vincent, Oxford 1994

Epistolae saeculi XIII e regestis pontificium romanorum selectae, ed. Carl Rodenberg, MGH, Epistolae, Berlin 1883–94

Extraits du Collier de perles, in *Receuil des historiens des croisades: historiens orientaux*, ii, Paris 1880

F. Nicholai de ordine fratrum praedicatorum annales, ed. T. Hog, London 1845

Filippo da Novara, *Guerra di Federico II in oriente, 1223–1242*, ed. S. Melani, Naples 1994

Flores historiarum, ed. H. R. Luard (RS, 1890)

Foedera, conventiones, litterae et cujuscunque generis acta publica, ed. Thomas Rymer, new edn, i/1, ed. A. Clark and F. Holbrooke, London 1816

Fontes rerum germanicarum, ed. J. F. Böhmer, Stuttgart 1843–68

Forschungen zur Reichs- und Rechtsgeschichte Italiens, ed. J. Ficker, Innsbruck 1868–74

Gascon register A (series of 1318–1319), ed. G. P. Cuttino and J.-P. Trabut-Cussac, London 1975

Gerardi maurisii cronica dominorum Ecelini et Albrici fratrum de Romano, ed. Giovanni Sorazzo, RIS viii/4, Citta di Castello 1913

213

Gervasii cantuarensis gesta regum continuata, in *The historical works of Gervase of Canterbury*, ed. W. Stubbs (RS, 1879–80)

Gesta abbatum trudonensium, continuatio, MGH, SS x, Hanover 1852

Gesta treverorum continuata, MGH, SS xxiv, Hanover 1879

Gestes de chiprois, ed. G. Raynaud (Publications de la Société de l'orient latin: série historique, v, 1887, repr. Osnabrück 1968)

Gilberti catalogus pontificum et imperatorum romanorum ampliatus et continuatus, MGH, SS xxii, Hanover 1872, 359–67

Gotfrid Hagen, *Dat Boich van der stede Colne*, ed. C. Schröder and A. Birlinger, in *Die Chroniken der deutschen Städte vom 14. bis ins 16. Jahrhundert*, XII/1: Die Chroniken der niederrheinischen Städte: Cöln Leipzig 1875

Hamburgisches Urkundenbuch: erster Band, ed. J. M. Lappenberg, Hamburg 1842

Hampe, K., 'Ungedruckte Briefe zur Geschichte König Richards von Cornwall aus der Sammlung Richards von Pofi', *NA* xxx (1905), 673–90

——— 'Ein ungedruckter Bericht über das Konklave von 1241 im römischen Septizonium', *Sitzungsberichte der Heidelberger Akademie der Wissenschaften: Philosophisch-Historische Klasse* (1913), 1–34

Hansisches Urkundenbuch, ed. K. Höhlbaum, Halle 1876–1907

Hartmann, H., 'Die Urkunden Konrads IV', *AfD* xviii (1944), 38–163

Heidemann, J., *Papst Clemens IV: eine Monographie*, I: *Das Vorleben des Papstes und sein Legationsregister*, Münster 1903

Heinrici de Heimburg Presb. Gmundensis annales, MGH, SS xvii, Hanover 1861

Herde, P., 'Ein Pamphlet der päpstlichen Kurie gegen Kaiser Friedrich II von 1245/46', *DA* xxiii (1967), 468–538.

Hermanni abbati altahenses annales, MGH, SS xvii, Hanover 1861

Hessische Urkunden aus dem Grossherzoglich Hessischen Haus- und Staatsarchiv, Darmstadt 1873, ed. L. Bauer, vol. vi [register] 1979

Historia diplomatica Friderici Secundi, ed. Alphonse Huillard-Breholles, Paris 1852–61

Huillard-Brehouilles, J.-L.-A., 'Examen des chartes de l'eglise romaine contenues dans les rouleaux de Cluny', *Notices et extraits des manuscrits de la Bibliothèque Imperiale* xxi/2 (1865)

Inventaire des chartes et cartulaires des duchés de Brabant et de Limbourg des pays d'Outre-Meuse, ed. A. Verkooren, Brussels 1910–66

Jacob, E. F., 'Complaints of Henry III against the baronial council in 1261', *EHR* xli (1926), 564–71

John of Wallingford, MGH, SS xxviii, Hanover 1888

Joinville, Sir Jean de, *Histoire de Saint Louis*, ed. N. de Wailly, Paris 1890

Kaiser, H., 'Ein unbekanntes Mandat König Richards und die Anfänge der Landvogtei im Elsass', *Zeitschrift für Geschichte des Oberrheins* xix (1904), 337–9

Kleve-Mark Urkunden, 1223–1368, ed. W.-R. Schleidgen, Siegburg 1983

Kronika Pulkakova, in *Fontes rerum bohemicarum*, v, ed. J. Emler and J. Gebauer, Prague 1893

Layettes du Tresor de Chartes, ed. H.-F. Laborde and A. Teulet, Paris 1863–1909

Liber de rebus memorialibus sive chronicon Henrici de Hervordia, ed. A. Potthast, Göttingen 1859

Liebermann, F., 'Zur Geschichte Friedrichs II. und Richards von Cornwall', *NA* xiii (1888), 217–20

———— 'The annals of Lewes Priory', *EHR* xvii (1902), 83–9

The life of St Edmund by Matthew Paris, trans. C. H. Lawrence, Stroud 1996

Litterae Walliae preserved in liber A in the Public Record Office, ed. J. G. Edwards, Cardiff 1940

Lupprian, K. E., *Die Beziehungen der Päpste zu islamischen und mongolischen Herrschern im 13. Jahrhundert anhand ihres Briefwechsels*, Vatican City 1981

Magistri tolosani chronicon faventium, ed. Guiseppe Rossini, RIS xxviii/1, Bologna 1936–9

Matthew Paris, *Chronica maiora: the Chronica maiora of Matthew Paris*, ed. H. R. Luard (RS, 1872–4)

———— *Historia anglorum*, ed. F. Madden (RS, 1886–9)

Mecklenburgisches Urkundenbuch, Schwerin 1863–1977

Memoirs of a Syrian prince: Abu'l-Fida, sultan of Hamah (672–732/1273–1331), ed. P. M. Holt, Wiesbaden 1983

The memoranda roll of the king's remembrancer for Michaelmas 1230–Trinity 1231 (E. 159.10), ed. C. Robinson, Princeton 1933

Memoranda rolls 16–17 Henry III preserved in the Public Record Office, ed. R. Allen Brown, London 1991

Monumenta boica, xxx, Munich 1834

Monumenta erphesfurtensia, ed. O. Holder-Egger, MGH, SS sep. ed., Hanover–Leipzig 1899

Nicolai de Jamsilla historia de rebus gestis Friderici II imperatoris ejusque filiorum, ed. L. A. Muratori, Milan 1726

Notae historicae sangallenses, MGH, SS i, Hanover 1826, 70–1

Nürnberger Urkundenbuch, Nuremberg 1959

Pagnotti, F., 'Niccolò da Calvi e la sua vita d'Innocenzo IV', *Archivio della Reále società romana di storia patria* xxi (1898), 7–120

Petri Cantinelli chronicon, ed. F. Torraca, RIS xxviii/2, Città di Castello 1902

Planctus destructionis regni Hungariae per Tartaros, ed. L. Juhàsz, SRH ii, Budapest 1938, 589–98

Pokračowatelé Kosmowi, in *Fontes rerum bohemicarum, II: Cosmae chronicon boemorum cum continuatoribus*, ed. J. Emler, Prague 1874

Political songs of England from the reign of John to that of Edward II, ed. T. Wright (Camden, 1839), repr. with new introduction by P. Coss, Cambridge 1996

Pontificia hibernica: medieval papal chancery documents concerning Ireland, 640–1261, ed. M. Sheehy, Dublin 1962–5

Quellen zur Geschichte der Herrschaft Landskron a. d. Ahr, ed. T. Zimmer, Bonn 1966

Quellen zur Geschichte der Stadt Köln, ed. L. Ennen and G. Eckertz, Cologne 1860–79

Quellen zur Geschichte der Stadt Worms, ed. H. Boos, Berlin 1886–93

Receipt and issue rolls for the twenty-sixth year of the reign of King Henry III, 1241–2, ed. R. C. Stacey, London 1992

Receuil des actes des comtes de Provence appartenant à la maison de Barcelone, ed. F. Benoit, Monaco 1925

Receuil des historiens des Gaules et de la France, ed. M. Bouquet, Paris 1738–1904

Regesta diplomatica nec non epistolaria bohemiae et moraviae, 600–1253, ed. K. J. Erben, Prague 1854

Regesta Honorii papae III, ed. P. Pressutti, Rome 1889

Regesta imperii: die Regesten des Kaiserreiches unter Philipp, Otto IV., Friedrich II., Heinrich (VII.), Conrad IV., Heinrich Raspe, Wilhelm und Richard, 1198–1272, ed. J. F. Böhmer, E. Winkelmann and J. Ficker, Innsbruck 1881–1901

Regesta regni hierosolymitani (1097–1291), ed. R. Röhricht, Innsbruck 1893–1904, repr. New York n.d.

Regesten der Prämonstratenserabtei Wadgassen bis zum Jahre 1571, ed. J. Burg, Saarbrücken 1980

Regesten der Reichsstadt Aachen, ed. W. Mummenhoff, Bonn 1937–61

Regestes des empéreurs latins de Constantinople (1204–1261/1272), ed. B. Hendrickx, Thessalonika 1988

Regestum Innocentii III papae super negotio romani imperii, ed. F. Kempf, Rome 1947

Les Registres d'Alexandre IV, ed. C. B. de la Roncière and others, Paris 1895–1959

Les Registres de Clement IV, ed. E. Jordan, Paris 1893–1945

Les Registres de Gregoire IX, ed. L. Auvray, Paris 1896–1955

Les Registres d'Innocent IV, ed. E. Berger, Paris 1884–1919

Les Registres d'Urbain IV, ed. L. Dorez and J. Guiraud, Paris 1899–1958

Reinado y diplomas de Fernando III, ed. J. Gonzalez, Cordoba 1980–6

Ridgway, H., 'King Henry III's grievances against the council in 1261: a new version and a letter describing political events', *BIHR* lxi (1988), 227–42

Rishanger, William, *The chronicle of the Barons' War,* ed. J. O. H. Halliwell (Camden, 1860), repr. New York 1968

Roger of Wendover, *Flores historiarum,* ed. H. O. Cox, London 1841–4

Rogerii carmen miserabile, ed. L. Juhasz, SRH ii, Budapest 1938, 543–88

Röhricht, R., 'Acte de soumission des barons du royaume de Jérusalem à Frédéric II (7 mai 1241)', *Archives de l'orient latin* ii (1881), 402–3

Rolandini patavini cronica in factis et circa facta marchiae trivixane, ed. A Bonardi, RIS viii/1, Citta di Castello 1903–8

Roll of divers accounts for the early years of the reign of Henry III, ed. F. Cazel, London 1982

Rolls of the fifteenth of the ninth year of the reign of Henry III for Cambridgeshire, Lincolnshire and Wiltshire and rolls of the fortieth of the seventeenth year of the reign of Henry III for Kent, ed. F. Cazel and A. Cazel, London 1983

Rotuli litterarum clausarum in Turri Londoninensi asservati, ed. T. Duffus Hardy, London 1833–4

Ryccardi de S Germano notarii cronica, MGH, SS xix, Hanover 1866

Sächsiche Weltchronik und ihre Fortsetzungen, MGH, Deutsche Chroniken 2, Hanover 1877, 296–7

Schaller, H. M., 'Die Antwort Gregors IX auf Peter de Vinea I, I: "Collegerunt pontifices" ', *DA* xi (1954/5), 140–65

———— 'Eine kuriale Briefsammlung des 13. Jahrhunderts mit unbekannten Briefen Friedrichs II. (Trier, Stadtbibliothek Cod. 859/1097)', *DA* xviii (1962), 171–213

———— 'Das letzte Rundschreiben Gregors IX gegen Friedrich II', in P. Classen and P. Scheibert (eds), *Festschrift Percy Ernst Scharmm,* Wiesbaden 1964, 309–21

Some new sources for the life of Blessed Agnes of Bohemia, including a XIV century Latin version and a XV century German version of her Life, ed. W. W. Seton, Aberdeen 1915

Sweeney, J. R., 'Unbekannte Briefe Kaiser Friedrichs II. im Codex Indianensis der Werke Senecas', *DA* xlv (1989), 83–108

Thesaurus novus anecdotorum, i/2, ed. E. Martène and U. Durand, Paris 1717, repr. New York 1968

Thomas de Papia (Tuscis, ordinis minorum) gesta imperatorum et pontificum, MGH, SS xxii, Hanover 1872

Thomas Wyke's chronicle, ed. H. R. Luard, AM iv, London 1869

Treaty rolls, 1234–1325, ed. P. Chaplais, London 1955

Urkundenbuch der Abtei Heisterbach, ed. F. Schmitz, Bonn 1908

Urkundenbuch des Stiftes St Gereon zu Köln, ed. Joerres, P., Bonn 1893

Urkunden zur älteren Handels- und Rechtsgeschichte der Republik Venedig mit besondere Beziehung auf Byzanz und die Levante, ed. G. L. Tafel and G. M. Thomas, Vienna 1856–7

Urkundenbuch zur Geschichte der Bischöfe von Speyer, ed. F.-X. Remling, Mainz 1852–3

Urkundenbuch zur Geschichte der Herzöge von Braunschweig und Lüneburg und ihrer Lande, ed. H. Sudendorf, Hanover 1859–83

Urkundenbuch zur Geschichte der mittelrheinischen Territorien, ed. H. Beyer, L. Eltester and A. Goerz , Koblenz 1874

Urkundenbuch für die Geschichte des Niederrheins, ed. T. J. Lacomblet, Düsseldorf 1840–58

Urkundenbuch des Hochstifts Hildesheim und seiner Bischöfe, ed. H. Hoogeweg and K. Jänicke, Hanover–Leipzig 1896–1911

Die Urkunden der oberdeutschen Städtebünde vom 13. Jahrhundert bis 1549, ed. K. Ruser, Göttingen 1979–88

Urkunden- und Quellenbuch zur Geschichte der altluxemburgischen Territorien bis zur burgundischen Zeit, ed. C. Wampach, Luxemburg 1935–55

Urkunden und Quellen zur Geschichte von Stadt und Abtei Siegburg, ed. E. Wimplinghoff, Siegburg 1964–85

Urkundenbuch der Reichsstadt Frankfurt, ed. J. F. Böhmer and F. Lau, Frankfurt 1901–5

Urkundenbuch der Stadt Friedberg: erster Band, 1216–1410, ed. M. Foltz, Marburg 1904

Urkundenbuch der Stadt Strassburg, ed. W. Wiegand and H. Witte, Strasbourg 1879–1900

Urkundenbuch des Stiftes Fischbeck, ed. H. Lathwesen and B. Poschmann, Rinteln 1978–9

Urkundenbuch des Stiftes und der Stadt Hameln bis zum Jahre 1407, ed. O. Meinardus and E. Fink, Hanover 1887–1903

Veterum scriptorum et monumentorum, historicorum, dogmaticorum, moralium amplissima collectio, ed. E. Martène and U. Durand, i, Paris 1724, repr. Westmead 1969

Vie et correspondence de Pierre de la Vigne, ministre de l'empéreur Frédéric II, ed. A. Huillard-Breholles, Paris 1865

Vita Gregorii IX, in *Le 'Liber censuum' de l'église romaine*, ed. P. Fabre, L. Duchesne and G. Mollat, Paris 1889–1952, ii. 8–36

Vita Henrici episcopi altera, MGH, SS xxiv, Hanover 1879

Weiland, L., 'Sieben Kaiserurkunden', *Forschungen zur deutschen Geschichte* xviii (1878), 204–10

Die Welfenurkunden des Tower zu London und des Excheqer zu Westminster, ed. H. Sudendorf, Hanover 1844

Westfälisches Urkundenbuch, Münster 1847–1977

Eine Wiener Briefsammlung zur Geschichte des deutschen Reiches und der österreichischen Länder in der zweiten Hälfte des XIII. Jahrhunderts, ed. O. Redlich,Vienna 1894

Willelmi Chronica andrensis, MGH, SS xxiv, Hanover 1879

William de Nangis, *Gesta sanctae memoriae Ludowici regis Franciae*, RHGF xx. 309–465, Paris 1840

———— *Historia albigensium*, RHGF, Paris 1839–40, xix. 193–225; xx. 764–76

Winkelmann, E., 'Zwölf Papstbriefe zur Geschichte Friedrichs II. und seiner Nachkommen', *Forschungen zur deutschen Geschichte* xv (1875), 373–89

———— 'Reisefrüchte aus Italien und anderes zur deutsch-italienischen Geschichte', *Forschungen zur deutschen Geschichte* xviii (1878), 469–92

Wirtembergisches Urkundenbuch, Stuttgart 1849–1913

Wittmann, F. M., *Monumenta wittelsbacensia: Urkundenbuch zur Geschichte des Hauses Wittelsbach: erste Abtheilung von 1204 bis 1292*, Munich 1857

Secondary works

Abulafia, D., *Frederick II: a medieval emperor*, London 1988

Ahlers, J., *Die Welfen und die englischen Könige, 1165–1235*, Hildesheim 1987

Allsen, T. T., 'Prelude to the western campaigns: Mongol military operations in the Volga–Ural region, 1217–1237', *Archivum Eurasiae Medii Aevii* iii (1983), 5–24

Angermeier, H., 'Landfriedenspolitik und Landfriedensgesetzgebung unter den Staufern', in Fleckenstein, *Probleme um Friedrich II*, 167–86

Antonelli, R., 'La corte "italiana" di Federico II e la letteratura europea', in *Federico II e le nuove culture*, 319–46

Arnold, B., 'England and Germany, 1050–1350', in Jones and Vale, *England*, 43–52

———— *Princes and territories in medieval Germany*, Cambridge 1991

———— 'Germany and England, 1066–1453', in N. Saul (ed.), *England in Europe, 1066–1453*, London 1994, 76–87

———— *Medieval Germany, 500–1300: a political interpretation*, London 1997

———— 'Emperor Frederick II (1194–1250) and the political particularism of the German princes', *JMH* xxvi (2000), 239–52

Aurell, M., 'Chanson et propagande politique: les troubadours Gibelins, 1255–1285', in *Le forme della propaganda politica el due nel trecento*, Rome 1994, 183–202

Aziz, M. A., 'La Croisade de l'Empereur Frédéric II et l'orient latin', in M. Balard (ed.), *Autour de la Première Croisade*, Paris 1996, 373–8

Baaken, G., 'Der deutsche Thronstreit auf dem IV. Laterankonzil', in Herbers, Kortüm and Servatius, *Ex ipsis rerum documentis*, 509–21

———— *Ius imperii ad regnum: Königreich Sizilien, imperium romanum und Römisches Papsttum vom Tode Heinrichs VI. bis zu den Verzichtserklärungen Rudolfs von Habsburg*, Cologne–Vienna–Weimar 1993

———— 'Die Verhandlungen von Cluny (1245) und der Kampf Innocenz' IV gegen Friedrich II', *DA* l (1994), 531–79

Baldwin, J. W., *Aristocratic life in medieval France: the romances of Jean Renart and Gerbert de Montreuil, 1190–1230*, Baltimore 2000

Bappert, J. F., *Richard von Cornwall seit seiner Wahl zum deutschen König, 1258–1272*, Bonn 1905

Barone, G., 'La propaganda antiimperiale nell'Italia federiciana: l'azione degli ordini mendicanti', in Toubert and Paravacini Bagliani, *Federico II*, 278–89

Barraclough, G., 'The English royal chancery and the papal chancery in the reign of Henry III', *MIÖG* lxii (1954), 365–78.

Bartlett, R., 'The impact of royal government in the French Ardennes: the evidence of the 1247 enquête', *JMH* vii (1981), 83–96

Battenberg, F., *Herrschaft und Verfahren: politische Prozesse im mittelalterlichen römisch-deutschen Reich*, Darmstadt 1996

Baylen, J. O., 'John Maunsell and the Castilian treaty of 1254: a study of a clerical diplomat', *Traditio* xvii (1961), 482–91

Bayley, C. C., 'The diplomatic preliminaries of the Double Election of 1257 in Germany', *EHR* lxii (1947), 457–83

———— *The formation of the German college of electors in the mid-thirteenth century*, Toronto 1949

Belperron, P., *La Croisade contre les albigeois et l'union du Languedoc à la France (1209–1249)*, Paris 1967

Bemont, C., 'La Campaigne de Poitou, 1242–1243: Taillebourg et Saintes', *Annales du Midi* v (1893), 289–314

Benson, R. L., 'Political *renovatio*: two models from Roman antiquity', in R. L. Benson and G. Constable (eds), *Renaissance and renewal in the twelfth century*, Oxford 1982, 339–86

———— 'Libertas in Italy, 1152–1226', in G. Makdisi, D. Sourdel and J. Sourdel-Thomine (eds), *La Notion de liberté au moyen âge: Islam, Byzance, occident: Penn-Paris-Dumbarton Oaks colloquia*, Paris 1985, 191–213

Berg, B., 'Manfred of Sicily and Urban IV: negotiations of 1262', *Mediaeval Studies* lv (1993), 111–36

Berg, D., *England und der Kontinent: Studien zur auswärtigen Politik der anglo-normannischen Könige in 11. und 12 Jahrhundert*, Bochum 1987

———— 'Imperium und regna: Beiträge zur Entwicklung der deutsch-englischen Beziehungen im Rahmen der auswärtigen Politik der römischen Kaiser und deutschen Könige im 12. und 13. Jhdt.', in P. Moraw, (ed.), *'Bündnissysteme' und 'Aussenpolitik' im späten Mittelalter* (Beiheft der Zeitschrift für Historische Forschung, v, 1987), 13–37

———— 'Staufische Herrschaftsideologie und Mendikantenspiritualität', *Wissenschaft und Weisheit* li (1988), 26–51, 185–209

———— *Deutschland und seine Nachbarn, 1200–1500*, Munich 1997

———— 'Papst Innocenz IV und die Bettelorden in ihren Beziehungen zu Kaiser Friedrich II', in F. J. Felten and N. Jaspert (eds), *Vita religiosa im Mittelalter: Festschrift für Kaspar Elm zum 70. Geburtstag*, Berlin 1999, 461–81

———— M. Kintzinger and P. Monnet (eds), *Auswärtige Politik und internationale Beziehungen im Mittelalter (13. bis 16. Jahrhundert)*, Bochum 2002

Berger, É., *Saint Louis et Innocent IV: étude sur les rapports de la France et du Saint-Siège*, Paris 1893

———— *Les Origines de la domination angevine en Italie*, Paris 1909

Beumann, H., 'Friedrich II und die heilige Elisabeth: zum Besuch des Kaisers in Marburg am 1. Mai 1236', in *Sankt Elisabeth: Fürstin-Dienerin-Heilige*, Sigmaringen 1981, 151–66, repr. in his *Ausgewählte Aufsätze, 1966–1986*, ed. J. Petersohn and R. Schmidt, Sigmaringen 1987, 411–26

Bienemann, F., *Conrad von Scharfenberg: Bischof von Speier und Metz und kaiserlicher Hofkanzler, 1200–1224*, Strasbourg 1886

Bisson, T. N., *The medieval crown of Aragon: a short history*, Oxford 1986

Blochet, E., 'Les Relations diplomatiques des Hohenstaufen avec les sultans d'Egypte', *Revue historique* lxxx (1902), 51–64

Boehm, L., '*De Karlingis Imperator Karolus, princeps et monarcha totius Europae*: zur Orientpolitik Karls I. von Anjou', *Historisches Jahrbuch der Görres-Gesellschaft* lxxxviii (1968), 1–35

Borchardt, K., 'Der sogenannte Aufstand Heinrichs (VII) in Franken 1234/35', in K. Borchardt and E. Bünz (eds), *Forschungen zur bayerischen und fränkischen Geschichte: Festschrift Peter Herde*, Würzburg 1998, 53–119

Boshof, E., 'Die Entstehung des Herzogtums Braunschweig-Lüneburg', in W.-D. Mohrmann (ed.), *Heinrich der Löwe*, Göttingen 1980, 249–74

Bosl, K., *Die Reichsministerialität der Salier und Staufer*, Stuttgart 1950–1

———— 'Europäischer Adel im 12./13: Jahrhundert: die internationalen Verflechtungen des bayerischen Hochadelsgeschlechtes der Andechs-Meranier', *Zeitschrift für Bayerische Landesgeschichte* xxx (1967), 20–52

Brentano, R., *Two churches: England and Italy in the thirteenth century*, Berkeley 1968, repr. with additional essay 1988

———— 'Western civilization: the Middle Ages', in H. D. Lasswell, D. Lerner and H. Speier (eds), *Propaganda and communication in world history*, Honolulu 1974, i. 552–95

Brezeanu, S., 'Notice sur les rapports de Frédéric II de Hohenstaufen avec Jean III Vatatzès', *Revue des études sud-est européennes* xii (1974), 583–5

Bromiley, G. N., 'Philip of Novara's account of the wars between Frederick II of Hohenstaufen and the Ibelins', *JMH* iii (1977), 325–38

Brown, M., 'Henry the Peaceable: Henry III, Alexander III and royal lordship in the British Isles, 1249–1272', in Weiler and Rowlands, *England and Europe*, 43–66

Brunner, H., 'Das Turnier von Nantes: Konrad von Würzburg, Richard von Cornwall und die deutschen Fürsten', in J. Kühnel and others (eds), *De poeticis medii aevi quaestiones: Käthe Hamburger zum 85. Geburtstag*, Göppingen 1981, 105–27

Brunner, K., 'Zum Prozess gegen Herzog Friedrich II von 1236', *MIÖG* lxxviii (1970), 260–73

Bühler, H., 'Die frühen Staufer im Ries', in I. Eberl, W. Hartung and J. Jahn (eds), *Früh- und hochmittelalterlicher Adel in Schwaben und Bayern*, Sigmaringendorf 1988

Buisson, L., *König Ludwig IX, der Heilige, und das Recht: Studie zur Gestaltung der Lebensordnung Frankreichs im hohen Mittelalter*, Freiburg im Breisgau 1954

Bulst-Thiele, M. L., 'Templer in königlichen und päpstlichen Diensten', in P. Classen and P. Seibert (eds), *Festschrift Percy Ernst Schramm zu seinem siebzigsten Geburtstag*, Wiesbaden 1964, 289–308

———— 'Zur Geschichte der Ritterorden und des Königreichs Jerusalem im 13.

Jahrhundert bis zur Schlacht bei La Forbie am 17. Okt. 1244', *DA* xxii (1966), 197–226

Bund, K., 'Studien zu Magister Heinrich von Avranches, I: Zur künftigen Edition seiner Werke', *DA* lvi (2000), 127–79

Burnett, C., 'An apocryphal letter from the Arabic philosopher al-Kindi to Theodore, Frederick II's astrologer, concerning Gog and Magog, the enclosed nations, and the scourge of the Mongols', *Viator* xv (1984), 151–67

Burton, J., 'The monastic world', in Weiler and Rowlands, *England and Europe*, 121–36

Buschmann, A., 'Landfriede und Verfassung: zur Bedeutung des Mainzer Reichslandfriedens von 1235 als Verfassungsgesetz', in *Aus Österreichs Rechtsleben in Geschichte und Gegenwart: Festschrift Ernst C. Hellbling*, Salzburg 1971, 449–72

—— 'Der Rheinische Bund von 1254–1257: Landfriede, Städte, Fürsten und Reichsverfassung im 13. Jahrhundert', in H. Maurer (ed.), *Kommunale Bündnisse Oberitaliens und Oberdeutschlands im Vergleich*, Sigmaringen 1987, 167–212

Busson, A., *Die Doppelwahl des Jahres 1257 und das römische Königthum Alfons X. von Castilien*, Münster 1866

Carpenter, D. A., 'The fall of Hubert de Burgh', *Journal of British Studies* xix (1980), 1–17, repr. in his *Reign of Henry III*, 45–60

—— 'The gold treasure of Henry III', *TCE* i (1983), 61–88, repr. in his *Reign of Henry III*, 107–36

—— 'What happened in 1258?', in J. Gillingham and J. C. Holt (eds), *War and government in the Middle Ages: essays in honour of J. O. Prestwich*, Woodbridge 1984, 106–19, repr. in his *Reign of Henry III*, 183–98

—— 'Kings, magnates and society: the personal rule of King Henry III, 1234–1258', *Speculum* lx (1985), 39–70, repr. in his *Reign of Henry III*, 75–106

—— 'Chancellor Ralph de Neville and plans for political reform', *TCE* ii (1987), 69–80, repr. in his *Reign of Henry III*, 61–74

—— *The minority of Henry III*, London 1990

—— 'England in the twelfth and thirteenth centuries', in Haverkamp and Vollrath, *England and Germany*, 105–26

—— *The reign of Henry III*, London 1996

Cazel, F. A., 'The fifteenth of 1225', *BIHR* xxiv (1961), 67–79

—— 'The legates Guala and Pandulf', *TCE* ii (1987), 15–21

—— 'Intertwined careers: Hubert de Burgh and Peter des Roches', *Haskins Society Journal* i (1989), 173–81

Chaplais, P., 'The making of the Treaty of Paris and the royal style', *EHR* lxvii (1952), 235–53

—— *English diplomatic practice in the Middle Ages*, London 2003.

Chapuisat, J.-P., 'A Propos des relations entre la Savoie et l'Angleterre au XIIIe siècle', *Bulletin philologique et historique Comité Traviens* i (1960), 429–34

Chevalier, J., *Quarante Années de l'histoire des évêques de Valence au moyen âge: Guillaume et Philippe de Savoie (1226 à 1267)*, Paris 1889

Chiffoleau, J., 'I ghibellini de regno di Arles', in Toubert and Paravacini Bagliani, *Federico II*, 364–88

Choffel, J., *Louis VIII le lion: roi de France méconnu, roi d'Angleterre ignoré*, Paris 1983

Chone, H., *Die Beziehungen Kaiser Friedrichs II. zu den Seestädten Venedig, Pisa, Genua*, Berlin 1902

Church, S. D. (ed.), *King John: new interpretations*, Woodbridge 1999

Clanchy, M. T., 'Did Henry III have a policy?', *History* liii (1968), 203–16

———— *England and its rulers, 1066–1272*, London 1983

Costen, M., *The Cathars and the Albigensian Crusade*, Manchester 1997

Cox, E. L., *The eagles of Savoy: the house of Savoy in thirteenth-century Europe*, Princeton 1974

Crouch, D., *William Marshal: court, career and chivalry in the Angevin empire, 1147–1219*, London 1990

Csendes, P., *Heinrich VI*, Darmstadt 1993

Cuttino, G. P., *English diplomatic administration, 1259–1339*, 2nd edn, Oxford 1971

———— *Medieval English diplomacy*, Bloomington 1985

Daumet, G., *Mémoire sur les relations de la France et de la Castile de 1255 à 1320*, Paris [1913/14]

Davies, R. R., *The age of conquest: Wales, 1063–14125* (originally published as *Conquest, coexistence and change: Wales 1063–1415*, Oxford 1987), Oxford 1991

Decker-Hauff, H., 'Das Staufische Haus', in *Die Zeit der Staufer: Geschichte-Kunst-Kultur* (exhibition catalogue), Stuttgart 1977–9

Demandt, K. E., 'Der Endkampf des staufischen Kaiserhauses im Rhein-Main-Gebiet', *Hessisches Jahrbuch für Landesgeschichte* vii (1957), 102–64

Denholm-Young, N., *Richard of Cornwall*, Oxford 1947

Dept, G. G., *Les Influences anglaises et françaises dans le comté de Flandre au début du XIIIme siècle*, Ghent–Paris 1928

Dickson, G., 'The flagellants of 1260 and the crusades', *JMH* xv (1989), 227–67

Döberl, M., 'Berthold von Hohenburg', *Deutsche Zeitschrift für Geschichts-wissenschaft* xii (1892), 201–78

Doran, J., 'Rites and wrongs: the Latin mission to Nicaea 1234', in R. N. Swanson (ed.), *Unity and diversity in the Church* (SCH xxxii, 1996), 131–44

Duby, G., *The legend of Bouvines: war, religion and culture in the Middle Ages*, trans. C. Tihanyi, Berkeley 1990

Dunbabin, J., *Charles I of Anjou: power, kingship and state-making in thir-teenth-century Europe*, London 1998

Duncan, A. A. M., 'John king of England and the kings of Scots', in Church, *King John*, 257–71

Eaglen, R. J., 'The evolution of coinage in thirteenth-century England', *TCE* iv (1991), 15–24

Eales, R., 'Castles and politics in England, 1215–1224', *TCE* ii (1987), 23–43

———— 'The political setting of the Becket translation of 1220', in D. Wood, *Martyrs and martyrologies* (SCH xxx, 1993), 127–39

Edbury, P. W., *The kingdom of Cyprus and the crusades, 1191–1374*, Cambridge 1991

———— *John of Ibelin and the kingdom of Jerusalem*, Woodbridge 1997

———— 'The de Montforts in the Holy Land', *TCE* viii (1999), 23–32

Egger, C., 'Henry III's England and the *curia*', in Weiler and Rowlands, *England and Europe*, 215–32

Ehlers, J., 'Die französische Monarchie im 13. Jahrhundert', in E. Boshof and F. R.

Erkens (eds), *Rudolf von Habsburg, 1273–1291: eine Königsherrschaft zwischen Tradition und Wandel*, Cologne–Weimar–Vienna 1993, 165–84

Engels, O., 'Der Vertrag von Corbeil (1258)', *Spanische Forschungen der Görresgesellschaft. Erste Reihe: Gesammelte Aufsätze zur Kulturgeschichte Spaniens* xix (1962), 114–46

———— *Die Staufer*, 6th edn, Stuttgart 1994

Ennen, E., 'Erzbischof und Stadtgemeinde in Köln bis zur Schlacht von Worringen', in F. Petri (ed.), *Bischofs- und Kathedralgeschichte des Mittelalters und der frühen Neuzeit*, Cologne–Vienna 1976, 27–46, repr. in her *Gesammelte Abhandlungen*, Bonn 1977, 388–404

Erkens, F.-R., *Kurfürsten und Königswahl: zu neuen Theorien über den Königswahlparagraphen im Sachsenspiegel und die Entstehung des Kurfürtenkollegiums*, Hanover 2002

Esch, A. and N. Kamp (eds), *Friedrich II: Tagung des deutschen Historischen Instituts in Rom im Gedenkjahr 1994*, Tübingen 1996

Favreau, R., 'Otto von Braunschweig und Aquitanien', in *Heinrich der Löwe und seine Zeit: Herrschaft und Repräsentation der Welfen, 1125–1235* (exhibition catalogue), Munich 1995, 369–76

Federico II e le nuove culture: atti del XXXI convegno storico internazionale, Todi, 9–12 ottobre 1994, Spoleto 1995

Fichtenau, H., 'Akkon, Zypern und das Lösegeld für Richard Löwenherz', *Archiv für Österreichische Geschichte* cxxv (1966), 11–32

Ficker, J., *Engelbert der Heilige: Erzbischof von Köln und Reichsverweser*, Cologne 1853, repr. Aalen 1985

———— 'Herr Bernhard von Horstmar', *Zeitschrift für vaterländische Geschichte und Alterthumskunde* iv (1853), 291–306; v (1855), 401–2

———— 'Die Reichshofbeamten der staufischen Periode', *Sitzungsberichte der Philosophisch-Historischen Klasse der (k.k.) Österreichischen Akademie der Wissenschaften zu Wien* xl (1862), 447–549

Fischer, B., 'Engelbert von Berg (1185–1225): Kirchenfürst und Staatsmann', *Zeitschrift des Bergischen Geschichtsvereins* xciv (1989–90), 1–47

Flachenecker, H., 'Herzog Ludwig der Kelheimer als Prokurator König Heinrichs VII', *Zeitschrift für Bayerische Landesgeschichte* lix (1996), 835–48

Fleckenstein, J. (ed.), *Probleme um Friedrich II*, Sigmaringen 1974

Folz, A., *Kaiser Friedrich II und Papst Innozenz IV: ihr Kampf in den Jahren 1244 und 1245*, Strasbourg 1905

Folz, R., *The concept of empire in western Europe from the fifth to the fifteenth century*, trans. S. A. Ogilvie, London 1969

Forey, A., 'The crusading vows of English King Henry III', *Durham University Journal* lxv (1973), 229–47

———— 'The military orders and holy war against Christians in the thirteenth century', *EHR* civ (1989), 1–24

Frame, R., 'Ireland and the Barons' War', *TCE* i (1985), 158–67

———— 'King Henry III and Ireland: the shaping of a peripheral lordship', *TCE* iii (1991), 179–202

Frech, K. A., 'Ein Plan zur Absetzung Heinrichs (VII): die gescheiterte Legation Kardinal Ottos in Deutschland 1229–1231', in Lorenz and Schmidt, *Von Schwaben bis Jerusalem*, 89–116

Freed, J. B., *The friars and German society in the thirteenth century*, Cambridge, Mass. 1977

Fryde, N., 'Deutsche Englandkaufleute in frühhansischer Zeit', *Hansische Geschichtsblätter* xcvii (1979), 1–14

—— 'Silver recoinage and royal policy in England 1180–1250', in E. van Cauwenberghe and F. Irsigler (eds), *Münzprägung-Geldumlauf und Wechselkurse; Minting, monetary circulation and exchange rates*, Trier 1984, 11–19

—— 'Hochfinanz und Landesgeschichte im Deutschen Hochmittelalter', *Blätter für deutsche Landesgeschichte* cxxv (1989) 1–12

—— *Ein mittelalterlicher deutscher Grossunternehmer: Terricus Teutonicus de Colonia in England, 1217–1257*, Stuttgart 1997

—— 'King John and the empire', in Church, *King John*, 335–46

—— 'How to get on in Henry III's England: the career of three German merchants', in Weiler and Rowlands, *England and Europe*, 207–14

Fuiano, M., *Napoli nel medioevo (seculi XI–XIII)*, Naples 1972

Gebauer, G. C., *Leben und denckwürdige Thaten Herrn Richards Erwählten Römischen Kaysers, Grafens von Cornwall und Poitou*, Leipzig 1744

Geh, H.-P., *Insulare Politik in England vor den Tudors*, Husum 1964

Geldner, F., 'Konradin und das alte deutsche Königtum: Opfer der hohenstaufischen Italienpolitik', *Zeitschrift für bayerische Landesgeschichte* xxxii (1969), 495–524

Gelsinger, B. F., 'A thirteenth-century Norwegian–Castilian alliance', *Medievalia et Humanistica* n.s. x (1981), 55–80

Georgi, W., '*intra* und *extra*: Überlegungen zu den Grundlagen auswärtiger Beziehungen im früheren Mittelalter: Wahrnehmung, Kommunikation und Handeln', in Berg, Kintzinger and Monnet, *Auswärtige Politik*, 47–86

Gerlich, A., 'Rheinische Kurfürsten und deutsches Königtum im Interregnum', *Geschichtliche Landeskunde*, III/2: *Festschrift Bärmann* (1967), 44–126

Ghazarian, J. G., *The Armenian kingdom in Cilicia during the crusades: the integration of Cilician Armenians with the Latins, 1080–1393*, Richmond, VA 2000

Giese, W., 'Der Reichstag vom 8. September 1256 und die Entstehung des Alleinstimmrechts der Kurfürsten', *DA* xl (1984), 562–90

Giles, K. R., 'Two English bishops in the Holy Land', *Nottingham Medieval Studies* xxxi (1987), 46–66

Gillingham, J., *Richard I*, New Haven 1999

Giunta, F., 'Federico II e Ferdinando III di Castiglia', in P. Grierson and J. Ward-Perkins (eds), *Studies in Italian medieval history* (*Papers of the British School at Rome*, xxiv/n.s. xii, 1956), 137–41

Goez, W., 'Friedrich II. und Deutschland', in K. Friedland, W. J. Müller and W. Goez (eds), *Politik, Wirtschaft und Kunst im staufischen Lübeck*, Lübeck 1976, 5–38

—— 'Möglichkeiten und Grenzen des Herrschers aus der Ferne in Deutschland und Reichsitalien, 1152–1220', in Kölzer, *Staufer*, 93–112

Görich, K., *Die Ehre Friedrich Barbarossas: Kommunikation, Konflikt und politisches Handeln im 12. Jahrhundert*, Darmstadt 2001

Gottschalk, H. L., 'Der Untergang der Hohenstaufen', *Wiener Zeitschrift für die Kunde des Morgenlandes* liii (1957), 267–82

—— *Al-Malik al-Kāmil von Egypten und seine Zeit: eine Studie zur Geschichte*

Vorderasiens und Egyptens in der ersten Hälfte des 7./13. Jahrhunderts, Wiesbaden 1958

Grauert, H., 'Meister Johann von Toledo', *Sitzungsberichte der königlich-bayerischen Akademie der Wissenschaften* (1901), 111–325

Gross, W., *Die Revolutionen in der Stadt Rom, 1219–1254,* Berlin 1934

Groten, M., 'Konrad von Hochstaden und die Wahl Richards von Cornwall', in Vollrath and Weinfurter, *Köln,* 483–510

———— *Köln im 13. Jahrhundert: Gesellschaftlicher Wandel und Verfassungsentwicklung,* Cologne–Weimar–Vienna 1995

Grundman, J. P., *The popolo at Perugia, 1139–1309,* Perugia 1992

Hack, A. T., *Das Empfangszeremoniell bei mittelalterlichen Papst- Kaiser-Treffen,* Cologne–Weimar–Vienna 1999

Hageneder, H., 'Die Beziehungen der Babenberger zur Kurie in der ersten Hälfte des 13. Jahrhunderts', *MIÖG* lxxv (1967), 1–29

Hägermann, D., 'Studien zum Urkundenwesen König Heinrich Raspes (1246/7)', *DA* xxxvi (1980), 487–548

Halfter, P., 'Die Staufer und Armenien', in Lorenz and Schmidt, *Von Schwaben,* 187–208

Hamilton, B., 'King consorts of Jerusalem and their entourages from the west from 1186 to 1250', in H. E. Mayer (ed.), *Die Kreuzfahrerstaaten als multikulturelle Gesellschaft,* Munich 1997, 13–24

Hampe, K., 'Über die Flugschriften zum Lyoner Konzil von 1245', *Historische Vierteljahresschrift* xi (1908), 297–313

Harding, A., *England in the thirteenth century,* Cambridge 1993

Hartmann, H., 'Die Urkunden Konrads IV.', *AfD* xviii (1944), 38–163

Hartmann, W. (ed.), *Europas Städte zwischen Zwang und Freiheit: die europäische Stadt um die Mitte des 13. Jahrhunderts,* Regensburg 1995

Hasse, C.-P., *Die welfischen Hofämter und die welfische Ministerialität in Sachsen: Studien zur Sozialgeschichte des 12. und 13. Jahrhunderts,* Husum 1995

Hausmann, F., 'Kaiser Friedrich II und Österreich', in Fleckenstein, *Probleme um Friedrich II,* 225–308

Hauss, A., *Kardinal Oktavian Ubaldini: ein Staatsmann des 13. Jahrhunderts,* Heidelberg 1913

Haverkamp, A. and H. Vollrath (eds), *England and Germany in the high Middle Ages,* Oxford 1996

Heinemeyer, W., 'Studien zur Diplomatik mittelalterlicher Verträge vornehmlich des 13. Jahrhunderts', *AfD* xiv (1935–6), 321–413

Helle, K., 'Trade and shipping between Norway and England in the reign of Håkon Håkonsson (1216–63), *Skofartshictorik Arbok* (1967), 7–34

———— 'Norwegian foreign policy and the Maid of Norway', *Scottish Historical Review* lxix (1990), 142–56

Helmholz, R. H., *The spirit of classical canon law,* Athens, GA–London 1996

Herbers, K., H. H. Kortüm and C. Servatius (eds), *Ex ipsis rerum documentis: Beiträge zur Mediävistik: Festschrift H. Zimmermann,* Sigmaringen 1991

Herde, P., *Karl I von Anjou,* Stuttgart 1978

Heupel, W. E., *Der sizilische Grosshof unter Kaiser Friedrich II: eine verwaltungsgeschichtliche Studie,* Stuttgart 1940

Hiestand, R., 'Precipua tocius christianissimi columpna: Barbarossa und der

Kreuzzug', in A. Haverkamp (ed.), *Friedrich Barbarossa: Handlungsspielräume und Wirkungswesen des staufischen Kaisers*, Sigmaringen 1992, 51–108

——— 'Von Bouvines nach Segni', *Francia* xxii/1 (1995), 59–78

——— 'Friedrich II. und der Kreuzzzug', in Esch and Kamp, *Friedrich II*, 128–49

——— 'Ierusalem et Sicilie rex: zur Titulatur Friedrichs II', *DA* lii (1996), 181–9

——— 'Kingship and crusade in twelfth-century Germany', in Haverkamp and Vollrath, *England and Germany*, 236–65

Hillen, C., *Curia regis: Untersuchungen zur Hofstruktur Heinrichs (VII.) 1220–1235 nach den Zeugen seiner Urkunden*, Frankfurt am Main 1999

Hillenbrand, C., *The crusades: Islamic perspectives*, Edinburgh 1999

Hillgarth, J. N., *The problem of the Catalan mediterranean empire, 1229–1327*, London 1975

——— *The Spanish kingdoms, 1250–1516, I: 1250–1410: precarious balance*, Oxford 1976

Hilpert, H.-E., 'Richard of Cornwall's candidature for the German throne and the Christmas 1256 parliament at Westminster', *JMH* vi (1980), 185–98

——— *Kaiser- und Papstbriefe in den Chronica majora des Matthaeus Paris*, Stuttgart 1981

Hilsch, P., 'Der Deutsche Ritterorden im südlichen Libanon: zur Topographie der Kreuzfahrerstaaten in Sidon und Beirut', *Zeitschrift des deutschen Palästina-Vereins* xcvi (1980), 174–89

Hintze, O., *Das Königtum Wilhelms von Holland*, Leipzig 1885

Holbach, R., 'Die Regierungszeit des Trierer Erzbischofs Arnold II. von Isenburg: ein Beitrag zur Geschichte von Reich, Territorium und Kirche um die Mitte des 13. Jahrhunderts', *Rheinische Vierteljahresblätter* cxlvii (1983), 1–66

Holt, J. C., *Magna carta*, 2nd edn, Cambridge 1992

Holt, P. M., 'The treaties of the early Mamluk sultans with the Frankish states', *Bulletin of the School of Oriental and African Studies* xliii (1980), 67–76

——— *The age of the crusades: the Near East from the eleventh century to 1517*, Harlow 1986

Holzapfel, T., *Papst Innozenz III, Philipp II August, König von Frankreich und die englisch-welfische Verbindung, 1198–1216*, Frankfurt am Main 1991

Höroldt, U., *Studien zur politischen Stellung des Kölner Domkapitels zwischen Erzbischof, Stadt Köln und Territorialgewalten, 1198–1332: Untersuchungen und Personallisten*, Siegburg 1994

Houben, H., *Roger II von Sizilien: Herrscher zwischen Orient und Okzident*, Darmstadt 1997

Housley, N., *The Italian crusades: the papal–Angevin alliance and the crusades against Christian lay powers, 1254–1343*, Oxford 1982, repr. 1986

Howell, M., *Eleanor of Provence: queenship in thirteenth-century England*, Oxford 1998

Hubatsch, W., 'Der deutsche Orden und die Reichslehnschaft über Zypern', *Nachrichten der Akademie der Wissenschaften zu Göttingen (Philosophisch-Historische Klasse)* (1955), 245–306

Hucker, B.-U., *Kaiser Otto IV*, Hanover 1990

Huffman, J. P., 'Anglicus in Colonia: die rechtliche, soziale und ökonomische Stellung der Engländer in Köln während des 12. und 13. Jahrhunderts', *Jahrbuch des Kölnischen Geschichtsvereins* lxi/ii (1990–1), 1–62

——— 'Prosopography and the Anglo-imperial connection: a Cologne *ministerialis* family and and its English relations', *Medieval Prosopography* xi (1990), 53–134

———— *Family, commerce and religion in London and Cologne: Anglo-German emigrants, c. 1000 – c. 1300*, Cambridge 1998

———— *The social politics of medieval diplomacy: Anglo-German relations, 1066–1307*, Ann Arbor 2000

Humphreys, R. S., *From Saladin to the Mongols: the Ayyubids of Damascus, 1193–1260*, Albany, NY 1977

Huyskens, A., 'Der Plan des Königs Richard von Cornwallis zur Niederlegung eines deutschen Krönungsschatzes in Aachen', *Annalen des Historischen Vereins für den Niederrhein* cxv (1929), 180–204

———— 'Noch einmal der Krönungsschatz Königs Richard von Cornwallis', *Annalen des Historischen Vereins für den Niederrhein* cxviii (1931), 136–43

Jackson, P., 'The crisis in the Holy Land in 1260', *EHR* xcv (1980), 481–513

———— 'The end of Hohenstaufen rule in Syria', *BIHR* lix (1986), 20–36

———— 'The crusades of 1239–41 and their aftermath', *Bulletin of the School of Oriental and African Studies* l (1987), 32–60

———— 'The crusade against the Mongols (1241)', *Journal of Ecclesiastical History* xlii (1991), 1–18

Jacob, E., *Untersuchungen über Herkunft und Aufstieg des Reichsministerialengeschlechts Bolanden*, Giessen 1936

Jacoby, D., 'The kingdom of Jerusalem and the collapse of Hohenstaufen power in the Levant', *Dumbarton Oaks Papers* xl (1986), 83–101

———— 'La dimensione imperiale oltremare: Federico II, Cipro e il regno di Gerusalemme', in M. S. C. Mariani and R. Cassano (eds), *Federico II: immagine e potere*, Bari 1995, 31–5

Jones, M. and M. Vale (eds), *England and her neighbours, 1066–1453: essays in honour of Pierre Chaplais*, London 1989

Jordan, E., *Les Origines de la domination angevine en Italie*, Paris 1909

Jordan, W. C., *Louis IX and the challenge of the crusade: a study in rulership*, Princeton 1979

Joris, A., 'La Visite à Huy de Richard de Cornouailles, roi des Romains, 29 décembre 1258', in his *Villes: affaires-mentalités: autour du pays mosun*, Brussels 1993, 457–66

Käser, G., 'Papst Innozenz IV und der deutsche Gegenkönig Heinrich Raspe', in W. Müller, W. J. Smolka and H. Zedelmaier (eds), *Universität und Bildung: Festschrift Lätitia Boehm*, Munich 1991, 25–31

Kammerer, H., 'Strassburg: das Selbstverständnis einer Stadt im 13. Jahrhundert: Stadtwerdung – Stadtbild – Geschichtsbewusstsein', in Hartmann, *Europas Städte*, 63–82

Kamp, H., *Friedensstifter und Vermittler im Mittelalter*, Darmstadt 2001

Kamp, N., *Kirche und Monarchie im staufischen Königreich Sizilien*, Munich 1973–82

———— 'Friedrich II im europäischen Zeithorizont', in Esch and Kamp, *Friedrich II*, 2–22

Kantorowicz, E. H., *Kaiser Friedrich II*, Berlin 1924, repr. Stuttgart 1991, trans. by E. O. Lorimer as *Frederick II*, London 1931

———— 'Peter de Vignea in England', *MIÖG* li (1937), 43–81

Karst, A., *Geschichte Manfreds vom Tode Friedrichs II. bis zu seiner Krönung, 1250–1258*, Berlin 1897

Kaufhold, M., 'Norwegen, das Papsttum und Europa im 13. Jahrhundert: Mechanismen der Integration', *HZ* cclxv (1997), 309–42

—— *Deutsches Interregnum und europäische Politik: Konfliktlösungen und Entscheidungsstrukturen, 1230–1280*, Hanover 2000

Keilmann, B., *Der Kampf um die Stadtherrschaft in Worms während des 13. Jahrhunderts*, Darmstadt–Marburg 1985

—— 'Papst Innozenz IV und die Kirche von Worms: Anmerkungen zur päpstlichen Personalpolitik am Beginn des Interregnums', *Archiv für mittelrheinische Kirchengeschichte* xl (1988), 43–66

Keller, H., 'Mailand zur Zeit des Kampfes gegen Kaiser Friedrich II.', in Hartmann, *Europas Städte*, 273–96

Kempf, F., 'Die Absetzung Friedrichs II im Lichte der Kanonistik', in Fleckenstein, *Probleme um Friedrich II*, 345–60

Kempf, J., *Geschichte des deutschen Reiches während des grossen Interregnums, 1145–1273*, Würzburg 1893

Kettering, M., 'Die Territorialpolitik des Kölner Erzbischofs Konrad von Hochstaden (1238–1261)', *Jahrbuch des Kölnischen Geschichtsvereins* xxvi (1951), 1–84

Kienast, W., *Die deutschen Fürsten im Dienste der Westmächte bis zum Tode Phillips des Schönen*, Utrecht 1924–31

—— *Deutschland und Frankreich in der Kaiserzeit (900–1270): Weltkaiser und Einzelkönige*, Stuttgart 1975

Kiesewetter, A., 'Die Heirat zwischen Konstanze-Anna von Hohenstaufen und Kaiser Johannes III. Batatzes von Nikaia (Ende 1240 oder Anfang 1241) und der Angriff des Johannes Batatzes auf Konstantinopel im Mai oder Juni 1241', *Römische Historische Mitteilungen* xli (1999), 239–50

Kintzinger, M., *Westbindungen im spätmittelalterlichen Europa: Auswärtige Politik zwischen dem Reich, Frankreich, Burgund und England in der Regierungszeit Kaiser Sigmunds*, Stuttgart 2000

Kirfel, H. J., *Weltherrschaft und Bündnispolitik: Untersuchungen zur auswärtigen Politik der Staufer*, Bonn 1959

Klebel, E., 'Zur Abstammung der Hohenstaufen', *Zeitschrift für die Geschichte des Oberrheins* cii (1954), 137–85

Klingelhöfer, E., *Die Reichsgesetze von 1220 1231/32 und 1235: ihr Werden und ihre Wirkung im deutschen Staat Friedrichs II*, Weimar 1955

Kluger, H., *Hochmeister Hermann von Salza und Kaiser Friedrich II: ein Beitrag zur Frühgeschichte des Deutschen Ordens*, Marburg 1987

Knöpp, F., *Die Stellung Friedrichs II und seiner beiden Söhne zu den deutschen Städten*, Berlin 1928

Koch, H., *Richard von Cornwall: erster Teil, 1209–1257*, Strasbourg 1887

Köeppen, H., 'Die englische Rente für den deutschen Orden', in *Festschrift Herman Heimpel*, Göttingen 1977, 402–21

Koller, H., 'Zur Diskussion über die Reichsgesetze Friedrichs II', *MIÖG* lxvi (1958), 29–51

Kölzer, T., 'Ein Königreich im Übergang? Sizilien während der Minderjährigkeit Friedrichs II', in K. R. Schnith and R. Pauler (eds), *Festschrift Eduard Hlawitschka*, Kallmünz 1993, 341–57

——— 'Magna imperialis curia: die Zentralverwaltung im Königreich Sizilien unter Friedrich II', *Historisches Jahrbuch* cxiv (1994), 287–311

——— *Die Staufer im Süden: Sizilien und das Reich*, Sigmaringen 1996

Kosztolnyik, Z. J., *Hungary in the thirteenth century*, New York 1996

Kowalski, W., *Die deutschen Königinnen und Kaiserinnen von Konrad III bis zum Ende des Interregnums*, Weimar 1913

Kracht, H. J., *Geschichte der Benediktinerabtei St Pantaleon in Köln, 965–1250*, Siegburg 1975

Kraus, J., 'Die Stadt Nürnberg in ihren Beziehungen zur Römischen Kurie während des Mittelalters', *Mitteilungen des Vereins für die Geschichte der Stadt Nürnberg* xli (1950), 1–153

Krieger, K. F., 'Obligatory military service and the use of mercenaries in imperial military campaigns under the Hohenstaufen emperors', in Haverkamp and Vollrath, *England and Germany*, 151–70

Lachaud, F., 'Liveries of robes in England, c. 1200–c. 1330', *EHR* cxi (1996), 279–98

La Roche, E. P., *Das Interregnum und die Schweizerische Eidgenossenschaft*, Bern–Frankfurt am Main 1971

Lawrence, C. H., *St Edmund of Abingdon: a study of hagiography and history*, Oxford 1960

Leach, H. G., *Angevin Britain and Scandinavia*, Cambridge, MA. 1921

Le Goff, J., *Saint Louis*, Paris 1996

Leicht, P. S., 'L'Empereur Frédéric II de Souabe et les parlements', *Tijfschrift voor Rechts Geschiedenis* iii (1922), 408–18

Lemcke, G., *Beiträge zur Geschichte König Richards von Cornwall*, Berlin 1909

Lewis, F. R., 'Beatrice of Falkenburg, the third wife of Richard of Cornwall', *EHR* lii (1937), 279–82

——— 'The election of Richard of Cornwall as senator of Rome in 1261', *EHR* lii (1937), 657–62

——— 'Ottokar II of Bohemia and the Double Election of 1257', *Speculum* xii (1937), 512–15

Lewis, S., 'Henry III and the Gothic rebuilding of Westminster Abbey: the problematics of context', *Traditio* l (1995), 129–72

Leyser, K. J., 'Some reflections on twelfth-century kings and kingship', *EHR* xc (1975), 481–506

Lloyd, S., 'Gilbert de Clare, Richard of Cornwall and the Lord Edward's crusade', *Nottingham Medieval Studies* xxix (1985), 46–64

——— ' "Political crusades" in England, c. 1215–7 and c. 1263–5,' in P. W. Edbury, (ed.), *Crusade and settlement*, Cardiff 1985, 113–20

——— *English society and the crusade, 1216–1307*, Oxford 1988

——— 'King Henry III, the crusade and the Mediterrenean', in Jones and Vale, *England*, 97–119.

Lloyd, T. H., *The English wool trade in the Middle Ages*, Cambridge 1977

——— *England and the German Hanse, 1157–1611*, Cambridge 1991

Lomax, J. P., 'Frederick II, his Saracens and the papacy', in J. V. Tolan (ed.), *Medieval Christian perceptions of Islam*, London–New York 2000, 175–98

Longnon, J., *L'Empire latin de Constantinople et la principauté de Morée*, Paris 1949

Lorenz, S., *Kaiserswerth im Mittelalter: Genese, Struktur und Organisation königlicher Herrschaft am Niederrhein*, Düsseldorf 1993

────── and U. Schmidt (eds), *Von Schwaben bis Jerusalem: Facetten staufischer Geschichte*, Sigmaringen 1995

Lothmann, J., *Erzbischof Engelbert I. von Köln, 1216–1225: Graf von Berg, Erzbischof und Herzog, Reichsverweser*, Cologne 1993

Loud, G. A., 'The case of the missing martyrs: Frederick II's war with the Church, 1239–1250', in D. Wood (ed.), *Martyrs and martyrologies* (SCH xxx, 1993), 141–152

────── 'Il regno normanno-svevo visto dal regno d'Inghilterra', in G. Musca (ed.), *Il mezzogiorno normanno-svevo visto dall'Europa e dal mondo mediterraneo: atti delle tredicesime giornate normanno-sveve, Bari, 21–24 ottobre 1997*, Bari 1999, 175–95, published in English as 'The kingdom of Sicily and the kingdom of England, 1066–1266', *History* lxxxviii (2003), 540–67.

Lucas, H. S., 'John of Avesnes and Richard of Cornwall', *Speculum* xxiii (1948), 81–101

Lunt, W. E., 'The sources for the First Council of Lyon', *EHR* xxxiii (1918), 72–8

────── *Financial relations of the papacy with England to 1328*, Cambridge, MA. 1939

Lupprian, K.-E., 'Papst Innocenz IV. und die Ayyubiden: diplomatische Beziehungen von 1244 bis 1247', in W. Fischer and J. Schneider (eds), *Das Heilige Land im Mittelalter: Begegnungen zwischen Orient und Okzident*, Neustadt an der Aisch 1982, 77–82

Lustig, R. I., 'Some views on Norwegian foreign service', *Medieval Scandinavia* xi (1978–9), 212–41

Maddicott, J. R., *Simon de Montfort*, Cambridge 1994

────── 'A multitude of nobles: knights in the early parliaments of Henry III's reign', *TCE* vii (1997) 1–18

Maier, C. T., *Preaching the crusades: mendicant friars and the cross in the thirteenth century*, Cambridge 1994

────── 'Crusade and rhetoric against the Muslim colony of Lucera: Eudes de Chateauroux's *Sermones de rebellione sarracenorum Lucherie in Apulie*', *JMH* xxi (1995), 343–85

Maleczek, W., 'Das Frieden stiftende Papsttum im 12. und 13. Jahrhundert', in J. Fried (ed.), *Träger und Instrumentarien des Friedens im hohen und späten Mittelalter*, Sigmaringen 1996, 249–332

Manselli, R., 'Onorio III e Frederico II, revisione d'un giudizio?', *Studi Romani* xi (1963), 142–59

Marc-Bonnet, H., 'Le Saint-Siège et Charles d'Anjou sous Innocent IV et Alexandre IV', *Revue historique* cc (1948), 38–65

────── 'Richard de Cornouailles et la couronne de Sicile', in *Mélanges d'histoire du moyen âge à Louis Halphen*, Paris 1951, 483–9

Marinesco, C., 'Du Nouveau sur Constance de Hohenstaufen, impératrice de Nicée', *Byzantion* i (1924), 451–9

Marsh, F. B., *English rule in Gascony, 1199–1259, with special reference to the towns*, Ann Arbor 1912

Martín, A. P., 'Federico II (1194–1250) y Alfonso X el Sabio (1221–1284)', in *Federico II e le nuove culture*, 113–51

Martin, J.-M., 'L'Administration du royaume entre Normands et Souabes', in Kölzer, *Staufer im Süden*, 113–40

Matthew, D., *The Norman kingdom of Sicily*, Cambridge 1992

—— *The English and the community of Europe* in *the thirteenth century: the Stenton lecture 1996*, Reading 1997

Mattoso, J., 'La Crise de 1245', in his *Portugal medieval: novas interpretaçoẽs*, 2nd edn, Lisbon 1992, 57–76

Maurer, H., 'Die Anfänge der Stadt Tiengen und das politische Kräftespiel am Hochrhein um die Mitte des 13. Jahrhunderts', *Alemannisches Jahrbuch* (1964/5), 119–58

Mayer, H.-E., 'Kaiserrecht und Heiliges Land', in H. Fuhrmann, H. E. Mayer and K. Wriedt (eds), *Aus Reichsgeschichte und nordischer Geschichte*, Stuttgart 1972, 193–208

—— *Geschichte der Kreuzzüge*, 7th edn, Stuttgart 1989

—— *Die Kanzlei der lateinischen Könige von Jerusalem*, Hanover 1996

Melani, S., 'Lotta politica nell'Oltremare franco all'epoca di Federico II', in *Federico II e le nuove culture*, 89–111

Menzel, K. L., *Geschichte des Rheinischen Städtebundes im 13. Jahrhundert*, Hanover 1871

Meuthen, E., 'Die Aachener Pröpste bis zum Ende der Stauferzeit', *Zeitschrift des Aachener Geschichtsvereins* lxxviii (1966–7), 5–95

Michels, A., *Leben Ottos des Kindes, ersten Herzogs von Braunschweig und Lüneburg*, Einbeck 1891

Miranda, A. di, *Richard von Cornwallis und sein Verhältnis zur Krönungsstadt Aachen*, Bonn 1880

Mitteis, H., *Die deutsche Königswahl: ihre Rechtsgrundlagen bis zur Goldenen Bulle*, Brünn–Munich–Vienna 1944, 2nd rev. edn, Darmstadt 1987

Möhring, H., 'Zu einem Brief des Sultans as-Sâlih Aiyûb an den Papst: Beweisstück Innocenz IV. gegen Friedrich II.', *DA* xli (1985), 549–67

Moody, T. W., F. X. Martin and F. J. Byrne (eds), *A new history of Ireland*, IX: *Maps, genealogies, lists*, Oxford 1984

Morgan, D., *The Mongols*, Oxford 1986

—— 'The Mongols and the eastern Mediterranean', in B. Arbel, B. Hamilton and D. Jacoby (eds), *Latins and Greeks in the eastern Mediterranean after 1204*, London 1989, 198–211

Naumann, C., *Der Kreuzzug Kaiser Heinrichs VI*, Frankfurt am Main–Berlin 1994

Neininger, F., *Konrad von Urach († 1227): Zähringer, Zisterzienser, Kardinallegat*, Paderborn 1994

Neumann, F., 'Der Markgraf von Hohenburg', *Zeitschrift für deutsches Altertum und deutsche Literatur* lxxxvi (1955/6), 119–60

Nicholas, D., *Medieval Flanders*, London 1992

Nicholson, H., 'The military orders and the kings of England in the twelfth and thirteenth centuries', in A. V. Murray (ed.), *From Clermont to Jerusalem: the crusades and crusader societies (1095–1500): selected proceedings of the international medieval congress, University of Leeds (10–13 July 1995)*, Turnhout 1998, 203–17

Nitschke, A., 'Konradin und Clemens IV', *Quellen und Forschungen aus italienischen Archiven und Bibliotheken* xxxviii (1958), 268–77

O'Callaghan, J. F., *The learned king: the reign of Alfonso X of Castile*, Philadelphia 1993

Ohlig, M., *Studien zum Beamtentum Friedrichs II.: in Reichsitalien von 1237–1250 unter besonderer Berücksichtigung der süditalienischen Beamten*, Kleinheubach am Main 1936

Oldoni, M., 'Pier della Vigna e Federico', in *Federico II e le nuove culture*, 347–62

Ollendiek, H., *Die päpstlichen Legaten im deutschen Reichsgebiet von 1261 bis zum Ende des Interregnums*, Freiburg 1976

Opll, F., 'Wien um die Mitte des 13. Jahrhunderts', in Hartmann, *Europas Städte*, 233–55

Otto, H., 'Alexander IV und der deutsche Thronstreit', *MIÖG* xix (1898), 75–91

———— 'Zu den Formelbüchern aus der Kanzlei Rudolfs von Habsburg', *NA* xxvi (1901), 217–28

Page, M., 'Cornwall, Earl Richard and the Barons' War', *EHR* cxv (2000), 21–38

Painter, S., 'The crusade of Theobald of Champagne and Richard of Cornwall 1239–41', in K. M. Setton (ed.), *A history of the crusades*, iv, Madison–Milwaukee–London 1969, 463–86

Paravacini Bagliani, A., 'La storiografica pontificia del secolo XIII: prospettive di ricerca', *Römische Historische Mitteilungen* xxviii (1976), 45–54

Partner, P., *The lands of St Peter: the papal state in the Middle Ages and the early Renaissance*, Berkeley 1972

Patschowsky, A., 'Zur Ketzerverfolgung Konrads von Marburg', *DA* xxxvii (1981), 641–93

Peters, E., *The shadow king: rex inutilis in medieval law and literature, 751–1327*, New Haven 1970

Petersohn, J., 'Kaisertum und Kultakt in der Stauferzeit', in J. Petersohn (ed.), *Politik und Heiligenverehrung im Hochmittelalter*, Sigmaringen 1994, 101–46

———— 'Über monarchische Insignien und ihre Funktion im mittelalterlichen Reich', *HZ* cclxvi (1998), 47–96

Pfeiffer, F., *Rheinische Transitzölle im Mittelalter*, Berlin 1997

Pfeiffer, G., 'Der Aufstieg der Reichsstadt Nürnberg im 13. Jahrhundert', *Mitteilungen des Vereins für die Geschichte der Stadt Nürnberg* xliv (1953), 14–24

Pispisa, E., 'Federico II e Manfredi', in *Federico II e le nuove culture*, 303–17

Powell, J. M., 'Frederick II and the Church in the kingdom of Sicily, 1220–1224', *Church History* xxx (1961), 28–34

———— 'Frederick II and the Church: a revisionist view', *Catholic Historical Review* xlviii (1962), 487–97

———— *Anatomy of a crusade, 1213–1221*, Philadelphia 1987

———— 'Frederick II, the Hohenstaufens, and the Teutonic Order in the kingdom of Sicily', in M. Barber (ed.), *The military orders: fighting for the faith and caring for the sick*, Aldershot 1994, 236–44

———— 'Frederick II and the Muslims: the making of an historiographical tradition', in L. J. Simon (ed.), *Iberia and the Mediterranean world of the Middle Ages: studies in honour of Robert I. Burns, S.J.*, Leiden 1995, 261–9

Powicke, F. M., *King Henry III and the Lord Edward: the community of the realm in the thirteenth century*, Oxford 1947

———— *The thirteenth century, 1216–1307*, 2nd edn, Oxford 1962

Prawer, J., *The Latin kingdom of Jerusalem: European colonialism in the Middle Ages*, London 1972

Prestwich, M., *Edward I*, London 1988

———— 'Money and mercenaries in English medieval armies', in Haverkamp and Vollrath, *England and Germany*, 129–50

Pryce, H., 'Negotiating Anglo-Welsh relations: Llywelyn the Great and Henry III', in Weiler and Rowlands, *England and Europe*, 13–30

Purcell, M., *Papal crusading policy: the chief instruments of papal crusading policy and crusade to the Holy Land from the final loss of Jerusalem to the fall of Acre, 1244–1291*, Leiden 1979

Queller, D. F., *The office of ambassador in the Middle Ages*, Princeton 1967

Rauch, G., *Die Bündnisse deutscher Herrscher mit Reichsangehörigen vom Regierungs- antritt Friedrich Barbarossas bis zum Tod Rudolfs von Habsburg*, Aalen 1966,

Redlich, O., 'Die Anfänge König Rudolfs I', MIÖG x (1889), 341–418

Reilly, B. F., *The medieval Spains*, Cambridge 1993

Reisinger, R., *Die römisch-deutschen Könige und ihre Wähler*, Aalen 1977

Reitemeier, A., *Aussenpolitik im Spätmittelalter: die diplomatischen Beziehungen zwischen dem Reich und England, 1377–1422*, Paderborn 1999

Reuter, T., 'The origins of the German *Sonderweg*? The empire and its rulers in the high Middle Ages', in A. Duggan (ed.), *Kings and kingship in medieval Europe*, London 1993, 179–211

———— 'Die Unsicherheit auf den Strassen im europäischen Früh- und Hochmittelalter: Täter, Opfer und ihre mittelalterlichen und modernen Betrachter', in J. Fried (ed.), *Träger und Instrumentarien des Friedens im hohen und späten Mittelalter*, Sigmaringen 1996, 169–202

Rey, M., *Les Diocèses de Besançon et de Saint-Claude*, Paris 1977

Richard, J., 'The Mongols and the Franks', *Journal of Asian History* iii (1969), 45–57

———— 'Pairie d'Orient latin: les quattres baronnies des royaumes de Jérusalem et de Chypre', *Revue historique de droit français et étranger* (1950), 67–88, repr. in his *Orient et occident au moyen âge: contacts et relations, XIIe–XVe s.*, London 1976

———— *La Papauté et les missions d'orient au moyen âge, XIIIe–XVe siècles*, Rome 1977

———— *The Latin Kingdom of Jerusalem*, trans. Janet Shirley, Amsterdam–New York–Oxford 1979

———— *Saint Louis: roi d'une France féodale, soutien de la Terre Sainte*, Paris 1983

Richard, J.-F.-N., *Histoire des diocèses de Besançon et de Saint-Claude*, Besançon 1847–51

Ridgeway, H., 'King Henry III and the "aliens", 1236–1272', TCE ii (1987), 81–92

———— 'Foreign favourites and Henry III's problems of patronage, 1247–58', EHR civ (1989), 590–610

———— 'William de Valence and his *familiares*, 1247–72', *Historical Research* lxv (1992), 239–57

Riley-Smith, J., *The feudal nobility and the kingdom of Jerusalem, 1174–1277*, London 1973

———— 'The Templars and the Teutonic knights in Cilician Armenia', in T. S. R. Boase (ed.), *The Cilician kingdom of Armenia*, Edinburgh 1978, 92–117

Roberg, B., 'Der Konzilsversuch von 1241', *Annuarium Historiae Conciliorum* xxiv (1992), 286–319

Rodenberg, C., *Innocenz IV und das Königreich Sicilien, 1245–1254*, Halle 1892

———— 'Die Friedensverhandlungen zwischen Friedrich II und Innocenz IV, 1243–1244', in *Festgabe für Gerold Meyer von Knonau*, Zurich 1913, 165–204

Rodríguez García, J. M., 'Henry III (1216–1272), Alfonso X of Castile (1252–1284) and the crusading plans of the thirteenth century', in Weiler and Rowlands, *England and Europe*, 99–120

Röhricht, R., *Die Deutschen im Heiligen Lande: Chronologisches Verzeichnis derjenigen Deutschen, welche als Jerusalempilger und Kreuzfahrer sicher nachzuweisen oder wahrscheinlich anzusehen sind, c. 650–1291*, Innsbruck 1894, repr. Aalen 1968

———— *Geschichte des Königreichs Jerusalem (1100–1291)*, Innsbruck 1898

Ronzani, M., 'Pisa e la Toscana', in Toubert and Paravacini Bagliani, *Federico II*, 65–84

Roscher, H., *Papst Innocenz III. und die Kreuzzüge*, Göttingen 1969

Rotthoff, C., 'Die politische Rolle der Landfrieden zwischen Maas und Rhein von der Mitte des 13. Jahrhunderts bis zum Auslaufen des Bacharacher Landfriedens Ludwigs des Bayern', *Rheinische Vierteljahresschrift* xlv (1981), 75–111

Rousseau, C. M., 'A papal matchmaker: principle and pragmatism during Innocent III's pontificate', *JMH* xxiv (1998), 259–71

Rowlands, I. W., 'King John and Wales', in Church, *King John*, 273–87

Rudolf, K., 'Die Tartaren 1241/1242: Nachrichten und Wiedergabe. Korrespondenz und Historiographie', *Römische Historische Mitteilungen* xix (1977), 79–107

Runciman, S., *The Sicilian Vespers: a history of the Mediterranean world in the later thirteenth century*, Cambridge 1958

Sanders, I. J., 'The texts of the Treaty of Paris, 1259', *EHR* lxvi (1951), 81–97

Sayers, J. E., *Papal government and England during the pontificate of Honorius III (1216–1227)*, Cambridge 1984

Schaller, H. M., 'König Manfred und die Assassinen', *DA* xxi (1965), 173–93

———— introduction to *Peter de Vinea Friderici II imperatoris epistolae: novam editionem curavit Johannes Rudolphus Iselius*, Basle 1740, repr. Hildesheim 1991

———— 'Die Frömmigkeit Kaiser Friedrichs II', in *Das Staunen der Welt: Kaiser Friedrich II. von Hohenstaufen 1194–1250: Schriften zur staufischen Geschichte und Kunst*, xv, Göppingen 1996, 128–51

Schein, S., *Fideles cruces: the papacy, the west, and the recovery of the Holy Land, 1274–1314*, Oxford 1991

Schlunk, A. C., *Königsmacht und Krongut: die Machtgrundlage des deutschen Königtums im 13. Jahrhundert und eine neue historische Methode*, Stuttgart 1988

Schmidt, H.-J., 'Vollgewalt, Souverän und Staat. Konzepte der Herrschaft von Kaiser Friedrich II', in P.-J. Heinig, S. Jahns, H.-J. Schmidt, R. C. Schwinges and S. Wefers (eds), *Reich, Regionen und Europa in Mittelalter und Neuzeit: Festschrift für Peter Moraw*, Berlin 2000, 3–19

Schneidmüller, B., *Die Welfen: Herrschaft und Erinnerung*, Stuttgart 2000

Schnith, K., *England in einer sich wandelnden Welt (1189–1259): Studien zu Roger Wendover und Matthäus Paris*, Stuttgart 1974

Schramm, P. E., 'Kastilien zwischen England-Frankreich-Deutschland-Italien: König Alfonso X. el Sabio (1252–84), deutscher Gegenkönig: ein Beitrag zur spanischen "Kaiseridee"', in P. E. Schramm, *Kaiser, Könige und Päpste:*

Gesammelte Aufsätze zur Geschichte des Mittelalters, Stuttgart 1968–71, iv/1, 378–419

Schulz, K., '*Denn sie liebten die Freiheit so sehr . . .*': *Kommunale Aufstande und Enstehung des europäischen Bürgertums im Hochmittelalter*, Darmstadt 1992

Schwab, I., 'Kanzlei und Urkundenwesen König Alfons' X. von Kastilien für das Reich', *AfD* xxxii (1986), 569–616

Schwarz, J., 'Der römische Reichsbegriff in der Auseinandersetzung des Papsttums mit Kaiser Friedrich II', in Thumser, Wenz-Haubfleisch and Wiegand, *Studien zur Geschichte des Mittelalters*, 200–21

Schwerin, U., *Die Aufrufe der Päpste zur Befreiung des Heiligen Landes von den Anfängen bis zum Ausgang Innozenz IV: ein Beitrag zur Geschichte der kurialen Kreuzzugspropaganda und der päpstlichen Epistolographie*, Berlin 1937

Schwind, F., *Die Landvogtei in der Wetterau: Studien zu Herrschaft und Politik der staufischen und spätmittelalterlichen Könige*, Marburg 1972

Segl, P., ' "Stabit Constantinopoli": inquisition und päpstliche Orientpolitik unter Gregor IX', *DA* xxxii (1976), 209–20

——— 'Die Feindbilder in der politischen Propaganda Friedrichs II. und seiner Gegner', in F. Bosbach (ed.), *Feindbilder: die Darstellung des Gegners in der politischen Publizistik des Mittelalters und der frühen Neuzeit*, Cologne–Weimar–Vienna 1992, 41–71

Siebert, J., 'Graf Hermann von Henneberg als Bewerber um die deutsche Königskrone', *Zeitschrift für deutsche Philologie* lvii (1932), 215–23

Smets, G., *Henri I duc de Brabant, 1190–1235*, Brussels 1908

Smith, B., 'Irish politics, 1220–1245', *TCE* viii (1999), 13–22

Smith, J., 'Religion and lay society', in R. McKitterick (ed.), *The new Cambridge medieval history*, II: *c. 700 – c. 900*, Cambridge 1995, 654–80

Smith, J. B., *Llywelyn ap Gruffudd, prince of Wales*, Cardiff 1998

Snellgrove, H. S., *The Lusignans in England, 1247–1258*, Albuquerque 1947

Socarras, C. J., *Alfonso X of Castile: a study of imperialistic frustrations*, Barcelona 1976

Sommerlechner, A., *Stupor mundi? Kaiser Friedrich II und die mittelalterliche Geschichtsschreibung*, Vienna 1999

Spence, R., 'Gregory IX's attempted expeditions to the Latin empire of Constantinople: the crusade for the union of the Latin and Greek Churches', *JMH* v (1979), 163–76

Sperle, C., *König Enzo von Sardinien und Friedrich von Antiochia: zwei illegitime Söhne Kaiser Friedrichs II. und ihre Rolle in der Verwaltung des Regnum Italiae*, Frankfurt am Main 2001

Spiegel, G., 'Defence of the realm: evolution of a Capetian propaganda slogan', *JMH* iii (1977), 115–33

Spufford, P., *Money and its use in medieval Europe*, Cambridge 1988

Stacey, R. C., *Politics, policy, and finance under Henry III, 1216–1245*, Oxford 1987

——— 'Crusades, crusaders and the baronial *gravamina* of 1263–4', *TCE* iii (1989) 137–50

Staniland, K., 'The nuptials of Alexander III of Scotland and Margaret Plantagenet', *Nottingham Medieval Studies* xxx (1986), 20–45

Stehkämper, H., 'Konrad von Hochstaden, Erzbischof von Köln (1238–1261)', *Jahrbuch des Kölnischen Geschichtsvereins* xxxvi/vii (1961/2), 95–116

—— 'England und die Stadt Köln als Wahlmacher Ottos IV. (1198)', *Mitteilungen aus dem Stadtarchiv Köln* lx (1971), 213–44

—— 'Geld bei deutschen Königswahlen im 13. Jahrhundert', in J. Schneider (ed.), *Wirtschaftskräfte und Wirtschaftswege: Festschrift Hermann Kellenbenz*, Stuttgart 1978, i. 83–115

—— 'Der Reichsbischof und Territorialfürst 12. und 13. Jahrhundert', in P. Berglar and O. Engels (eds), *Der Bischof in seiner Zeit: Bischofstypus und Bischofsideal im Spiegel der Kölner Kirche: Festschrift Joseph Kardinal Höffner*, Cologne 1986, 95–184

—— 'Die Stadt Köln und die Päpste Innocenz III bis Innocenz IV', in J. Dalhaus and A. Knell (eds), *Papstgeschichte und Landesgeschichte: Festschrift Herman Jakobs*, Cologne–Weimar–Vienna 1995, 361–400

Steinbach, H., *Die Reichsgewalt und Niederdeutschland in nachstaufischer Zeit*, Stuttgart 1968

Stickler, A., ' Imperator vicarius papae: die Lehren der französich-deutschen Dekretistenschule des 12. und beginnenden 13. Jahrhunderts über die Beziehungen zwischen Papst und Kaiser', *MIÖG* lxii (1954), 165–212

Stimming, M., 'Kaiser Friedrich II und der Abfall der deutschen Fürsten', *HZ* cxx (1919), 210–49

Stoob, H., 'Bruno von Olmütz, das mährische Städtenetz und die europäische Politik von 1245 bis 1281', in H. Stoob (ed.), *Die mittelalterliche Städtebildung im südöstlichen Europa* , Cologne–Vienna 1977, 90–129

Strayer, J. R., *The Albigensian Crusades: with a new epilogue by Carol Lansing*, Ann Arbor 1992

Stubbs, W., *The constitutional history of England*, 6th edn, Oxford 1903

Studd, R., 'The marriage of Henry of Almain and Constance of Bearn', *TCE* iii (1989), 161–79

—— 'Reconfiguring the Angevin empire, 1230–1259', in Weiler and Rowlands, *England and Europe*, 31–41

Sturler, J. de, *Les Relations politiques et les échanges commerciaux entre le duché de Brabant et l'Angleterre au moyen âge*, Paris 1936

Stürner, W., *Friedrich II*, Darmstadt 1992–2000

—— 'Der Staufer Heinrich (VII) (1211–1242): Lebensstationen eines gescheiterten Königs', *Zeitschrift für Württembergische Landesgeschichte* lii (1993), 13–33

Tabacco, G., *The struggle for power in medieval Italy: structures of political rule*, trans. R. B. Jensen, Cambridge 1989

Tenckhoff, F., *Papst Alexander IV*, Paderborn 1907

Thirteenth Century England i (1985), *Proceedings of the Newcastle-on-Tyne Conference 1985*, ed. S. D. Lloyd and P. R. Coss, Woodbridge 1986

—— ii (1987), *Proceedings of the Newcastle-on-Tyne Conference 1987*, ed. S. D. Lloyd and P. R. Coss, Woodbridge 1988

—— iii (1989), *Proceedings of the Newcastle-on-Tyne Conference 1989*, ed. S. D. Lloyd and P. R. Coss, Woodbridge 1991

—— iv (1991), *Proceedings of the Newcastle-on-Tyne Conference 1991*, ed. S. D. Lloyd and P. R. Coss, Woodbridge 1993

—— v (1993), *Proceedings of the Newcastle-on-Tyne Conference 1993*, ed. S. D. Lloyd and P. R. Coss, Woodbridge 1995

—— vi (1995), *Proceedings of the Durham Conference 1995*, ed. M. Prestwich, R. H. Britnell and R. Frame, Woodbridge 1997

—— vii (1997), *Proceedings of the Durham Conference 1997*, ed. M. Prestwich, R. H. Britnell and R. Frame, Woodbridge 1999

—— viii (1999), *Proceedings of the Durham Conference 1999*, ed. M. Prestwich, R. H. Britnell and R. Frame, Woodbridge 2001

Thorau, P., 'Territorialpolitik und fürstlicher Ehrgeiz am Niederrhein zur Zeit Kaiser Friedrichs II und König Konrads IV: das Lütticher Schisma von 1238', in Herbers, Kortüm and Servatius, *Ex ipsis rerum documentis*, 523–36

—— *König Heinrich VII, das Reich und die Territorien: Untersuchungen zur Phase der Minderjährigkeit und der 'Regentschaften' Erzbischofs Engelberts I von Köln und Herzog Ludwigs I von Bayern (1211) (1220–1228)*, Berlin 1998

—— 'Der Krieg und das Geld: Ritter und Söldner in den Heeren Kaiser Friedrichs II.', *HZ* cclxviii (1999), 599–634

Thum, B., 'Öffentlichkeit – Öffentlich machen – Recht: zu den Grundlagen und Verfahren der politischen Publizistik im Spätmittelalter, mit Überlegungen zur sog. "Rechtssprache" ', *Zeitschrift für Literaturwissenschaft und Linguistik* x (1980), 12–14

—— 'Öffentlichkeit und Kommunikation im Mittelalter: zur Herstellung von Öffentlichkeit im Bezugsfeld elementarer Kommunikation im 13. Jahrhundert', in H. Ragotzky and H. Wenzel (eds), *Höfische Repräsentation: das Zeremoniell und die Zeichen*, Tübingen 1990, 65–889

Thumser, M., *Rom und der römische Adel in der späten Stauferzeit*, Tübingen 1995

—— 'Friedrich II und der römische Adel', in Esch and Kamp, *Friedrich II*, 425–38

—— 'Der König und sein Chronist: Manfred von Sizilien in der Chronik des sogenannten Nikolaus von Jamsilla', in *Die Reichskleinodien: Herrschaftszeichen des Heiligen Römischen Reiches*, Göppingen 1997, 222–42

—— 'Die Briefsammlung des Thomas von Gaeta', in Thumser, Wenz-haubfleisch and Wiegand, *Studien zur Geschichte des Mittelalters*, 187–99

—— 'Adel und Popolo in Rom um die Mitte des 13. Jahrhunderts', in Hartmann, *Europas Städte*, 257–71

—— A. Wenz-Haubfleisch and P. Wiegand (eds), *Studien zur Geschichte des Mittelalters: Jürgen Petersohn zum 65. Geburtstag*, Stuttgart 2000

Tibble, S., *Monarchy and lordship in the Latin kingdom of Jerusalem, 1099–1291*, Oxford 1989

Tinnefeld, F., 'Byzanz und die Herrscher des Hauses Hohenstaufen', *AfD* xli (1995), 105–27

Toomaspoeg, L., 'Les Premiers Commandeurs de l'ordre teutonique en Sicile (1202–1291)', *Mélanges de l'École française de Rome: moyen âge* cix (1997), 443–61

Toubert, P. and A. Paravacini Bagliani (eds), *Federico II e le città italiane*, Palermo 1994

Tout, T. F., 'Wales and the march during the Barons' War', in T. F. Tout and J. Tait (eds), *Historical essays*, 2nd edn, Manchester 1907, 77–136

Trabut-Cussac, J. P., 'Don Enrique de Castilla en Angleterre (1256–1259)', *Mélanges de la Casa de Velázquez* ii (1966), 51–8

Trautz, F., *Die Könige von England und das Reich, 1272–1348*, Heidelberg 1961

——— 'Richard von Cornwall', *Jahrbuch des Vereins zur Geschichte von Stadt und Kreis Kaiserslautern* vii (1969), 27–59

Treharne, R. F., *The baronial plan of reform, 1258–63*, Manchester 1932

Tremp, E., 'Auf dem Weg in die Moderne: Peter II von Savoyen und die Anfänge von Territorialstaatlichkeit im 13. Jahrhundert', *Zeitschrift für Historische Forschung* xxv (1998), 481–507

Turner, R. V., *King John*, London 1994

Tyerman, C., 'Some English evidence of attitudes to crusading in the thirteenth century', *TCE* i (1985), 168–74

——— *England and the crusades, 1095–1588*, Chicago 1988

Unverhau, D., *Approbatio-reprobatio: Studien zum päpstlichen Mitspracherecht bei Kaiserkrönung und Königswahl vom Investiturstreit bis zum ersten Prozess Johanns XXII. gegen Ludwig IV*, Lübeck 1973

van Cleve, T. C., *The Emperor Frederick II of Hohenstaufen: immutator mundi*, Oxford 1972

van Eickels, K., *Die Deutschordensballei Koblenz und ihre wirtschaftliche Entwicklung im Spätmittelalter*, Marburg 1995

——— 'Die Grafen von Holland und das Reich im 12. und 13. Jahrhundert', *Rheinische Vierteljahresblätter* lx (1996), 65–87

——— 'Vom freundschaftlichen Konsens zum lehensrechtlichen Konflikt: die englisch-französischen Beziehungen und ihre Wahrnehmung im Wandel an der Wende vom Hoch- zum Spätmittelalter', in Berg, Kintzinger and Monnet, *Auswärtige Politik*, 87–111

——— *Vom inszenierten Konsens zum systematisierten Konflikt: die englisch-französichen Beziehungen und ihre Wahrnehmung an der Wende vom Hoch- zum Spätmittelalter*, Sigmaringen 2002

Varanini, G. M., 'La marca trevigiana', in Toubert and Paravacini Bagliani, *Federico II*, 48–64

Vaughan, R., *Matthew Paris*, Cambridge 1958

Vincent, N., 'Simon de Montfort's first quarrel with King Henry III', *TCE* iv (1991) 167–77

——— *Peter des Roches: an alien in English politics, 1205–1238*, Cambridge 1996

——— *The holy blood: King Henry III and the Westminster blood relic*, Cambridge 2001

——— 'England and the Albigensian Crusade', in Weiler and Rowlands, *England and Europe*, 67–98

Voci, A. M., 'Federico II imperatore e i mendicanti: privilegi papali e propaganda anti-imperiale', *Critica storica* xxii (1985), 3–28

Vollrath, H. and S. Weinfurter (eds), *Köln: Stadt und Bistum in kirche und Reich des Mittelalters: Festschrift Odilo Engels*, Cologne–Weimar–Vienna 1993

Voltmer, E., 'Nel segno della croce: il carroccio come simbole del potere', in *Militia Christi e crociata nei secoli XI–XIII: atti della undecima settimana internazionale di studio, Mendola, 26 Agosto–1 Settembre 1989*, Milan 1992, 193–207

——— 'Deutsche Herrscher in Italien: Kontinuität und Wandel vom 11. bis zum 14. Jahrhundert', in S. de Rachewitz and J. Riedmann (eds), *Kommunikation und Mobilität im Mittelalter: Begegnungen zwischen dem Süden und der Mitte Europas (11.–14. Jahrhundert)*, Sigmaringen 1995, 15–26

Voss, I., *Herrschertreffen im frühen und hohen Mittelalter: Untersuchungen zu den Begegnungen der ostfränkischen und westfränkischen Herrscher im 9. und 10. Jahrhundert sowie der deutschen und französischen Könige im 11. bis 13. Jahrhundert*, Cologne–Vienna 1987

Wachtel, A., 'Die sizilische Thronkandidatur des Prinzen Edmund von England', *DA* iv (1940), 98–178

Waley, D., *The papal state in the thirteenth century*, London 1961

Wand, K., 'Die Englandpolitik der Stadt Köln und ihrer Erzbischöfe im 12. und 13. Jahrhundert', in J. Engel and H. M. Klinkenberg (eds), *Aus Mittelalter und Neuzeit: Festschrift Gerhard Kallen*, Bonn 1957, 77–95

Watt, J. A., 'The theory of papal monarchy in the thirteenth century: the contribution of the canonists', *Traditio* xx (1964), 178–317

—— *The Church and the two nations in medieval Ireland*, Cambridge 1970

—— 'Spiritual and temporal powers', in J. H. Burns (ed.), *The Cambridge history of medieval political thought, c. 350–c. 1450*, Cambridge 1988, 367–423

Weiler, B. K. U., 'Image and "reality" in Richard of Cornwall's German career', *EHR* cxiii (1998) 1111–42

—— 'Henry III's plans for a German marriage (1225) and their context', *TCE* vii (1999), 173–88

—— 'Frederick II, Gregory IX and the liberation of the Holy Land 1231–9', in R. N. Swanson (ed.), *Holy Land and holy lands in Christian history* (SCH xxxvi, 2000), 192–206

—— 'Matthew Paris, Richard of Cornwall's candidacy for the German throne, and the Sicilian Business', *JMH* xxvi (2000), 70–91

—— 'The *Rex renitens* and the medieval ideal of kingship, c. 950 – c. 1250', *Viator* xxxi (2000), 1–42

—— 'Henry III and the Sicilian Business: a reinterpretation', *Historical Research* lxxiv (2001), 127–50

—— 'Henry III through foreign eyes: communication and historical writing in thirteenth-century Europe', in Weiler and Rowlands, *England and Europe*, 137–62

—— 'The *negotium Terrae Sanctae* in the political discourse of Latin Europe 1215–1311', *International History Review* xxvi (2003), 1–36

—— with I. W. Rowlands (eds), *England and Europe in the reign of Henry III (1216–1272)*, Aldershot 2002

Werner, M., 'Prälatenschulden und hohe Politik im 13. Jahrhundert', in Vollrath and Weinfurter, *Köln*, 511–70

Wieruszowski, H., *Vom imperium zum Nationalen Königtum: vergleichende Studien über die publizistischen Kämpfe Kaiser Fiedrichs II und König Phillips des Schönen mit der Kurie*, Munich–Berlin 1933

—— 'The Norman Kingdom of Sicily and the crusades', in *Politics and culture in medieval Spain and Italy*, Rome 1971, 1–50

Wilkinson, B., 'The council and the crisis of 1233–4', *Bulletin of the John Rylands Library* xxvii (1942–3), 384–93

Williamson, D. M. 'Some aspects of the legation of Cardinal Otto in England, 1237–41', *EHR* lxiv (1949), 145–73

Wilshire, L. E., 'Boniface of Savoy', *Analecta Cartusiana* xxxi (1977), 4–90

Winkelmann, E., ' Reisefrüchte aus Italien und anderes zur deutsch-italienischen Geschichte', *Forschungen zur deutschen Geschichte* xviii (1878), 469–92

———— 'Die Legation des Kardinaldiakons Otto von S. Nicolaus in Deutschland, 1229–31', MIÖG xi (1890), 28–40

Wissowa, F., *Politische Beziehungen zwischen England und Deutschland bis zum Untergang der Staufer*, Bresslau 1889

Wojtecki, D., 'Der Deutsche Orden unter Friedrich II', in Fleckenstein, *Probleme um Friedrich II*, 187–224.

Wolf, A., 'The family of dynasties in medieval Europe: dynasties, kingdoms and Tochterstämme', *Studies in Medieval and Renaissance History* xii (1991), 183–260

Wolf, G., 'Anfänge ständigen Gesandtschaftswesens schon zur Zeit Kaiser Friedrichs II?', *AfD* xxxvii (1991), 147–53

Wolf di Cecca, C., 'Der Brautschatz der Isabella von England 1235 mit besonderer Berücksichtigung der Brautschatzkrone', *AfD* xli (1995), 137–45

Wolff, R. L., 'Baldwin of Flanders and Hainault, first Latin emperor of Constantinople: his life, death and resurrection, 1172–1225', *Speculum* xxvii (1952), 281–322

———— 'Mortgage and redemption of an emperor's son: Castile and the Latin empire of Constantinople', *Speculum* xxix (1954), 45–84

Wolfram, H., 'Meinungsbildung und Propaganda im österreichischen Mittelalter', in E. Zöllner (ed.), *Öffentliche Meinung in der Geschichte Österreichs*, Vienna 1979, 13–26

Zeller, G., *König Konrad IV. in Italien, 1252–54*, Bremen 1907

Zöller, S., *Kaiser, Kaufmann und die Macht des Geldes: Gerhard Unmaze von Köln als Finanzier der Reichspolitik und der 'Gute Gerhard' des Rudolf von Ems*, Munich 1993

Zöllner, E., 'Das Projekt einer babenbergischen Heirat König Heinrichs III. von England', *Archiv für Österreichische Geschichte* cxxv (1966), 54–75

Zorzi, A., 'La giustizia imperiale nell'Italia communale', in Toubert and Paravacini Bagliani, *Federico II*, 85–103

Zug Tucci, H., 'Il carroccio nella vita communale Italiana', *Quellen und Forschungen aus italienischen Archiven und Bibliotheken* lxv (1985), 1–104

Unpublished theses

Hurst, Jeanette Jones, 'Franciscan preaching, communal politics and the struggle between papacy and empire in northern Italy, 1230–1268', PhD diss. Cornell 1987

King, James R., 'The English clergy and Simon de Montfort's rebellion', PhD diss. Iowa 1972

Index